Born in Newcastle, New South Wales, in 1928, Peter Cabban joined the Royal Australian Navy as a cadet midshipman in 1942 and served in ships and establishments of the Royal Navy and RAN before specialising as a Fleet Air Arm pilot and maintenance test pilot. In 1962, following an appointment as executive officer of HMAS *Sydney*, he joined HMAS *Voyager* as second in command and retired five weeks before the destroyer met its fate in collision with HMAS *Melbourne* in February 1964.

In civilian life, Peter Cabban worked as a management consultant, primarily in health care management, and formed a non-profit foundation, which he directed for twenty years. The foundation was responsible for identifying areas of danger to patients' lives as well as improvement of quality of care and facilitated the saving of millions of dollars in health expenditure. He retired from full-time employment in 2004.

David Salter is an independent television producer and journalist. After a stint on *The Bulletin* magazine, he joined the founding team of the pioneer ABC-TV current affairs program *This Day Tonight*. His television work includes three years at the BBC, the historical series *This Fabulous Century*, *Geoffrey Robertson's Hypotheticals*, *Media Watch* and a recent documentary on the *Voyager* disaster titled *Unfit to Command*. Salter has also run sport for the Seven Network, Channel Nine and the ABC and writes regularly on yachting and rugby.

Breaking
RANKS

PETER CABBAN and **DAVID SALTER**

To Ben Whitten,

Thanks for friendship and for
interest in this story.

Peter Cabban
9/17/09.

RANDOM HOUSE AUSTRALIA

Random House Australia Pty Ltd
Level 3, 100 Pacific Highway, North Sydney NSW 2060
http://www.randomhouse.com.au

Sydney New York Toronto
London Auckland Johannesburg

First published by Random House Australia 2005

National Library of Australia
Cataloguing-in-Publication Entry

Cabban, Peter T. (Peter Thomas).
Breaking ranks.

ISBN 978 1 74051 315 9.
ISBN 1 74051 315 0.

1. Cabban, Peter T. (Peter Thomas). 2. Stevens, Duncan
Herbert, d. 1964. 3. Voyager (Destroyer : 1952–1964).
4. Melbourne (Aircraft carrier). 5. Collisions at sea –
Australian Capital Territory – Jervis Bay. 6. Marine
accidents – Investigation – Australian Capital Territory –
Jervis Bay. I. Salter, David. II. Title.
359.32540994

Cover photos by Corbis and Fairfaxphotos
Cover design by Darian Causby/www.highway51.com.au
Map by Caroline Bowie
Typeset by Midland Typesetters, Maryborough, Victoria
Printed and bound by The SOS Print and Media Group

10 9 8 7 6 5 4

For Sue

Contents

Foreword ix
Introduction xi

PART 1 1

1 Childhood Years 3
2 Naval College 7
3 Battleships Midshipman 19
4 Destroyer Training 30
5 Naval Undergraduates 38
6 Pompey Courses 42
7 First RAN Ship 48
8 Flying Training 57
9 Early Squadron Flying 64
10 Flying Ashore and Afloat 73
11 Testing Times 78
12 Studying Work 91
13 Executive Management 102
14 Introduction to *Voyager* 108

PART 2 **115**

15 Enter Duncan Stevens 117
16 The Gathering Storm 123
17 *Caine Mutiny* Revisited 128
18 Operation Sea Serpent 134
19 Hong Kong Farewell 137
20 Karatsu 140
21 Ship Handling 145
22 Crisis in Tokyo 149
23 Five Days in Command 156
24 Subic Bay 160
25 Singapore Finale 164

26 Sydney   168
27 Final Sea Command   174

PART 3   **181**
28 Out of the Navy   183
29 The *Voyager* Inquiry   189
30 The *Voyager* Debate   199
31 Preparing for an Ordeal   217

PART 4   **227**
32 The Cabban Statement   229
33 Witness   244
34 Sir John Spicer's Assistants   262
35 Medical Evidence   274
36 Admirals' Hypotheticals   290
37 Conflicting Evidence of Japan   302
38 Variations on a Theme   312
39 Recalled to the Witness Box   324
40 *Melbourne*'s Case   333
41 A Question of Loyalty   339

PART 5   **343**
42 The Royal Commissioners' Report   345
43 Parliamentary Post-mortem   352
44 Aftermath   363

Acknowledgements   369
Index   370

Foreword

In 2003 David Salter wrote and directed a brilliant TV feature *Unfit to Command* about the *Voyager–Melbourne* collision of 10 February 1964. He produced powerful evidence, which was not before the second 1967 royal commission into the Cabban Statement, which showed that that statement was very much closer to the truth than the findings made by the royal commission. The dreadful cover-up, which was only partially revealed in 1967, is now only too apparent. In order to protect the reputation of the Navy and the captain of *Voyager*, numerous naval persons told half-truths or lied, urged on by their naval superiors, despite the fact that the collision had cost eighty-two lives with many more injured. Captain Robertson, who captained *Melbourne*, became a scapegoat.

Yet despite implacable naval opposition, Peter Cabban was a successful whistleblower. The evidence revealed that the essence of his allegations had to be reluctantly accepted by the royal commission. Captain Duncan Stevens was found to be unfit to command. The findings against Captain Robertson were reversed and he was exonerated. He received $60,000 compensation.

More importantly, all three services were taught a vivid lesson; that a good-natured, cricket playing alcoholic could not be permitted to control modern war machinery. If that lesson was learned the second royal commission was worthwhile, even if it only revealed a comparatively small part of the truth.

I met Peter Cabban at the very beginning of his legal ordeal, as his barrister, junior to my leader J.T. Hiatt QC. Peter and I worked together for nearly seven months and during that time we became friends, our wives became friends, and our children became friends. Many a whistleblower has been cruelly and unfairly destroyed. Peter survived.

Yet he was still haunted by the feeling that he should have reported a sick and alcoholic captain to higher authority, even though he had reported the facts to a senior captain who chose to cover up everything. It is now manifestly obvious that had his report gone higher still, he would have been rebuffed and destroyed with all the ruthless force demonstrated in the second royal commission. This book clearly shows that no man could have usefully done more than he did.

The problem of the whistleblower destroyed by authority before wrongs can be exposed is still with us.

Peter has now told the whole story in this book, a book of exceptional interest. It gives a revealing account of the old method of official training of boys aged fourteen years. It describes some of the thrills and dangers of Australia's one-time Fleet Air Arm. It tells a true story which (despite the sneers of the royal commissioners) eclipses the fictitious *Caine Mutiny*.

Peter is a whistleblower who suffered but survived. The support of his wife Sue made all the difference when things looked very black indeed. It is fitting that this book is dedicated to her.

David Salter, with whom I have worked myself, was good enough to help Peter and co-wrote this book. Peter was lucky indeed to receive such capable assistance.

Chester Porter QC

Introduction

Had I really shot the albatross? The wedding guest of Coleridge's *Rime of the Ancient Mariner* was beset by the heart-wrenching story of a man's unbearable guilt as he unfolded the events leading up to and following his fateful act of stupidity. Wearing the decaying carcass of the symbolic omen of fair winds as his shipmates died about him, he suffered eternally that his sin should be known far and wide and the punishment be seen as appropriate.

My albatross was less visible, but equally compelling. My audience was not a wedding guest, but any hapless and halfway-interested acquaintance foolish enough to let me tell my story. The slightest encouragement was all it took. I would be off, talking and reliving the tragi-farce that was so vividly imprinted on my memory. I became ever more emotional as it proceeded, and ever more anxious to catch the details that prompted matching emotions. I was driven. The need to speak of it was overwhelming and never to be denied. I believed that I should write it all down and thereby purge it from my soul, but could never settle to the task and did not know why.

The wellsprings of all this emotion were stark. Five weeks after I had relinquished my appointment as executive officer and second-in-command of the destroyer HMAS *Voyager* it sank off Jervis Bay in New South Wales, after colliding with the aircraft carrier HMAS *Melbourne* at 8.56 p.m. on 10 February 1964. The captain, Duncan Stevens, together with my successor, Lieutenant Commander Ian Macgregor, and eighty officers and sailors, died in the collision and subsequent sinking. The survivors were scarred for life.

I was in Khancoban, in the Snowy Mountains, when the first sketchy news of the collision reached me from my wife, who had telephoned from Sydney. There was no television and only poor-quality radio reception in the chalet, but I knew the identity of the ships immediately.

I neither went to bed nor slept that night as I sat alone and relived events aboard *Voyager* during the previous year. I recoiled with horror from the thought that those who had been killed might still be living had I behaved differently. By morning, the most critical incident of that year had been erased from my immediate memory and buried deep within my subconscious. There it would reside, to torture me with unaccounted guilt, for the next twenty years.

It was, perhaps, not surprising that during the ordeal of the Royal Commission that I was to endure, I was largely sustained by the constant silent repetition of the words of William E. Henley's epic poem, *Invictus*, learned with awe and admiration at the Naval College:

> *Out of the night that covers me,*
> *Black as the pit from pole to pole,*
> *I thank whatever gods may be*
> *For my unconquerable soul.*
>
> *In the fell clutch of circumstance*
> *I have not winced nor cried aloud.*
> *Under the bludgeonings of chance*
> *My head is bloody, but unbowed.*
>
> *Beyond this place of wrath and tears*
> *Looms but the Horror of the shade,*
> *And yet the menace of the years*
> *Finds, and shall find, me unafraid.*
>
> *It matters not how strait the gate,*
> *How charged with punishments the scroll,*
> *I am the master of my fate:*
> *I am the captain of my soul.*

Far East Cruise HMAS Voyager 1963

Port	Arrive	Depart
Sydney		31.01.63
Darwin (1st)	07.02.63	08.02.63
1. Singapore (1st)	13.02.63	25.02.63
2. Trincomalee (1st)	01.03.63	05.03.63
Trincomalee (2nd)	08.03.63	10.03.63
Singapore (2nd)	19.03.63	25.03.63
3. Hong Kong (1st)	29.03.63	15.04.63
Singapore (3rd)	21.04.63	23.04.63
4. Pulau Tioman	27.04.63	29.04.63
5. Manila	08.05.63	10.05.63
Hong Kong (2nd)	13.05.63	20.05.63
6. Karatsu	24.05.63	28.05.63
7. Tokyo	05.06.63	10.06.63
8. Subic Bay	17.06.63	19.06.63
Singapore (4th)	24.06.63	04.07.63
9. Langkawi	07.07.63	08.07.63
Singapore (5th)	11.07.63	20.0763
Darwin (2nd)	25.07.63	25.07.63
Fitzroy Island	29.07.63	29.07.63
Sydney	03.08.63	10.08.63
Williamstown	12.08.63	23.01.64

Hong Kong (3)

Trincomalee (2)

Langkawi (9)

Pulau Tioman (4)

Singapore (1)

INDIAN OCEAN

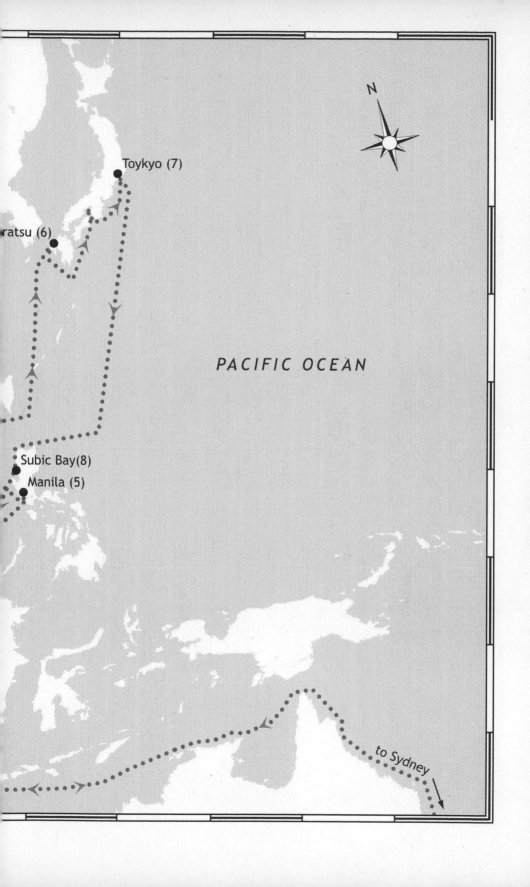

N

Toykyo (7)

ratsu (6)

PACIFIC OCEAN

Subic Bay(8)

Manila (5)

to Sydney

PART 1

1
Childhood Years

My father and grandfather were both master butchers, Dad in Islington, suburban Newcastle, while his father owned a business opposite Newcastle Beach. Dad was born in Batlow and attended Sydney Boys' High School before his parents and younger sister moved to Newcastle, where he met my mother. His parents had intended that he continue to university but he preferred to pursue his own path, learning his trade and being his own boss as early as he could. He loved sport and was a good golfer, tennis player and amateur boxer. My mother was a shy girl who was born in Curlewis, the third of five children who all rode horses to school from their farm. When her father was defeated by drought the family moved to Newcastle, and she left school at fourteen to attend business college.

I was born on 12 March 1928 in Newcastle, the younger, by two years, of two sons. My elder brother Laurie was exceptionally bright academically so that I was able to plod along at school with no great expectations as to my progress. While my brother created mayhem in the playground, with a knack for initiating fights with older and bigger boys, I stuck to my own classmates and joined him only when he was on the receiving end of a beating. When I was six, my father introduced me to the concept and practice of working for pocket money. At the back of his butcher shop there was a large pile of logs, which were burned for the rendering of fat. Every Saturday morning my job was to stack the logs neatly along one wall of the shop. This took me some time, and I clearly remember my anxiety once the task was complete and I waited for Dad to inspect the finished work and approve it. I received sixpence for my efforts, and was very pleased to add these weekly earnings to my savings. When I was seven or eight I would often help in my grandfather's butchery in the city on Sunday mornings, delivering meat to the hotel next door and helping to clean up the shop. I would be rewarded with a large breakfast (which cost a shilling at a nearby café), my tram fare, plus a shilling to save. If this was capitalism, I was all for it! Sometimes I would borrow threepence from my grandfather to buy an ice-cream, but always ensured that I repaid the debt the next time I saw him. Years later I was told that this impressed him greatly.

As my size and strength increased I graduated to other jobs, including mincing fat for lard, and meat for mince and sausages. The importance of safety around the large mincer was drummed into me through the most frightening stories of what had supposedly happened to boys whose neckties had been caught or who had used their hand to force meat through the large opening. Such scare tactics are effective on young and impressionable minds, and those images made me extremely careful. I sliced a thumb only once, cutting meat with a razor-sharp knife. My father immediately pushed my thumb into a jar of pepper, which certainly stopped the bleeding and prevented infection while also ensuring that I never went near the business end of a butcher's knife again. By the time I could ride a bike safely, meat delivery was a daily task before or after school and every Saturday morning. There was a washing basket filled with parcels on the handlebar. The job required early rising, and the steep hills and heavy loads made it physically demanding.

Childhood in the 1930s entailed clear-cut moral lessons. Once, when feeling tired and rebellious on a Saturday morning, I deliberately allowed my delivery load – bicycle and all – to fall on to the road outside the shop. My father's reaction was swift and effective. He reloaded the basket and gave me a quick warning of the hiding that another such episode would merit. I suddenly found the strength and incentive to pedal the heavy load of meat parcels over the nearby rail crossing bridge and out on my run.

An introduction to institutional discipline came during my early education at Cook's Hill Public School. The headmaster, George Blair, was a strict disciplinarian, but he matched his high standards with uncommon perception and humanity. He practised the old maxim of 'spare the rod and spoil the child'. During a lesson one morning, when I was eight, George Blair entered the classroom and wrote the numbers one to nine on the top corner of the blackboard. We all watched expectantly when he produced a tall tin and unscrewed the lid to reveal its contents. Boiled sweets! He said that the first pupil to raise a hand with the correct answer to a simple addition test, which he would set by pointing a ruler to one number after another, could take as many sweets as his hand could hold. The excitement was electrifying. Blair tapped a sequence of numbers and paused for reaction. Hands shot up, and the boys who were indicated by the ruler shouted their answers. We learned to be fast and accurate as our consumption of boiled sweets expanded. The astute headmaster would often turn a blind eye to the first upraised hand so as to encourage all, and we soon realised that this was fair. Maths became my best subject, undoubtedly influenced by this unique spur to learning.

At the age of nine I joined the junior ranks of the Australian Air League, meeting weekly at night, advancing by examination to the exalted rank of Squadron Commander. The parade ground drill and the discipline involved came easily, and were probably a reflection of my father's influence. My brother and I knew that if we pushed our mother too far she would, reluctantly, hand us over to Dad for a memorable thrashing by razor strop. Living within easy walking distance of a good surf beach with a rock-encircled pool, I spent many hours swimming and surfing after school and work. Most nights saw me up late, striving to complete homework for school the following day. My brother always helped me if asked. He showed me a trick of how to draw a map of Australia accurately by calculating offsets from an atlas. When I proudly submitted the result to my teacher, the headmaster appeared and accused me of tracing it. I was distressed and outraged at this false allegation, for it had taken me more than three hours, late at night, measuring distances with a wooden ruler, to locate the capes and other prominent landmarks on which the framework was built. My denials fell on deaf ears, but I never changed my precise method of mapping.

Late in the final year of primary schooling I overheard my parents discussing me. They were deciding the likely course of action when I failed to achieve a sufficient pass in the qualifying examination to join my brother at Newcastle Boys High. I was shocked but not dispirited when they concluded that I should repeat the year. I had never been placed worse than third or fourth in my class, and had seen no need to work any harder than was required to complete my assignments in homework and periodic tests. In the event, I found the qualifying examination to be quite straightforward and duly attended the same school as my brother. Having to accept junior billing to a notorious schoolyard terror was a familiar situation, and I was accepted for myself and formed my own group of friends. I enjoyed school, and looked forward to each day. My father encouraged me to elect Latin, with medicine or law in mind – in his mind of course, not mine. But after getting only 68 per cent in the first-year Latin exam – a good indication of how little the language of the Romans interested me – I changed to combined history–geography. I also chose technical drawing, on my brother's advice, and was glad that I did when years later it served me well both in and out of the Navy.

At the outbreak of war in 1939 my father was already an officer in the militia. He transferred to the AIF as soon as age restrictions were lifted. In the same year, when I was eleven, my father told me that he and my mother would divorce as soon as I was independent. I was devastated and heartbroken. He asked for my commitment to join him, but I was emphatic that I would stay with my mother, although I loved them both fiercely. Having given my word to keep this to myself, I did not discuss it with my brother or disclose it to my mother, which was an agonising experience.

At around this time, I asked my father for ten shillings, the price of a five-minute flight from the aerodrome at Broadmeadow. Joy flights were offered at weekends on the open space on which the most famous Australian aviator, Sir Charles Kingsford Smith, had landed and displayed his great three-engined Fokker, the *Southern Cross*, an event I had witnessed. My first flying experience was in an open-cockpit, low-wing monoplane. It was exhilarating, and my desire to become a pilot was born.

2
Naval College

During his first year in high school my brother told our parents that he was interested in entering the Royal Australian Naval College (RANC) at Flinders Naval Depot, Victoria. His application was forwarded too late for consideration. He was bitterly disappointed, and I observed his emotions with a mixture of compassion and my own dawning interest in the Navy. I determined that I should take early steps to apply for entry. My parents agreed to my application in good time, perhaps because they were confident it was a harmless exercise that would come to nothing.

The age of application was thirteen, in the year of examination, so that entry to the college was at the beginning of the year in which entrants turned fourteen. The academic examination included compulsory subjects, including mathematics, English, history and geography, and a voluntary subject, for which I elected French. I passed, and was invited to the next stage, the medical examination. The guidelines for the medical prompted our family doctor to suggest that I undergo a tonsillectomy, which had me discharged from hospital two weeks before the naval doctor passed me fit. Immediately after this test was the personal inter-view – the real hurdle to be cleared for anyone wanting a career as an RAN officer.

The interview lasted nearly fifty minutes and held my interest from the first moment. Seated behind a long table in a wooden building in the grounds of HMAS *Rushcutter*, a shore establishment on Sydney Harbour, were two naval commanders, a naval medical officer and a civilian (who, I learned much later, was Director of Studies at the college). One of the commanders was Commander S. H. K. Spurgeon DSO, captain of the destroyer HMAS *Stuart*, which was moored within sight of the interview room. The other was the commander of the college. My early nervousness was soon dispelled as I warmed to the challenge of the queries and propositions put to me. There were several trick questions in the form of riddles, which were easily answered, together with tests of observation and concentration. I was asked to look out the window. Then I was directed to read a passage from a book. Next I was interrogated on what I had observed from the window. Finally I had to answer questions about the book passage.

My results must have been fine because on completing the test I was asked, 'Did anyone tell you what to expect at the interview?' Of course they had. I told of a cadet midshipman whom I had approached in the street some months before and of my next-door neighbour, a naval reserve officer, both of whom said that observation would be important. When asked if I knew how many applicants were involved, I recounted an earlier conversation with another applicant whose reference number was 851, and replied, 'About 850, Sir', and was asked how many would be selected. 'Sixteen,' was information I had also learned from my casual conversation with the cadet. 'What chance do you think you have?' That was easy. 'As much as every other applicant, no more and no less.'

When they were finished, my interviewers asked if I would like to see the establishment. As we emerged, my mother, who had waited anxiously with deepening conviction that I had been successful, felt her heart would break. She was convinced that her 'baby' would soon be leaving home. She told me that the other interviews had been ten to fifteen minutes long. In the mail, we received forms for self-measurement for uniforms, together with instructions for a detailed eyesight examination. The family assumed that I was almost certainly selected, but this was not quite correct. The RAN had to ensure that they had sixteen fully fit applicants, and sent those papers to at least eighteen. My selection was formally announced in the Newcastle *Sun* on the same day the confirming letter from the Navy arrived at home, and there was great excitement, including that of my brother who was genuinely happy for me. (He later applied successfully for admission to Duntroon Royal Military College and withdrew to join the AIF before the cessation of hostilities, which upset my father greatly, and spent most of his life in the permanent Army.)

The process of becoming a midshipman in the Royal Australian Navy is much more than vocational training. It is a thoroughly planned process for turning boys into young officers and shaping them into an elite. Their characters are carefully forged – sometimes forced – into a common set of values and disciplines. These highly select groups live and work together closely, sharing personal habits, aspirations and pastimes. It is with good reason that each graduating year is called a 'cohort'. A large, high-pressure institution such as the Navy can only function if its managerial class all operate in a consistent, obedient and predictable manner. An insight into how this was achieved is essential to understanding the behaviour of my colleagues and me many years later during the dramas of *Voyager*.

The Naval College was set in the grounds of the RAN's principal training establishment at Flinders Naval Depot, Westernport, Victoria, and had a four-year curriculum. The training was designed to transform thirteen-year-old schoolboys into junior naval officers through a disciplined academic and sporting regimen, separated almost entirely from outside influences. New entry cadet midshipmen, classified as subordinate officers, arrived at the college a week ahead of returning cadets to be outfitted and orientated before the academic year commenced. Clothes sizes and tailored uniform measurements, which had been supplied by parents weeks earlier, enabled the issue of correct service kit on the day of arrival. If a cap were too large, it was adapted to size by stuffing it with newspaper. The clothes we wore on arrival were packed away until the first term ending, when we returned home and disposed of them. They would never fit again. Pocket money from home had to be banked, and cadets relied on a tiny weekly payment, which commenced at one shilling a week and rose by threepenny increments to reach the heady sum of two shillings by fourth year. A clothing allowance was paid into an account for each cadet, and purchases were debited until, on leaving the college, the outstanding balance was paid into the cadet's Commonwealth Savings Bank account. My father sent me regular payments of a pound each fortnight and this money provided for my spending during recreation leave, three times a year.

The introduction to college rules and regulations was firm and hard from the outset. There was a chief cadet captain and house cadet captain and four cadet captains (equivalent to prefects in civilian schools), one to each year's intake of cadets, with responsibility for discipline, appearance and morale. Each fourth-year cadet chose a fag from among the first year, and Tony George chose me. He was a good fagmaster in that he expected no more of me than appeared reasonable: daily cleaning of boots and shoes, and brushing uniforms before parades. Some fagmasters were much more demanding, and I was grateful for the treatment I received. John Matthew, who was to become my best man, fagged for Ian Sinclair, who was to feature as a barrister in both *Voyager* royal commissions and later become a judge. There were cleaning jobs, which had to be done on a rostered basis to a strict timetable, such as scrubbing the wooden boot boards, sweeping specified areas and standing by them for inspection at nightly rounds. All of this was excellent preparation for life at sea, where we would be supervising and inspecting the cleaning of ships.

Every cadet had a cold shower, twice a day, regardless of weather. These drenchings possibly helped to protect us from severe colds and influenza, both of which were rare among cadets. (I continued the twice-daily ritual of cold showers until I decided to stop sixty years later.) Dressing afterwards would commence on command and be timed by stopwatch up to an absolute limit of three minutes. Similarly, undressing and folding clothes for inspection, every night except Saturday, was liable to be timed. Not doing all buttons up or properly tying laces would be cause for punishment. Pockets were not allowed in trousers until fourth year, so carrying handkerchiefs was difficult, being confined to discreet tucking in a sleeve.

All routine parades, meals and activities were announced by a cadet who was designated quartermaster for a week. He 'piped' a distinctive and instantly recognisable tune on a boatswain's call to announce each activity. (The boatswain's call is a whistle made of a hollow spherical ball at one end and a curved pipe about eight centimetres long.) The tunes – all fixed by naval regulation – ranged from a simple monotone of four seconds to a variety of short notes ending with a long trill, which signified a meal. Being unable to roll my 'Rs', I was in torment whenever I had to perform this pipe.

Corporal punishment was official and regulated. Punishment by a cadet captain in the form of beating cadets on the buttocks, while they were bent from the waist, was meted out after a formal presentation of a complaint against the offender and his opportunity to plead an excuse or explanation. Four or six whacks were the maximum permitted at this level on any occasion. Two such beatings was the maximum to be applied to an individual within a week. A third offence that merited a punishment was referred to a term officer, a lieutenant or lieutenant commander who each had a more complete responsibility for training in naval matters and responsibility for the welfare of two cadet intakes. Every cadet had to submit his own written record of offences and punishments received each week in which he was punished. A scale of physical punishments in the form of prescribed hours of drill on the sports field under the direction of a chief petty officer was the usual punishment for minor referred offences, with dismissal from the Navy the ultimate penalty for major offences. I only once endured the spectre of the latter, having arrived a day late from leave after missing a train in my senior year. Informal punishment, in the form of kicks to the behind with the side of a senior cadet's shoe while bent over, was often offered as an alternative to appearing before a cadet captain. This option was accepted readily by most of us, and it was a practice to which authorities turned a blind eye.

By and large, the system worked well and prepared the cadets for their roles as prosecutors and defenders of the sailors under their authority in later life. It also taught them to accept pain and indignity without flinching or complaint, even when feeling hard done by, and recognising mercy and compassion when they were shown. Homesickness and shock combined to produce acute depression in many young boys during the first few days. Sobbing could be heard at night from some who were deeply affected by the sudden change in their lives. I was punished both informally and formally for what appeared to us as the most trivial offences, such as slightly imperfect dress or not dressing in the allotted time. Learning to accept punishment was vital to self-respect and survival.

There was an initiation ceremony for all entries, conducted with no warning by the term ahead of them after they had settled in. It was always quite rough, although to my knowledge no one was ever hurt physically through intent. An accusation was made when we were in second year that a cadet had been injured by toe stomping. This was not substantiated, although it did see an end to the practice of initiation, which I felt was a pity. There was a public uproar when the mother of one of the same term complained in a newspaper about the punishment by cadet captains, but fortunately that did not stop that aspect of discipline as it was all recorded and authorised. The identity of the cadet was protected so only those directly involved knew his name, but our whole term resented the intrusion of the outside world into what we regarded as a very private situation. Twenty years later the Navy's system of handling and recording punishments would become a crucial factor during my service on *Voyager*.

The academic curriculum at the college was basically similar to that of civilian schools, with graduates being accepted at all Australian universities if they wished to proceed to tertiary education. The fourth-year standards for mathematics and science corresponded to Sydney University first-year levels. Interspersed with the usual school subjects were naval subjects such as navigation, spherical trigonometry, naval French, seamanship, signals (which I liked enormously) and marine engineering. Naval history was important, and a senior cadet was nominated to present to the entire college a summary of famous British naval victories on their anniversaries. Engineering was taught in classroom and workshops. Each cadet had a formal introduction and practical training in every trade from fitting and turning to pattern-making and foundry work. The aim was to ensure that future officers could assess demands when breakdowns occurred at sea and to encourage cadets to consider specialisation in an engineering career in the Navy. Like all schoolboys of that era we made ashtrays, cast-iron pokers, wooden serviette rings and other simple products of our training to take home as proud evidence of our growing skills.

The harsher realities of separation from my family were never far away. I remember receiving a letter from my mother's closest friend, telling me that Mum was in hospital with pneumonia and might not live. My father was posted to Darwin at the time and was unaware of her illness. I did not know what I could do, and it never occurred to me that I could request leave to go to her. I did not share my anxiety with another soul. It transpired that Mum was delusional as well as critically ill, trying to throw herself from a balcony in the fever-induced belief that she was on a burning boat and calling on everyone to abandon ship! To compound these horrors, my grandmother was dying in the same hospital, following surgery for cancer. It was a tremendous relief when I received a letter from my much-improved mother, who had not known that I was aware of her dramatic episode in hospital. My grandmother died while I was on leave. When my father's Dad died I was informed by the commander and granted permission to go to the chapel, where I prayed alone and grieved in silence.

First and second years at the college were not really enjoyable. I remember well the simple relief of being at studies and therefore away from the constant threat of committing an offence to the Navy and being subject to punishment or harassment from seniors. Once each year the cadets, a term at a time, embarked on a corvette for practical experience in seamanship and orientation to ship routines, sleeping in hammocks and all the other discomforts of crowded life at sea. In the years 1942–45 the presence of Japanese submarines in Australian waters sometimes made these cruises hazardous, dangers we brushed aside with the supreme confidence of youth. Our destinations were either in Tasmania or other Victorian ports. My term had its initial experiences of seasickness during our first Bass Strait crossing, with all cadets (and 95 per cent of the officers and crew) succumbing to the effects of a gale. I held out until a seaman who was on the helm suddenly parted company with his dinner. I was splashed, and immediately joined him in being sick. Those experiencing real seasickness for the first time often declare that they wished they could die. I was no exception. I lay curled on the upper deck in darkness, nevertheless responding to an instinct for survival by making certain that I was in a safe position. We learned more than we realised on these cruises, and they were certainly worth the cost and effort expended in preparing us for our later lives in the service.

Every cadet played organised sport on six afternoons each week. There were two 'houses' for competition, Cook and Flinders, in red and green jumpers. The cadet captains chose from newcomers those whom they expected to enhance their house's prospects of winning. We also played regular representative games against teams from the Melbourne private schools as well as against adult teams from the depot. Cadets played rugby against the wardroom (officer's mess), the New Entry School (new adult recruits to the Navy undergoing training) and the Officer Training School (selected sailors being given intensive short-term training for commission as officers). These were always extremely hard-fought matches in which no quarter was given. With an age disadvantage of as many as five years, the cadets soon learned to rely on fitness and courage to persevere, and we managed to win our fair share of these encounters.

Physical training figured largely in the studies program and was later incorporated in sub-lieutenants' specialist courses, with a designated petty officer physical training instructor in charge of all cadets' instruction. Rope climbing, with and without the assistance of feet, was a valuable skill learned for immediate practical application. The fire escapes at college consisted of rope hawsers anchored to the floor and just thrown out of the nearest window. At the only evacuation drill conducted in our four years, I flew through the window, failed to grasp the rope firmly and dropped like a stone to the ground below, somehow unscathed. This caused consternation among the officers conducting the drill, but merely amused my term mates and me. I would soon put this new-found talent for falling to profitable use.

Each Saturday night we could attend the cinema performance in the depot drill hall. The entrance fee was threepence, collected before the cadets were formed into one group and marched to the hall (and double-marched home). One night, not having the money, I offered to jump from the gunroom window to the rose garden below if six cadets of my term paid a halfpenny each. As this was both illegal and involved the risk of broken limbs, there were plenty of eager takers. I was over the window ledge and falling through the darkness as soon as I had the money in hand, landing unhurt between the rose bushes. I then raced through the clothes drying room to emerge again and blended into the normal traffic. Mission accomplished.

The regime of college was certainly strict, but not without its lighter moments. One of the chief petty officers had acquired a rooster, which he named Charley. Each morning in the summer that wretched bird crowed, wakening us all well before our need for sleep had been sated. I vowed, as a butcher's son (and rather too loudly), that I would chop off its head if it happened once more. It did, of course. Now under intense challenge to 'put up or shut up', I parcelled Charley into a hessian bag and, with the rest of my term baying like banshees, spirited him away to the back of the cricket pavilion. Poor Charley was decapitated, plucked and prepared for cooking very quickly, and we tried in vain to spit-roast him in the gunroom fireplace. One of the term officers got wind of what was happening and joined in the spirit of the caper. He took Charley to the galley, where he was to be seasoned and roasted for service at dinner that evening. Meanwhile, we could hear anguished cries of 'Charley!' from outside the building as the owner scattered seed and called to his missing bird. Then a rousing cheer went up as the chef ceremoniously carried the poultry platter to the table and the college commander used his sword to slice the first drumstick. The bereaved CPO burst through the door and shouted, 'Cannibals!' before hurling the remaining seed on the floor in disgust. This triumph of the axe over our pre-dawn tormentor soon passed into college legend.

Camping under canvas on the Mornington Peninsula or at Cowes, on Phillip Island, was undertaken over the long weekends that served as mid-term breaks. We sailed or were towed in whalers to Cowes and went by buses to Mornington. Issued with tents and food (consisting of lots of eggs, bacon, chops, tinned foods, flour, milk and potatoes), together with frying pans and saucepans, we were expected to fend for ourselves, with no officers in the vicinity. These were enjoyable passages of relief from the strict discipline of college life. There were spirited inter-term fights to which no disciplinary restrictions applied. Eggs and legs of lamb were the most popular weapons, while pancakes were our favourite meal. Nobody went hungry. Swimming, walking and visits to movies occupied much of the time.

The final year at the college was a watershed for me. During the previous spring vacation, spent in Newcastle, I met and fell in love with a sensationally beautiful girl, Suzanne Hill, seven months younger than me, almost sixteen years old. She was lying on the sand, under a beach umbrella, propped on her elbows, wearing a red Jantzen bathing costume, white canvas hat and glasses, listening to a university student studying some lines for examination. There was a circle of young men and boys around her, and she looked to me like a blue-eyed, blonde angel. My mother told me, years later, that when I arrived home from the beach that day and told her I had met the girl I was going to marry, she was certain that I had.

Yet outwardly, at least, Sue gave no sign of acknowledging my presence. Had I made the slightest impression? Meeting her leaving the surf at the same beach on the very next day, she failed completely to recognise me when I greeted her. A friend invited me to play tennis, and when I declined, he said, 'Suzanne Hill will be there.' I could not grab my racquet fast enough and joined him. It was enough to establish an acquaintance. When a young crowd was meeting to go to Lake Macquarie for the afternoon, I suggested that I should first phone Sue, ask her to join us and catch up later. When she met me I suggested instead that we go to the nearby cinema and watch *The Fleet's In*.

Later, I took her home to introduce her to my mother. Mum did not make a fuss, but they established a relationship that was to grow to love and last for more than fifty years. Meeting Sue's mother was uncannily like her meeting with mine. No fuss was made of either of us, and our friendship quietly grew with more and more planned (and contrived) meetings. We were accepted by our friends and families as a pair and soon became inseparable. Like all sociable youngsters, we did not constrain ourselves to seeing only each other, but whenever possible we ensured that we were both at the same place at the same time. In that way we could meet, apparently innocently, and stay together throughout a dance or whatever was happening, even if arriving and leaving with someone else.

Love works strange miracles. While I had been only a spasmodic church-goer from childhood Sunday school through to confirmation in the Anglican Church, my interest in religion heightened when I learned that Sue attended evening service at Christ Church Cathedral in Newcastle on most Sundays. I joined a group of boys who attended and sat in the back pews, waiting for refreshments with the young girls in the church hall afterwards. I hoped to impress Sue with my burgeoning snooker and billiards skills in competition with some of the local lads, and was lucky in that I did. Our taste in music was identical, and probably typical of our generation.

We danced to the records of Glenn Miller, Tommy Dorsey, Jimmy Dorsey and Harry James. Sue was a divine dancer and had no trouble following my limited range of steps, awkwardly learned at a dance studio in the city and practised on my mother. Mum's trusty hand-wound gramophone was constantly in use as we clung together in the lounge and moved to our favourite slow foxtrots and quicksteps. Records were in short supply during the war, but my mother would buy one frequently, always choosing dance music with vocals, the most popular choice of the 1940s. At the college, when I proclaimed that Frank Sinatra (whose early recordings I thought expressed everything I felt for Sue) would be remembered when Bing Crosby was long forgotten, I was treated with angry contempt by the entire term.

Back at the college I became the stereotypical love-struck young swain. I spent my Sunday afternoons writing letters and love sonnets to Sue and used my pocket money to buy quarter-pound blocks of chocolate, always scarce in wartime, to send in parcels to her. The joy of romance yielded a quite unexpected bonus for me as a cadet. Whereas I had been performing well below my potential, probably through my despair at my parents' underlying conflict, a new confidence made me suddenly competitive in every aspect of sport and studies. I was awarded colours for rugby in my initial game for the First Fifteen and was suddenly performing at a higher level in track events, cross-country running and tennis. I fought a draw in the boxing competition with a much heavier opponent, and began to leap ahead in academic subjects. Having earlier been told that I would be considered for dismissal if my maths did not improve, I now moved from sixteenth to second place in my year, being beaten for first by one mark.

During the week of our final exams, when our routine was informal, I went to bed early each night and rose at 1.00 or 2.00 a.m. to study for the day's papers. I also analysed the papers from previous years, set by the same examiners, to detect patterns and restricted my cramming to what I felt were the 90 per cent certainties. This fundamental trick of pre-examination technique paid off, and I finished the four years greatly improved on my average performance in all subjects. The passing out parade took place about a week following the cessation of hostilities in World War II.

After graduation, we went on leave, and I continued working for my father to earn the money for lunches, tennis, swimming, movies and dances with Sue. I approached Sue's parents one day when they were in their lounge with, 'Mr and Mrs Hill, I would like to ask you an important question.'

'My daughter's hand in marriage, I presume?' replied Mr Hill.

'Oh no, Sir, not yet. I shall be asking that later. I just want to take her to the Great Northern Hotel for dinner!'

Permission was granted, and Sue looked radiant in the dining room sitting with her obviously entranced young beau in uniform. We must have presented a picture of young happiness because a waitress came over to say that a gentleman sitting with a lady at another table wished to buy us a drink. We accepted, and each had a gin sling. My mother was then working at the Northern as office manager, and was given a full description the following Monday. Mum was, in fact, a great source of discreet advice, only when asked, on etiquette, flowers, gifts and even kissing.

Returning to the depot, we lived at the college while attending courses at the Gunnery and Torpedo Schools. During the gunnery course, our instructor, Petty Officer Gunner's Mate George Cheadle, introduced us to thunder flashes, a pyrotechnic simulator for hand grenades. At the conclusion of the course he had a bucket of surplus thunder flashes and said, turning his back, that he did not expect to see any when he looked next. Naturally, they disappeared in an eye blink.

That night, as the three terms of cadets were returning in the dark from 'prep', a multitude of explosions erupted among them as thunder flashes were hurled with accuracy from the cypress hedges that flanked the path. We learned later that a mess dinner was in progress in the depot wardroom, and the explosions startled the officers, many of whom thought that hostilities had been resumed! The following morning we were all sitting innocently in a classroom when our term officer, 'Nobby' Clarke, entered. Without preamble he demanded that everyone who threw thunder flashes stand. I stood with three others, while twelve of my term remained motionless at their desks, giving no hint of admitting their involvement. We upright four were appalled. The entire term had been in the hedge. It was soon obvious that the term officer was after poor George Cheadle. We were asked how we obtained the fireworks and said that we had stolen them. Then each of us was told that we had been recommended for expulsion, but instead were subjected to a savage caning. Not surprisingly, that incident affected my long-term respect for and trust in many of my term mates. I had learned a painful lesson about honesty and closing ranks in the armed services.

3
Battleships Midshipman

Four years of college training were now behind me. Ahead lay the exciting vista of service in the 'real' Navy. In late 1945 the RAN was still essentially subsumed into the Royal Navy, and it was on ships of the Royal Navy that most Flinders graduates did their initial sea time. The imposing HMS *King George V*, a 48,000-ton battleship, was to be my home for the next fourteen months, along with five other Australian midshipmen.

The 'sub of the gunroom' (president of the mess), John Wilson, introduced us to our gunroom messmates, a mixture of thirty Royal Navy and Royal Naval Reserve midshipmen and sub-lieutenants. The sleeping accommodation was in the midshipmen's 'chest flat', a congested space located a deck below the gunroom, where we slung our hammocks and stowed our clothing in metal chests of drawers. Hammocks had to be taken down each morning to make room for dressing and free movement. Each of us was allocated to a seaman division under the direction of its divisional officer, in my case Lieutenant Bernard Skinner RN (whom I was to meet again in 1949, in vastly different circumstances). The system was designed to educate us in the core responsibilities of a naval officer and to understand the nature and needs of the sailors under leadership and direction. Midshipmen were expected to take command of powerboats and their crews for the routine running of officers and liberty men between ship and shore, communication between units of the fleet and other *ad hoc* journeys.

An officers' dance was held on the quarterdeck on the Friday night before we sailed, and Sue was able to travel from Newcastle with my mother and to stay overnight in Sydney. She looked sensational in a navy blue evening gown with white polka dots, and all of the Australian midshipmen fell under her spell. It was a magical night of dancing followed by strolling and kissing on the deserted Balmoral beach. We pledged our love for each other and had already agreed that we would marry when we could. Sue told her mother on returning home that she was going to marry me and was told, graphically and often, of the type of life that would mean for her! We knew that during three years of separation it was inevitable that we had to see others, but were confident our love would last.

Our passage to England was slow, reflecting the change from unfettered fuel expenditure in wartime to the sudden stringency of peacetime. We travelled at the stately but economical speed of twelve knots. Visits were made to Fremantle and Cape Town in good conditions, but the passage up the African coast was exceptionally uncomfortable with stifling heat and humidity.

Every midshipman was required to undertake practical navigation training, fixing the ship's position at noon each day by sextant. A complete set of about six fixes, using sun, stars, moon and land, was required for the midshipman's exam at the conclusion of our capital ship training. The navigator took it extremely seriously, checking every calculation against his own, more accurate, fix. But anyone could make a mistake, as became obvious during a night watch when I woke the navigator from a sound sleep to inform him that there was land on the radar. 'Balls!' he shouted.

'I'm sorry, Sir, but it is distinct,' I said.

'Balls! It can't be! Don't say anything to the captain.'

'The captain has been looking at it for ten minutes, Sir,' I said, before he was up, racing to the bridge.

We finally arrived in the Solent in early March 1946, passing the Isle of Wight during a blizzard. The crew was lined up on the upper deck, dressed in greatcoats, anticipating returning home to Portsmouth. This was the first experience of snow for many of us, and I found it depressing, making three years of being separated from Sue seem like a lifetime. The captain had told us that a representative from Australia House would visit the ship, accompany us to London and tell us of arrangements for a three-week leave. Sloane Square was the location of Lady Francis Ryder's Organisation, founded as a charitable entity for attending to the recreational needs of Rhodes scholars and Dominion service officers while in the United Kingdom. The widowed Lady Ryder and her associate, Miss McDonald of the Isles, had developed a formidable network of stately homes and other accommodation where the owners were willing to welcome strangers as live-in guests. The offices of the Ryder Organisation were modest and, after introductions and afternoon tea, Miss Fry briefed us on the domestic rules of the organisation, including 'no tipping' of servants and writing promptly to thank our hosts for their hospitality. Ernest (Gus) Grey and I were given precise instructions concerning three homes where we would be expected. Rail warrants were issued in Australia House, and having packed before departing the ship, we proceeded directly to the railway stations for the first leg of our journeys.

Mrs Darsie Watson, an elegant and handsome lady in her fifties, met us at Hayward's Heath station in Sussex. She was dressed sensibly for the robust weather in tweeds with ribbed woollen stockings and drove a station wagon. We were driven to an Elizabethan mansion, Bedales, set in a beautiful estate on the outskirts of the town. The grounds were spacious, including vast strawberry and vegetable gardens, fields of hay, two lawn tennis courts and one hard court, and a discreetly hedged swimming pool with attendant change rooms. The stables had been converted to garages for the family cars. Our welcome was warm and sincere, so that we settled in immediately, and our hostess had made arrangements for our entertainment, including meetings with neighbours and notables. The outstanding memory of the latter is of Captain Duncan W. Grant CBE RN (Retd), who entertained us to tea and recounted some epic moments of his career. Grant was a key figure in the history of the RAN College, first as a lieutenant commander when the college commenced in 1913, then as a commander in 1914–15 and as captain in 1917–19. Earlier, he had been a term officer at Royal Naval College, Dartmouth, when Edward, Prince of Wales, was a cadet midshipman. At the week's end we were told that we must consider Bedales our home whenever we had the opportunity to visit.

By contrast with the very full days in Sussex, our next experience was extremely quiet. Staying in country Hampshire with two middle-aged wives of British Army colonels who were currently serving in India, we were very much left to our own devices as regards entertainment. I explored the surrounding area and found it ideal for cross-country running. Prestbury in Cheshire, our third destination, was the home of the couple who influenced my life more than any others I met in England, and who became among the very special people in my life. Sir Robert Burrows was chairman of the London, Midland and Scottish Railway and owner and chairman of Lancashire Collieries as well as filling several other directorships.

Sir Robert had conceived and founded the Limbless Soldiers' Organisation as well as the Duke of York's Boys' Camps, a vacation and physical development organisation for the children of Britain's poor families. Through the latter he had direct contact and friendship with the Duke, soon to become King George VI, and the Duke had stayed at the Burrows' home, Bonis Hall, as a guest on two weekends. Collie and Border collie dogs were Sir Robert's companions, and he trained them to do simple tricks. 'Die for your king!' and the dog would fall and close its eyes. 'Fight for your country!' and he or she would leap up.

Invited to return to Bonis Hall whenever we wished, I accepted the invitation and after my second visit, this time alone, Lady Burrows asked me to continue 'as one of our family'. My relationship with them strengthened to deep affection and even greater respect for these wonderful, generous people.

Admiral Sir Neville Syfrett had hoisted his flag in *King George V* when we returned from leave, so we were flagship carrying the staff, including the fleet navigating officer (FNO), Commander Ian Hogg DSC RN. Hogg had survived a court martial following the First Battle of Narvik where his ship, HMS *Penelope*, struck an uncharted pinnacle of rock at thirty knots and was disabled. Although they escaped back to England in the repaired cruiser, he and Captain G. D. Yates were found guilty of hazarding their vessel.

A vacancy occurred for the position of navigator's tanky, a midshipman attached to the navigator, responsible for keeping charts up to date and attending the bridge whenever Special Sea Duty men (SSD) were summoned. (SSD comprised the specialist officers and sailors who manned the wheelhouse, bridge, signal deck, sounding gear and other positions, such as the anchor cable party, when entering or leaving harbour or in hazardous situations that demanded experienced crewmen.) I volunteered for the 'tanky' role, well aware of perks that far outweighed the heavy workload, and was appointed. The most tangible benefit was possession of a cabin located at the rear of the admiral's bridge, but not designated on the ship's plans. Few on board knew of its existence. This bolt-hole was sheer luxury after the stuffy, crowded life of the chest flat. I had a telephone (number unpublished), a desk, washstand, and reading and shaving lamps. A discreet scuttle (port hole) at the rear of the cabin did not excite the interest of other crew using the ship's super-structure. When I invited the FNO for a cup of cocoa on a cold night he joked that my cabin was better than his!

To offset this privilege, the work was demanding beyond any I had experienced before. All the time I was not on watch, boat running or attending training was occupied with the never-ending chore of meticu-lous correction of charts, following the lists in Admiralty Fleet Orders. I enjoyed the work and saw no reason to request relief or assistance. But, as flagship, we carried charts of the entire Atlantic and associated seas, and the task of keeping up to date with corrections was becoming insur-mountable. When I was busy at three o'clock one morning the FNO appeared in the bridge charthouse where I worked and asked why I was still working. I showed him my current progress, and he arranged for my release from quarterdeck watch-keeping to give me more time.

Leaving Portland Harbour en route to Devonport one morning, the captain drew the attention of FNO to a buoy that was not marked on the chart. The captain referred to a recent Naveam, a signal from the Admi-ralty alerting ships to chart amendments. I received these signals in profu-sion and, acting on the advice of my predecessor, had filed them all in the wastebasket! There was initial consternation, but I was treated with understanding and sympathy. On our arrival in Devonport, a current set replaced the ship's entire portfolio of outdated charts, and a qualified navigator's yeoman, a sailor whose job centred on the current accuracy of charts, joined us and took that responsibility from me.

King George V had several power boats, each painted in a distinctive colour to signify their role and ownership. Green was for C in C (commander in chief), navy blue for the chief of staff (COS). There were two 45-foot picket boats, which were black and white, twin screw with a bridge and fore and aft cabins; two launches, which were black and single screw; and two 35-foot motor boats. Midshipmen were required to be adept in the handling and command of the picket boats, launches and motor boats, but never manned the barges, each of which had an individual coxswain and crew, on the commander in chief's staff. Boat running in harbour became a passion, and I endeavoured to be the first of my crew of five to reach the lower boom and man the picket boat whenever we were called away. I would haul the boat by its hawser to the Jacob's ladder, leap on board, start the powerful engines and move to the boom.

On one particularly rough day, I was ordered to collect the staff of Commander in Chief Home Fleet from shore and return them before the fleet was to sail. The sea was running so high that the rise and fall alongside the companion ladder was between six and ten feet and extremely hard to read. As I waited for an opportune moment and the senior officers in the cabin of the boat became anxious, the fleet operations officer, a commander, ventured out and began giving me orders. Without hesitation, I said, 'The boat is yours, Sir!' and moved to vacate my position on the bridge. I did not hear what the other officers said to him, but he immediately said, 'No, Mid, it's yours!' I continued judging the moment until I could safely come alongside and get them out. Commander Fisher, who had observed the entire incident, merely said, 'Well done', as I reported to the officer of the watch after the boat was hoisted aboard.

I learned that conceit has its price when, in St Peter Port, Guernsey, I was detailed to carry a vice admiral from *King George V* to the city for an official function, the admiral's barge preceding me with the commander in chief aboard. A crowd of curious sightseers witnessed the boat come alongside the barge and discharge our VIP passenger. As they looked on, admiringly I thought, I shifted gears and opened throttles to speed away. 'Look at the stern, Sir!' shouted the cox'n. In horror, I saw that the barge was lifting out of the water as our gunwale was wedged under its rubbing strake. Inevitably, something had to give, and a large piece of highly polished timber broke away as the barge settled back into the water. The admiral's cox'n watched in dismay, and after apologising to him, I proceeded with humility to face the music in the flagship. Reporting to the commander, who was on the quarterdeck at the time of my return, I said, 'I broke a piece of timber off the barge, Sir.'

'What piece of timber?'

'A piece on the starboard quarter next to the stern, Sir,' I replied, ingenuously.

'Your leave is stopped until you know the correct name, and the barge is repaired!'

I sought out the fleet shipwright officer and apprised him of my plight. He worked a minor miracle and had the barge hoisted and repaired as soon as it returned. So, within less than an hour, I was able to inform the now calm commander, 'The quarter badge of the barge has been replaced, Sir,' and was dismissed without rancour.

All six RAN midshipmen played rugby for the ship, and the team performed well, winning the season fleet championship in a memorable final. I had attended a mess dinner in the wardroom the previous night as a guest of the FNO. My host and his colleagues, who appeared to enjoy my resultant condition, had plied me with a mixture of wines and spirits. A large Royal Navy midshipman, Gordon Crosbie, woke me to a shocking hangover with the threat that if I were not eating breakfast and prepared for my role as hooker of the rugby team within thirty minutes, he would thump me. Crosbie then took me to the sick bay where a compliant medical officer dosed me with a 'wonder tonic', after which I recovered, miraculously, and was later told that I played 'the game of your life'. An instant convert to the restorative powers of pharmacy, I obtained the recipe for the wonder drug and had a large bottle dispensed so that I could have it handy at all times. A civilian pharmacist, who made up the prescription some months later, asked if it were for a horse!

Shortly after, when returning to Portsmouth for ship's company leave, I witnessed an alarming incident that would have a tragic echo almost twenty years later. A pilot, the King's Harbourmaster, joined the ship at Spithead and, in keeping with regulations for all capital ships entering dockyard ports, took control of the ship's navigation for docking. This regulation applied notwithstanding the presence and qualifications of both the captain and FNO. It was my task to record proceedings, and I was careful to write in the navigator's note book each and every comment and order uttered by all members of the command team present on the bridge. The FNO had already told me of the pre-war event in which HMS *Nelson* had grounded on the Portsmouth Harbour mud banks, resulting in the suicide of her captain. This was to be a similar scenario.

As the ship entered the extremely narrow channel, which lies close to the shore on the starboard side with massive mud flats to the port side, it was obvious that he was tending to steer the ship off centre to starboard, as if to avoid the mud. This had the effect of slowly building up the pressure of water between ship and shore. The pilot was chatting away while the captain maintained a stony silence, constantly observing the ship's position and reaction. Soon the ship began a lateral movement to port – towards the mud bank. Stepping swiftly to the voice pipe at the side of the compass, the captain ordered, 'Full speed astern both engines! Hard a' starboard!'

The pilot panicked as, too late, he recognised the predicament of the ship and proposed in a shaking voice, 'Could we have some more revs, Sir?'

'Get out of my way, you bloody fool!' responded the captain, as the ship continued slow ahead towards a vessel that was moored in our path.

With our speed reducing ever so slowly, and within a few feet of collision, *King George V* thankfully lost momentum and the captain manoeuvred it safely into the centre of the channel and then to its berth. Both he and the FNO would have been court-martialled had the ship grounded, because theirs is the ultimate responsibility. The handwritten account that I had made in the navigator's note book of each command given was the only record of the incident, a powerful demonstration of the importance of accurate documentation.

We had further first-hand experience of the dangers of sloppy navigation, especially at night. By late spring, the fleet was engaged in exercises in Moray Firth, Scotland. In the middle watch one night, the fleet of twelve ships was steaming in single line between the Orkney Islands and the coast when the FNO walked on to the bridge and glanced at the illuminated horizontal strip of film that relayed the reading of the compass within fifteen degrees either side of the ship's heading. The strip was moving rapidly as he watched, indicating that the helmsman, in the wheelhouse two deck levels below the bridge, was 'chasing the strip' – putting the wheel in the opposite direction to that which he should to correct a deviation from course. Giving direct orders via the voice pipe to reverse the wheel, the navigator stepped quickly to the wing of the bridge to observe the line of ships, all blindly following the flagship towards an island on which many would probably have grounded had he not intervened. He ordered the signalman to signal, 'You are standing into danger', and then 'Act independently', so that the officers of the watch turned their ships to the correct course – and safety.

Midshipmen – universally nicknamed 'snotties' by their superior officers – had plenty of opportunities to blow off the steam that built up from the pressures of their role. We did this with the boundless energy of youth and physical discipline that had been developed over our four years as cadets. Early in the twentieth century, midshipmen serving in the capital ships of many navies began to prize traditional red-and-white striped barber's poles as souvenirs. They were wrested from their rightful places, usually in foreign ports, and smuggled back to the ships. There, in the gunroom mess, the history of the pole would be displayed with pride by the list of ships' names carved into the wood to indicate the succession of the pole's owners. Such displays were, of course, a goad to visitors from other ships. Raids were launched upon the host mess with the intention of capturing the pole and taking it to a more deserving place of display. Immediately following a successful raid, the name of the ship acquiring it was carved below that of its former owner. Any gunroom that had a barber's pole therefore also had constant need to be vigilant for possible raids by the envious snotties of other ships in port.

Our own 'Saga of the Pole' began in Portland Harbour when Royal Navy midshipmen from the aircraft carrier HMS *Colossus*, which had just been decommissioned, joined the gunroom, bringing with them their prized French barber's pole. This trophy had originally been acquired by midshipmen in the French battleship *Richelieu* and then, in succession, was taken by HM Ships *Glasgow*, *Colossus*, *Vengeance* and *Colossus* again. In *King George V* the pole was displayed together with two belisha beacons (liberated by midshipmen in Liverpool) and historically significant photographs. On a Saturday night in Portland Harbour, the ships of the Home Fleet were secured to buoys. The midshipmen of *King George V*, except for two who remained in the gunroom, attended a movie show on board. After the film we returned to the gunroom, only to find that the two who remained behind had been victims of a raid. They were tied up securely in the mess and all our trophies were missing. The culprits were midshipmen of HMS *Howe*, a sister battleship of the same class as *King George V*, who had come aboard as if visiting friends, and left with their booty undetected by our gangway staff.

Quite clearly, a recovery operation was necessary to restore the ship's honour. It would be unwise to attempt a frontal attack on the same night as the 'enemy' would be expecting us and be well prepared. But we recognised that there was one great advantage of our being virtually identical ships: as the flagship, we had a duplicate set of keys for *Howe*, including to the gunroom mess. A plan was developed, predicated on the assumption that we could approach and board *Howe* without detection. After midnight the mess would be clear of staff and midshipmen, and security would depend on occasional patrols and the watch-keeping quarterdeck staff. But first we had to get aboard. If any boat were seen approaching, the officer of the watch (OOW) or the midshipman of the watch in *Howe* would alert the midshipmen who would, in turn, soon repel us with fire hoses rigged for this purpose. The only way we could board undetected was by a small rowboat with muffled oars, with no moonlight and at a time when the crew was sleeping. The completed plan was discussed with Commander Fisher as well as with the gunnery officer, the 'snotties' nurse'. This was necessary as we needed the 'unofficial' use of one of the picket boats to recover the raiders.

At 12.30 a.m. on the moonless night of the raid, a fishing boat's dinghy, barely able to carry six including two rowing, was taken by indirect route to *Howe*. Five midshipmen scrambled on to the large anchor buoy and climbed the cable. Initially hidden from view of the deck by the overhang of the ship's bow, they crawled through the hawse pipe on to the forecastle, where they hid behind the breakwater and waited while the dinghy returned for the second group. I rowed the dinghy back to *King George V* and collected the next five. Up we went after securing the dinghy to the buoy with a slip knot. The anchor cable was freshly painted, so it was tricky to climb without ruining our battle dress uniforms. With the complete raiding party now safely assembled on the forecastle, we used a torch to signal to the recovery party aboard *King George V* that we should be ready for pick-up in thirty minutes. We then descended two sets of ladders into the battleship's middle deck, confident that there would be no activity at that time. As we carefully crept past sailors sleeping in hammocks no one was disturbed. Using the borrowed key we were inside the gunroom within five minutes. Silently procuring the loot, we nevertheless felt vulnerable because if our presence were even suspected there would have been little time to escape.

After half an hour of waiting for the recovery boat we became extremely nervous. After an hour we were anxious to the point of alarm, concluding that our signal had not been seen. A volunteer was needed to retrace our steps and signal to *King George V* again. Stupidly, I offered. Before long it was obvious that our raid had been discovered as I heard an unholy noise of running and shouting from behind. My knowledge of the ship's geography gave me an advantage, and I hit the forecastle deck about ten yards ahead of the nearest pursuer, jumped into the hawse pipe and slid down the cable (ruining my uniform with the wet paint), landing on the buoy as a cry of 'There he is!' rang out. I leapt into the dinghy and cast off while pushing myself into the current. Almost immediately, a picket boat was alongside with a midshipman reaching for the painter so the dinghy could be towed. My relief was overwhelming. We made a provocative circuit of *Howe*, where chaos was now reigning as the frustrated midshipmen were joined by other officers in shouting and making a useless effort to hose us. We taunted them from long range, holding up the trophies – both theirs and ours – and returned to the flagship in triumph to be greeted by the commander and gunnery officer, both of whom were as proud of our effort as we were relieved to be back. It transpired that the picket boat's engine would not start when it had been due to recover us. The chief of staff to our admiral had even offered his barge when he became aware of our plight.

The next morning evidence of our successful raid was on display for the whole fleet to see. *Howe's* starboard side, outside the gunroom, bore the scars of ten pairs of feet. We showed off our trophies, including a Japanese Zero fighter propeller. A series of signals was exchanged between the two battleships. The first, addressed from *Howe's* commander to our commander, demanded that the *King George V* midshipmen involved be sent to paint *Howe's* side. Our commander replied that he had provided the recovery boat and supported his midshipmen. Signals between captains established that our captain agreed with his commander. The incident was escalating to flag officer level. Finally, Rear Admiral Training Battleships, Rear Admiral Harold Hickling, in command of three battleships of the Home Fleet, complained about all of us: the *King George V's* midshipmen, commander and captain! The commander in chief replied that he was proud of his midshipmen and that his chief of staff had offered his barge to assist. Eventually, no doubt wishing to end the matter, C in C told us to return the propeller. We duly sent back the trophy, now permanently engraved with the story of the raid and its aftermath.

4
Destroyer Training

At the conclusion of my leave I arrived in Devonport to join HMS *Sluys*, a Battle Class destroyer of the Fifth Destroyer Flotilla, commanded by Commander Tom Larkin OBE RN. (BBC announcers were supplied with a helpful ditty, composed by a former captain, which warned: 'When you announce something so choice, don't mispronounce HMS *Sluys*!') I found Pat Burnett already arrived, while Midshipman Drax RN had sent a telegram announcing his intention to join a day late. This was unpopular with the captain, but meant that we two Australians secured the only bunks in our cabin while Drax had a camp stretcher. The skipper then expressed his further displeasure by ordering Drax, when not in the mess for meals, to dress in seamen's work clothes as he had behaved with 'a sailor's attitude'.

When it came to choice of duties I was happy to take the ship's office, assisting a delightful lieutenant in the administration and secretarial matters of the ship, as well as torpedo and anti-submarine action stations. The more relaxed atmosphere of a smaller ship was in sharp contrast to the formality of a battleship like *King George V*. There were only fourteen officers in *Sluys*, including us three midshipmen. This was a period largely spent learning more of the conditions of the sailors, dealing with their pay matters, their discipline and welfare, as well as working directly with seamanship situations, such as anchor work and ship handling. The captain supervised on the bridge while we undertook the duty of OOW. As in *King George V*, we took 'tricks' on the wheel, steering the ship for an hour or so at a time.

We were given the task of making a small model of the Battle of Sluys to replace an inferior existing model over the wardroom fireplace. When the ship joined the Home Fleet in Portland, I was delegated the task of taking the model to a friend of the captain at the Admiralty. It was one of the coldest winters in history, and the railway trip to London commenced disastrously for me when I slipped crossing the ice-covered gangway and almost fell into the freezing waters. Fortunately, the precious package was undamaged. The sole redeeming feature of this woeful journey was a small bottle of navy issue rum, which had been pressed on me by a petty officer of the seamen's division to which I was attached. What a kind gesture it was, and how perceptive! After seven hours in the train, I stayed overnight at the home of Sue's aunt in Hampstead, and glumly learned that I could not afford West End cinemas.

The Home Fleet units, comprising four battleships, four cruisers, a carrier and eight destroyers, entered the English Channel on 1 February 1947, in two lines through which HMS *Vanguard* was to pass with the royal family. *Vanguard* had only recently joined the fleet, and looked magnificent in its paintwork and general appearance as she sailed between the two lines. The fleet 'cheered ship'; that is, the officers and men lined the sides looking towards *Vanguard* and, as she passed abreast of each ship, raised their caps and gave 'three cheers for His Majesty the King', while the King returned their salutes. It was a stirring reminder of the close historic connection between British royalty and their navy. A signal was received from the King to Commander in Chief Home Fleet, 'All ships splice the mainbrace.' A full tot of rum was issued free to every man in the fleet, except for midshipmen and boys under eighteen. Commander Larkin, exercising his discretion, invited the three midshipmen in *Sluys* to have a tot of rum from his bar.

During this period we were introduced to the skills of station-keeping, whereby ships are required to take and maintain a position at designated distance and bearing from a nominated guide ship. This is no simple matter, and judgement was passed on an officer's ship-handling ability when he, as officer of the watch, responded to orders requiring a change of station. Those who reacted instantly, with the correct degree of rudder and speed adjustment, were more highly regarded than any who dithered or miscalculated. It was vital never to lose sight of any ship in the vicinity and to take frequent compass bearings of all close ships as well as that on which station is kept. Diligent observation yielded a reliable grasp of the 'tactical situation'. For example, if a bearing between two ships that are closing remains constant, a collision is inevitable unless the subordinate ship, or the ship not having the 'right of way' according to the Rule of the Road, alters course.

In the Bay of Biscay, notorious for its rough conditions, the fleet took a terrible pounding. *Duke of York*'s bow rose out of the sea until her hull, up to the bridge superstructure, was clear of water, and then she plunged so that the sea cascaded over her forward gun turrets and lapped at the admiral's bridge. I watched as one of our fellow escort destroyers rose from the sea, exposing her Asdic dome located below the bridge, and then dived into the ocean with water rising to the bridge level, thinking, 'Thank God that's not us.' A few seconds later I realised that we were doing exactly the same.

The weather calmed in the Straits of Gibraltar, and we entered harbour under the shadow of the famous Rock and secured to a wharf. Here, I heard of an exchange of signals between the captain of a cruiser and the admiral in command of Gibraltar. The cruiser entered harbour and had attempted to secure alongside a wharf, but repeatedly failed to manoeuvre adequately. While this relatively simple task of ship handling should typically have taken no more than fifteen minutes, the admiral (and all fleet units already in the harbour) watched, unimpressed, as it took an hour and a half. A signal, sent by the admiral to the cruiser, said, 'Good!' The cruiser captain sighed with relief and went to his cabin to rest and have a drink. One and a half hours later a second signal from the admiral was received. It said: 'To my last, add "God!" '

A visit from Admiral of the Fleet Lord Fraser of North Cape, Commander in Chief Portsmouth, was a highlight of our stay at Gibraltar. As cadets we had met the admiral when he was Sir Bruce Fraser, Commander in Chief British Pacific Fleet. He had joined us in the college mess at our mid-morning break and had a rock cake and cup of milk with us. This meeting was very different. The captain introduced each of us in turn, thus: 'This is Midshipman Burnett, Sir. He's Australian,' then, 'Midshipman Cabban, Sir. He, too, is Australian.' And, 'This is Midshipman Plunkett-Ernle-Erle-Drax, Sir.'

The admiral did not miss a beat as he asked Drax, 'Are you an Australian, too?' It was so beautifully done!

Drax's father had been an admiral before and during World War II, and Fraser would at some time have served under his command. The captain had made the only deference to snobbishness of which I was aware in all the time I was in *Sluys*, and it immediately embarrassed him, as it did Drax. The full, grandly hyphenated surname is a result of socially contracted marriages in the past. Admiral Sir Reginald Aylmer Ranfurly Plunkett-Ernle-Erle-Drax was one of England's wealthiest men, and 'Plunkett', as we called Drax, was the youngest child of five, his only son and heir, and a good shipmate to Burnett and me, even if he was carrying the ballast of three hyphens and surnames too many.

The fleet proceeded into the Mediterranean for different destinations. Two destroyers went to Casablanca in Morocco, *Duke of York* to Villefranche in France, and three destroyers, including *Sluys*, proceeded to Oran in Algeria. Our greeting was extremely warm and generous. There was an invitation for all officers to attend an Admiral's Ball, as part of the Mardi Gras festivity, which coincided with our visit. Burnett and I attended and danced with heavily chaperoned young girls through the night. I realised at once that my dancing partner spoke far better English than I did French, in spite of my six years of study of the language. Although she spoke English for some time, she begged me to speak French. Always trying to be the gentleman, I attempted to comply with her wish. Each time (and it was often) that I stepped on her toes, I said 'Je suis heureux!' intending to say 'I am sorry'. Later I discovered that I was actually telling her 'I am happy'!

I was fortunate to serve under an unorthodox type of captain. When the destroyers received an invitation for ten officers and thirty sailors to visit the Foreign Legion headquarters at Sidi bel Abbès it was understood that the officer in command of the flotilla was bound to accept and that three officers of each of the ships would accompany him. In *Gabbard* and *Cadiz*, quite reasonably, the three most senior officers were nominated. But on board *Sluys* Commander Larkin had all officers called to the wardroom mess and told us that he would leave the selection of attendees largely to chance. He asked for the roulette wheel, owned by the mess, and directed that each officer was, in order of rank and seniority, to spin the wheel. The three officers who spun the highest numbers would be chosen. If two or more spun the same number, then seniority would determine who went. So the captain spun, and then the first lieutenant (second-in-command) and the others until I, the most junior of fourteen officers, was last to take my turn at the roulette wheel. I spun thirty-six, the highest possible number, and my excitement was extreme.

Early on the morning of 17 February the first lieutenant, the torpedo officer and I joined the other officers for a wild drive through the desert to the fortress at Sidi bel Abbès. When we arrived at the gates the naval officers waited until our hosts were ready, while the petty officers and men were spirited away to tour separately. We were joined by the British ambassador and the colonel of the Legion, together with other senior Legion officers. Moving into the main street of the fort, we stood to attention and saluted while the legion band, 120 members strong, played the national anthems of England and France and a guard of honour presented arms for inspection by the colonel and captain. I had, as a schoolboy, read every novel written by P. C. Wren, starting with *Beau Geste*, and harboured a reverential regard for the very idea of the Legion and its extreme standards of discipline and courage.

A parade of a regiment, more than a thousand men, who were to leave for French Indo-China (now called Vietnam), marched past the colonel. The men wore full woollen winter uniforms, complete with heavy overcoats and backpacks full of their gear, and carried rifles on their shoulders. The temperature was high and we were feeling the heat, so the discomfort of the marching men must have been extreme. When I commented on this to a host, he replied, 'It is winter. They are wearing winter uniform.' (If you ask stupid questions, expect stupid answers!)

Following the parade we were taken to a large hall where 250 officers were seated at trestle tables, on which were plates of *hors d'oeuvres*, carafes of wine and glasses. We were seated at a table on a dais at the head of the hall. Assuming that we were at lunch, I made a meal of the delicious fare. The colonel stood and made a speech of welcome to the visitors, in French, while our young guide translated. When his ability in English clearly failed him, he said, 'It's the same in English.' This drew howls of laughter from the thronged hall, and from the colonel, whose English was excellent. The ambassador replied in French, expressing pleasure and gratitude for the honour shown us.

After applause for the speeches, the senior officers led us to a dining room, while the remaining French officers returned to their work. The room we entered was relatively small and was dominated by a polished timber table set with beautiful dinnerware, complete with five dinner plates at every place. I was aghast at the thought that we were to be served a five-course meal after our previous hour's feast. I was wrong. What was served was a splendid nine-course meal! My hosts on either side of me were both lieutenant colonels and delighted in insisting that I eat every morsel.

Before coffee and cognac were served the adjutant opened a locked safe, removed a velvet-lined tray and handed it to the colonel. The colonel addressed us and invited us to accept honorary membership as officers of the French Foreign Legion, presenting us each with a gilt and enamel brooch on which was the name and crest of the Legion. After the adjutant had returned the tray to the safe and resumed his seat, I felt his hand on my thigh and looked down in alarm, only to see that he was holding, out of sight of the others in the room, another brooch. He said in a whisper, 'This is for your sweetheart!' It disappeared into my pocket as quickly as I could say, 'Thank you, Sir!'

A few days later we rejoined other units of the fleet and, after two days of exercises, returned to Gibraltar to replenish before sailing to Lagos, in Portugal, and back into bad weather. One last visit to Gibraltar, followed by more exercises in the wild Atlantic, was all that remained until we returned to England.

Entering Portland Harbour on my nineteenth birthday, I was anticipating a pleasant evening, having invited a school friend of Elizabeth Watson of Bedales for cocktails and dinner aboard. The officers even prepared a special cocktail, which they assured me would work wonders on my guest's resistance when we went ashore. Alas, these best-laid plans were about to come unstuck. As we approached our buoy in the teeth of a blizzard, the captain proceeded to make a dog's breakfast of manoeuvring to secure the ship. Other crews already passing on their way ashore made us the subject of ribald comment and gestures as we repeatedly failed to secure. Three pairs of sailors – called 'buoy jumpers' – whose task was to climb on to the buoy from a boat and then secure the anchor cable to the ring of the buoy, were dumped unceremoniously into the icy harbour as the bow hit the buoy. They had to be rescued and given tots of rum to warm them after hot showers. I was on the bridge, checking that we did not drag our anchor, which had been dropped while we were delayed. In the wardroom the officers were already all drinking my health, on my wine bill, following the custom of 'shouting the mess' on one's birthday. Even the captain compounded my misery by calling 'Happy birthday' through the voice pipe!

The snow fell all day, and when I finally got ashore there was no sign of my guest. A taxi driver told me she had waited for four hours at the landing but had just been driven to another town where she was spending the night with her sister. I certainly could not contemplate following in a taxi and returned to *Sluys*, despondent, and proceeded to drink the 'seduction syrup', all the while complaining to the amused officers about the captain's abysmal ship handling. 'Don't tell us, tell the captain!' one officer suggested, and before I had paused to evaluate the consequences, I was knocking on his cabin door. 'What do you want, Cabban?' he asked. After I had blundered in and reminded him of his performance (and, in particular, its effect on my social life), he asked, 'What do you want me to do about it?'

'Let me go to Lyme Regis tomorrow, Sir, so I can explain and clear things up,' I replied.

'Off you go then, and come back when you sort it out!' he said.

I was off early in the morning and caught a bus to Lyme Regis, stopping in the town in which my friend had stayed. By a remarkable coincidence she joined the same bus. She then led me to her school where I met her headmistress and explained my presence. I was directed to a charming inn where I lodged for three nights, while we were allowed to meet each afternoon. Money inevitably ran out, and I returned to the ship to be met on deck by the captain saying, 'Nice of you to come back, Cabban. Did you sort everything out?'

'Yes, Sir! I gave her gifts from our cruise and explained my late arrival, and everything was all right.'

'If you'd given me the gifts, you could have stayed the week!' he said.

A few days later, I met Commander and Mrs Larkin approaching *Sluys* as I was heading off towards Weymouth. As I passed them, saluting, the captain asked, 'Off to Lyme Regis, Cabban?' and I responded with a muttered, 'No, Sir, just into town.' As I scampered on my way, I heard their happy laughter at my obvious embarrassment.

Not all our experiences at the time were so carefree. HMS *Nelson* was anchoring in Portland after exercising in Weymouth Bay when the starboard anchor flew out of the hawse pipe followed by the entire length of cable. The port anchor followed, then the secondary sheet anchor, and finally the stream anchor and cable were left on the harbour bed as the battleship lumbered on. This was not only a very public lapse but also one with serious implications for the officers in command of the ship. It is the duty of the navigator to observe, at first hand, the securing of the cables to the cable clenches in the cable lockers on completion of every refit. That episode saw the end of a navigator's career, as the ship was ordered by the admiral to return to Weymouth Bay and continue steaming in circles until all anchors and cable were recovered by boats and then reinstated correctly. This was a mammoth task, taking several days to complete. It also had us all reading our *Manual of Seamanship* again, studying the evolution (recovering an anchor and cable from an open boat and securing it in its ship), which we had not had the misfortune to experience.

Returning to Devonport for leave and refit, we completed our training with the ship in the dockyard. I became acutely aware, at this time, why we were restricted from drinking spirits in the gunroom messes when I found myself swallowing cigar smoke when inhaling after having consumed too much brandy and ginger ale. The pain was self-inflicted, but it taught me how potentially dangerous the loosening effect of spirits can be. This had been a fairly free-drinking mess, but without any major loss of control or drunkenness. In small ships, with absolutely no drinking at sea, the opportunity to imbibe several drinks slowly on long evenings in harbour was welcome. Still, I decided to cut down on my drinking, even foregoing the Algerian wine that we had bought in casks and decanted into washed-out beer bottles, at threepence a bottle.

Late in this destroyer phase of training, Commander Larkin told me that Commander Fisher of *King George V* had written in my E190 (the record of a midshipman's training) that I worked 'as hard as is necessary, but may get over this'. Larkin was extremely angry at this slight, saying that I was an exemplary worker and he was very impressed by my diligence and results. Privately, I thought that Fisher was spot on! *King George V* represented a challenge by naval bureaucracy to the individual spirit. Every opportunity to resist blind obedience to ritual, such as attending boring parades, seemed important, while attractive activities such as boat running and tanky's duties were to be relished. *Sluys*, on the other hand, was supremely enjoyable and whetted my growing thirst for learning and experience.

5
Naval Undergraduates

After another four-week leave period in London we were reunited with our seaman colleagues from the RAN College for two terms of four months at the Royal Naval College, Greenwich. It was now May 1947, and we were proud acting sub-lieutenants. Through the continuing benevolence of Lady Ryder, I had spent a week in the New Forest, riding ponies from the stables of Joe and Betty Taylor, a delightful and generous childless couple who lavished affection and comfort on countless RAAF aircrew during the war and continued this tradition with young RAN officers.

The Royal Naval College was an advanced general education establishment between sea training and the technical naval courses that would follow immediately afterwards. Its milieu was like that of a university, which it has since become. Some subjects, such as advanced mathematics, nuclear physics, electronics and current affairs, were mandatory. Formal writing of submissions, logic, and strategic and tactical analysis were also expected to be learned, the latter in extended workshop situations. Considerable unallocated time was also available for research. At least one extra-curricular subject for study was nominated during the first term and could be carried over. Two informal subjects were required in the second term.

Our tenure coincided with several major international sporting events of great interest to me, including the Wallabies playing England at Twickenham, which I watched, having been to primary school with the Australian scrum half, Cyril Burke. Later there was Wimbledon, and the Australian Davis Cup team playing beforehand at the Queens Club tournament. I established where the team was staying and, by telephone, invited them to a mess dinner. Since they did not have dinner suits, I was obliged to get dispensation from the president for them to come in business suits. John Bromwich, Geoff Brown and their manager joined us. It was a big occasion for us all as we showed them around the facility.

With payment being monthly, balancing income and expenditure was always a delicate task. Having been introduced to London nightclubs and good restaurants, I found that it was possible to afford one night a month on which I could take a partner to dinner and a club if the next three weekends were spent in the country. This became a pattern of activity for months. Entry to Churchill's, my favourite nightclub, cost only one pound each, and a large jug of fruit punch was fifteen shillings. So, if no alcohol was consumed, a night of dancing to two top-rate orchestras (one playing foxtrots and the other Latin music) could cost as little as three pounds, including a five-shilling tip for the squash. Pat Burnett and I had pooled resources for rumba and samba lessons as midshipmen in Portsmouth, and this was pay-off time! Members at Churchill's were able to buy bottles of spirits, on which the level of remaining content was marked on their departure, usually at about 4.00 a.m., and the bottle could be redeemed on the next visit.

While staying at Bedales with several other young house guests, we often congregated in a small lounge in the basement level to conduct séances, using an inverted glass on a highly polished table with the letters of the alphabet on paper squares, placed at random in a wide circle. Everyone would place a finger on the glass and someone would ask a question, either aloud or silently, and the glass would move from letter to letter, spelling out the response. Belief or disbelief did not matter. It was riveting, as the identity of the muse or whatever was answering was consistent, and we enjoyed it. We were given the winner of a horse race, although nobody risked backing it, because we had never heard of the nag! But I was convinced that at least one reply, which was consistent, was true: that I would marry Sue.

Two incidents that will live with us always came during social occasions. While speaking to two young ladies at a cocktail party one evening, David Leach, subsequently RAN Chief of Naval Staff, turned to one whose glass was empty and asked, 'May I get you another drink?' The words were no sooner spoken than a crusty old retired admiral to whom we had been introduced said, 'Young man! You don't ask a lady if she would like *another* drink. You ask if she would like a drink!'

Poor David quickly asked, 'May I get you a drink?'

'I've already had one!' was the immediate response.

A few nights later, our host took us to the home of the chaplain of the fleet. In the absence of her husband, who was serving at sea, the chaplain's wife had invited us to dinner. As we were naval officers, she kindly provided suitable company for us in the person of our old friend, the admiral. She was charming and eager to make us comfortable, commencing by giving us each a half pint pewter tankard full of gin and vermouth, and drinking hers swiftly as she finalised the meal. Although I don't pretend to remember the menu, caviar was passed and, as I helped myself, 'It's not jam, boy!' was bellowed at me. There was game bird and accompanying fine wines and dessert, followed by aged Napoleon Cognac, in great quantity, served in brandy balloons. 'Pearls before swine!' trumpeted the flushed 'guest of horror'. We retired to the lounge for coffee. Our hostess, having poured and passed the cups, settled into her chair and promptly passed out cold. We looked at her and at each other and, with tacit agreement, crept silently out and closed the door.

My mother's brother had asked some Rotarians in Newcastle-upon-Tyne to look after me for a visit, and I travelled there by train to be met by three enthusiastic businessmen who had sent their wives away for the week in order to concentrate on me. The visit consisted of a succession of lunches, dinners, sightseeing and drinking at their favourite pubs and restaurants, with happy stories and exchanges of experiences scattered throughout. We seemed to end up each night drinking and eating winkles at the home where I stayed. Then I would wake late and ring a bell, which led to my bath being run and breakfast being served. After breakfast, usually near 11.00 or 11.30, I would telephone a number that reached my host, who would send his chauffeur to collect me, and it would start all over again. At the end of the week, when the wives returned, they were a little shocked at my appearance, but I was able to assure them that I was fine.

The following week, in Bury St Edmonds, Suffolk, I stayed with the brother of my Newcastle harbour pilot neighbour and his wife, who were very concerned at my condition and cosseted me. It was a week of long sleeps, leisurely walks and pub conversation, which saw me recover for the final lap of my leave. Returning to London, I had only five pounds remaining and a week to go. The oppressive summer weather in London was finishing, and there were still plays to be seen at the Arts Theatre Club and the Players Club, and events at the Royal Albert Hall, courtesy of Lady Ryder. Ballroom dancing, a passion of both Sue's and mine, was available nightly at the Palladium, at minimal prices. There were very good and affordable dance halls with excellent music and well-behaved patrons in every town and city I visited. Prearranged partners were not a necessity as there were always as many young women unattached as partnered.

Returning to Greenwich for the second and final term, we were briefed for a current history examination, in the form of a thesis. I chose to write on 'The End of the British Raj in India', having met a brigadier and his brother, a wing commander in the Indian services, who were fellow guests in Sussex. I gave a copy of my paper to these senior officers to read, and it became obvious that they had a widely differing view. I received not a word of comment and was therefore not unduly surprised to obtain only a B+ for my effort.

On the upper deck of a London bus one evening I sat next to a highly decorated senior RAF pilot, and we struck up a conversation. This was Group Captain 'Dixie' Dean DSO DFC, president of the Pathfinder Association, and I invited him to attend a guest night at the Royal Naval College. He enjoyed the dinner and was popular with the sub-lieutenants, who heard him describe his exploits flying Mosquitos over Europe during World War II. At the end of the evening I was invited to join the Pathfinder Club, situated in Berkley Square, despite the fact that there were no members at the time who were not associated with the Pathfinder Association. I duly joined and met the many delightful members, introduced to me by Squadron Leader Alex Thorne, the club secretary. He was a firm friend for many years, and the club became special to me, both for relaxation and its comfortable accommodation.

6

Pompey Courses

The year ended with a further three weeks of leave, taken entirely in Sussex, before commencing the much more disciplined ten months of specialist courses and exams for qualification for the rank of lieutenant. We undertook this instruction at Portsmouth, or 'Pompey' as it is known colloquially. Groups of about fourteen subs of mixed nationalities had fixed schedules for attending the various schools to undergo training in each of the specialist branches of the Navy. These consisted of Aviation, Gunnery, Navigation, Torpedoes and Anti-submarine (TAS) and Signal Communications. The subordinate, but still important, subjects were Divisional Duties and Atomic/Biological/Chemical Warfare and Damage Control (ABCD). For the duration of each course we were accommodated at the training establishment at which it was held, each unit being commissioned with a ship's name; for example HMS *Excellent* was the Gunnery School. The one exception was ABCD, which had no school with dedicated accommodation, so we lived in the old and uncomfortable royal yacht *Victoria and Albert* for two weeks.

Study for the examinations for each of the courses was undertaken with varying degrees of seriousness by the young officers, although the results would determine our seniority as lieutenants and could affect careers and income. I concede readily that during this period I tried to balance working sufficiently hard to pass all of the exams with the once-in-a-lifetime social opportunities available. No doubt I forwent higher passes by a few marks in some courses. My guiding philosophy was 'I may pass this way but once, so if I can do any good for myself, I must, for I'll never pass this way again!' It was a variation on the old theme of 'Eat, drink and be merry, for tomorrow we (may) die'.

The one course I enjoyed with a passion was Aviation. Along with Gunnery, Navigation and Torpedo, the Aviation course was of six weeks' duration. Subject to weather, it involved around twenty hours of flying. This included three hours solo, piloting a De Havilland Tiger Moth aircraft at HMS *Siskin*, the Royal Navy air station at Gosport. Royal Navy lieutenants who were qualified flying instructors (QFIs) taught the principles of flight sufficiently for their pupils to undertake the basic flying routines of taxiing, taking off and landing from a grass field. Lectures on the structure and operation of the Fleet Air Arm filled many more hours, introducing us to the concepts of air navigation, communication and combat. The effects of weather, darkness and distance had special significance in the air. Those pupils who were sufficiently advanced, at about ten hours' experience, were then 'checked out' by the chief flying instructor (CFI), Lieutenant Lunberg. If he was satisfied with their capability they were cleared for their first solo flight. This took place immediately, with a short briefing from the pupil's regular instructor.

During early training I had learned to judge the height of my aircraft by reference to the clarity of the blades of grass as they appeared beneath the wings. When the time approached for my solo check I was horrified to discover that the grass had been freshly mown, and I had to adjust quickly to other means of height estimation. Despite this initial unease my solo check proceeded well until, on the final approach to land, maintenance staff testing the engines of a Beaufighter close to the airfield boundary suddenly opened throttles, sending slipstream across our path and turning the plane on its side. The CFI took the joystick, saying, 'I have control', and immediately righted the aircraft, still on its glide path for landing at about three metres altitude. The landing was completed gently. 'Well done!' he said. 'You can go solo.' I did not enlighten him that I had not landed the plane at all. It had apparently landed itself without any human intervention.

The preflight briefing by Lieutenant Des Russell, my instructor, was simple enough. I was to take off, fly a circuit of the airfield, then land. The thrill of being airborne alone was indescribable. All of the instructors were standing outside the crew room as I approached to land, although I was unaware of them. As I touched the ground the aircraft bounced up into the air again. My heart fell as much as the plane rose, but without hesitation I opened the throttle wide and climbed away, in deep disappointment. The next landing was better. I touched on three points and allowed the Tiger Moth to come to a halt. Lieutenant Russell was on the wing speaking to me as soon as I had taxied back to the crew hut. 'If you hadn't gone around again, you'd not have flown solo again.'

After I had accumulated about fifteen hours, including two and a half hours solo, I was assessed as ready to undertake the A Licence test. This licence, qualifying the holder to fly as a pilot, even with passengers, required only a total of twenty hours' flying, including three solo hours, and passing a test by a qualified tester. Many young officers qualified and were issued with their A Licence, although I know of none who took advantage of it, probably because of the great expense of hiring an aircraft. Yet the 'A' was another desirable benchmark I wanted to achieve. The CFI briefed me to take off, climb to 200 feet, fly in a figure-of-eight pattern between two prominent points on the airfield, followed by a glide approach and landing, then another circuit ending with a precautionary landing. (The latter involves using engine power and a shorter approach and landing pattern.) I had completed all of these procedures in dual flight instruction, so I was confident. My confidence was misplaced.

When commencing the turning pattern I was blown off the line by a stiff crosswind. That complication had not occurred during training, so I tried to adjust while gazing at the nominated points below me. I turned with the aircraft on its side to stay within the tight constraints of the figure of eight. At the same time I unwittingly closed the throttle, which actually needed to be opened fairly wide to support this manoeuvre. Suddenly the aircraft spun towards the ground in what I later discovered was an incipient spin. Without alarm I corrected the situation, climbed to my height again and recommenced the turning pattern. As I passed over the control tower, a red Verey Pistol cartridge appeared in the air near me. 'Some poor bastard's in trouble,' I thought, as I kept turning. A few minutes later, aware that a red Aldis lamp was now focused on me from the tower, I was devastated to realise that I was 'it' and had to abort the test and land immediately. As I came to rest, Des Russell climbed on the wing and asked, 'What the bloody hell were you trying to do – kill yourself?'

Like an idiot I replied, 'No. Doing an A Licence test!'

'Don't be bloody smart,' he retorted. 'The CFI has just vomited!'

That was the last of the test for me. I was obliged to shout drinks to all of the instructors in the wardroom mess that evening – pass or fail – as was the custom. While I licked my wounds, Lunberg came up to me and said, 'Cabban, we're recommending you, highly, for specialisation. Anyone who gets out of what you did today has to be a pilot.' They were prophetic words.

Most of the courses were enjoyable, although many of my group found HMS *Vernon*, the Torpedo School, dreary. But two sporting events coincided with our six weeks there and made the period memorable. Our course officer had accepted a challenge, on our behalf, from the subalterns of the Royal Marine Barracks, Eastney, to a whaler rowing race over two miles – informing us only after it was accepted! We were appalled, considering our current state of physical fitness unlikely to suffice, but set about training daily at the crack of dawn. Of our group, Frank Morrell and I were the two most experienced in these boats. By crew consent, Frank stroked while I coxed over three hard weeks of galley-slave training. To everyone's great surprise we won by a length, and kept the Navy's pride intact.

Meanwhile, Don Bradman's 1948 team was playing a Test match at Lord's, and David Leach invited me to accompany him as a guest of a young Royal Navy lieutenant who was a member of the MCC. Australia was fielding, and we were privileged to watch as Lindwall and Miller bowled Australia into a good position against England. At lunchtime I carefully hand-printed a note to Bradman, inviting him and his team to a mess dinner at HMS *Vernon*, and passed it to an usher. I later received a very nice note of thanks in reply, indicating that their schedule precluded acceptance.

One of our sorties to London during our Gunnery training at Whale Island featured a dinner dance party at the Savoy Hotel, where several subs and our partners occupied a prominent large circular table. We had just settled and were warming up for the evening when Admiral of the Fleet Lord Fraser, Commander in Chief Portsmouth, entered with a large group of senior officers and their ladies. As they were about to be directed to their table I said glibly to my partner, 'There's my old mate, Bruce.'

'If he's your "old mate", invite him to join us,' she responded.

Before anyone could react, I was standing before the admiral saying, 'Good evening, Sir. Would you care to share a drink with the boys?'

'Do I know you?' he asked.

'I doubt it, Sir, but I know you,' I replied.

Without missing a beat, he said, 'Are those young people gawking at me "the boys"?'

'I'm sure they are, Sir.'

'If you will first allow me to seat my guests, I will join you in a few minutes.'

True to his word, he joined us and was introduced to everyone. He was extremely animated and moved around the table chatting with each couple in turn until he gracefully returned to his guests. On the following Monday I was admonished for my impertinence, but the exuberant irreverence of youth can be difficult to curb.

During summer leave, Sir Robert Burrows told me that he had received an invitation to take his family to the London Olympic Games and to share the box of the president of the IOC, Lord Templeton, and take meals with Lord Burleigh, the chairman of the British Olympic Committee. He had replied that his family was unable to attend, but he had a young Australian guest whom he would like to take if this were acceptable, and it was approved. He later told me that his family could in fact have gone, but they could afford to see the Olympics anywhere in the world, whereas I might never have the opportunity. He assured me that they all concurred with his action. His chauffeur drove us to London and to the most exciting sporting event of my life.

We were adjacent to the Royal Box, occupied by the royal family. So much was happening that it now seems a blur, but back then it was crystal clear. That night, as we were enjoying our customary nightcap, I was asked, 'Tell me about the Olympic Games, Peter.' It flowed from me like a gusher. The highlight had been seeing an Australian, John Winter, set a new world record for the high jump, winning the gold medal.

All of the RAN sub-lieutenants joined HMS *Glory*, the accommodation aircraft carrier for the crew standing by HMAS *Sydney*, which was to commission in Devonport, following courses. This was our first opportunity since graduating from college to meet and serve with other Australian officers. The executive officer, Commander O. H. Becher DSC RAN, a tall slim man of stern demeanour, was a firm and canny disciplinarian whom I liked instinctively. He had been gunnery officer at Flinders Naval Depot during my time as a cadet, but other than a basic awareness of his identity, I had no knowledge of him. He was also a keen bridge player, as was the dental surgeon, Surgeon Commander Wolcott, father of the career diplomat who went on to head the Department of Foreign Affairs. We played many games in the evenings as we awaited our passage home. Six of us were to sail in RMS *Orcades* on its maiden voyage and the others in RMS *Strathaird*.

When our sailing dates were known and it looked as though we would have no further opportunity to farewell our friends in the UK, I was nominated by the subs to ask Becher for some pre-embarkation leave. He did not make this easy, but I eventually asked at what I thought was the best moment, during a bridge game, only to be rebuffed and rebuked. I could not disagree with his contention that all we thought about was leave, and I did not argue or say another word to press our cause. The following day, with a wry grin, he said that a week's leave was granted us before embarkation. I stayed in Hayward's Heath for a few days, taking with me Rory Burnett, Pat's younger brother, who was at Greenwich at the time, and finally spent a night in London visiting the Pathfinder Club.

The experience of being on board a passenger liner was new to us, and we soon established friendships with many passengers, some of which survived the passage. The senior RAN officer aboard, Captain D. H. 'Darbo' Harries, summoned us and assured us that he did not wish to see us unless we were in trouble, and I do not recall sighting him again. On the other hand, we met Surgeon Lieutenant Commander Robert Coplans, later to feature prominently in my life, and eventually to become Surgeon Rear Admiral. After leaving Port Said, in the Red Sea, I had cause to seek his advice for gippy stomach. His bland prescription was, 'Drink straight Scotch whisky!' It worked. Fifteen years later, witnessing that volatile combination of spirits and stomach trouble at sea would become my nightmare.

7
First RAN Ship

I was met in Sydney by my mother and, after a night in Balmoral, was whisked off to Newcastle for six weeks leave. Safely home, I was sitting in the kitchen in a bay window when, to my utter delight, I saw Sue entering by the back gate. I was out the door and had gathered her into my arms in seconds. The long time apart disappeared in an instant as we clung to each other. The following days were precious as we filled in the unknown gaps in each other's lives so that nothing could come up later to mar our joy. We were often able to borrow a car so that we could travel more widely. We picnicked and surfed on the beaches as well as dancing and dining often, trying to capture as much as possible before we would part again, this time for at least a year.

Jane Hill had admonished Sue not to become involved with me to the exclusion of anyone else, but could just as well have been speaking to herself. We were young and in love. We had no doubts about our future together, so parting was even more difficult than it had been three years earlier. Our feelings were now even more intense and urgent. Sue was to accompany her parents and siblings to England soon after I sailed north. Her parents had given them the option of staying home and having a gift of money, or accompanying them. They all chose to go, never thinking that they would all secure jobs, travel extensively and, for Sue, be attracted to another man.

To join my first RAN ship, HMAS *Shoalhaven*, I had to sail to Japan. The passage to Kure was aboard HMAS *Westralia*, a World War II troopship. Also aboard and joining *Shoalhaven* was Lieutenant Murray Fowler, appointed to relieve the navigator, a handful of sailors and soldiers, some of whom were bound for New Guinea, and some Army nurses. The ship was slow, averaging about twelve knots, and very hot. It was mid-summer and we were entering the tropics with no air-conditioning. The weather deteriorated as we arrived in the Coral Sea with a hurricane developing, causing the ship to slow, and eventually sustain damage.

After one engine failed at night, in the worst of the storm, two soldiers were skylarking, racing around the upper deck as the ship rolled and pitched uncontrollably. *Westralia* lurched violently, and one soldier was pitched over the guardrail into the sea. 'Man overboard!' was called, and a lifebuoy was thrown to the soldier, who swam towards it. As fate would have it, there was no lamp attached to that buoy, while several others that did have lamps were also thrown, causing confusion. The ship slowed and circled to approach him, but could not close sufficiently to throw a line. A colonel attached to the ship, who had been a champion swimmer, immediately readied himself to swim to the soldier, but the captain refused to allow it, citing the difficulty of recovering them if they survived. Murray Fowler and I volunteered to take a lifeboat with four sailor volunteers if we could be lowered in the lee of the ship. That, too, was ruled out because of the unpredictable nature of the sea, which was unbelievably disturbed. The captain was in an impossible position. While the storm raged he had no accurate fix of the ship's position, but knew that uncharted reefs surrounded us and that we were drifting at the whim of wind and sea. Although we could see the soldier, still cheerfully clinging to the buoy, the captain made the courageous decision to sail off and leave him rather than hazard his ship and passengers.

Two days later, the captain approached me quietly and asked if I thought he should have let us try a boat rescue. The poor man was distraught. I should have consoled him, and have always regretted that I could not. Murray and I believed that we had a good chance in the lifeboat. The captain was right, of course. He had no way of knowing our capabilities, and would have been culpable had we all been drowned, which I now accept was possible, if not probable.

My twenty-first birthday arrived while we were in the hottest and most humid part of the passage. I was sleeping in the afternoon when one of the ship's officers silently entered my cabin and left a bottle of gin and a birthday cake on a chair near my bunk. I was missing Sue madly and, in the boredom of the tropical torpor, was wishing my life away until we could be together again. That evening all the officers played poker, which was not unusual, and I lost as much as I could afford and begged to be excused. The purser would not hear of it and offered to lend me ten shillings. I refused to borrow to gamble and declined, but he insisted that it be a gift for my birthday, and that it would spoil the night if I left. The next hand dealt to me was a Royal Straight Flush. I could not bet on that! I immediately tabled it, and everyone threw two shillings into my cash pile. By the night's end I had won ten pounds after repaying the purser.

Kure was a major naval port in Japan, quite close to Hiroshima, and the British Commonwealth Occupation Force had a full presence there, mostly Australian servicemen and women. *Shoalhaven* was a River Class frigate, with nine officers and about ninety petty officers and men. Its main activity was 'showing the flag' and conducting a specified number of searches for contraband of Japanese merchant vessels. Our time on station alternated between Japanese waters and Shanghai, where we blended with the British Far East Fleet. I was designated quarterdeck officer, and my action station was the four-inch X Gun, located on the quarterdeck.

Peter Rees, another of my term, was already aboard, and had been installed in the cabin close to the quarterdeck, known as 'Nagasaki' because it resembled an atomic bomb site. Murray and I had to join Rees and Clem Schmitzer (an ex-RAAF pilot) in 'Nagasaki', but there were only three bunks. An extra bunk, for me, was installed by hanging a wire mattress on chains over the clothes lockers. It probably cost two cakes of bath soap to have the extra bunk installed, as that was the currency for quick, unofficial jobs done by Japanese workers. Soap was a scarce commodity in Japan at the time. Whoever was going ashore first from this cabin was usually best dressed, as most clothes fitted us all and it was hard to keep them separate.

On the day after I joined, a message was broadcast for all officers to report to the first lieutenant in the wardroom. As I made to respond, another officer told me sharply to ignore it. I recoiled at this attitude, but found that I was the only officer to answer the call. The lack of respect for the first lieutenant was ingrained, and he was referred to as 'Charley Horse'. By contrast, respect and liking for the captain, Lieutenant Commander Keith Tapp, was as high as for anyone with whom I served, from officers and the lower deck alike. This was illustrated dramatically one evening at the RAAF base in Hiroshima when officers and men of the ship were being entertained. An air force man, the worse for drink,

accidentally threw his glass of beer over 'Tappy' and was promptly flat-
tened by a sailor, saying, 'That's our captain, you bastard!' Fortunately, a
brawl was avoided.

We sailed for Shanghai shortly after I joined, and secured to a buoy in
the Huang Pu River, opposite the Bund, the waterfront plaza of
Shanghai. Our routines here were determined by the Royal Navy, and
included armed patrols of the city and suburbs, made in a Land Rover.
On return to the ship after one such patrol I heard that a Chinese soldier
had thrown a hand grenade into a cinema, killing and wounding many
patrons, and had been shot dead by a passing Chinese officer. The futility
of these patrols was not lost on us, but 'ours not to reason why' was the
inescapable policy.

The political situation in China during March–April 1949 was explosive as the Communist forces moved relentlessly against the Nationalists
towards Shanghai. It was rumoured that the Nationalist Chinese soldiers
were selling their ammunition to the enemy for sixpence a bullet as they
had to pay threepence for each bullet they fired! None of this was reassuring for the locals. They were a mixture of nationalities, many of
whom could not expect to receive any sympathy from the Red Army.

On our return to Kure, *Shoalhaven* was replenished before sailing to
other ports to show the flag, and visited the real Nagasaki as our first port
of call. The devastation of an atomic bomb is breathtaking when
confronted at ground zero. I stood with other officers at the crumbled
rock walls of the jail over which the detonation occurred and then visited
the nearby hospital where glass test tubes were fused in one room and
intact in the next.

I was able to accompany the captain to Yokohama while he called on
senior US Navy officers. Our driver and I made a beeline for the post
exchange store to buy a turkey and other special food for a surprise
birthday dinner for the captain. The birthday dinner was a success. The
residents of our cabin had formed a band, the Nagasaki Shithots, using
castanets, tambourines and bongos as well as singing raucously while
wearing silk Chinese skullcaps and a plastic bunch of grapes in our
buttonholes. The songs in our repertoire were mostly adult and/or naval
in nature, although we did give a fair rendition of 'Cigarettes and Whisky
and Wild, Wild Women'. We entertained not only the wardroom but also
half of the crew, who clustered happily around the open scuttles on the

upper deck, enjoying the unusual spectacle of officers letting their hair down in a great cause.

Our wardroom was the proud custodian of a signed, steel-framed photograph of Esther Williams, a famous American bathing beauty, which was secured above the fireplace. The signal, 'Where's Esther?' was routinely circulated when new ships arrived on station, and she was as much a coveted target as any barber's pole. One attempted raid was successfully repelled in Kure, but when we proceeded to Sasebo, where the US Navy had a large presence, she was lost at the end of what was a very active cocktail party. On our last night in Sasebo (and I think, Japan) that hospitality was returned in spades. Every officer except the CO, who was suffering from influenza, and me as officer of the day, attended the US Navy mess ashore. They returned on board with less than an hour remaining before we were due to sail.

I attempted to keep those whose roles were key to our sailing awake and more or less vertical. Fortunately, I had prepared the charts for the navigator (usually Peter Rees' job as officer of the watch entering and leaving harbour), and had the cable party called to the forecastle to prepare to slip from our buoy. 'Pilot' was almost without uniform when assisted over the side by a zealous boat's crew, and turned in immediately. I commenced sending a messenger to call him to the bridge every five minutes. The message that came back was always the same two words, courteously advising what I should get. The response from Rees was a little better. I knew when 'Speed' Gordon had arrived on the forecastle by the loud and colourful shouting that emanated from the scrum of bodies clustered around the capstan.

The captain, who had arrived on time but was clearly not well, looked around for everyone. Assured that we were almost ready to proceed, he transferred his attention to the forecastle and called on the loud hailer, 'Gordon, what's wrong?' The reply has remained with me over the intervening years: 'The fucking fucker's fucked!' No more was said. Suddenly, Murray appeared alongside me at the screened chart table, shouldered me aside and cheerfully said, 'Fuck off!' Which I did, with some relief. Then the captain, not having observed anything to warn him, put his head under the chart table screen, at which the navigator turned, not seeing who it was (but assuming it was Rees), exhaled mightily in his face, saying, 'That'll fix you, you bastard!' and laughed madly as the captain reeled backwards. It said a great deal for the mutual liking and respect between Tapp, Gordon and Fowler that the situation was allowed to play itself out with good humour. Murray was completely capable of performing his duties, but was playing the situation for maximum effect, as was Speed. The ship left Sasebo Harbour without mishap, although the number of ships moored between us and the entrance required excellent night pilotage by the navigator. Before leaving the bridge, when we were safe at sea, he told me, 'The bastard knows its own way out!'

After we returned to Sydney I found Newcastle had lost its glow without Sue. Nevertheless, taking Peter Rees with me for a couple of weekends, we had a lot of fun. Jane and Eric Hill had not yet returned, and I had no idea that Sue would not return with them but had chosen to stay with her siblings.

The promotion of Keith Tapp to commander meant that we had a new commanding officer in *Shoalhaven*. Newly promoted Captain A. W. R. McNicoll OBE GM became captain of the First Frigate Flotilla and our CO. We also had a new first lieutenant (executive officer), Lieutenant Sangster RN. I had been appointed to HMAS *Culgoa* at a time that clashed with my impending specialist flying course so Peter Rees took my place, returning to Japan and eventually going to Korea. The number of qualified bridge watch-keeping officers had been reduced to three, comprising the first lieutenant, the navigator and me. The change in atmosphere in the ship was dramatic. We had just been awarded the Gloucester Cup as the most efficient ship in the Navy, and morale was incredibly high. There had been deep and genuine respect between the officers and crew at all levels, but it suddenly seemed to disappear as the 'small ship' camaraderie of the wardroom was displaced by more rigid attitudes.

A consequence of this sharp reduction in experienced watch-keeping officers meant that Murray Fowler and I suddenly found we had to keep all of the bridge watches as officer of the watch. Also, we were both required on the bridge whenever special sea dutymen were at their stations, and at action stations during fleet exercises. These duties could stretch for hours. The situation reached a climax on a night when the fleet was off the South Coast of New South Wales. At midnight the captain asked me, 'Who has the middle watch, sub?'

'I have, Sir,' I replied.

'But you've been on the bridge all day,' he observed.

'So has the navigator, Sir,' I said.

He then said, 'I shall do the middle!'

'No, Sir! The navigator and I can cope.'

'Then call me if you can't keep awake!' he replied.

The first lieutenant had been present throughout that exchange but then left the bridge. Two minutes later, I had a phone call from Lieutenant Sangster, who said, 'I'll keep the middle, Sub.'

'No you won't,' I replied. 'Fowler and I will sort out our own problems!'

For almost two weeks we endured that pressure, and averaged less than four hours sleep a night each, arriving in Melbourne for Cup Week absolutely exhausted.

Murray was an incredibly successful punter, and we spent many a pleasant hour poring over the form guides, selecting 'good things'. I had extremely limited resources and a mounting mess bill to address. On the day of the Mooney Valley Cup I gave him my meagre cash to place on two selections. Both horses won at long odds, and I joined others of my college term at Flemington on the pre-Cup Saturday and backed more winners.

Some of my winnings went on an expensive overseas phone call to Sue in England. It became clear that she was not returning in the foreseeable future, and I felt totally empty. Others were in the room while she took the call, so little was said, but her lack of enthusiasm for the conversation came through to me and I was devastated. I had not been prepared for that. We had drifted apart again, and although we continued writing frequently, as close friends, there was a distinct lack of truly personal news. So things took their course, and I endeavoured to get over my sense of loss.

My experience with McNicoll was, on the whole, unpleasant. I found his attitude towards me to be demeaning, while he found me immature, which I undoubtedly was. McNicoll told us several times, in the wardroom, that as an acting sub-lieutenant he had obtained five first-class certificates and that the only college graduate since the beginning of the war who was 'worth a pinch of shit' was Tony Sallmann, who also had five. When I informed him that Sallmann had not attended Greenwich, which had not been utilised for subs during the war, he withdrew his endorsement and included Sallmann in his derogatory assessment. Later, I could not help myself when, during a mess dinner in his honour, I challenged McNicoll by saying that courses must have been easier in his time. There was a shocked silence, and then he said, 'I hope you can justify that remark!'

I said that he would not be repeatedly trumpeting his five firsts if there were not only five courses. 'We had seven courses, Sir,' I said. Then I asked, 'And what did you know about radar?'

'This has gone far enough, sub!' finished it.

Murray told me afterwards what I already knew: that I had been an idiot!

Shoalhaven steamed north through the Barrier Reef, carrying Rear Admiral Sir John Collins KBE CB RAN, Chief of Naval Staff, and Commander R. I. Peek OBE DSC RAN, *en route* to Dreger Harbour, New Guinea. The admiral occupied the captain's day cabin, which irritated McNicoll, who had to use his much smaller sea cabin for the extended period. I found the presence on board of the guests quite refreshing. Admiral Collins was on the bridge when, as OOW, I altered course decisively to avoid a whale that had suddenly surfaced close to our bow. 'Well done, sub! If that had been a submarine, you'd have hit amidships!' he said with a huge grin.

When the ship was near our destination, I had already prepared the charts for entry to Dreger Harbour and sent a message to the exhausted Murray Fowler to come to the bridge, only to be rewarded with the usual responses. But this time the admiral and CO were alongside me on the bridge. I continued manoeuvring the ship towards the wharf without any corrective orders from the captain, nor any comment on the navigator's absence. Just when I concluded that I was going to have to take her alongside the wharf, Murray materialised quietly beside me, telling me (in his usual way) to go.

I was pleased to receive an appointment to HMAS *Sydney* for a few weeks to become familiar with aircraft carrier operations, before commencing my pilot's training at the RAAF air station at Point Cook. It was exciting and totally different as I watched the Firefly and Sea Fury aircraft taking off and landing in varying weather conditions. I even witnessed deck landing accidents at close quarters, including a 'Grand National' where an aircraft bounced over the crash barriers and onto the back of another plane in which the pilot was still seated. The propeller narrowly missed decapitating the lieutenant who was about to leave his cockpit. Not surprisingly, he resigned his commission and left the Navy soon afterwards.

One night in Jervis Bay during this brief appointment I was standing as OOW at the boat ladder and was joined by a decidedly drunk captain who was shedding tears because his pilots were still ashore attending a mess dinner at HMAS *Albatross*, and would be affected by alcohol when flying the following day. I never drank any alcohol within twenty-four hours of planned flying. This was not a moral decision or the dutiful following of some strict doctrine. I simply felt that I had enough to overcome without adding another handicap to a hazardous undertaking. But I did not try to impose my decision on others.

Some years later Captain Peek told me that 'the finest captain who served in the Navy', J. M. Armstrong, had been permanently injured after falling from a tram. His career was ended just as he was about to take command of *Sydney*. His place had been taken by the inebriated captain I had met at the boat ladder.

8
Flying Training

I arrived at Point Cook in February 1950, along with Alan Cordell, who had been serving in *Sydney*, and John Matthew, also of our term at college.

The flying was more than enjoyable – I absolutely loved it. We learned the elements of navigation in cross-country flying as far as the safe range of the Tiger Moth would permit, plus simple aerobatics, loops and rolls. My first instructor was distinguished for having unwittingly allowed a pupil to land on an aircraft that was about to take off. Fortunately, I was not destined to be his pupil for long, but on my first check flight with the chief flying instructor I 'stretched the glide' on approaching to land, a major sin of flying that can cause the aircraft to stall and crash. I never did it again. In four and a half months we flew fifty hours, almost thirty of them solo.

After a brief period of home leave we commenced training in Wirraway aircraft. Throughout the six months of Wirraway flying I was most fortunate to be instructed by Flight Lieutenant Jim Gooch DFC, an extremely experienced and brave wartime bomber pilot and a post-war test pilot of Meteor jet fighters. Jim Gooch was awarded an immediate Distinguished Flying Cross, by King George VI, after mining the Konigs-berg Canal in World War II. His was the only surviving aircraft of a secret raid, returning after having suffered horrendous damage but with his crew intact.

Gooch told me, after the final tests, that I was the best pilot on course on Fridays – and the worst on Mondays! That reflected my weekends in Melbourne, burning the candle at both ends, and sounded fair enough to me. None of us had a car, so the RAAF bus would drop us on Friday evening and pick us up again on Sunday night at Spencer Street Station. I had met a lovely young student nurse who had visited Point Cook with a senior RAAF officer's daughter. I had been asked to entertain them, and had subsequently become friendly with the nurse's family and visited them regularly. From the very beginning I was open about my enduring love for Sue, but we became very close.

In January 1951 we converted to the twin-engine Oxford trainer aircraft, having logged more than 200 hours on single-engine Tiger Moth and Wirraway trainers. I was paired with Alan Cordell for this phase. We would change position at the controls halfway through each session of flying after landing on a satellite airfield at Werribee, about twenty miles from Point Cook. Later, if no one was able to see us, we trimmed the aircraft for level flight and changed positions in the air. This was fun, seemed completely safe and allowed us just a few more precious minutes at the controls. We graduated and were awarded our wings and granted a brief home leave before our scheduled departure aboard the liner RMS *Orcades* for the UK and operational flying training. During my leave, I visited Mr and Mrs Hill, who had left their three children working in England, and asked if there were anything I might take from them for Sue. A pair of fine stockings was duly purchased, and they were to give me at least a reason for an early meeting and a resolution of our feelings towards each other.

Our three-berth cabin in *Orcades* was shipside and much more comfortable than that to which we were entitled as sub-lieutenants. The passage was an enjoyable break from the discipline of training and studying for the previous year. On arrival in London we were given four weeks leave and substantial back pay, which was most welcome. The moment we met, I knew I was still hopelessly in love with Sue. It was overwhelming, and it was mutual, although Sue was cautious and wanted time to really evaluate our feelings before committing to marriage. I needed no more time, after seven years of loving her. We had been apart for two years, but this long period of separation just melted away. After an intense week of courtship, dining, night clubbing and persuasion, we became engaged. Sue was working in London, through an agency, as a chauffeuse to movie stars, executives, tourists and dignitaries. I had proposed on our first night in London, after dinner at the Mayfair Hotel and a nightcap at Churchill's in New Bond Street. We finished up at

Churchill's after a dinner dance every night except Sunday, for a week. Sue still worked each day and said that she finally accepted me in order to get some sleep!

Having agreed on an August wedding, Sue suggested that we tie the knot in the church near the flat that she and her sister shared with some other Australian girls in South Kensington. On closer inspection we discovered the church was a bombed-out shell. Told of our dilemma, Lady Burrows suggested the King's Chapel of the Savoy, off the Strand. Its compact size and character suited the modest number of guests we would have. The availability of the nearby St Paul's Cathedral men's choir was an added attraction. After we had met the deacon and arranged the details, Sue duly lodged a suitcase, labelled with her name, in the precinct of the chapel and attended the reading of banns. We travelled to Bristol so that I could meet Sue's relatives, who insisted on buying the bridal gown. I then took her to Portsmouth where we met other RAN officers who had served at the college while I was there and whom we invited, with their wives, to the wedding. A carefully crafted letter to Mr and Mrs Hill, asking their blessing on our engagement and wedding plans, received a prompt and considered reply from my soon-to-be father-in-law.

We did not agree on the purchase of an engagement ring until a time when Sue was with me when I visited Gieves, the naval outfitters, to buy some uniform clothes. (She had, in fact, expressed a strong preference for a movie camera instead of a ring.) There was a jewellery display cabinet at Gieves that she studied while I was busy with my uniform purchases. When I rejoined her she said, 'If you can pick the ring I like, you may buy it for me.' It was a snip! I pointed to a simple sapphire, diamond and platinum ring that matched her eyes, and when it fitted her ring finger, we borrowed it 'for half an hour' while we went to a small café to consider it seriously. Five minutes later we were back, and I bought it. We ordered the wedding ring to match, and all was settled.

At the conclusion of leave, I travelled by train and bus to Royal Naval Air Station (RNAS) *Lossiemouth*, via Aberdeen. It was here that pilots underwent conversion to fighter or anti-submarine (AS) aircraft. To my delight, 'Wings', the commander (in charge of all flying operations) was Charles Lamb, and although we had only cursory contact, it was pleasing to know that he had been promoted. I requested that he ask the captain on my behalf for permission to marry, and this was forthcoming. He told me later, in a letter, that he and the captain had laughed at the thought of what my reaction would have been to a refusal.

Cordell, who was designated a fighter pilot, continued on Supermarine Seafires, while Matthew and I were anti-submarine pilots on Fairey Firefly aircraft. Our days were occupied by interspersed sessions of briefing, dual instruction and solo flights as we gained experience in these aircraft. This was more interesting, exciting and fulfilling than earlier training.

While we were living at Lossiemouth I became so concerned at the inequity of the living conditions and status of rating pilots that I submitted a paper, 'The Recruitment, Training and Promotion of Aircrew in the RAN'. It was forwarded through the captain of the air station to the Australian Commonwealth Naval Board (ACNB) after which I thought no more about it. At the conclusion of Phase 1 training the flying ability of all pilots was assessed and I was pleased to receive an 'Average' assessment of five, on a scale of one to nine. I did not know at the time that any higher assessment than this was uncommon for junior naval pilots.

We were separated for the final phase of operational flying training, with fighter training being undertaken in Sea Fury aircraft at RNAS *Culdrose* at Land's End and anti-submarine training in Firefly aircraft in Northern Ireland at RNAS *Eglinton*, outside Londonderry. Close to the eve of our departure from *Lossiemouth*, a stag party was given for me, and I was persuaded to extend my legendary acquaintance with Lord Fraser, now First Sea Lord, by sending him an invitation to our wedding. The audacity of that action hit home the following morning, so I wrote a hurried letter to the flag lieutenant to the Admiralty, explaining my sequence of contacts with the admiral of the fleet and asking his discretion in intercepting the invitation and evaluating the prudence of either presenting or destroying it. A delightful, hand-written letter from Lord Fraser wished us every happiness and expressed his regret at not being able to attend at short notice because of a staff meeting.

On the wedding day, 1 August 1951, after buying and despatching my gift to Sue (a string of pearls), I had a haircut at Harrod's, requesting that it be cut to look a week old. We married at the Savoy Chapel, with many of Sue's relatives among the guests. Her sister Elizabeth was bridesmaid, John Matthew was my best man and Sue's brother John gave her away. The Burrows acted as my virtual parents, sitting in the front row on the 'groom's side'.

As Sue entered the chapel and John Matthew and I stood looking ahead, Lady Burrows leaned towards me and said, 'Peter, if you want to enjoy your own wedding, turn around and look at your bride. She's beautiful!' I did, and she was more than that. (Although there were photographers galore, and we still have some really good photographs, it was Harrod's that captured the true depth of Sue's beauty that day in her full crinoline gown, which they'd made of 150-year-old Brussels lace. They proudly displayed that portrait until I bought it five years later.) A Reuters photographer was among a throng who delayed Sue before the service and kept the honour guard standing much too long afterwards. His photographs were published the next day in the national papers in Britain, and later in Australia. We were thrilled to have Charles Lamb as senior officer in the guard of honour, with five lieutenants.

The reception was held at the Pathfinder Club. A camera crew from Bristol recorded the proceedings for our families at home in an hour-long colour movie, which Eric Hill had commissioned. The Rothes Glen Hotel, a former county seat of the Countess of Sutherland, was the site of our honeymoon. Sue and I had chosen the hotel during her visit to Elgin in June, for the reading there of our banns, and found it and its surrounds to be idyllic. The hotel staff were wonderfully attentive and made us splendid picnic lunches every day. We drove to secluded havens, one of which was in the grounds of a laird whom I had phoned with the request that we might enter his estate. All he asked was that we close the gates behind us so as not to be disturbed! When we returned to London there was a letter from my mother saying, 'I know that you will be broke,' with a cheque to pay for a night at Churchill's night club.

The next stage of my flight training was preparation for the specific demands of fleet air operations: flying on and off aircraft carriers. Instruction was to be in Northern Ireland, so off we drove to Londonderry via the Liverpool–Belfast car ferry. When we commenced assisted dummy deck landings (ADDLS) at a satellite airfield, Sue drove there each day in time for a picnic lunch at the side of the runway. Each pilot would complete a series of curved approaches and landings, controlled by a landing signals officer (LSO, or batsman) who indicated the attitude of the aircraft to the pilot by means of circular bats held at arm's length. With about ten minutes between successive sessions for each pilot, we left the engine idling as we changed over, sharing one plane between two. I could sleep on the grass alongside the bitumen runway and then wake without prompting for the next session. During those days our most valued possession was a portable gramophone on which we played Nat King Cole's 'Too Young' as Sue and I danced around the kitchen until the disc was almost worn out.

The culmination of this stage of training came after three months when we embarked in HMS *Triumph* in the Irish Sea, off Bangor, County Down. Each pilot completed sixteen take-offs and deck landings during a six-day period. The weather was dismal. It has often been said that at first sight, from the cockpit of an aircraft due to land on its deck, an aircraft carrier appears like a postage stamp. It is indeed a very small stamp when seen for the first time, and it is a relief when nearing the carrier that it grows until the pilot is so preoccupied with flying to the LSO's signals that the initial apprehension fades to nothing. But this type of flying is undeniably dangerous.

One pilot panicked after his aircraft had engaged an arrestor wire while bouncing from the flight deck, and he opened his throttle fully. The plane rose vertically on the wire and then fell sideways over the ship's side, into the sea. The aircraft submerged immediately, and he was not recovered. As we were going ashore that evening Lieutenant Johnny Pope, an Australian serving in the Royal Navy, was directed to telephone the pilot's wife (whom Pope had never met) and inform her of her husband's death. We were appalled at the Royal Navy's attitude, and I accompanied Johnny as we called the police station in the pilot's home town and arranged for a minister of religion to counsel his widow. We then adjourned to a local club to meet up with the other pilots for a wake. Later in the evening I was thrilled to see Sue, who together with Audrey Pope, surprised us with a visit. Sue and Audrey had made a spontaneous decision to drive to Bangor in the hope of finding us, and had chanced on the club on the only night we were ever there.

Before I had to rejoin *Triumph* on the following morning, Sue and I decided that if a child resulted from our desperation (and lack of preparedness), it would be named Bangor. The commander (air) of the carrier told me, 'I'm not being personal, Cabban, when I say that you are the ugliest deck-landing pilot whom I've ever seen!' I was neither surprised nor resentful. I considered it nothing short of a miracle every time I arrived on the deck in an intact aircraft. It is no coincidence that the Fleet Air Arm song is named 'The A25' after the code number of the Navy's official Report of Aircraft Accidents form. The first verse is:

> They say in the Air Force the landing's OK,
> If the pilot gets out and can still walk away.
> But in the Fleet Air Arm the prospects are grim,
> If the landing's piss poor and the pilot can't swim.
> Cracking show! I'm alive!
> But I've still got to render my A25!

I embraced that sentiment forever after HMS *Triumph* and the rough weather in the Irish Sea.

One day, while at *Eglinton*, I was summoned to the office of lieutenant commander (flying), the officer responsible for the day-to-day operation of the airfield. He read to me a letter from the Naval Board, informing me that I had been awarded a Naval Board commendation for my paper on aircrew selection, etc. He told me that the Royal Navy, as well as the Australians, appreciated my paper. The recommendations were implemented by the time we returned home, and I felt relief and satisfaction that the service was able to accommodate constructive criticism.

9
Early Squadron Flying

The passage home in *Orontes* was wonderful. It was a second honeymoon, so soon after the first, and we relished it, aware of the many partings soon to come.

Also aboard *Orontes* was Lord Nuffield, the former William Morris, manufacturer of the Morris automobiles, whose gifts built and maintained dozens of servicemen's and women's clubs throughout the British Isles. The RAN officers aboard invited Lord Nuffield to a party, which he graciously attended. He responded with a reception in his cabin for our wives and us, and when Sue and I entered the crowded space, he took a perfect peach from a brimming fruit bowl and presented it to her, saying, 'Such a perfect peach must only go to a perfect beauty.' We were thrilled by that chivalrous remark.

Home leave preceded our journey in February 1952 to Nowra, where I was to join HMAS *Albatross*, the RAN air station, for service in 816 Squadron. Accommodation was virtually non-existent and the waiting list for married quarters at the airfield was more than twelve months, so we rented an extremely small room in a boarding house in Nowra.

Throughout my flying career we could not afford life insurance premiums, and no compensation was paid to the next of kin of servicemen killed in accidents. During an intensive period of night flying two pilots and two observers were lost when their aircraft crashed, presumably into the sea, without trace. While the squadron searched for any sign of the missing aircraft there was no opportunity for me to contact Sue to assure her of my own safety. A malicious Royal Navy officer, another tenant of the boarding house, told her, 'Someone's been killed, and they're searching.' He knew I was safe.

When I could find transport and finally arrived at our room, Sue was sobbing uncontrollably, convinced that I was dead and no one was going to tell her. My disgust for that officer – and for the unfeeling attitude of the senior staff at Nowra who gave no thought to the wives and families of those who were kept flying through the night – was total. This was not an isolated incident, and it demonstrated the appalling indifference of the Fleet Air Arm at the time.

I was transferred to 817 Squadron in mid-April, after the return from the Korean War of HMAS *Sydney* and her Air Group of three squadrons. Each squadron had twelve aircraft and was commanded by a lieutenant commander, almost always a pilot. The CO of my squadron was Lieutenant Commander Lunberg, formerly CFI at Gosport, who was serving with the RAN on exchange duty. There were several Royal Navy pilots and observers who were either on loan from the Royal Navy or on exchange. I flew with this squadron, gaining experience and learning more techniques, until, in June, we were to embark in *Sydney* for a short work-up cruise to Hervey Bay and back to Jervis Bay.

The ugly feeling in my stomach at the prospect of once more landing on a carrier after ten months is difficult to describe. I was not landing well, in spite of dozens of ADDLS sessions at Jervis Bay airfield. I found that I did not see the carrier's deck for long enough to perform the same calm landings that were routine for me ashore. It was pretty much a case of 'One, two, three, pull the stick back and hope for the best!' I survived, but had some hairy arrivals, entering the steel wire crash barrier on one landing after missing the arrestor wires.

Captain H. J. Buchanan had recently assumed command of HMAS *Sydney*. He was completely new to carrier operations, and the first deck landing accident he witnessed was, regrettably, my meeting with the crash barrier. That established in him an attitude towards me that I soon realised was never going to change. He was convinced that I should not be a pilot and suggested that I might specialise in gunnery, his own specialisation. I was pleased to return to Nowra, having made a further six deck landings. As my pilot's flying log books attest, I had only two deck landing accidents in 1952, yet the word was swiftly passed around that I was 'accident prone'.

Early in 1953, while Sue and I were enjoying dinner at Chequers nightclub in Sydney, we were joined by the commander of *Albatross*,

John Robertson, and his wife Bettine. We liked what we saw of both Robertson and Bettine, not having an inkling of how closely our lives were to be linked later in life. John impressed me with his whole bearing, a fine sense of humour, firmness in expressing his opinions and an ease with his position in life. I thought him a very good example to which a naval officer might aspire, and had no doubts as to his rapid progress along the path to Chief of Naval Staff.

Travelling a week or so later by train to Nowra after a family visit, Sue was told by a senior officer that I would be going on the coronation cruise of HMAS *Sydney* to England. Only 817 Squadron was embarked in Sydney for the cruise, and we flew on board on 21 March 1953. John Robertson had joined the carrier as executive officer and second-in-command, and his cheerful demeanour shone like a beacon throughout the cruise.

On completion of an anti-submarine bombing exercise in the Indian Ocean I completed my landing with my port wheel adjacent to the edge of the flight deck. Captain Buchanan seized upon this incident as a reason to refuse to allow me to fly from the ship again. Despite the vigorous and emotional objections of my commanding officer, I was grounded until we arrived in England. This afforded me the unwelcome opportunity to observe other deck landings from the safety of the 'Goofers', an area astern of the funnel, above the flight deck, where non-flyers would 'goof' at the landings and give their uninformed opinions. The second verse of the 'A25' song is pertinent:

When the batsman says 'Lower!', I always go higher,
I drift off to starboard and prang a Seafire.
The boys in the Goofers all think that I'm green,
But I get my commission from Supermarine!
Cracking show! I'm alive!
But I've still got to render my A25.

As a qualified sea watch-keeping officer I performed bridge watches in *Sydney*, while as a squadron officer I was also rostered as air officer of the day. This was an excessive workload at those times when both duties over-lapped. The ship docked at Port Suez, at the southern end of the canal, and the captain called formally on the Governor of Suez. When the

Governor returned the call, I was officer of the watch at the gangway, with the captain, the side party of quartermaster and boatswain's mate and a bugler, all ready to greet him. As the Governor's boat pulled alongside the gangway I ordered the bugler to sound 'the Still', calling the ship's company to attention. The young man put the bugle to his lips and promptly vomited over the area where all were gathered. Buchanan turned scarlet and shouted at me, 'If this happens in Malta, Cabban, I'll hang you from the yard arm!'

As we then proceeded towards Port Said, an Egyptian ran along the canal side, calling out, 'I'm Australian bastard! Herby Buchanan's my father!' My unspoken but heartfelt congratulations went out to whichever genius had instigated this exquisite prank.

As fate would have it, when the ship secured in Port Said, I was again OOW for the forenoon watch. I relieved Lieutenant Andrew Robertson at the gangway at 8.00 a.m., and the ship was a hive of industry with ropes stretching from several points to Egyptian traders' boats. Goods and money passed busily from one to the other. The captain arrived in the ladder space, quickly assessed the situation and raised his voice to me. 'Cabban, this is supposed to be a ship of war, but under your command it has become a trading vessel. Get rid of them!'

One unfortunate trader was almost directly alongside, and I instructed the quartermaster to prepare the fire hose, which was rigged in readiness for such a need. I called on the trader to back off, but my warning went unheeded. Sensing another outburst from Buchanan, I ordered the hose turned on. The water exploded sideways out of the nozzle, which was not properly connected, and soaked the captain. He snarled at me that he was going to change and then see if I could perform any duties competently, which he doubted.

Arriving in the Straits of Gibraltar, a signal was received by *Sydney*, with a message from the Governor of Gibraltar asking if I were on board. Sir Robert and Lady Burrows were guests of the Governor and invited me to afternoon tea with them at the Rock Hotel. After coming to anchor in Gibraltar Harbour I obtained the captain's permission to invite them aboard later in the day. We had a very pleasant reunion ashore, and it transpired that Sir Robert had never visited a naval vessel before, in spite of many invitations, because he felt it would be an abuse of privilege. He was delighted to accept my invitation. At the boat steps in the dockyard, the boat's coxswain told us that all boats were being recalled because of deteriorating weather, so my guests could not go aboard. Undaunted, I excused myself for a minute and used a dockyard telephone to call HMS *Ark Royal*, which lay nearby. As luck would have it, the OOW was Lieutenant John Wilson, my former gunroom sub from *King George V*, who readily agreed to my request to take my guests aboard his ship and show them around. Thus I was able to show my friends through the hangar and the flight deck of this much larger ship. As we parted, Sir Robert assured me that I would 'definitely be an admiral!' and Lady Burrows told me I could not know how happy I had made her husband.

The English Channel was calm as we approached the Isle of Wight, and I was at last back in the cockpit of my Firefly on the way to one of my old haunts, HMS *Siskin*, Gosport. David Robertson, our senior pilot, and I shared a cabin at *Siskin*, where the squadron was accommodated for the following six weeks. I have never known a more compatible cabin mate. It was at about this time that I received a cryptic telegram from Sue, which made no sense to me, advising (I finally learned) that she was pregnant. She was trying to avoid anyone else knowing before I did, but I could not decipher her *ad hoc* code, so I had to await her letter a week later. We were both ecstatic, and I took the opportunity, when in London, to buy a pram and all manner of baby accessories from nappies to an inflatable potty.

Each Saturday morning for the next six weeks all Fleet Air Arm squadrons in the British Isles joined together at Spithead to rehearse the formation fly-past, which was part of the post-coronation review of the fleet. Ships of all the world's navies had already arrived and taken their designated anchorages in the Solent, preparatory for the review. In each fly-past rehearsal more than 200 propeller-driven aircraft flew in close formation at a height between 100 and 200 feet. The turbulence for those not leading made accurate positioning extremely difficult. There was one aircraft emergency on each occasion, but none from 817, and it was chilling to hear some of the distress calls.

Once they were qualified to sign (QS) for daily and weekly inspections for all aspects of maintenance, naval pilots could be permitted to take their aircraft to any other service airfield in the UK that would provide facilities at weekends or overnight. This was considered to be excellent navigation and maintenance experience, but it was also a wonderful perk. I arranged to spend the coronation long weekend with close friends of Sue's family, at Yatton, Somerset, leaving my plane at the RAF Reserve airfield, Weston-Super-Mare, which was located nearby. I borrowed the required radio frequency crystal from an RAF unit at Gosport and had permission to refuel and depart immediately following the Saturday rehearsal. But the Solent Tower called all aircraft to announce that the West of England was closed to air traffic and that those squadrons affected were to spend the weekend at Lee-on-Solent. Without a word, I refuelled and took off, calling Gosport Tower to advise them that I was airborne and changing radio channel to the Weston frequency. Without allowing time for any counter instructions, I then set off for the West.

My smugness quickly changed to concern when the cloud was so low that navigation by careful reference to my map became increasingly difficult. I was at about 100 feet when I decided that discretion dictated that I 'go by rail' and took the simple option of flying along the Great Western Railway line, expecting to recognise a major station around the time that I calculated I should be turning to the north. At last, at about 80 feet, I came to a large city, lowered my flaps to reduce speed and descended to fly between the platforms and read the station name. At 120 knots, the only sign I could read said, 'VIROL – ANAEMIC GIRLS NEED IT!'

There was no way that I could turn and try again, so, with rising dismay, I climbed into the cloud and began calling Weston Tower. My anxiety turned to relief when, at 10,000 feet and still in cloud, I heard, 'Unknown station say again call sign.' We established communication, and I was given a course to steer and instructed to maintain my altitude. I was controlled in a descent and approach into the Bristol Channel and then back through cloud, to the airfield. As I approached the field I was told that the cloud base was 200 feet and that the ridge of trees before me was on the hill, just in front of the field. The controllers congratulated me and told me that the last pilot they directed, on the same route, had disobeyed instructions and crashed fatally into the sea. I pushed the plane into a hangar, was picked up, and spent a peaceful and pleasant four days in Yatton, where I watched the Coronation on television.

Captain Buchanan ordered me to undergo an evaluation by the Central Air Medical Board of the Fleet Air Arm, in Lee-on-Solent, to determine my suitability as a pilot. The board consisted of three surgeon captains who were air medical specialists. They examined my flying log book and questioned me at length. At the conclusion the chairman told me, 'Return to your squadron and continue flying. There is nothing wrong with you. But don't believe that your captain is as bad as you think!' I was tremendously relieved but replied that they did not know him.

In the meantime, the LSO had identified my problem with deck landing. I was oriented towards the LSO to the extent that I was aiming the aircraft at his position and not the centre line of the deck. I overcame this tendency immediately I was made aware of it. In spite of completing ADDLS successfully, and the pleas of Les Oakley and the LSO as well as my clearance by the CAMB, I was not to fly aboard a carrier commanded by Buchanan again.

The review fly-past was a success, and we sailed for Halifax, Nova Scotia, following a last day on which the Duke of Edinburgh had lunch aboard *Sydney*, at anchor off Spit Head. The Atlantic Ocean, during our crossing, showed how angry it could be. Small icebergs, called growlers, were detected as we sailed north, but none was threatening. The ship drove into huge seas, with deep water surging furiously over the flight deck and the spray beating on the bridge windows. We were fortunate not to lose aircraft, many of which were lashed to the deck and subjected to the seawater deluge.

Our visit to Halifax was uneventful and brief. But the next destination, Baltimore, Maryland, was much more interesting. This was my first experience of the USA, and I was delighted to be there. The ship was opened to the public, and thousands of Americans accepted the opportunity to inspect it. Walking about the flight deck so that I could answer any questions or give guidance, I was asked by one lady, 'Queen Elizabeth owns your ship, doesn't she?' I replied, 'Yes, ma'am,' for the sake of simplicity, and was then asked, 'She owns your country, too, doesn't she?' Too far in for long explanations, I answered 'Yes' again, and was told, 'She sure owns a lot!', which amused me enormously and illustrated the depth of ignorance of the monarchy that prevails outside the British Commonwealth.

Kingston, Jamaica, was the next port of call with the visit scheduled for only twelve hours. I joined other officers going to a club overlooking the harbour. It was a small tropical jewel, with a rock swimming pool, a pleasant area of seating by a bar and an overwhelming sense of tranquillity. I felt refreshed and much happier than I had been for a long time when we returned to the ship.

The passage to Hawaii was placid, allowing me too much time for introspection over my status. I had again received a classification of five – Average – for flying, which must have further angered the captain.

Pearl Harbor was a revelation. I had never seen naval personnel work so well or more effectively than the US sailors appeared to be doing as the morning watch ended at 8.00 a.m. Our crew had not even started, and the Americans had been busy from 7.00 a.m. Commander Robertson was invited to join a US destroyer for a day of evolutions at sea and had accepted. But, at a late moment, he was required aboard *Sydney* and asked me if I would like to replace him. It was a memorable experience. The destroyer's captain, a USN commander, invited me to perform a simulated rescue of a man overboard, using a dan buoy as the target. Without hesitation I ordered, 'All engines ahead, full; hard right rudder!' and then, 'All engines stop: all engines astern, full!' followed by 'All engines stop!' and we were alongside the buoy, still in the water. The captain was delighted, and said, 'I wish my officers would handle the ship like that!'

'But Sir, they have more to lose than I, don't they?' I replied.

Sue believed that I might not find her attractive, in her advanced state of pregnancy, when I returned and had booked herself into a room at the Nowra Hotel so that we would not meet in public. She had even sent me a photograph in which she had a pillow stuffed under her jeans and T-shirt, to prepare me for the shock. I don't believe a more beautiful woman existed than Sue in the full radiance of pregnancy and I adored her. We went immediately to our dear little fibro cottage Mutmutbilly, on the edge of Huskisson, on Jervis Bay. We had negotiated the purchase just before my departure, and Sue had recently taken possession. It was white with a blue fibro roof and yellow window frames, and it had slip rails instead of gates. We relied on tank water and had six chooks, an abundant vegetable garden, an open wood fire and no car, and we thought it was heaven. I purchased four lengths of six-by-four timber and built a double bed frame on which I placed a steel spring mattress. Sue still needed convincing that this was strong enough to hold her pregnant body and me. It would have supported a Lancaster bomber.

The most magical aspect of the house was the window in the wall separating our bedroom from the children's room. There was a Holland blind that we could move to view them, unnoticed, when they were waking and talking to each other. When I practised aerobatics for air displays I would ensure that Sue saw that the display was safe by circling above the house until she appeared in the garden, waved a towel, and then performing my routines. No one in Huskisson ever complained.

Sue finally gave birth to David, eight pounds of red-haired baby boy. When the telephone rang in the early hours, following an extended labour and instrument delivery, I was certain that the nurse who spoke to me said that he was a 'flat baby'! Having passed this information on to the new grandmother, who was as sleepy as I, we both went back to our beds wondering what that meant. The following morning I was taken to the hospital but only had enough time to see Sue and her 'fat baby' briefly before being driven straight to the airfield. The separation was heart-breaking for both of us. I had to head off for some inconsequential flying when we really needed to be together, but compassion of that type was unknown in the Navy of the time.

10
Flying Ashore and Afloat

I flew with 817 only twice after disembarkation in Jervis Bay at the conclusion of the coronation cruise. Through Buchanan's influence I was transferred to a second-line, fleet support unit. I was to prepare for a flying test and assessment in a Wirraway, presumably with a view to vindicating the captain's opinion that I should be permanently grounded. Lieutenant Commander Gill Campbell DFC RAN, commanding officer of 723, was a fighter pilot who had been decorated in the Western Desert for destroying enemy aircraft in aerial combat. I had got to know him more recently on HMAS *Sydney*. Gill was another fine officer who had fallen foul of Captain Buchanan, and had poor career prospects. I was delighted to be under his command and was to learn much from him, although I first had to survive a flying test.

During two hours in the air, over three days, Lieutenant Peter 'Bras' Cooper, a recently qualified flying instructor and a college graduate a year senior to me, took me through the entire range of flying in the Wirraway. The process concluded when, hopelessly underconfident, I did a ground loop on landing – the final ignominy. I was convinced that I had been set up by Buchanan to fail and had made Cooper's sad task so much simpler. To my utter astonishment, Cooper endorsed my ability, with the rider that I was underconfident and required a period of retraining before returning to a first line squadron. I had breathing space.

Late in October, I was briefed by Gill Campbell to fly a Sea Fury fighter, and had seven hours of flying them in a week. The Fury was the fastest single piston-engine fighter ever built and was a thrill to fly, although difficult to land on carriers. They handled beautifully in the air and I flew them at every opportunity, particularly performing aerobatics.

In November I commenced flying Vampire Trainer aircraft and was 'checked out' (approved to fly solo) by Lieutenant Peter Goldrick who, with Peter Cooper and Bill Dunlop, all from the same 1941 college term, had qualified as a flying instructor at the RAAF Central Flying School. Having a drink at the wardroom bar after flying, Goldrick made the extraordinary observation that if he were ever in a position to affect adversely the career of an officer whom he considered a threat to his promotion, then he would consider it an obligation. That was the most amazing and incomprehensible statement I could recall hearing, but I should have heeded it.

In June 1954 the commanding officer of 808 Squadron, Lieutenant Commander G. A. Beange DSC RAN, permitted me to join a weapons training program by flying his squadron's spare Sea Fury. My first experience of rocket firing and strafing from the Sea Fury on the naval firing range at Beecroft Head was absorbing, although I was not privy to my results. The following week I flew the same fighter in a joint RAN–RAAF weapons display off the coast near RAAF Williamtown.

On the following day, Guy Beange came to my crew room, told me to get my parachute and to follow him. His expression was dour, which was normal when I was in his company. With no idea what was to follow, I lined up my aircraft alongside his and, taking off in formation, flew past Jervis Bay to perform the most intensive and hazardous formation flying that I had ever undertaken, at extremely low altitude above the ocean. I had to be conscious of the proximity of the water at every moment, and there was certainly no time for introspection. We performed the complete range of aerobatics in different formation dispositions, changing frequently without warning each time I began to feel settled. We climbed several thousand feet, and he indicated to me that we were to dogfight. I managed to evade his Fury and to get into a firing position behind him. In combat I would have destroyed his aircraft from that position. Just as quickly, I was signalled to form on him again, and we descended to sea level for more rapid manoeuvres, ending with a last-second climb to clear the cliff edge, with no warning, as we crossed the coast towards Nowra. I could see the pebbles scattering below his propeller as I barely avoided striking the ground. I was then confronted by a tree, which he would miss, but over which I quietly lifted before resuming my position alongside him. We landed in formation, and I signed the aircraft log. Nothing was mentioned about the flight, or my results in any of the weapons firing, until he told me the whole story in HMAS *Melbourne*, in 1961.

In December 1954 I received a six assessment – 'Above average' – and was appointed to join 817 Squadron as senior pilot on 2 January 1955. The squadron embarked in *Sydney*, now commanded by Captain G. C. Oldham DSO, early in February. During deck landing practices (DLPs), I made what Oldham – a naval observer – described as the best deck landing he had ever seen. That was all news to me. I had felt no impact with the deck and, as the aircraft was obviously not stopping, I thought I was 'floating' – airborne above the arrestor wires. I lowered the nose, hoping to feel the deck, as the plane rolled into the crash barrier and only damaged the propeller. My hook was still housed!

Three people were responsible for ensuring that no aircraft lands without the hook being lowered. They were the lieutenant commander (flying), referred to as 'Little F', on the wing of the bridge, who watched the aircraft flying around the 200 feet altitude landing circuit of the ship, checking the hook; and the landing signals officer (LSO) and the LSO's caller, who stood directly to the side of the LSO and whose only job was to watch the incoming aircraft through binoculars and report, 'Hook down, Sir! Wheels and flaps down, Sir!' after confirming that status. If any of the wheels, flaps or hook is not down, the pilot is alerted early by hand signals, or else 'waved off', to circuit again.

The post-mortem revealed that the caller realised his error after he had called wrongly, then lost his voice through shock. He was repeatedly mouthing the word, 'Hook!' but no noise emerged. The captain reprimanded 'Little F', the LSO and me to save us from further punishment.

By now I had been flying for six years and wished for a short break in small ships. I wrote to Commander V. A. T. Smith, then the officer responsible for aircrew appointments at Navy Office, and requested a twelve-month appointment to a destroyer. I wished to refresh my small ships experience, and I wanted to undertake the examinations for command of a destroyer, the formal recognition of eligibility for sea command, one of which I had already completed. In reply, 'Vat' informed me that as a result of the reports of my flying from Nowra, I was to be trained as a maintenance test pilot (MPT), and would travel to England in HMAS *Vengeance* when she was returned to the Royal Navy after HMAS *Melbourne* was commissioned.

When Sue and I discussed this situation she decided that she wanted to become pregnant again, so that she would not feel lonely in my absence. By the time I was home again we would have another baby. Sue duly became pregnant. But by now we did not want to be separated while I was overseas, so we borrowed the fare from our bank for her and David to travel by sea to join me in England.

Passage in HMAS *Vengeance* provided me ample opportunity to play chess, solo and contract bridge in the evenings and to study for destroyer command exam subjects when off watch. Three of these exams were held and passed before reaching Portsmouth. The captain had sought special permission of the Naval Board to conduct the exams.

Monsoon winds and very heavy swells prevailed in the Indian Ocean. When I logged the wind as 'Force 4', Captain Otto Becher took issue with me because he had to reduce speed to avoid damage to the ship. He maintained that he could not justify this action to the Naval Board in a Force 4 wind (about twelve to eighteen knots with 'white horses'). As diplomatically as I could, I quoted the Beaufort Scale description of the wind force, with which my record complied, and the scale of sea swell. He was convinced, and admitted his error with some relief. His prudent lessening of speed could now be justified because of the swell, not the wind.

While playing solo whist on the quarterdeck in the evening, as the ship left the Suez Canal, I looked up sharply as a large oil tanker passed close down our port side, and remarked, 'I wonder if anyone has told the captain about that?' On the following morning it was clear that no one had until it was almost too late. Lieutenant David Martin, on his first day in that rank, was officer of the watch, accompanied by an inexperienced sub-lieutenant understudy. Martin saw the green starboard bow light of a ship approaching the canal on his starboard bow, and, following the Rule of the Road at Sea adage, 'Green to green or red to red, perfect safety, go ahead', felt relaxed.

Martin left the bridge to the junior officer and walked out of the port side door. He was hoping for a glimpse of the loom of the Pharaoh's Light. When he returned to the bridge proper he found it bathed in red light from the port bow light of the oncoming ship, which had altered course and now represented an imminent danger. Before you could say, 'If to starboard red appear, it is your duty to keep clear!' the OOW ordered, 'Starboard 20, half speed astern both engines!' and pressed the call bell for the captain. Racing to the bridge, Becher said, 'God! It's too late,' then, 'Hard a-starboard, full speed astern both engines!' while seizing the lever for the ship's steam whistle to sound the signal for 'my engines are going astern'. Miraculously, *Vengeance* swung out of the path of the tanker and the two ships passed safely. But oh, so close!

Becher made his thoughts known to every officer in *Vengeance* at 8.00 a.m. the following day when he addressed them all on the flight deck. He said, after describing the debacle of the near-miss, that whenever he stepped on to the bridge he found 'the OOW's arse sticking out of the radar screen'. The safety of the ship could be guaranteed only 'by using a Mark 1 eyeball'! He concluded that Martin, had he not been promoted the day before, would never have been promoted.

I scored the middle watch in the English Channel. The Channel is a madhouse of ships moving in all directions. At about 1.30 a.m. I watched a ship fine on our starboard bow approaching almost head-on. I reckoned that if I continued on course he would be bluffed by our size and move aside to port and leave me – and the captain – in peace. The ship did move slightly, and I was confident of my bluff until the signal light of the oncoming ship flashed the challenge, 'What ship, where bound?' I froze with the realisation that a Royal Navy cruiser was less than 300 yards off our starboard bow. I had to tell the captain. Pushing the button, I said, '*Birmingham*'s on our starboard bow, Sir!'

'I'll be right there. Ask permission to proceed,' he responded.

'You can see him from your cabin, Sir!' (I was trying to keep the skipper off the bridge and from seeing how close we were.)

But he was there in an instant and demanded, 'Who challenged first?'

'He did,' I confessed.

'Bad show, Cabban! He's senior to us, but you should have been quicker off the mark.'

The proximity was not raised as an issue, and I was just happy that we did not challenge first. It was yet another lesson painfully learned about the dangers of large ships moving at close quarters during the hours of darkness.

11
Testing Times

I travelled to HMS *Gamecock*, a shore establishment near the Armstrong Siddeley factory and airfield in Coventry, to undertake an engine-handling course before my flying course. Tommy Frost, the newly appointed chief test pilot of the company, and I were the only students on the course. He insisted on entertaining me to drinks and meals to set a precedent for the use of his expense account, and I was content to be listed as an Australian admiral on his 'cheat sheet'. I bought Tommy's car, an old Austin 12 with a fourteen-horsepower engine, when he took delivery of a company car.

I drove to London and met Sue and David as they arrived in *Orcades* at Tilbury docks. Not having seen David for three months I could hardly believe that this beautiful little blond boy was ours. Sue was radiant, and I was overjoyed to see them. I took them back to Stretton where we stayed in a hotel for a week before moving to 'The Love Nest', a small rental cottage on the station. Meanwhile, Lady Burrows again helped by finding us a flat in a house owned by her niece but which was not immediately available. Sue was 'due' with our second child in four weeks. We found the obstetrician who was recommended from home and, although Sue had reservations about him, she did not share them with me. For the final week of pregnancy we were obliged to rent a room that had previously been an apple store in a house where the owner complained that not only did we bathe every evening but also we did not use the same water!

On the afternoon before Sue was due for confinement I was ordered to fly to South Wales, carrying a referee for a game of rugby. I could not contact Sue to tell her that I might not return that day. The weather was poor and deteriorating, with gale force winds at the destination, but I was assured that I would be back in time to drive home at the normal time. The trip took 105 minutes, with almost full throttle, into the worsening wind. On landing, ten naval airmen ran on to the runway and held the wings as I taxied to shelter and for refuelling. I was told that the airfield was now closed and I would have to stay overnight. The local commander told me, when I insisted that I would return, that the airfield would remain closed and that if I took off it was at my own risk. He said, further-more, that Stretton would be closed when I returned.

I succeeded in taxiing and taking off without mishap and, with full throttle, set course for 'home', becoming aware that the light had faded only when another aircraft's navigation lights appeared close by me. As my wheels touched the lighted runway, all of the lights were immediately extinguished, leaving me to complete the landing in total darkness, taxi to the apron and even tie the aircraft to concrete blocks for security, with no light and no sign of a living soul. I guessed that someone was angry with me!

Our second son, Christopher John, was born in Warrington Hospital two days later, half an hour before 21 October 1955, the 150th anniver-sary of the Battle of Trafalgar. Sue had declared that she refused to spend another night in the room with its strong apple smell when suddenly, at about 8.00 p.m., she commenced labour. It was snowing heavily, and it was only with great difficulty that I was able to get the car started and drive the three of us to the hospital. There was no waiting room, so I drove David back to our room for our last night there.

Early the next morning the doctor told me, as if it were my fault, that my wife had almost died. The midwife had failed to call him in time, and he had arrived literally at the last possible moment to save both mother and baby. I won't repeat my side of that conversation. Christopher was black-haired, and we were both thrilled to have him, although we had expected a daughter and now had to agree on a name other than Sally.

The village of Ditchling was the home of Sue's aunt and we rented the next-door house for Sue and the boys until they sailed, in RMS *Himalaya*, for home. It was a delightful time while I had some leave and settled them. When I joined HMAS *Melbourne* for the return voyage I arranged to prepare for more destroyer command exams, and passed them on arrival in Jervis Bay, leaving only gunnery and navigation outstanding. The passage was slow, at an economical steaming speed of fourteen knots, and boring. When we were passed at sea by RMS *Himalaya* and *Arcadia*, we felt that better management of the schedule, and some compassion, might have enabled a brief reunion between spouses travelling in those ships and their husbands in *Melbourne*. It was ten weeks before I was in Nowra again, attached to the Air Engineering Department, responsible to the air engineering officer for test flying, with the call sign 'Nowra Test One'. My position was unique in that I was the authorising officer for my test flights, and was captain of any aircraft flown in that capacity, regardless of the rank of passengers. Time on the ground was occupied checking aircraft before and after flying, meeting maintenance staff and discussing issues raised in the tests. Flying mainly involved testing problem aircraft – those with major modifications or repairs – and practising aerobatics when the opportunity presented.

Home life was disrupted one afternoon while I was on leave when a naval car drove on to our property while Sue was changing for dinner. It looked ominous, and it was. We had enjoyed a pleasant dinner with Bill and Dorothy Dunlop in their Huskisson home on the previous evening. Bill was assessed as an exceptional pilot when he qualified as an instructor at East Sale. While instructing in a Vampire trainer on that day, Bill and a pupil had been killed. It was later determined that Bill failed to connect the lanyard of his dinghy, carried with the parachute on the pilot's seat in the cockpit, to his Mae West jacket. It had dropped to the aircraft floor area and jammed the elevator control. This resulted in the aircraft looping out of control and striking the ground vertically.

I was asked if we knew Dorothy and then asked if Sue would inform Dorothy of Bill's death. I hated to do this, but poured a strong whisky and took it to Sue and told her to drink it without questioning. She complied, and I explained what she was being asked to do. When she returned a long time later, Sue broke down and beseeched me to stop flying. 'I'd rather be dead,' was my honest reply, although my heart broke for her. It was the only time that Sue ever asked that, and I could not have been more selfish in my attitude, but I was not thinking that at the time.

A double fatality occurred while Sea Venoms were operating from HMAS *Melbourne*, resulting in the squadron disembarking to Nowra for investigation of the aircraft. After being launched by the carrier's steam catapult, a Venom dropped towards the sea, barely missing it before gaining sufficient speed to climb away. The next aircraft launched hit the sea, killing the pilot and observer instantly. The 'near miss' plane was grounded while the elevators and ailerons were sent to Sydney to be submitted to rigorous testing by De Havilland while all controls and systems were examined minutely in the Nowra workshops. An armed guard was posted over the aircraft, and an atmosphere of mystery prevailed as engineers attempted to link the two incidents to mechanical or electrical failure.

The squadron commanding officer, George Jude, flew Venoms with varying and improbable fuel distributions to eliminate the possibility of ground crew error. The commander (air) of *Melbourne*, 'Butch' Hain, an ex-Royal Navy pilot, took extreme interest as every possible aircraft deficiency that might have caused these deaths was analysed. Meanwhile, the suspect aircraft being cleared of defect, the squadron was ordered to re-embark. The telephone rang in my office an hour before the take-off time and Jude ordered me to test-fly the 'rogue' aircraft half an hour after his squadron cleared the circuit. 'I'll test it now, Sir!' I replied, being deliberately provocative, because I had predicted that this would happen.

'No, you won't. You will do as I have ordered!' End of conversation.

That was the only time I had taken off in an aircraft with an intimation that I might be killed, but it was not frightening. I had test-flown every plane in that squadron and was confident of their safety and serviceability. I had offered at the outset to test each of them when they disembarked, but was rebuffed. Commander Hain recommended Jude for a decoration for bravery, but none was forthcoming. I was relieved at that, knowing more than anybody else about the risks involved. Nor was there an official conclusion as to the cause of the accident.

That summer was very hot and decisions concerning flying depended on the engine requirements together with weather conditions. In the case of a Gannet trainer, which I was to test following the fitting of a new propeller assembly, the engine power was marginally above the minimum requirement. To test the controls and instruments in the instructor's cockpit I asked the senior instructor to accompany me. As we climbed after take off, the port propeller became uncontrollable, and at 5,000 feet I closed both throttles and reduced speed. As I opened them again, the port revolutions rose further, and I immediately attempted to shut the engine down and feather the propeller. The propeller continued to rotate in superfine pitch, and I tried to relight the engine to provide control. At

6,000 feet, I levelled the Gannet and was able to operate the port engine and control it partially through throttle application. I advised the control tower of the situation, and asked for a clear circuit in case of further cause for concern in landing.

I found that I needed to leave flaps and undercarriage lowered in order to induce drag while maintaining engine control for descent. I entered the landing circuit downwind at about 130 to 140 knots, and reached to engage the emergency flight pitch stops to prevent reverse torque in case of engine failure. As I did, there was a sudden change of engine noise and an increase in revs on the port engine. 'We'll never make it,' my passenger shouted, referring to the distance to the duty runway and, aware that there was no time to hesitate, I turned to the non-duty runway. Then he shouted, 'Lower the undercarriage!' to which I replied, 'Jesus, no!' as we were still descending and unsure of aligning with the runway in a safe position for landing. Our speed was 105 knots when the aircraft became uncontrollably wing heavy as the torque took control. It rolled beyond ninety degrees and appeared to be rolling on to its back. My passenger was screaming, 'Pick it up! Pick it up!', which was heard over the radio by the tower and other aircraft.

At fifty feet, now believing that I was about to die, I applied full rudder and full aileron, and ran the electrical aileron trim through full travel. The aircraft began to level and, as it slowly responded to the controls and the wings were level, I decided that the only chance for my passenger to survive was to avoid hitting the ground with one wing first. As the wings levelled, cutting both throttles, I pushed the control column fully forward, and the Gannet hit the ground alongside the runway. I was thrown into the instrument panel as my seat fragmented under the 17G impact force recorded on the accelerometer as it jammed. Instantly discharging the fire extinguishers into the engines, I switched off the fuel and electrics, jettisoned my hood and helped my passenger, who was unscathed, out of his cockpit. As I led him away, I said, 'Thank God I did not lower the undercarriage!' He did not reply. The medical officer examining me later said that I did not suffer shock because I had accepted death.

I was grounded, pending an inquiry. When I gave a full account of the incident to Lieutenant Commander Gill Campbell, acting commander (air), I told him that we would have been killed if I had lowered the undercarriage. He said, 'The undercarriage was down, Pedro!' Gill later assured me of his belief that the undercarriage had not been lowered by me, and offered to testify on my behalf to that effect.

While awaiting the board of inquiry, I studied for the navigation component of the destroyer command exams, a challenging task when not serving at sea, and passed. Giving up smoking was another challenge I tackled during this time, from more than eighty cigarettes a day to none. It almost drove my family to distraction, and they begged me to start again. I carried cigarettes and matches in my pocket for a year, offered them freely, and knew that it was only my willpower that mattered.

My family's support kept me going while I waited for the inquiry and watched as Gill Campbell, my staunchest supporter, was appointed else-where. Then the composition of the board of inquiry was published. It was not good news. My judges would comprise Acting Commander R.T. 'Potter' Power, from Admiral Buchanan's staff, Lieutenant Commander Peter Goldrick and Lieutenant Bill Caws, an air engineer whom I trusted and respected. Of the three, only Goldrick was a pilot, and Power was a passed-over lieutenant commander; that is, he had not been promoted to commander within the period of eligibility. He, too, was largely ignorant of flying. Yet I still naively expected that truth and justice would result from the inquiry.

The engineers from De Havilland acknowledged that the propeller had been assembled incorrectly and the control fluid drained during take-off, causing the entire episode to occur. I requested that one who offered to give evidence on my behalf be called, but it was denied. Gill Campbell was not questioned on the position of the undercarriage. Junior pilots who were airborne and heard the hysterical voice of my passenger, and the control tower staff who recorded him, were not called. I made a detailed statement about the problems I had encountered in my relationship withthe commanding officer of 724 Squadron, in response to vitriolic evidence he had given about my flying ability and attitude.

Left to ponder the outcome, I had occasion to visit Admiral Buchanan's headquarters in Sydney. Lieutenant Commander Jimmy Bowles, an experienced pilot, ex-squadron commanding officer and the aviation adviser to the admiral, showed me, in complete confidence, a copy of the transcript of evidence. He said, 'You'd better read this and see what you're up against.' He took a risk, and I respected his confidence. The transcript, typed by a WRANS writer, had been altered in ink, so that my responses were changed from positive to negative and vice versa in critical parts. I was appalled, but could do nothing without disclosing the source of my information. Before leaving, Gill Campbell had endorsed my log book with a 'six' assessment.

The Navy eventually reached its decision. I was stripped of my flying qualification and appointed to HMAS *Warramunga*, a Tribal Class destroyer, commanded by Commander A. M. Synnot RAN. Assuming that I had been deemed responsible for the accident, I then protested officially to the new captain of HMAS *Albatross*, Captain V. A. T. Smith, and expected his support. I asked that I be charged and tried by court martial if I were adjudged guilty of causing the accident. Smith just assured me that he thought it was a misunderstanding and that I should raise the matter through my new captain in *Warramunga*. But I could not let this slur on my conduct go unanswered. I gained an interview with Rear Admiral Gatacre, deputy Chief of Naval Staff, at Navy Office, who said that although sympathetic to my problem, he was powerless to help. Who then did have the power, and from where did it derive?

Joining *Warramunga*, I sought to approach the flag officer commanding the Australian fleet, Rear Admiral Harries, and although an interview was arranged, I accepted Commander Synnot's offer to represent my complaint on my behalf. This intervention was successful only in achieving a reversal of the retrospective cancellation of my flying pay, which had been maliciously dated from shortly after the accident. It was reinstated to the date of my new appointment. Admiral Harries believed, I was told, that I would not get justice in the Navy and should get out.

Tony Synnot was a highly competent commanding officer. We had enjoyed a brief friendship while I was learning to fly at Point Cook, and he had been my guest at an officers' mess dance. Now, in *Warramunga*, I was designated gunnery officer and succeeded in passing the destroyer command exam in that subject, completing all of the requirements. It must have been a difficult situation for Tony for I bore a deep resentment and bitter disappointment in the Navy for the actions to which I had been subjected. I was waiting until I could resign. I believed that when I was thirty years old I was free to leave the Navy. My father had signed a form of indenture, guaranteeing that I would serve for twelve years after turning eighteen. I told Synnot of my intention and planned accordingly. I remained diligent in carrying out my duties, and tried to ensure that my problems never interfered with my professional conduct.

When I telephoned Huskisson one evening to check how my family was coping, an anxious Sue wanted advice on how to handle a snake in our garage, obviously drawn by the presence of shelter and the chicken feed that was stored there. I instructed her to borrow a shotgun from a neighbour, place a saucer of milk at the door and sit on a log outside until the snake came for the milk, then shoot it. She shook for days after blowing the head off a red-bellied black snake. When she then explained the dangers of snakes to David, he informed her brightly, 'Boy plays with snake.' (He referred to himself as 'Boy'.) He was apparently referring to the presence of a snake in the garden while he was fossicking happily, and Sue was totally unaware of its proximity.

Sailing south via Adelaide and Fremantle, we collided with the wharf at Port Adelaide sufficiently hard to dent the side adjacent to my cabin. This was not reported as it was repaired locally. I paid my first visit to Hong Kong in *Warramunga* when we were briefly attached to the Far East Strategic Reserve. I found the city enchanting, particularly at night when the harbour and lights were magical, and I made a point of standing on the upper deck before retiring to my cabin. An admiral's inspection was scheduled while we were in company with the flotilla leader, HMAS *Tobruk*, and Captain R. I. Peek was delegated to conduct it. On the evening before the inspection, Commander Synnot was dressed in overalls painting the superstructure, while the executive officer hosted a mess dinner in the wardroom, with women present, as guests of the supply officer and a civilian stores officer who was embarked. This attitude was not lost on the commanding officer, who had a deepening disrespect for his first lieutenant. Heavy rain began falling during one of the evolutions that was part of the next day's inspection and, led by the executive officer, the crewmen involved ran for cover, to be promptly called out to continue by the irate and embarrassed CO. Captain Peek looked on disbelievingly. So many lessons on how not to behave, in such a short time!

On the eve of his taking up another appointment Commander Synnot called me to his cabin and told me that there was a custom, to which he would adhere, that an outgoing captain always left his wine cupboard empty. It was up to me to join him in the task, and so we set about it with a will. I reiterated my intention to resign, and he very kindly asked what he could do to assist my future as a civilian. I asked that, if he believed it to be a fair statement, he should describe me as proving to be adaptable when he wrote my 'flimsy', the brief summary of the officer's confidential report. He confided his poor opinion of his executive officer and the wish that he could have had me replace him, an opinion that he was kind enough to repeat when I called to congratulate him on his knighthood when he was Chief of Naval Staff, some years later. More was discussed that night, in confidence, and we parted as we began with mutual liking and respect.

I wrote to Commander Keith Tapp, who was now at Navy Office and responsible for seaman officers' appointments, advising him of my intention to resign. I requested a shore posting in the Jervis Bay area, close to my home, so that I could prepare for the transition to civilian life. He granted my wish, and I was appointed to HMAS *Creswell* as officer-in-charge, Jervis Bay Airfield, and for the Marine Section, the Air Sea Rescue Unit. This was ideal for my purposes, as I thought that I would now have only a few months in the service, spent in enjoyable circumstances. *Creswell* was once again the site of the RAN College, having been transferred back from Flinders Naval Depot.

Admiral Harries conducted the annual admiral's inspection of *Creswell* and the airfield while I was there. Captain Bill Dovers, CO of *Creswell*, had already informed all involved that when Harries asked a question he already knew the answer. True to form, the admiral came directly to the point, asking, 'How much time do you spend here, Cabban?'

'About two to three hours each month, Sir,' I replied.

'That's what I would have thought,' he said.

My duties were no more than checking that the runway was clear, that there were no fire hazards and that firefighting facilities were present and serviceable for emergencies. All of that was accomplished in about half an hour weekly. The command of the high-speed search and rescue craft was another thing entirely, but there was a capable lieutenant commander who was officer in charge of the Marine Section of just three boats.

Submitting my resignation on the day I was promoted lieutenant commander, 16 March 1958, I was confident that my remaining time would be short. But Captain Dovers called me to his office in *Creswell* to discuss the matter urgently. Rear Admiral Harrington, Second Naval Member, had phoned him and directed that I be asked my real reason for resigning. (The reason stated in my formal letter was that, stripped of my specialist qualification without redress, my opportunity for promotion had been finished.) I told Dovers that the real reason was that I had lost confidence in the Naval Board, and when Harrington phoned again a few minutes later, he relayed that statement. 'Arch' Harrington replied, via Dovers, 'That's what we thought. Tell him that if he withdraws it, he'll get the best job for a lieutenant commander at Navy Office.'

'My respect for the Naval Board has just sunk further,' I said.

'Then he'll get the worst job in the Navy for a lieutenant commander!' was the final outburst. The fact that my resignation could not be accepted was a mystery. I was unaware at the time that regulations had been introduced to prevent an officer resigning within three years of the completion of an overseas course. My appointment as ship's company divisional officer and blocks officer at Flinders Naval Depot was received soon afterwards, and I sensed that the description fitted the job. When asked by the commanding officer, Commodore J. Plunkett-Cole, what I thought of it, I replied without hesitation that a competent sub-lieutenant should be able to do the job satisfactorily.

The standard of discipline at this, the basic training establishment of the RAN, appalled me from the outset. Very soon after arriving I approached the executive officer, Commander David Wells, intending to tell him of my concerns. Invited to sit, I said, 'I think I had better stand while I say what I have to, Sir.'

'Go on,' he replied.

'Sir, the standard of discipline in this depot is disgraceful, and I blame you for it,' I charged, giving a number of convincing examples.

'What are you going to do about it?' he asked.

'Nothing!' I replied. 'Every time that I complain about anything, I face lack of interest and support.'

'If you can find a solution, I can guarantee that the commodore and I will give you full support,' he said.

It was a worthwhile challenge. 'I won't come back until I have one,' I promised.

I was due for leave, and while sitting on the train to Newcastle, a plan began to materialise in my mind. By the end of my leave I had the outline of a solution and put it to the commander. 'There's a germ of genius in what you're recommending,' he said. 'Put it in writing and I will forward it to the Naval Board.'

'They will never read it,' I commented. 'Busy men won't read more than one page, and this will take many pages.'

'They will read every word of what you are proposing, I'll guarantee,' he concluded.

He was right. On his appointment to Navy Office, shortly afterwards, he presented it to the Naval Staff and I received a Naval Board commendation for the paper, titled 'The Standard of Officers in the Navy'. It contained two alternative solutions, titled 'Evolution' and 'Revolution'. Briefly, the first proposal offered remedial action by taking drastic measures to weed out those who were a hindrance to the proper conduct of the Navy and to improve the recruitment and introduction to the Navy of such professionals as dentists, doctors, graduate teachers and others so that they were not expected to uphold disciplinary responsibility attached to their rank without adequate preparation and assimilation. The second proposal included a new treatment of the promotion ladder, with early recognition of prospects being disclosed honestly, and allowing officers to make a choice to continue or leave the service in a timely manner. This summary is a gross oversimplification, but suffice it to say that a very high percentage of the recommendations contained in the 'Evolution' section were implemented.

Soon after, the newly constructed but not yet commissioned destroyer HMAS *Vendetta* was driven into the dry dock gate at Williamstown, Victoria. There was considerable damage, and the embarrassing mishap was featured prominently in the press. Captain John Robertson had been seconded to the dockyard management to conduct the ship's trials, and he had a crew borrowed from various ships and establishments. One of these was an able seaman from my division at Flinders who had been on duty as telegraphsman at the time of the ramming.

Summoned by the executive officer to his office on a Friday morning shortly after the accident, I was told that the able seaman was to be charged with negligence on the Monday morning and that it was my duty to defend him. It was also said that my career prospects would be totally destroyed should the man be found responsible. I had to inform the unfortunate sailor of the impending charge and the maximum punishment, which was ninety days' imprisonment and dismissal (service no longer required, or SNLR). Anything I requested was to be made available to assist me in preparing the defence.

A car took me to the dockyard where I was able to see the wheel-house, and was amazed by its unfamiliar features. There was no view outside the cramped room, except behind to a passageway if the door were open. The cox'n, when steering, could not see the telegraph on his right-hand side, as the body of the telegraphsman obscured it. The telegraph itself moved, not forward for 'ahead' and backwards for 'astern', but right and left. There was no natural sense of which way to move the lever when ordered.

I studied the *Manual of Court Martial Proceedings* to understand the circumstances in which a man could be judged negligent, and ascertained that he must fail to perform a duty that any adequately trained and experienced man should perform. I also studied the Regulations and Instructions for the RAN and procured the Hansard covering the debate on the *Vendetta* accident in the House of Representatives. The Prime Minister had stated that it was 'a simple human error, and no one can be blamed for a human error'. So why was the case initiated?

There were rumours aplenty concerning the real target of ministerial anger, but none of this was going to help the able seaman. When I briefed the defendant I instructed him that if the charge were found to be established and he were to be punished, he must immediately say that he wished to appeal. The charge was read, and I immediately produced and quoted Hansard, asking for the matter to be dismissed as the Prime Minister had already prejudged the incident. The case was stood over while the commodore contacted Navy Office and sought a ruling. 'Nice try, Cabban, but it won't wash,' he said as the case resumed.

I called witnesses to establish that the ship had been alongside a wharf, facing the dry dock in which HMAS *Quickmatch*, commanded by Commander Andrew Robertson, was undergoing a refit, with her hull opened for repairs, and that the inrush of water had jeopardised the safety of the crew sleeping aboard. As securing lines were cast off from *Vendetta*, the order was given by Captain John Robertson, 'Slow astern both engines.' The ship moved slowly ahead, and the order was given, 'Stop both engines. Half speed astern both engines.' The ship accelerated ahead, then the final orders 'Stop both engines. Full speed astern both engines!' as the ship leapt ahead under full power into the caisson, which it breached. At no time did the navigator consider using the broadcast system to advise the engine room that the ship was going ahead, instead of astern. This was, as everyone present knew, the responsibility of the captain, but he had not made himself available as a witness. (The captain and navigator are the 'usual suspects' in any ship-handling mishap.)

The cox'n then confirmed that he had never served in a ship with a wheelhouse of *Vendetta*'s design and cramped quarters, and supported the contention that there was no natural sense of direction, which was normal to the telegraph movements. The day of the ramming had been the able seaman's first day on the telegraph in *Vendetta*, and the cox'n could not give normal visual supervision to his actions. Neither man had any idea that the ship was going in the wrong direction because the design of the wheelhouse was such that they could not see outside. The commodore closed the case by saying 'Admonished', which meant that a temporary notation would appear in the able seaman's history for twelve months, and there would be no permanent record of the offence. I trod on the unfortunate able seaman's toes to prevent any appeal, and he understood.

After lunch, the commander said to me, 'The commodore said that if any officer in the Navy earned his pay today, you did.'

12
Studying Work

I was now a lieutenant commander, but with no clear sense of what my future in the Navy would be. One morning I was asked whether I would like to go to England to undertake a course in work study. In response to my question, 'What is work study?' I was told that it was an alternative to being a lavatory sweeper for the remainder of my career. With such a persuasive recommendation I asked, and was granted, a naval car and driver to take me home to collect Sue so that she could accompany me to Navy Office, in Melbourne, where I was to be interviewed by Admiral Harrington. Not keen to commit myself to anything in the Navy at that stage, I wanted to discuss what little I knew with Sue and be sure that we agreed on my approach to the meeting.

'Arch' Harrington gave me an inkling of what would be involved in my appointment as officer-in-charge, fleet work study team. Following my training I would be responsible to Commander R. H. Thompson, who was the first head of fleet work study. Thompson would be at Navy Office, responsible for advising the Naval Board and for overseeing the methods and results of studies, but would not participate in the process of the studies. The course was to be attended at a civilian engineering establishment in Bristol, under Royal Navy sponsorship. Practical experience would then be gained in a major study with a Royal Navy work study team. On my return, the subjects and the locations of studies would be determined by the Naval Board (meaning Admiral Harrington in practical terms), and I would have a team consisting of two chief petty officers and a writer to work with me. The selection of the chief petty officers would be my choice from volunteers, and they would undergo six months' training at the Royal Melbourne Institute of Technology while

I was overseas. Asked if I had any questions, I queried why I was being given a choice rather than being told what to do. 'Because you make so much bloody trouble when you're told!'

'How long is this for?' I wanted to know.

'Five years.'

That would be the finish of any career prospects I might still have retained, and I said two years was the maximum I would consider. We settled on three, including training.

'You have divided the Navy into two halves,' the admiral said to me. 'Those who like you and those who hate you!' (This was clearly in reference to my paper on the standard of officers.)

'That doesn't concern me, Sir,' I replied.

'No, that's obvious,' he finished.

The meeting lasted about an hour. After I left his office, intending to rejoin Sue in the waiting car, I was only a few feet down the corridor when I was called back to the Second Naval Member's office. 'Cabban, we're trying to make up for what we've done to you,' he said, sincerely.

I almost choked. 'Don't ever say that again, Sir!' I said. 'I was prepared to die for you, and you were not prepared to support me.'

I flew as a commercial passenger for the first time when travelling to Sydney to interview applicants for the two chief petty officer positions. The work of the two men I selected to work closely with me for the next two years was outstanding and worthy of their selection and training.

My respect for my new boss, Commander Ron Thompson, was not enhanced on arrival at Heathrow at 5.00 p.m. when I received a message saying that I need not report to Australia House until the next morning. Fortunately, I had arranged accommodation with Sir Robert and Lady Burrows in their home, now adjacent to Hampstead Heath, and was warmly welcomed. To my complete surprise and delight my hosts had procured stalls seats for *My Fair Lady* at the Drury Lane Theatre, including two for me and a partner, so I was able to repay Sue's aunt in Ditchling, Sussex, by taking her.

After a few days in London, during which I was able to attend an 'Introduction to Work Study' seminar, I joined HMS *Dolphin*, the Royal Navy submarine base in Gosport, Hampshire. We were introduced to Ron Burns, a lecturer at the Engineering and Allied Employers Association, who briefed us on the subject that had been chosen by the

Admiralty to be our practical project during our course. It was essential that we collect every piece of information, every form and every reference, which would allow us to recreate the processes involved in 'the foreign service drafting of submarine ratings'. One week was a brief period in which to accomplish this. But it was done so successfully that we did not have any occasion to telephone for more information during the next four weeks in Bristol.

The course was intensive, involving living in a guest house in suburban Clifton Hill, walking distance from the school, and progressively learning and applying new techniques of recording and analysing information to describe and solve a problem. After four weeks, our projects had advanced to a stage at which we had recorded the present method, identified and critically analysed the key operations and produced alternatives. We were then sent back to our factories to sell the solutions. In Gosport, we gave a presentation to captain (SM4), the captain of *Dolphin* commanding the 4th Submarine Squadron, and all of the individual captains and senior officers of the squadron. Our proposals effectively saved half a submarine's crew through a dramatic and realistic reduction of unproductive time, which was achievable through integrated planning and co-ordination between naval and civil authorities, medical procedures and transport arrangements. All of this enhanced the lives of the submariners and their families.

I had the opportunity to visit London for weekends, and my enthusiasm for work study as the panacea for all of the world's industrial problems was so evident to Sir Robert Burrows that he asked me, 'Peter, tell me about work study.' Looking at this dear, now elderly friend and benefactor through younger and wildly enthusiastic eyes, I decided to simplify and gave a summary of the salient points as I saw them. He listened attentively. When I finished he thanked me and said, 'I think I knew a man once who knew a little bit about that. I brought him over from the United States to help me in my coal mines. His name was Frank Gilbreth [famously portrayed in *Cheaper by the Dozen*]'.

Thoroughly and suddenly mortified, I said, 'Sir Robert, I feel the size of threepence!'

'So you should, young man!' he retorted, 'Don't teach your grandfather to suck eggs!'

As students at Bristol we had been fed on the history of Frank Gilbreth, the Father of Method Study, and read his books. All the time my host not only knew of him and his incredible talent but also had employed and witnessed his work at first hand. Lady Burrows told me after Sir Robert's death that he often chuckled when recalling the incident, 'I got him that time.'

Late in this period, Sue's mother suffered a heart attack, and was treated in Royal Newcastle Hospital. I bought a portable tape recorder and recorded warm messages from every relative in England whom I could reach. Flying home, it was a joy to be met by Sue and our boys at Melbourne Airport. But in next to no time a list of preliminary work studies to be undertaken at Flinders Naval Depot was being given to me, commencing with the indoctrination of recruits into the New Entry School.

The processes of introducing eighteen- or nineteen-year-olds to the Navy, including outfitting them with uniform clothing, initial drill, disciplinary instruction and medical requirements, was scheduled to occupy their first nine working days at the base. My team and I managed to prove, during the duration of two cycles, that this time could be reduced to two and a half days by some practical modifications of routines and simple adaptation of existing facilities. I was threatened with physical violence by the commander of the school if I reported our findings, which he was convinced reflected poorly on his management ability. Not only did I report the findings but also we were able to show that, in three and a half days, many additional and desirable processes could be included with the co-operation of the school's management.

It was Admiral Harrington's intention that next we 'Do the Electrical School', a prospect that, by the very implication of his loaded language, I dreaded. Meanwhile, I had already been approached by Surgeon Captain Coplans, medical officer in charge of Flinders Naval Hospital. His staff of sick berth attendants was 50 per cent below the approved establishment for the 212-bed hospital, and he had asked me, in the wardroom, if we could help him. This was a crucially important moment in the prehistory of our little unit: it was the first request for help from the work study team that had come spontaneously from within the RAN, rather than the team being imposed on departments with the attendant resentment and resistance. Immediately, I approached Commodore Plunkett-Cole, who saw the issues clearly and represented them to a very perturbed Admiral Harrington, by telephone. To our combined delight, the request was approved, and we were able to agree terms of reference for the first hospital work study undertaken in Australia. It was, to my mind at least, a watershed decision on which the entire future of work study in the RAN would depend.

Our analysis precipitated a complete change of operational approach in the hospital over the next twelve months. The number of beds staffed was reduced dramatically, by consolidation of services and beds to reflect the medical history of the depot's population. The study of the operating theatre and recovery ward was a major success, demonstrating what could be achieved with total co-operation between the staff and our team. The first central sterilising department in a country hospital in Victoria was established as a part of the implementation. We relocated the surgical recovery room from the former Cadet Midshipmen's Ward, some distance from the operating theatre, to a newly vacated space adjacent to the theatre. Shortly afterwards this reform was credited with the saving of the life of a patient who had haemorrhaged following tonsillectomy. Immediate surgical intervention was now possible.

The Victorian Hospitals and Charities Commissioners visited Flinders to see the results and embraced the principles and practice of work study soon afterwards. During this period I proceeded on leave to Newcastle, staying with Sue's family, and attended a farewell party given for a dentist from the Royal Newcastle Hospital. The guest of honour asked whether I had ever visited that institution and told me, emphatically, that I should, as it was internationally famous for its innovative management and clinical practices. That night I mentioned this to my father-in-law, and he arranged for me to meet the chief executive officer and medical superintendent, Dr C. J. McCaffrey. That meeting changed my life, although I did not know it at the time. Chris McCaffrey showed me around the entire city campus of the hospital, explaining what they did and why, and I was captivated by the obvious efficiency and cleanliness achieved amid the sheer simplicity of the hospital design and lay-out. At the day's end I asked if I could spend a week with him, as I had only seen the 'tip of the iceberg'. He agreed, and to my great surprise my application for another week there was approved by the Navy shortly after my return to Flinders.

The time flew, being so full of startling new discoveries, each leading to better methods with total teamwork. It was awe-inspiring. 'Well, Peter, what are you going to do when you return to Flinders?' I was asked when I thanked my host for his wonderful generosity and patience with me.

'I hope that you will understand, Doctor, that I am not going to copy anything that you are doing, because the environment is completely different. But I am intending to apply the principles,' I replied.

'I anticipated your reply to my question, and obtained my board's permission, last night, to retain you as management consultant to this hospital,' he said.

Completely taken by surprise, I showed my stupidity by saying, 'But Doctor, I can't teach you anything!'

'I know that!' he continued, 'but I don't believe in owning a dog and barking! I want you to do the things which I don't have time to do.' And he outlined terms under which I would spend any time when I was free in Newcastle at the hospital, talking to the staff, seeing what they did and responding to any requests for help. My payment would be eight pounds for a full four-hour session. So for the remainder of my naval career, whenever I was on leave in Newcastle, with Sue's blessing, I spent as much time as possible at the Royal Newcastle Hospital.

My association with Dr McCaffrey was consolidated into one of the strongest friendships of my life. Chris later helped me in my approach to managing the crew of a warship, and visited each of the three in which I served as executive officer. The trust I placed in McCaffrey was to reap rewards when I joined *Voyager* and faced dilemmas of a much different kind.

Commodore F. Leveson George, an avid supporter of work study, joined Flinders early in the hospital study and discussed with me the general management of the depot. Very shortly afterwards he directed that I must study the management and organisation of training. But, as this assignment did not have Naval Board approval, it was to be accomplished in my own time.

The study commenced on 6 June 1960 (D–Day) and was reported four months later with a personal presentation to the Naval Staff at Navy Office in Canberra. This meeting was my only non–negotiable demand for the commitment to undertake such a task in my own time. Rear Admiral McNicoll, now Second Naval Member and Chief of Naval Personnel, was chairman of the meeting. Afterwards he assured Commodore George of my prospects for early promotion, but I did not hold my breath.

Our report was brutally objective, indicating that Flinders was a

miniature Portsmouth, with reproductions of each Royal Navy establishment within one depot. This was extremely inefficient and outmoded in
both structure and management practice. The recommended solutions
were simple, if not immediately popular. We proposed a 50 per cent reduction in the number of people reporting directly to the commanding
officer and a fundamental, functional reorganisation of the management of
training. Commodore George later wrote to me, when I was serving in
the fleet, to say that the visiting First Sea Lord had told him our report was
'the most devastating paper ever read at the Admiralty' and that the Royal
Navy was being restructured on the basis of its proposals. Meanwhile, the
RAN was dithering, and I never received any official intimation from the
Naval Board of their pleasure or otherwise.

Admiral Harrington was now Flag Officer Commanding Australian
Fleet (FOCAF) and insisted that he have us in the fleet as an adjunct to
his staff. Consequently, we were appointed to his flagship. Before I was to
embark in HMAS *Melbourne*, Sue told me that she intended giving me a
daughter. This was out of the blue, as we had been advised that she should
not have more children after the trauma of Christopher's delivery. I
objected strongly, for I could not bear the risk of losing her, but Sue's
decision was final. 'If it's another boy, I'll have a fourth baby,' she said, 'but
if it's a girl, you can have the fourth!' Once more, during my time at sea,
she would have close company.

The only study designated at the time was of the handling of signal
communications in the flagship. It appeared that it was taking several hours
for signals addressed to FOCAF to reach him. We were to study and speed
up the process. From previous experience I envisaged the actions on board
and the number of hands through which these signals would normally pass
en route to the admiral. I said that the recording would require the use of
three time-lapse cameras, fitted with non-standard reels of film specially
produced by Kodak for the purpose. (In truth, I hoped that this requirement would kill any enthusiasm for the study. There was still much to be
achieved in the far more fertile and receptive area at Flinders.) But, for
whatever reasons, Admiral Harrington was determined that we should be
in the fleet, at sea.

After observing the signal-handling process at first hand in *Melbourne*
I was able to solve the problem in less than a day. The original signals
arrived by telex, full of typing errors, yet always able to be understood.

Nevertheless, they were always retyped in duplicate or triplicate. Then, if there were no typing errors, they would finally be taken to the admiral and other addressees. The standard of typing by the telex operators was obviously poor, but they knew that their work was going to be retyped anyway and so clearly did not care. I took a signal as it was originally received and copied it on the duplicating machine in the same office. Finding the admiral in his cabin, I asked him if he could read and understand it. He could, and said he was quite happy to receive his signals in the same manner and condition. Case solved. (The standard of telex typing improved overnight when it became known that signals were no longer to be retyped and that the original senders would be identified.)

Melbourne sailed to the Far East for exercises with SEATO navies, and called into Singapore, Bombay, Karachi, Hong Kong and Manila during the cruise. On the evening before the Sea Venom squadron was scheduled to fly ashore to Butterworth airfield for the duration of the ship's stay in Singapore, I was told of a powerful rumour that was circulating. Commander Guy Beange, who was 'Wings' at the time, had committed himself to piloting the spare aircraft. The rumour was that it was going to be sabotaged so that it would crash on take-off. On the basis of acknowledged attitudes among the men towards this strict and taciturn man, this was no small thing to laugh off. When I knocked on his cabin door, I saw Guy sitting and reading, and asked if I could fly as his passenger the next day.

'Do you know what you're doing?' he asked.

'Yes, Sir, I do, and I know that nothing will happen if I'm with you,' I replied. I assured him that I was being neither brave nor stupid. I knew myself to be not unpopular with the ratings in the Fleet Air Arm so there was no way I would be in jeopardy. He accepted my offer. When we taxied to the catapult for take-off, poor Guy's leather gloves were soaked with perspiration as he showed a level of courage that I was quite sure I did not need. It was a short and pleasant flight to the RAAF–RAF base, from where I returned by car to the ship, which had docked by the time I was in Singapore.

Onboard *Melbourne* and again at sea, Beange invited me to have a beer in his cabin one evening and told me the story of my flying career as he knew it. He said that Bras Cooper had told him he had been instructed by Buchanan to fail me in my flying test, and why he had refused that order. The flight over the ocean that concluded the period of flying with Guy's Sea Fury squadron had been undertaken to confirm the opinion he had formed of my ability. Immediately after we had landed, he telephoned Commander Smith at Navy Office and told him, 'I want Cabban in my squadron and you can take anyone else for him.' He was refused, and I was sent to the UK for maintenance test pilot training. I was completely devastated, almost in tears from the emotions that now surged through me.

'Why didn't anyone ever tell me?' I asked. 'I always felt that I was below average.' I have lived with mixed feelings about the Navy ever since that day – of love and dedication to the ideals of the service, and a bitter resentment for the conspiratorial strength of the mediocrities who so often gain power.

In Hong Kong, I was pleased to meet two young women who had been Sue's neighbours in their childhood when their father was colonel-in-charge of Fort Scratchley, Newcastle. They were now married to Dutch businessmen, resident in Hong Kong, and would figure prominently in the events of 1963 and the royal commission of 1967. Both husbands were in China, separately, on business when I made contact. After a brief meeting I invited them to attend a cocktail party and witness the ceremonial sunset on the flight deck. When Adrian de Lange and Piet Liebenschutz returned to Hong Kong we formed a lasting friendship, and saw a great deal of each other at their homes and in my ships. Lieby was a dedicated bridge player, and arranged for me to be included in an evening of bridge with some reputedly fine Chinese players at his home one evening. During the afternoon I had been shopping with Robin de Lange and chosen the gemstones for an eternity ring to be made for Sue.

When I returned briefly to the ship to collect my shaver and a change of clothing, I was met on the gangway by the flag lieutenant to the admiral. He told me that all leave was cancelled. We sailed an hour later, in the face of Typhoon Alice, and wasted days circling in the South China Sea. Not only had the bridge-playing opportunity vanished but also my writer was enjoying himself ashore in Hong Kong, having watched us sail away after turning a deaf ear to the radio broadcasts that ordered a mass recall to the fleet. Fortunately, we docked again in the wake of the storm for just enough time to collect Sue's ring.

The executive officer asked that we undertake several projects, so I first proposed a series of short courses to enable his officers to solve the problems rather than us. The most spectacular success was to tackle the provisioning and storage of aircraft carriers. This task normally kept 600 men fully occupied for five days. The workforce employed was reduced to just sixty men for less than a day by incorporating a Bailey bridge and new hatches in the hangar deck. This solution was adopted by both the Royal Navy and the United States Navy with commensurate savings.

I was pleased that my three-year commitment to work study in the RAN would soon expire and approached Admiral Harrington. I requested that he personally write my AS206, the report on me for promotion. 'Arch' Harrington agreed to write my AS206 and asked what appointment I would prefer next. (He was soon to be Chief of Naval Staff and could confer my choice.) I said that I did not wish any favours, but assumed that I should be appointed executive officer of a fleet destroyer. He did not think that suitable but, when informed that I had passed every examination for command of destroyers, his attitude changed, and he agreed that it would be a most suitable appointment.

At lunch time on the day of our return to Sydney, I was approached, in the wardroom, by the fleet photographic officer, Lieutenant 'Soapy' McEwen, who asked, 'Are you a friend of Alan Cordell?' He explained that he had just returned from the new frigate HMAS *Parramatta*, where Alan was executive officer, and that he was concerned for Alan's welfare. Soapy had been given permission to leave his camera equipment, to be used to record the commissioning ceremony later that afternoon, in Alan's cabin. 'But I won't be here,' Alan had said, 'I've had a message from Jesus.' This was not normal behaviour for a talented lieutenant commander.

I found David Leach, who was fleet gunnery officer at that time, and said, 'Alan Cordell's in trouble and needs our help.' We hurried across the dockyard to *Parramatta* where 'Snow' Gafford, with whom I had served in *Shoalhaven*, was on the quarterdeck. 'Where's Alan?' I asked. Told that he had gone ashore in civilian clothes, I asked where I would find the captain and was directed to his cabin. Commander (later Rear Admiral) Guy Griffith said he was worried at Alan's behaviour and that, after he had told him of his 'message', Alan had gone ashore. Griffith did not know where he was! I was staggered. Cordell had in effect deserted his ship and was technically liable for disciplinary action, including court martial. But, worst of all, he was probably sick, yet no one knew where he was. I suggested that Father Grantly Lake, the Roman Catholic chaplain then located at HMAS *Penguin*, Balmoral, should be requested to go immediately to Cordell's local church to intercede.

Alan was not a Catholic, neither was David Leach nor I, but Father Lake had often served with us during the previous twenty years. He found Alan at his local Anglican Church, with the alarmed minister, and easily persuaded him to accompany him to Balmoral Naval Hospital for a rest. His treating psychiatrist requested, about a week later, that I visit Alan at Concord Hospital where he was now a patient. I had never visited a psychiatric ward and was totally unprepared for the experience. The door of the ward was unlocked to admit me and locked behind me again as I ventured in to be greeted cordially by a cheerful Alan. He told me that he had been receiving electroconvulsive shock treatment, and was quite content. Diagnosed as suffering schizophrenia, Alan was discharged from the RAN as medically unfit. His marriage dissolved. He had continuing treatment in a civilian hospital where I visited him. His condition is now controlled successfully, and he is a loyal friend. It was not hard to imagine that his dramatic breakdown had been caused by the pressures of a naval career, but the chilling spectre of shock therapy would soon figure in my own life.

13
Executive Management

My next appointment was as executive officer of HMAS *Tobruk*, a Battle Class destroyer, like *Sluys* then being transformed from 'mothballs' (reserve) to be recommissioned into the fleet within four months. I was to reside at HMAS *Penguin*, the Balmoral shore base, for the precommissioning period and travel daily to Garden Island.

Driving regularly past the site of the new AMP Building on Circular Quay, I was conscious that none of the construction workers on the building was idle or looking undirected in their activity. I asked Sue's father if he could acquire any information concerning the management of the project, and he arranged an on-site meeting for me with an American, Robert Thomas, the project manager, who was on loan to Civil and Civic from the Utah Construction Co. in the USA. The meeting was very productive, and I learned a great deal of the planning and management of large projects from Bob over the next few months while we maintained contact. Later, I referred to that meeting when I was at Royal Newcastle Hospital with Dr McCaffrey, and he immediately drew from a filing cabinet a dossier on Thomas that he had accumulated from newspaper articles in the previous few years. Bob had built the Eildon Weir and the St Mary's Munitions Factory with notable success, and had an unblemished industrial relations record, always coming in on time and on budget. McCaffrey was fascinated by him.

As *Tobruk* reached the required standard of readiness, Commander Vernon Parker, who had been two years my senior at the college, joined me as captain-designate for recommissioning. The crew had also joined and were as ready as the ship. We were all anxious to get going when, with only days to go, a signal was received directing that the ship be sealed again and placed in reserve once more. The commissioning was cancelled, and *Tobruk* was eventually scrapped. Everyone else was appointed elsewhere, while I was left to oversee the reversal. Devastated is not the word for my feelings, which were shared by the entire crew. 'We were too good for them, Sir!' was the summary of the chief boatswain's mate, speaking for the crew. 'They did not care' was nearer the mark. As far as I could ascertain the whole process had been a political ploy to keep the dockyard workers employed.

I had no doubt that I had been singled out for special treatment with my next appointment. As executive officer, I was to prepare the ageing aircraft carrier HMAS *Sydney* for recommissioning in its new role as a troop transport vessel. For four months I had watched the slow and slipshod efforts of men who were employed aboard the moth-balled carrier. I had thought, 'God help the poor bastard who has to commission her!' Well, it was me, and the task was enough to provoke paranoia. It was the only job I ever had in which I would go to sleep every night with the thought that one day I would wake up and it would all be over. The whole, huge recommissioning project had descended into a textbook example of how not to manage work of this complexity and scale. It was a living nightmare.

I was on leave when Sue was in Newcastle and due to give birth to Sally (the only name I had considered for all of our babies before birth). She was overdue by two weeks when her obstetrician told her that there was no such thing as being overdue. 'You've miscalculated,' he told her. She advised him to tell me himself as I had been overseas nine months earlier! On 11 November 1961 Sally Jane Cabban came into the world, 'like a steam train', the doctor informed me at Royal Newcastle Hospital, and she was the living image of the grandmother she would never see. When I took our boys to view their new sister, they first surveyed all of the babies in the nursery. Sally had not been washed, in keeping with McCaffrey's policy of not allowing anyone except the mother to handle newborns and allowing them to rest before bonding and being washed by the mother. One of the boys spoke for both of them and asked me, 'Why couldn't we have one of the clean ones?'

My mother recalled me phoning her with the news and said I was crying, of which I have no memory. I recall holding little Sally in my hands and looking upwards to thank God for her and her mother. My life was an unsettling mosaic of blissful family happiness and professional hell.

In order to protect the integrity of the refit as much as I could, I determined that I should live on board, despite the fact that there was no fresh water or toilet plumbing connected, no cooking facilities and no security except for routine dockyard patrols. The presence of one ship's officer aboard, albeit with no authority, would be a deterrent to theft from a free, open, unsupervised aircraft carrier full of saleable items, lying unoccupied from 4.00 p.m. to 7.00 a.m. daily.

To my surprise, the junior engineer officer appointed to stand by also asked to sleep aboard, accepting the same regimen as I, and getting a more productive day on board without the wasted travelling time to and from Balmoral. We showered in the cold water of the dockside bathrooms, twice daily, through summer and winter, and walked to the wardroom mess at HMAS *Kuttabul*, just outside the dockyard gates, for our meals and use of the bar.

Each day, I spent a considerable time just walking through the ship, observing the activity of the dockyard workers on board – or lack of it – and kept my counsel. The mounting frustration that came from witnessing over-staffing, slow work, base idleness and sloth, all with little or no supervision – even in the direct view of those charged with management – was barely tolerable. The amount of flammable waste throughout the ship was of major concern to me, until, when I judged it to be extremely hazardous, I directed my entire workforce of about sixty men to clean all waste material from the cafeteria flat, a very large open area in the centre of the middle deck, and dispose of it ashore. Approximately a ton of rubbish was removed, and there was a consensus among the crew that a major fire could have been ignited in the area.

By extraordinary coincidence, a fire broke out in the cafeteria flat the very next day and was detected and extinguished before it was out of control. The regulations stated categorically that any and every fire on board a ship in dockyard hands must be reported immediately to the flag officer in charge, eastern Australia (FOICEA). I waited for the report to be submitted, but in vain. It was never reported by the general manager as required, and no inquiry was conducted into the circumstances of the fire, as was also demanded by the regulations.

Christmas was approaching when I observed several dockyard workers walking over a gangway carrying cartons of beer and taking them into the aircrew briefing room, from which a considerable noise of partying emanated. Choosing my words with great care, I called the general manager's office and reported what I had seen. My report was heard without comment. Within ten minutes I received a visit from a civilian dockyard officer, who stated, 'I believe you have a complaint.'

'No!' I replied, 'I am not complaining, I am merely reporting what is happening in case no one knows. It is certainly not a complaint, because I have no right to complain.'

Without comment he left and, as far as I knew, did nothing. Partying continued unabated in the ship.

As soon as the Christmas public holidays had finished, I requested a formal meeting with FOICEA, and although I was nominally on leave, I drove from Newcastle and reported to the admiral that the management of Garden Island Dockyard was corrupt and in breach of regulations. I believed the quality and safety of the refit and conversion of *Sydney* was in jeopardy. Citing the fire, the party and misallocation of funds, as well as a raft of direct observations, I made my point with some force. Shortly afterwards, Captain F. Leveson George was appointed general manager, and the dockyard seemed to take on a different attitude.

We had an establishment, the number and designations of all officers, chief and petty officers and junior ratings, which was planned in Navy Office by a group who must never have been near an aircraft carrier, much less served in one. Their calculations were predicated on the theory that, while in a non-operational role, all crew, regardless of rank or rating, would reside, twenty-four hours a day, seven days a week, in the officers' quarters in the stern of the ship. The remainder of the ship, including living quarters, galleys, passageways, engine rooms and other compartments, would require no lighting, plumbing, cleaning, electrical or steam power, or heating. Then, when required to be operational, embarking 600 or more Army personnel and their equipment, the officers' quarters would revert to their designated use and the lower ranks would move to hammocks and general mess decks. None of the management gurus in Navy Office realised that without routine patrols, the salt water in the ring main (the source of water for fire-fighting throughout the ship) would quietly leak through the corrosion pieces interspersed throughout its length, and the ship would gradually fill with water and sink. Later experience proved my prediction to be entirely realistic. To great annoyance in Navy Office, because the budget was based on this fantasy, my submission for review prevailed, and we received a barely sufficient establishment of about 130 officers and men.

Captain R. I. Peek OBE DSC RAN joined as captain-designate, and immediately assessed the condition of the ship and its inadequacy for its scheduled commissioning a fortnight hence. He commented to me in disbelief, 'I don't know how you have stood it.' Nor did I. With Captain Peek's arrival, life in the ship took on a new vibrancy. He waited until the day prior to our planned commissioning before entering the general manager's office and demanding, 'Come and see what you expect me to commission tomorrow!' When Captain George had accompanied Peek around the ship, he proceeded directly to the dockyard gates and ordered them locked so that no employee could leave until *Sydney* was properly refitted. Men worked right through the night, sewing cushion covers, fitting furnishings and ensuring that every facet of the ship was adequate within twenty-four hours. I have never seen such a transformation, nor so much fear as showed in those dockyard officials who were being held responsible, for the first time, for the results of their inattention. The ship was commissioned on time.

Sue and I celebrated the christening of Christopher, who was now six years old, and our baby daughter Sally on the quarterdeck of *Sydney*. Their names were subsequently inscribed in the ship's bell, the traditional improvised font. David was in paroxysms trying to contain his laughter while Christopher was being splashed on the head with a handful of cold water from the bell. Sally had been completely unmoved by the same treatment.

Commander Ken Shands joined *Sydney* in midyear of 1962 as executive officer, leaving me to serve as first lieutenant. Captain Peek's reaction to Ken's appointment was swift and unequivocal. He signalled Navy Office, indicating that I had been fulfilling the role satisfactorily and that I should not be left in the junior position. I liked and respected Ken, and I enjoyed the few weeks of serving with him, having known him for four months at the college before his term were sent to sea. He was a good leader and sensitive to the situation contrived by Navy Office at the time. I was duly appointed to HMAS *Voyager*, as executive officer, to join on 3 September. Captain Peek had by then transferred to command of HMAS *Melbourne*, so I was again for a short time executive officer of

Sydney, with Ken Shands as commanding officer. Before leaving, Captain Peek had told me that although I was not due for a confidential report (AS206), he was submitting one to ensure that my efforts were recognised and that his action was endorsed by Rear Admiral Oldham.

This latter period associated with HMAS *Sydney* was the most rewarding of my career in terms of the leadership of my commanding officer. I was able to learn much from Richard Innes ('Peter') Peek about loyalty to those who serve with and under the command of officers of the Navy. He was, in my experience, an exemplary captain.

14
Introduction to *Voyager*

While Captain Peek was absent from *Sydney*, I invited *Voyager*'s captain, David Wells, aboard for dinner one evening. Neither of us knew that I was to be appointed to his ship in the near future. The conversation was generally about our experiences since I had joined him at Flinders Naval Depot, and he asked, 'What do you want to become, eventually?'

Without hesitating, I replied, 'A management consultant.'

'No, be serious. What do you want to be in the Navy?' he demanded.

'Chief of Naval Staff,' was my firm answer.

'Well, you will be. You're the only officer I have asked that question who has ever given that reply.'

There was no alternative to satisfy my ambition, and I was prepared to serve only as long as there was still a window of opportunity to fulfil it.

I had been in the Navy long enough to harbour no delusions as to the twists and turns that lay along that path to the top. I already had a fair idea of who the potential candidates were. Those who had the inside running were obvious, for I had watched their ill-concealed manoeuvres in obtaining plum appointments under the eye of influential admirals and senior officers. Some hopefuls practised the art of listening to brilliant ideas and then promoting them as their own. Alternatively, a snide innuendo cast against a feared contender for recognition was a good fall-back device, usually followed with a hearty laugh once the destructive seed was sown, indicating that it might all be just a joke.

Meanwhile, my own steady progress through the ranks continued. When appointed in August 1962 to HMAS *Voyager* as executive officer I was aware that Captain Wells had already left to take another job and that

Commander Alan Willis, two years my senior at the college, had assumed temporary command. I looked forward to serving with him as Willis had been a cheerful, fair and enthusiastic cadet captain. Not so encouraging was the knowledge that Willis would soon be replaced by the newly promoted Captain D. H. Stevens, when he returned from duty in England. Stevens was already known throughout the Navy as 'Drunken Duncan', but I accepted the prospect of serving under him with equanimity.

An incoming executive officer is allowed three days in which to confirm the presence on board of all equipment for which he will be held responsible. He is painstakingly led by his predecessor through the compartments where everything is stored or is shown it in current use. When this long process had been completed, the ship's officers celebrated their outgoing colleague's departure with him from 11.45 a.m. until 3.00 p.m. – in other words, before, during and after lunch.

I refrained from joining these celebrations on *Voyager* and instead continuously walked around the ship's upper deck so that the working crewmen would see an officer who was interested in their occupation. That not one other officer showed his face on the upper deck while the remainder of the crew was working could not go unnoticed by the sailors. The seamen's evaluation of their superiors should never be under-estimated, and I felt a deep unease about the officers with whom I was to be confined in a destroyer for the next eighteen to twenty-four months.

The ceremony of 'colours', the hoisting of the white ensign at the stern and the Australian blue ensign (or jack) at the bow, is performed at 8.00 a.m. daily in harbour. Both are lowered at sunset, while at sea the white ensign flies continuously from the masthead. Immediately follow-ing colours, normal practice was that the seamen would congregate in groups, or 'fall in', according to their divisional allocation. After their presence was confirmed the executive officer would specify the duties they were to perform. This activity was known as 'All watches of the hands, fall in', and in *Voyager* it took place on the quarterdeck.

Armed with my work study training, this process seemed patently inefficient. With time to plan thoroughly, I addressed the crew of *Voyager* and told them that commencing on the following Monday, the Forecastle Division would not be required to attend this (or the similar 1.00 p.m. after-lunch parade), but would now be expected to proceed directly to their duties. These would be published on the prior Thursday night. All necessary materials and equipment, such as paint and brushes, would be in place for them in advance. The new system was to be trialled for three months, then, with any necessary modification, to be introduced to the entire seaman division.

As I stood before the men I was aware of the sniggers and sly looks, which indicated that the wings on my sleeve signified me as being away with the birds. At this meeting I also said, 'You know my name but I don't know yours. Please forgive me if I ask your name each time I speak to you until I know it, because I'm determined to know all of your names.' This decision was to prove critical in my relationship with the crew – and to my survival in the 1967 royal commission.

Once I had dismissed the men, Petty Officer Donnelly, responsible for the forecastle, approached me directly with his concerns. 'Sir, I'll never find them!'

'How many men are in your division?' I asked, and was told thirty-three. 'How many don't you trust?'

Hesitating for a few seconds, he replied, 'Three, oh, probably only two.'

'I have just reduced from thirty-three to two the number of men you have to worry about. But don't worry; the other thirty-one will worry about them. You won't have to.'

Within a fortnight, there was a delegation from the seamen requesting that I expand the system to all of them. 'You weren't listening,' I told them. 'It's to be three months, because something will go wrong within three months, and thirty-three men will work with me to solve it. Then it will work for a hundred men.' The three months passed quickly, and it worked well.

On that same morning, I also called all officers to the wardroom and met some for the first time. By my appointment as executive officer I was also president of the wardroom mess, with total responsibility and authority for the conduct in the mess of all officers other than the captain, who was not a member of the mess. (The captain may enter the mess informally only if invited, while nothing prevents his entry in the normal course of duty.) While I spoke to them, a lieutenant addressed me by my Christian name. I turned to him and said, 'My name is "Sir", to you and every officer below my rank, and never forget that!' The mood instantly changed from inquisitiveness to shocked disapproval.

I then explained that there were new regulations governing the mess operation, commencing with meal hours. Officers would not be allowed to eat at a time when the crew was working, except when coming off watch or in other exceptional circumstances approved by me. The bar would not open at sea. In harbour, the bar would be open at lunch time until 12.30 p.m., and from 6.00 p.m. until 11.00 p.m. at night, unless I were aboard, when I might decide to extend the closing.

These new bar rules met with immediate challenge. 'You don't trust us!' was one accusation.

'You are wrong,' I replied. 'I don't know whether I trust you or not, but I don't have to trust you.' I was not about to leave my fate in the hands of men I hardly knew. From what I had seen of them, some might very well act in my absence in a manner that could result in my court martial – as well as theirs. But the *Voyager* wardroom veterans weren't about to give up their old ways without a rearguard action.

'Regulations and Instructions for the RAN say that there has to be a mess committee,' said the supply officer, a lieutenant commander.

I agreed, and expedited an on-the-spot election so that we all knew the committee's composition in a few minutes. 'When are we meeting?' I was asked.

'There is nothing in the regulations about meeting. There will be none,' I said.

'Then how will disbursement of mess funds be decided?'

'By meetings such as this, with every officer present and able to vote, in the open,' I responded. There were no meetings of committees, and there were no complaints about the disbursement of funds.

What was soon to become the most fateful passage of my life had rather mundane beginnings. We knew we would be undertaking an extended cruise of the Far East, but first *Voyager* sailed to Jervis Bay and commenced a work-up, having undergone a refit before I joined. The plan was to then proceed to Fremantle, arriving in time for the Commonwealth Games in Perth. But many of the rivets that secured the aluminium alloy superstructure to the steel hull were found to be corroding through a process of electrolysis. We were forced to return for remedial dockyard action. While at sea before this Commander Willis dislocated his shoulder, a recurrence of a chronic condition he was determined to hide from naval authorities. Willis was obviously in intense pain, but dismissed my entreaty that he should rest and insisted on retaining personal command on the bridge while perspiration poured down his face. A navigator by specialisation, Willis showed a distinct lack of respect for *Voyager's* own appointed navigator, Lieutenant Scott Griffith, and would not hand over control of the ship to him when manoeuvring alongside the wharf in Sydney Harbour.

At Christmas time, Sue and our children shared a week with me at a motel in Rushcutters' Bay. It was an idyllic few days, with the kids loving the novelty of a swimming pool outside the door. The boys even asked if we could live there, always. I took them on board *Voyager* for Christmas dinner in the wardroom with my fellow officers. As we were leaving, Sue remarked, 'They hate you!' referring to the officers who were present, many with families.

'They'll hate me much more before I'm finished with them,' was my heartfelt reply, for they still had much to learn and many attitudes towards their duty to change.

McCaffrey had impressed on me that people are products of their environment, and will always act in the same manner in the same circumstances. The only way to change their behaviour is by altering that environment, and this does not only mean their physical surroundings. On *Voyager*, the most important change I needed to make was to ensure the constant and timely supply of information that concerned the welfare and comfort of the crew. This would limit rumour and discontent, and rob troublemakers of a vital tool. To effect this, I announced everything of special interest to the ship's company over the ship-wide armament broadcast system as soon as convenient after I became aware of it. Routine, non-urgent information was disseminated through their officers and petty officers or in daily orders, while the welfare committee spread the word on any matters of general welfare that required feedback.

On the financial side, my introduction to Gus Pfafflin, New South Wales manager of Thomas Hardy & Sons, could not have been more timely or fortuitous for *Voyager's* wardroom wine cellar. They agreed to my proposal that we carry only Hardy's wines and purchase them on consignment, instead of by the usual practice of buying from local agents in the Far East. This gave far greater overseas exposure to the Australian wines, while we were also making a significant saving on price. Four years later the distinctive shape of the Hardy's brandy bottle would be an illuminating point of evidence in the royal commission.

In complete contrast to my state of mind while living aboard _Sydney_ (when I went to sleep each night with the thought that I would wake one day and it would all be over), I was now full of determination and confidence. My honest belief was that through trust and co-operation, I would eventually succeed in turning the officers and crew into the best in the Navy. From the outset I offered the officers the opportunity to be involved in my management experiment of work allocation, but they categorically declined to participate, so I warned them not to interfere. The reforms could, in any case, be realised through their petty officers. They were also informed that I would 'throw over the side' any officer whom I saw walk past a cigarette, match or any other rubbish on the deck without personally picking it up and disposing of it. Nobody commented on my colourful choice of words, but when I left the ship, one officer said that they had all thought I would do what I had threatened.

PART 2

15
Enter Duncan Stevens

Saluting Duncan Stevens as he stepped on to the gangway to join his new ship, his first as a captain, I was a little surprised that he failed to look at me directly or even acknowledge my presence. He just returned the salutes of the assembled side party and walked briskly towards the captain's cabin. But it was not long before my new captain had me in a motor boat, about a hundred metres from the ship, observing every aspect of its appearance from outboard. He taught me to view things with a 'seaman's eye', as it would be seen and judged by any passing ship's crew. Henceforth, I was always on deck before 7.00 a.m. daily, at sea or in harbour, and out in a boat when possible, ensuring that the ship was faultless.

The officers, having received no sympathy from Alan Willis, lost no time in representing their gripes against my dictates to their new captain. Stevens brought up the subject of the rigid mess rules, imposed by me, but I said that I was adamant that they would remain in force as long as I were president of the wardroom mess. He described the officers as the most miserable group that he had ever served with, to which I replied that they would be even more miserable before I changed my attitude towards them. Further, if he ordered me to alter my mess regulations I would resign, citing that as my reason. A heated discussion like this was hardly the best start to our relationship, but he had brought the subject to the fore so it had to be dealt with and, I hoped, only once. Although disappointed in his apparently surly attitude towards me, I expected it would lessen and ultimately change to respect when I could demonstrate success in managing the ship. I strove to ensure that no resentment or disrespect should emanate from my demeanour or bearing. There was still a great deal more for me to learn about my craft, and I was keen to show that I was able to learn from him.

One of the executive officer's most crucial roles is to take responsibility for discipline. He is placed in judgement over defaulters who have overstayed their leave or committed offences under the naval regulations. This part of the job was not new or unfamiliar to me, having experienced it in both *Warramunga* and *Sydney*, while temporarily in command or as executive officer. The second in command prosecutes the referred cases before the commanding officer, having first heard all the available evidence when the defaulter appeared routinely before him. My consistent practice was always to give the benefit of any doubt to the defaulter, and on the first occasion when a man was found to be guilty of a specific offence, to award the minimum punishment listed. On the second occasion, he would be awarded the maximum on the scale. The crew largely considered that this was a fair policy. (Some time later my father told me, after drinking with a sailor who had discovered Dad's relationship to his exec, that the seaman had described me as 'the hardest bastard in the Navy – but he was fair!')

The ship left the dry dock and spent a day in Sydney Harbour, steaming through the degaussing range off Steel Point where the ship's 'magnetic footprint' is mapped so that it can be protected from magnetic mines. On returning to Garden Island, Duncan Stevens was handling the ship as it struck HMAS *Vampire* heavily, breaking one of *Vampire*'s stanchions and scraping its paint. The collision impact was about as hard as Tony Synnot's bump on the wharf in Adelaide. Captain G. J. Willis of *Vampire* accepted an apology and the making good of the damage, but the effect on Stevens was lasting. He did not handle *Voyager* again, either entering or leaving harbour, but handed that responsibility to Lieutenant Griffith, the navigator. Later in the year Stevens also entrusted these duties to officers under training.

The ship was prepared for its forthcoming voyage to the Far East, together with *Vampire* as senior ship, and our itinerary was broadly promulgated. We were to exercise with other components of the Australian fleet as well as SEATO forces. When not with the Australian fleet, we were to operate under the command of Commander in Chief Far East Station, the Royal Navy vice admiral who was based in Singapore as part of the Far East Strategic Reserve. The Strategic Reserve was retained to provide support, if required, to British forces that were containing communist insurgents in Malaysia, mainly Borneo.

It might seem quaintly colonial now, but the standard practice on these detachments was for each ship to make independent arrangements to engage Asian tailors, shoemakers and launderers who would board the ship at the first port of call and disembark at our final point of departure. It was the responsibility of the first lieutenant, or 'Number 1' as the executive officer was alternatively known, to make these arrangements. The formal documents were lodged with Commodore Hong Kong, the naval officer in charge of the dockyard, to cover the movement of the contractors' employees through the dockyards. With more than 300 officers and men spending a high proportion of their wages on these services, Hong Kong-based merchants could make thousands of pounds. The cost of wages and materials were kept to a rock-bottom minimum through the employment of low-paid workers and use of duty-free goods.

It was the more informal arrangements that worried me, although I was well aware of their customary nature and origins. A range of inducements was offered to the executive officers of warships, depending upon the size of the crew, so that an aircraft carrier commander would be a most attractive target and could make high demands. I was offered free air passage and accommodation in Hong Kong for my wife, lavish entertainment, free clothing and laundry services for *Voyager*'s contract. The captain would enjoy free laundry and a lesser gift of clothing, as part of this package. My concern was that the sailors would be expected to pay a premium for their goods, in order to defray the cost of this largesse. I met Admiral Harrington in *Melbourne* and discussed the issue. He reminded me that I had total responsibility for the safety and security of the ship as far as these men were concerned, and that the price list was fixed as a part of the proposed contract, regardless of the benefits bestowed on specific officers. Harrington urged me to think carefully before breaking with custom. In the end I was able to negotiate a fair and satisfactory deal through a reputable firm.

There was also the question of which Chinese 'side party' would be allocated by Commodore Hong Kong. This group of about ten women would be occupied in painting *Voyager*'s hull, from sampans, with materials supplied by the ship at all times when in Hong Kong harbour. This labour was performed in exchange for all scrap food from the ship's

galleys and the concession to sell Coca Cola and Fanta, at a shilling a
bottle, to sailors on board between 8.00 a.m. and 6.00 p.m. daily. Such was
the nature of Hong Kong capitalism forty years ago. The 'side party'
women did not live on board and were restricted to the upper deck.
Voyager had Suzy's side party while *Vampire* had Jenny's, a precedent set
when the ships were previously in the port. I was to be offered a choice
of Suzy's girls for my pleasure, and one smiling woman was indicated to
me as the girl chosen by an erstwhile predecessor. I declined, politely.

On the Tuesday evening before our departure from Garden Island, a
farewell buffet party for wives and guests was held on board by the
officers. The forecastle was decorated with bunting under a canvas
awning. For me, the evening had a bitter-sweet beginning. The captain
had invited Admiral Gatacre who, quite unprompted, said to me, 'Cabban,
you did a magnificent job in *Sydney*.' Thanking him quietly, I refrained
from asking why I had not then been promoted, as was recommended by
Captain Peek and endorsed by Admiral Oldham. It would have been rude
and destructive to have pursued the issue.

The evening seemed to be a success and, after the captain and his wife
had farewelled the official party, the other officers and guests moved
forward on the forecastle to sit on chairs and talk quietly. We were joined
by the captain and, although he appeared mellow and a little the worse for
wear, I was not particularly conscious of the extent of his condition. Then
Beatrice Stevens appeared and said quite forcefully, 'Duncan, it's time to
go!' He looked at his wife in bewilderment before rising and leaving with
her. The remaining guests were then escorted from the dockyard. It was
unfortunate, in my view, that the captain's wife felt obliged to speak
publicly as she had, at Stevens' first social gathering with his officers.

The following morning I enquired of Griffith, who was wardroom
wine caterer, 'Were there any problems, last night?'

'Not really, Sir,' he replied. 'We ran out of Scotch, but I ordered a
steward to open a dozen of the bonded bottles.'

The implications of his action struck me like a hammer. All ships are
open to random inspection of their bonded stores, and the discovery of a
broken seal would have threatened the entire structure of duty-free privilege enjoyed by naval vessels at sea. There was no way that I was going to
violate the trust involved and jeopardise our good relations with customs.
Without a moment's hesitation I called the chief inspector of customs,

reported what had happened and asked how I could atone. He was courteous and pleasant, thanked me for my account and said that a customs officer would shortly call at the ship, collect the duty and reseal the store. When I reported my actions to Stevens he expressed horror and surprise, saying that he would never have been game to do as I did (and would rather have hoped the breach would not have been discovered). We were to reap the reward for my instinctive action on our return six months later.

Voyager finally sailed out on the Far East cruise in company with *Vampire* on 31 January 1963. The day was sunny and the sea placid so I was taken by surprise when Captain Stevens said he was feeling unwell and turning in. 'You have command, Number 1.' Innocently, I put his discomfort down to seasickness, as he had been in shore-based appointments for the two previous years. I signalled to *Vampire* that I had command and carried out my first jackstay transfer, the passing of a cylinder containing a message by a rope line between the two ships while under way. Later in the forenoon, I held the captain's requestmen and defaulters parade, which had been scheduled. When attending to the consequential records of punishment, I signed them as 'Lieutenant Commander for Captain (Sick)'. On returning to the bridge after twenty-four hours in his cabin, the captain resumed command and did not remark in any way on my conduct in his absence, but it was soon to have repercussions for both of us.

Darwin was our first port of call following a week of exercises and vital 'shaking down' after the prolonged period of inactivity in the dockyard. Despite the hot and steamy conditions, sport of every kind was played between the two ships' crews and by combined ships' teams against other services' teams. One of the stars of our rugby side was the doctor, Surgeon Lieutenant Michael (Mick) Tiller, a big bluff man who had a distinct disdain for naval customs and would challenge most situations, regardless of personal risk. He played rugby with impressive vigour and stirred the imagination of all those who took the field alongside him.

I played squash with 'Toothy', the dental surgeon, Allan Kyd. He was a good player as well as an excellent messmate, and as the cruise continued I was to find his company more and more enjoyable. 'Toothy' was discreet, mature, extremely patient and responsible, although not imbued with an automatic acceptance of the Navy.

Duncan Stevens was a good cricketer and joined the ship's team whenever they played, as did Jim Willis for his team. After playing cricket during our stay in Darwin, the captain visited an old college term mate. On the following morning, while supervising preparations for sailing, I had not been able to find him. Lieutenant Wright, the captain's secretary, sought me out and spoke to me with some urgency. Wright told me that the captain's steward had found the captain wandering around the deck, not knowing where he was, and had taken him to his cabin. We were due to sail in ten minutes, so I went to Stevens' cabin to check his condition. He agreed to my proposal that I should take the ship to sea and have command for the next forty-eight hours, then climbed the steps to his sea cabin and retired to his bunk.

Taking *Voyager* to sea for the first time should have been a thrill, but under these strained conditions my elation was subdued. After saluting Captain Willis when he appeared on his bridge, I deliberately ignored him until both ships were ready for sea. When Willis's look of concern finally demanded some explanation I held the captain's gold-braided cap aloft and rubbed my stomach to show that the skipper was sick. Stevens was widely known in the Navy to have a troublesome duodenal ulcer, but my conscience found it far from pleasant to perform this pantomime.

The passage continued with gunnery and torpedo exercises between the two ships. We passed through Sunda Strait, the site of the 1942 World War II battle in which HMAS *Perth* was lost. In Singapore we berthed ahead of *Vampire* and embarked our Chinese domestic workforce. For the next few months they would sleep on deck or in sheltered compartments, always out of the way of the crew, measuring for clothes, making and repairing footwear, and laundering. These men prepared their own food after the ship's cooks had completed the crew meals, and might have been able to supplement theirs with leftovers, but no open fire was tolerated.

Fuelling, storage work and hull maintenance occupied most of the sailors, and I insisted that their officers supervise and encourage them. It had become my habit to visit every accessible compartment of the ship where my seamen might be working at least once every hour between 8.00 a.m. and 4.00 p.m., and then to attend to my accumulated paperwork. Very soon I was able to recognise and address each of the crew by name, and to acquire a more intimate knowledge of their characters by observing and talking with them.

16
The Gathering Storm

Trincomalee, on the east coast of Sri Lanka (still Ceylon when we were there in 1963), was not my favourite harbour. Its tropical heat drains your energy and has a way of seeming even hotter, more humid and steamier than anywhere else in Asia. The locals adapt by moving very slowly and dressing suitably, although they did not appear any more enthusiastic about the conditions than we were after we had made the passage following our twelve days in Singapore. There was, however, one magical moment when a herd of elephants crossed from the mainland to a small island in the harbour, with each cow carefully holding the trunk of her submerged calf above the water throughout the trip.

The Royal Ceylon Navy hosted a cocktail party and supper for officers of the visiting ships, and this was an excellent opportunity to meet these interesting, hospitable and efficient officers and their wives. We invited a group to a buffet dinner in *Voyager* on the following night, a Saturday. During that morning the crew worked feverishly to erase the effects of seawater on our paintwork and brass so that the ship was fully prepared for the possibility of a snap inspection by the admiral.

Our guests for dinner that evening were most gracious, and never learned of a grotesque little scene that was hidden from their view. The officers gave us fascinating descriptions of their childhood development and the privileges of growing up within tea plantation society. In turn, they were interested in hearing of our way of life. The ladies looked gorgeous in colourful saris, and their husbands urged them to dance with our officers while they relaxed and watched.

The normal *Voyager* practice on such occasions, with the captain's concurrence, was to allocate the bathroom of the captain's day cabin, almost adjoining the wardroom, for the use of lady guests. Regrettably, Stevens returned aboard drunk after a dinner aboard HMS *Caesar* and vomited all over the bathroom, rendering it unfit for use. I helped the captain's leading steward, Freeman, to clean up the mess. That episode killed the party spirit in me, but I managed to hide my feelings when returning to our guests.

The captain's 'illness' had another direct consequence for both me and the ship. The next day, Sunday, a defaulter was paraded before me, charged with 'direct disobedience of orders', an offence carrying with it a penalty of imprisonment and possible dismissal. The seaman had refused to clean the captain's heads in the bridge superstructure, the toilet in which he had vomited the previous night after turning in. Under the prescribed conduct of such a case, I was obliged to have the order repeated to the offender in front of me. Instead, I asked him why he had refused. He said, 'The captain was drunk, Sir, and I won't clean up after him.' Obviously, Stevens' condition had been seen by the boat's crew conveying him back to *Voyager*, as well as gangway staff. The word had spread.

I asked, 'Where is your bucket?' When he told me, I said, 'Bring it to me. I'll clean the heads.'

'No, you won't, Sir,' he replied. 'I will.'

The case was dismissed. Duncan Stevens was never made aware of the incident.

'Divisions' and prayers were conducted every Sunday on board all ships. After his excesses the night before, the captain summoned me to say that he was ill and ordered me to assume command. I was to inspect the crew as they paraded in their best uniforms before conducting the morning prayer service. This was the first occasion when I had taken prayers and, in my ignorance, I pronounced the 'absolution' at the conclusion, to be confronted by an indignant sailor afterwards. I apologised and it was not mentioned again.

The commander in chief had invited all officers in the fleet aboard *Lion* for pre-lunch drinks immediately after divisions and prayers, and as we arrived I obeyed Stevens' order that I apologise on his behalf and report that he was ill. It was fortunate that I was never challenged as to the nature of his illness, because I was bereft of excuses. By the following day the captain was able to attend the briefings and planning meetings preparatory to proceeding to sea for a series of exercises, but made no reference to his illness and recovery.

By now enough time had passed for me to form a considered impression of the captain. On the one hand, Duncan Stevens presented to me as a mixture of maturity bred of the naval college background, parental influence and respect for rank – especially his own. On the other was gross insecurity and the need for reassurance that he really was a captain and deserving of that rank. I was certain that he was lonely, this being his first significant command, and experiencing the isolation imposed on all captains. For example, captains are not members of the wardroom mess, maintaining their own pantries with unique tableware, and drawing their beverages from the wardroom stocks as required. They usually eat alone, served by a leading steward, with domestic support from a cabin hand. It was also obvious that Stevens missed his wife, and wrote to her daily.

A genuine sympathy and desire to support his weakness and show respect for his strength prompted me to approach the captain ten days before his birthday. There was certainly no patronising intent when I said, 'Sir, the officers would be pleased if you would be our guest for the evening of your birthday.' The long notice provided time to ensure that he had no other engagements within his control, and for me to prepare both the officers and the meal arrangements. Soon after he joined, I had extended an invitation to Stevens to make casual use of the wardroom, and I appreciated that he did not avail himself of the offer. Instead, he waited for an invitation when I thought it appropriate for him to join us.

The officers were predictably hostile to the idea, as they wished to make other plans for a free Saturday night in Singapore. I gave them no option. The menu was designed with the captain's known gastric problem in mind, and commenced with sweet corn on the cob, then smoked salmon followed by turkey and ham with fresh local vegetables. The officers' cooks were superbly trained and responded well when good provisions were available. Similarly, the petty officer steward and his team were at their best when serving at a formal function, and they prepared conscientiously and with considerable pride. The cooks and stewards were informed in advance that an issue of two bottles of beer each would be made to them, courtesy of the officers, as soon as the port had been passed after dinner, so that any temptation to pre-empt this bounty was negated.

Saturday dawned and sport was again the popular choice for a large proportion of the crews, including me. As I spent the afternoon swimming at the officers' club and playing squash I was unaware that the captain had already laid the foundations of a disaster. He had invited all officers to share a drink with him in his cabin before lunch, and then entertained Bill Money and Lieutenant Commander Ian Blaikie, the supply officer, throughout the afternoon. (While I gave evidence of this as an observation and it was my honest belief, both of these officers later denied it.) As he preceded me into the mess before the birthday dinner one of the captain's erstwhile drinking companions told me, 'The old man's had a skinful – he may not make it.' Shocked, and with grave misgivings, I ordered a Scotch and water and waited for the officers to assemble.

Russell Vasey, a lieutenant commander in the Naval Reserve who served his annual training period aboard *Voyager* during its previous period in the Far East, had joined us once again. As a qualified and experienced bridge watch-keeper and a convivial messmate he was most welcome. He had been a prefect at Newcastle Boys High School when I was in first year, and it was good to have someone aboard with whom I could talk in confidence. He was in the mess when, everyone being present, I was about to invite our guest to join us.

Captain Stevens burst through the curtain at the doorway, with a florid, beaming smile, and proceeded to sit alongside me, on the club fender in front of the fireplace. Out of courtesy, but against my better judgement, I ordered a drink for him. His condition was deteriorating alarmingly by the second. The petty officer steward had already informed me that dinner was ready to be served. Just as I was rising to suggest that we should move to the table, Duncan Stevens dropped to his hands and knees and crawled rapidly to the table. It was so bizarre that Vasey, as a witness three years later, was convinced he had seen Stevens enter the mess on his hands and knees. I was appalled. Seeing the whole evening dissolving into farce, I hurried to my place at the head of the main table alongside the captain, who had somehow seated himself before anyone else could reach the table. Mixed emotions flickered across the faces of the officers – from mirth to shock and disbelief. The stewards began serving the first course. Stevens managed to get his corn on to the small forks but then failed miserably to find his mouth as his moving face and hands were uncoordinated. The display caused suppressed outbursts of hilarity among the watching stewards.

Succumbing completely to the influence of the alcohol he had consumed, the captain suddenly slumped forward onto his plate. I rose to my feet immediately, trying to steady the captain with a lift to his shoulders. The whole scene now took on an air of desperate absurdity. I gave a brief speech addressed to our guest of honour and presented him with the Ronson table cigarette lighter I had purchased on behalf of the wardroom. Saying that I believed he should now retire, I asked the doctor, Mick Tiller, to assist the captain from the mess and accompany him to his cabin.

The situation was far from comic. It required a firm expression of authority to restore a proper sense of discipline and respect within the officer team. When Tiller had returned and said that Stevens was asleep in his bunk, I spoke to the officers in the absence of stewards, ordering them never to speak a word outside the mess of what had occurred, and warned of dire consequences. David Martin (who'd been excused from attendance to meet his wife who'd flown in unexpectedly) told me later that Jim Dowling, a sub-lieutenant, had described the events to him in graphic detail. I then released any who wished to leave while a normal meal service was soon to follow. I addressed the stewards in the pantry that separated the wardroom from the day cabin and gave them a similar instruction, demanding loyalty to keep the matter from the remainder of the crew.

It had been an extraordinary night. Duncan was unwell for the next three days. He never made any acknowledgement of the gift to me or the officers, or mentioned the dinner.

17
Caine Mutiny Revisited

The captain was up and about again by the time we departed Singapore for Hong Kong on the morning of Monday, 25 March. *Vampire* left later to rendezvous with us at sea, and we sailed together with other units of the Far East Fleet and met *Melbourne*, under the command of Captain R. I. Peek. The carrier was accompanied by *Yarra* and wearing the flag of Rear Admiral A. W. R. McNicoll, who had succeeded Harrington as FOCAF. To everyone except me the situation was absolutely normal. We performed a standard repertoire of exercises during a routine passage.

Meanwhile, my unspoken concerns about the captain and his conduct were growing rapidly. I needed guidance, maybe even enlightenment, but was too well aware of the pitfalls that lay ahead for anyone who chose to expose perceived difficulties with senior officers. The book and film of *The Caine Mutiny* – understandable favourites among the world's navies – were a classic illustration of my dilemma. The knowledge of the proximity of Captain Peek, whom I believed I knew well enough to trust with my confidence, started a train of thought that was worth careful assessment. There was a valid pretext to call on my recent captain as a recognised courtesy. Any open discussion of my problems with Stevens would be clearly out of order, but perhaps an opportunity might present itself for me to raise the issues via a sequence of hypothetical questions, such as, 'How would you recommend that an executive officer should handle a situation where he believes that his commanding officer is unfit but won't admit it?' That would be a disaster! Blind Freddy would see where that was leading. Alternatively, could I simply say straight out, 'Sir, may I discuss, in the strictest confidence, a grave problem which I believe I have with my captain?' That, too, would burn my bridges, as there would be no turning back.

Countless scenarios passed through my mind, and in each of them I refused to implicate any other officer (just as Mr Maryk did not speak to his admiral about Captain Queeg). It would be unfair to jeopardise their careers. From a more self-interested standpoint, I also did not dare discuss it with any of them for fear of a charge of conspiracy to mutiny, which might well be upheld. But unless I discussed it with them, no other officer would be as knowledgeable as I of all the incidents that had led me to my conclusions. Even if I were to refer to any other officer in an informal discussion it would immediately change the nature of the meeting to formality, and no retreat. This was a dilemma with more than two horns! In the end I decided that I must do something – anything – if only to create an opportunity to seek advice. I approached Stevens for permission to call on Peek when in harbour. Permission was granted without comment.

Docking in Victoria Basin, Hong Kong, we were immediately under siege from all the would-be agents for local merchants. It required a few minutes of resolute and unpopular plain speaking to clear them from the area of the gangway and restore order. The side party duly appeared and, after Suzy had introduced herself, were issued with paint and rollers. They immediately went to work with their customary quiet efficiency. I remained on deck supervising for most of the time while the crew were occupied with replenishment, ship maintenance and training classes.

I had made it a habit in the tropics to change my clothes at least twice daily so as to always appear in clean whites as an example. All officers changed into Red Sea rig (white uniform short-sleeved shirt, black trousers and black silk cummerbund) before 6.00 p.m. each day. When formality dictated, officers wore No.10 uniform, a full white jacket and white trousers with medals, and sometimes swords by day. In the evenings, white mess undress (a uniform consisting of white mess jacket, dress shirt and black bow tie with a black silk cummerbund, black trousers and shoes) was the norm. These pedantries of service attire might seem faintly ridiculous today, but in the early 1960s the standard to which a naval officer 'turned out' was still considered a measure of his efficiency, morale and self-discipline. And the captain was always expected to set the standard.

Russell Vasey and I walked to the Star Ferry wharf and set out on a Kowloon floorshow crawl. This was an inexpensive form of nightclub tour we had devised to add a logistical challenge to our off-duty entertainment. We would buy a beer at each establishment and watch the show until it was time to move on, then another beer, and so on. It was innocent fun and good therapy after the tensions that I endured aboard, and I could not have wished for a better companion during our diversion. We must have visited at least eight establishments before deciding to call it a night and just caught the last ferry back to Victoria. Russ and I were feeling rather pleased with our little achievement, but that euphoria was short-lived. We discovered Duncan Stevens slumped, semi-aware and alone, on a ferry seat. We took him back to *Voyager* and saw him to his cabin before parting. I climbed to the bridge to contemplate the beauty of the night, and reflect on my increasing sadness and concern for the future.

My Dutch friends welcomed me back to Hong Kong enthusiastically, and at different times I introduced both Scott Griffith and David Martin to them and their generous hospitality. 'Lieby' – Piet Liebenschutz – was Far East manager of the Royal Dutch Inter-ocean Line and had enormous knowledge and experience of merchant shipping and protocol. He was a man of great wisdom and courage, and I was able to discuss any issue with him. We visited Lieby and Janice's new home on the mountainside, where we enjoyed games of table tennis and miniature bowls (with lots of good-hearted cheating), and conversation. These were very good and dear friends, and I knew that what was talked about there was held in confidence. I shared with them my concerns about Duncan Stevens and the safety of the ship.

On the Tuesday morning, the day following our arrival, Captain Stevens had doubled over with pain during the colours parade, complaining about his stomach ulcer. As we walked towards his cabin afterwards, I advised that he should see Dr Tiller. The captain vehemently responded that he would not see Tiller because to do so would threaten his career to the extent that he could lose his command. No, he would see Surgeon Commander McNeill instead. McNeill was *Melbourne*'s doctor and an old friend of Stevens, who in my view could be relied on to keep the examination unofficial. The episode only hardened my resolve to bring the matter before a superior officer.

At 10.45 on the same morning I went to the captain's cabin to inform him that I was leaving the ship to call on Captain Peek. He looked up and said, evenly, 'You might be interested that I have just had a complete medical by the fleet medical officer and am perfectly well!' That statement was as unexpected as it was disheartening. At a stroke, Stevens had made clear to me that he assumed I would raise the matter of his health with Peek. It also revealed his cunning: he now regarded me as an enemy, not to be trusted. In truth, he was not far off the mark in some respects, but his interpretation was misguided. The captain clearly had no appreciation of my earnest desire for him to overcome his problem and to command respect from the officers and men. Nor did he recognise the complete support I had been giving him. But the die was cast. I was committed to calling on Peek and walked around the basin towards *Melbourne*.

Captain Peek greeted me and invited me into his cabin. He was dressed in full No.10 uniform with medals and sword belt, and it was obvious that he was about to accompany the admiral to an official function fairly soon. The realisation that our time was therefore limited took me aback. All my pipe dreams of a cosy chat with plenty of opportunities to collect my thoughts and direct the conversation towards Duncan Stevens and my dilemma fell apart. When asked, 'How's *Voyager*, Peter?' the best I could manage, seeing my ship through his open scuttle being covered by smoke from *Vampire*, was some inane comment about the smoke! The meeting was brief and impersonal, through no fault of Peek, but because of a coincidence of factors that I could not have foreseen – all compounded by my own inadequacy. Could he have had the slightest inkling that I was unsettled? I left with an irrational sense that my former captain might have been saving me from my own precipitous action, but this was ridiculous. The failure was all mine.

I returned to *Voyager* and reported to the captain within twenty-five minutes of my departure. He made no comment nor did he question me.

Meanwhile, our stay in Hong Kong continued to provide opportunities for Duncan Stevens to endanger his health. The China Fleet Club is a place of relaxation and entertainment for sailors of all visiting ships. The crew invited the captain and officers to join them informally for a few drinks on Wednesday evening, and all of us who were off duty accepted. Before leaving the ship, I suggested that we should not outstay our welcome and that it might be best for us to leave after about forty-five minutes so the men could get on with their drinking without the encumbrance and expense of officers as guests. I thought that everyone agreed. It was a very pleasant occasion with a sincere welcome and generous hosting by the men in a respectful and friendly atmosphere. Very discreetly, I spoke to the senior officers and to the captain when I believed that it was approaching the time when we should decline any more drinks and take our leave. One or two others left with me, and we returned to the ship for dinner, where we were soon joined by most of the officers. But there was no sign of the captain.

On the following morning the petty officer in charge of one of the seaman divisions reported to me that later in the evening the captain had been found lying in the gutter outside the dockyard. He was then carried back aboard by the petty officer, with the assistance of others.

On Saturday morning the ship was moved from its berth, by tugboat and a Chinese dockyard pilot, to the West Arm wharf. We would still be within the dockyard, but outboard of *Vampire* and *Yarra*. During the move *Voyager* collided with a part of the dock wall, causing superficial damage. The mishap was observed by McNicoll and others in *Melbourne*, and caused Stevens untold fury. Although the impact was no greater than that which Tony Synnot had not reported in Adelaide, the fact of being observed resulted in a collision report being demanded by the Flag Officer Commanding the Australian Fleet, Admiral McNicoll. Stevens apparently felt that the incident somehow reflected on him, although it was absolutely beyond his control. As soon as the details had been settled with his secretary and he had finished lunch, the captain went ashore with Money and Blaikie, returning aboard around 6.00 p.m., and then having more drinks with them in his cabin.

I was in the wardroom, which was otherwise empty, when Money and Blaikie entered and told me that I should intervene with the captain to prevent him from attending a party organised for that evening by a group of resident Australians to raise money for a charity. The admiral and all the captains of RAN ships present were attending the party, but I was told that Stevens was too drunk to go, and they expected me to stop him. By then I was in no mood to pick up their broken pieces. 'You got him into this. You get him out of it!' I told them. Money and Blaikie left the wardroom – and left the captain to his fate. They knew that I had no intention of intervening. Both officers were later to deny this conversation.

I hoped fervently that Captain Stevens would go to the party without interference and be seen by the admiral and Captain Peek in the state that had become commonplace. The facts would speak eloquently for themselves, and I would not have to report my own captain. Sure enough, without either of his erstwhile drinking companions having the courage to speak to him, Duncan set off to the gangway, and I joined him to salute as he crossed to *Vampire* and on to *Yarra*. From there the Land Rover driver would take him to the party. With a sad feeling of the inevitability of what was unfolding, I said a small silent prayer for him to get to his destination safely, and returned to the wardroom.

All too soon, I was disillusioned. Stevens was carried back on board by a group of sailors who had found him aboard *Yarra*, locked in the sailors' toilets and calling out, 'You're not going to get me like this!' They had forced the door of the cubicle, released him and then lifted the captain, now quite unable to walk, off his feet to bodily bear him back.

The situation had now become so fraught that it required me to confront Stevens with the impossible position in which his behaviour was placing me as his second in command. When I reported to him the next morning, Stevens was feeling ill, but I tackled him head on, asking, 'Sir, what am I to do with you when you're drunk?'

He replied immediately and without embarrassment, 'Just say "Sir, you're drunk!" And I'll go to bed. But you must call me "Sir!"'

So it was agreed, and never discussed again between us.

Around this time I succumbed to a minor local medical condition and turned in for several hours. The captain was invited for drinks aboard HMS *Mull of Kintyre*, the Royal Navy ship of the senior captain serving in the port of Hong Kong at the time, which was secured alongside. He returned on board at about 8.00 p.m. and came into my cabin to see how I was before himself turning in. His voice was slurred, and he was obviously drunk and confused when he said, 'The funniest thing happened, Number 1! The captain told me that not only he and his officers, but also his entire crew think that *Voyager*'s crew are the hardest working, best-dressed, best-disciplined and happiest sailors they have ever seen! I can't understand it!'

Shaking his head, he departed. Soon afterwards, Susie and David Martin popped in to see how I was, and I repeated what Stevens had just told me. 'The ignorant bastard!' David exploded. 'Doesn't he know that it's in spite of him, and not because of him?'

18
Operation Sea Serpent

The prospect of a collision at sea is the worst recurring nightmare for any officer who carries responsibility for a ship's navigation. From the sheltered harbour of Hong Kong we now returned to Singapore in preparation for South East Asia Treaty Organisation (SEATO) exercises in the South China Sea. *Voyager* would be sailing in close company with ships from other nations in a complex series of exercises. Our capabilities as a modern destroyer in one of the world's leading navies were about to be put to the test on an international stage.

We rendezvoused with the other SEATO ships in late April and began Operation Sea Serpent, a program that involved almost every aspect of naval operations in a convoy situation, including submarine intervention. During a night encounter exercise I was at my action station on the bridge while the captain and the operations team were one level below in the operations room. *Voyager* was part of a formation of ships that were screening a convoy when we detected a submarine. At this point, the Thai Navy frigate *Pinklao* was close by us. As we signalled that we had the contact and were turning to starboard to attack, *Pinklao* turned in the wrong direction, across our path. Without a moment's hesitation, I ordered the engines to 'full speed astern' and the wheel 'hard a' port', then a further correction. *Voyager* passed between *Pinklao* and another ship in the convoy that had also been hazarded. At the same time, I switched on the navigation lights, which were blacked out for the exercises, so that all ships in the vicinity were alerted to our presence.

Over the armament broadcast, accompanying the sudden surge in engine power and the violent motion of the ship under wheel, came the captain's shout, 'Where in the name of Christ do you think you are going?'

I replied, 'I am avoiding a collision!'

To which he replied, 'Carry on!'

It was an extraordinarily near miss, and the effect on *Pinklao* was dramatic. She stopped in the water and did not move during the next several hours, taking no further part in the exercise. There was no comment or discussion by Stevens after the incident, at least with me, and nothing about it was reported to me by other officers. At the time I was annoyed at the effect his unconsidered outburst might have had on the morale of the crew. There was a secondary concern that he should have avoided any actions that could have distracted the officer of the watch while dealing with an obvious emergency. The sound of the captain's voice suddenly bellowing belligerently over the Tannoy is not normally conducive to calm navigation.

On the morning of Saturday, 27 April, *Voyager* anchored with the fleet off the island of Pulau Tioman, and some of the crew took the opportunity offered to go ashore to swim from the beach. The officers agreed to my proposal that we should perhaps establish a precedent for a destroyer and invite the Flag Officer Commanding Australian Fleet to dine with us in the wardroom. I signalled Lieutenant Baird, his flag lieutenant, enquiring whether McNicoll would be amenable to an invitation, and it was accepted. While I walked around the quarterdeck, wearing white mess undress, checking on the ship's appearance and looking out for the admiral's barge, I was surprised by a wolf whistle. Turning to see a smiling group of sailors, I was touched when one of them quietly commented, 'We're very proud of you, Sir.' The dinner was successful and enjoyable, except for Duncan Stevens himself, who sat opposite the admiral and appeared glum and totally devoid of any appreciation of the occasion.

The Sea Serpent exercises continued on the Monday as the mixed fleet sailed towards Manila. Our whole crew seemed to respond well to each challenge presented, taking pride in their performance. This type of intense activity, maintained by day and night, is what navies are trained to undertake – and far more interesting than the smaller operations that formed the bulk of our operational diet in Australian waters. One night we were closed up at action stations, stationed on the starboard wing of a screen of destroyers and frigates protecting the aircraft carriers HMS *Hermes* and *Melbourne*. Ordered to change station to the port wing, we turned to port and increased engine revolutions for the transition while

I calculated the required course and speed and then steadied on them.

Without any form of warning HMS *Caesar*, which was on the port wing, suddenly turned 180 degrees towards us and across our bow at very close distance. Again, I was obliged to order 'full speed astern both engines' and 'hard' wheel in order to avoid a collision. As with the *Pinklao* incident, I turned the navigation lights on to illuminate us. There was never, to my knowledge, any reference made by *Caesar* to this near collision, nor was there any suggestion by Duncan Stevens that it should have been investigated. Had I the gift of seeing into the future, my larger concern would have been that the navigator of *Caesar* then was Lieutenant Harry Cook RAN, who less than a year later would be the navigator of *Voyager* at the time of her collision with Melbourne.

FOCAF, with the other RAN ships, sailed for home waters, leaving us with *Vampire*, after an uneventful visit to Manila. Meanwhile, during these periods each ship was obliged to conduct exercises to prepare the crews for Atomic, Biological and Chemical Warfare and Damage Control (ABCD), reporting their results to the commander in chief. Each successive exercise was graduated so that ability and knowledge were required at a higher level, and the extent of simulated damage and severity of attack was reflected in the typed messages in envelopes, opened by team leaders around the ship, on command. The planning and execution of these drills was quite demanding, and I was mindful of the importance of the crew being trained to the highest level of competence in case of real emergency, so I never took short cuts. The forthcoming test at the admiral's inspection would also incorporate scenarios similar to those I created, and I was confident in the men's ability as they progressed. Duncan read the reports without comment.

19
Hong Kong Farewell

On completion of Sea Serpent we accompanied units of the Far East fleet back to Hong Kong, where we secured to a buoy alongside *Vampire*. Five days of tropical routine afforded the opportunity to do last-minute shopping and take advantage of the splendid recreational pursuits offered by the colony.

The captain was informed of my intention to invite a few officers of our Army liaison group, together with their wives, to a buffet dinner on the Wednesday evening, and invited to join us on the forecastle. Officers were also able to invite private guests, and the two Dutch–Australian families with whom David and I had forged such a close friendship both accepted our invitation to attend. Unfortunately, I was taken ill, possibly with food poisoning, and had spent much of the day resting in my cabin.

When a launch conveyed my friends to the ship, David Martin, Scott Griffith and I welcomed them as they stepped on to the deck. They were the first guests to arrive, and they had just been served with drinks when Captain Stevens appeared on deck. As was standard, our attire for dinner was white mess undress for the officers, and the guests wore evening dress. Suzy's side party girls and our stewards were all smartly attired for service. Captain Stevens arrived in a state of dress that caused instant and total embarrassment to all present. His cummerbund was drooping at the waist, and he was clearly unaware of his appearance. His speech was slurred and, after being introduced to the guests, he put two fingers in his mouth and whistled at a steward for a drink. The captain's unsteadiness on his feet, strange expression, unconstrained actions and dishevelled appearance left no doubt in anyone's mind that he was drunk.

Struggling against the effects of my illness, I remained while the party settled and the Army guests arrived, then excused myself, leaving Martin and Griffith as hosts while I retreated to my cabin for a brief rest. When I rejoined the party after about twenty minutes Stevens was still on deck but was gone within the hour. The impact his inebriated appearance had on all present lasted for years.

The following afternoon I was planning to go swimming at Repulse Bay with Martin after lunch. Stevens had been invited to a captains' lunch aboard HMS *Rothesay*, and I had changed into civilian clothes. As a matter of courtesy, I awaited his return before proceeding ashore. All the captains of naval vessels present were invited to the *Rothesay* lunch. I was surprised when I received a message, written on signal stationary, saying, 'YOUR CAPTAIN HAS PASSED OUT AND WILL BE RETURNED TO YOU WHEN HE RECOVERS.' I showed it to Martin before despatching a reply asking whether I should send a boat, to which the return signal simply said, 'NO.' About an hour later Stevens returned to *Voyager* looking pale but apparently sober. He ignored me as he made his way to his sea cabin. We went ashore and caught a bus for our swim.

Later in the week I saw Commander Peter Irwin, who invited me aboard *Rothesay*, where he was engineer officer. I later gave evidence that he told me that when Duncan had suddenly collapsed the other captains had wanted to send him back to *Voyager* in that state, but Irwin prevailed on his captain to allow him to put Stevens on his bunk to recover, which he did. (Irwin was later to deny all of this in evidence, apparently in conformity with pointed remarks contained in a letter from his former captain when they were both still serving in the Royal Navy. He supplied that letter, which was circulated to all counsel at the royal commission but never incorporated into the exhibits. No reference was made to it in the commissioners' report. Irwin recalled our meeting as being in *Voyager*.)

During the last four days before the fleet's departure, David Martin and I visited our friends ashore. The appearance and conduct of Duncan Stevens, and the shame we felt at his behaviour, was a major topic of conversation. Commiserations for my position were expressed all round. We made our farewells and subsequently communicated by air mail letters.

The ship was prepared for sea, and *Voyager* began the passage to Japan late on Tuesday, 20 May, in company with *Vampire*, *Rothesay*, *Caesar* and *Hermes*. As we were about to slip, I broadcast to the crew, 'We are leaving

Hong Kong for good, and even though the Mad Chemist says we will be back, the first lieutenant says we won't!' That had the desired effect of bolstering morale, and several sailors made appreciative comments as I proceeded through the ship.

'The Mad Chemist of Wanchai' was a mythical figure in Australian naval lore. Whenever ships approached the Far East rumours attributed to him would sweep the mess decks. 'The Mad Chemist says there will be a tiger hunt, and they're looking for volunteer beaters!' was a successful leg–pull in *Melbourne*, resulting in scores of names filling lists on a notice-board. Extra leave, cancellations of destinations and much more were claimed to be the pronouncements of this oracle-like figment.

As we passed from the harbour into the South China Sea, the medical officer reported to the captain that a seaman was suffering acute appendicitis, and the ship would need to return to harbour and disembark him for surgery. The entire crew was jubilant, and I was told by triumphant sailors, 'The Mad Chemist was right again!' Our delay was brief, and we caught up with the other ships the following day. Although we had planned on Nagoya being our destination, we were detached by the commander in chief to work with *Hermes* as plane guard destroyer. In hindsight there was a hint of doom about that change of orders. 'Plane guard' was precisely the same role *Voyager* would fill so fatefully for *Melbourne* just nine months later.

20
Karatsu

'**W**e're stupid, Sir, aren't we?' he asked. The slightly built, sandy-haired sailor looked up at me from his squatting position on the deck, which he was happily preparing for painting.

'Why's that?' I responded.

'We're working an hour a day more than the rest of the fleet.'

He was right, and I knew it. Our seamen were starting work as soon as they had finished their meals in the morning and at lunchtime, as they were not required to wait for the traditional parades to be told what to do. 'Yes, but do you want *Voyager* to look like the rest of the fleet?' I challenged him.

'No, Sir! That was a stupid question, wasn't it?'

I assured him that, on the contrary, it was a very fair and informed question. But I also recognised that he was speaking for the whole crew, presumably expecting me to acknowledge their efforts in a practical manner. He confirmed my insight with an expectant grin. 'But please tell the crew that I appreciate what they are doing and I shall make it up to them as early as I can,' I said, 'and explain to them that it's a court-martial offence for me to give them additional leave when the remainder of the fleet is working. That sort of action sows the seeds of mutiny, because you would know what it's for, but the others wouldn't! One day soon, we'll be detached and I'll show my gratitude.' Although this had been a good opportunity for an informal exchange between the upper and lower decks, I was taking a risk by acting on an instinctive belief that I could fulfil my undertaking. There were no scheduled unaccompanied visits to ports in our program, so 'detached' was a promise made in hope.

My gamble soon became reality. While the plan was for *Voyager* to accompany *Vampire* on a goodwill visit to Nagoya, sister city to Sydney, we were notified almost at the last minute to proceed alone to Karatsu, a city of about 150,000 inhabitants situated on the northwest corner of Kyushu. Karatsu was the first Japanese port to experience trade with China and is the birthplace of Japanese emperors. But the privilege of visiting as a single naval ship also carried with it additional responsibilities. The Far East General Orders, the regulations that governed the standards of conduct in foreign ports, were specific in directing that a shore patrol consisting of an officer and thirty men must be landed when leave was granted. The cox'n duly published the names for our five-day visit.

Arriving in steady rain, we moored alongside a wharf that was composed of packed coal (a unique experience for me), to be greeted by a school band playing the US Marines' Hymn, a musical selection that must have seemed appropriate to the citizens! The reception committee consisted of the mayor, councillors and the chief of police, with Captain A. N. Dollard DSC RAN, naval attaché, Tokyo, and Squadron Leader Maurice Farrelly RAAF, Japanese interpreter to the embassy. As soon as the gangway was secured, the captain welcomed the VIPs and led them to his day cabin where they exchanged greetings, had refreshments and discussed the arrangements for the visit.

The police chief waited until the others had gone before approaching me, bowing and asking could we speak. Taking him to my cabin, I invited him to be seated and asked how I could help him. He said, in perfect English, 'Sir, what size patrol do you intend to land, and how many extra police should I bring in from the provinces to control your crew?'

Without a moment's hesitation, I replied, 'I'm not landing a patrol, and you will need no police. I have the best-behaved crew in the Far East, and there will be no trouble.'

He rose, bowed politely and said, 'Thank you, Sir.'

We shook hands as he left my cabin, and I escorted him to the gangway. Walking to the nearest armament broadcast position, I drew the attention of the crew to my voice, saying, 'This is the first lieutenant. I have just had a meeting with the chief of Karatsu Police,' and continued by repeating, verbatim, what had transpired between us. Then I said, 'I am walking around the ship in one hour and if the ship is clean, I shall grant leave to the entire crew, except for the patrol who will remain on board as a fire-fighting patrol, until 0700 tomorrow. Tomorrow, and each day we are here, I shall walk around the ship at 0900 and if the ship is clean, I shall grant leave until 0700 on the following day. That is all!'

No sooner had I returned to my cabin than Captain Stevens appeared in his doorway, face scarlet and hissing in an angry but measured tone, 'I hope you know what you're doing, Number 1, because if this goes wrong, you're finished!'

'I know exactly what I am doing, Sir!' I replied, and he returned to his cabin without another word or acknowledgement. I thought, 'Jesus! What am I doing?'

With some trepidation I waited for the cox'n and quartermaster to call at my cabin to report the ship 'ready for inspection', as they did each evening before I accompanied them on mess deck rounds. It was an act of faith on my part, and the time for me to indulge in any introspection was now long gone. I chuckled to myself at the thought that I probably had the heaviest punishment return in the Far East yet still believed I had the best crew. So much had happened to us together. At least they knew what I thought of them. Now, what did they think of me?

You could have heard a pin drop as we made our way from one mess to the next, the leading hand or the president of each mess saluting and reporting his mess ready for inspection. I felt every eye on me as more than a hundred expressionless faces scrutinised me. The ship was spotless, and as I completed the inspection of the last passageway on the route, the responsible sweeper said, 'We are very proud of what you said about us, Sir, and we won't let you down!' And they did not. I was not really surprised by their exemplary behaviour (otherwise why would I have extended them my trust?), but they made me even more proud of them. It is still difficult to express the emotions evoked.

Within forty-eight hours every major TV network had crews in Karatsu, and on prime time television they showed the sailors participating in 'the most successful visit ever made to Japan by a foreign warship'. The citizens of Karatsu were inviting strange Australian sailors into their homes and showering them with hospitality and goodwill. I deputised for the captain (who was disabled by the effects of his indulgence) at a tea drinking ceremony at the town hall, and was described on television as 'the vice captain'.

On the evening of the second day I visited Maurice Farrelly at his local hotel, having followed his clear instructions and said, 'Mush mush,

Farrelly San deska', to the lady who answered the telephone. He offered me a drink, and I noticed that he had a bottle of Hardy's Black Bottle brandy. He said that Bill Money had given it to him when he called the previous evening, smuggled from the ship. (Money later claimed he had no recollection of this.) This made me extremely angry, as he had violated the trust of the local customs officials, putting the entire visit in jeopardy. Although still being careful not to be too specific, I found it a relief to unwind a little with Farrelly about my concerns with Money, Blaikie and the captain. Farrelly was of an equivalent rank and I assessed him as being discreet and trustworthy.

The only memorable incidents other than the captain's drinking to occur at Karatsu were happy ones. Ceremonial was intermingled with informality as official and private arrangements were made. Everything seemed to pass in a perfection of communication and fellow feeling between two diverse groups of people. I took the captain on a drive in the ship's Land Rover, hoping he might retain something of the almost mystical atmosphere that seemed to prevail during our visit. Several photographs were taken in which the captain appears happy and even ebullient in the company of the mayor and others, including Captain Dollard. But he was hardly ever truly clear of the influence of liquor during the entire visit, and certainly seemed to remain unaffected by the general aura of goodwill.

The wardroom mess invited the mayor and local councillors to cock-tails, and we wondered how they might react to our Western forms of entertainment. There was no need to be concerned as they came with wives, daughters and friends, the ladies dressed beautifully in kimonos, and mixed with dignity and grace. At the conclusion of the party the senior dignitaries invited me, together with a small group of officers, to share a meal with their daughters. They led us with great assurance to a local restaurant. We were seated upstairs with the young ladies, while their fathers ate at a discreet distance downstairs but sent up copious quantities of beer and food for us. This was a delightful experience, designed in part to help the sixteen- or seventeen-year-old schoolgirls to improve their already excellent English. With their fathers' permission, they invited us to remain and dance to pop music after dinner, until the city curfew bell rang at 9.00 p.m.

Later, on the evening before we left Karatsu, the boatswain's mate, who stands sentry with the quartermaster on the gangway, appeared at the wardroom door to inform me that two Japanese schoolgirls were at the bow, asking to see 'Rickie and Peter'. Richard Carpendale and I went to the gangway, and standing happily in the pouring rain were two bright-eyed high school girls in uniform. June and Hiroko, who had sat by us at dinner on the previous night, presented us with little gifts for our families. There was a tiny porcelain vase for my wife and an umbrella for me. We were humbly grateful and, after giving them a soft drink in the wardroom, we took them home in the Land Rover. These were typical, enchanting moments from a visit that we knew would never be repeated.

We had arrived to a wharf almost devoid of citizens, yet there was a packed throng to farewell the ship. A continuous stream of people came aboard quietly and left gifts on the deck, bowed and left. Men wept openly as emotion ran higher than I ever experienced with a ship's crew. A dream was ending, and it was blessed by nature as the rain stopped and the sun finally shone through. We all felt that we had shared something special. Typically, as the ship slipped from the wharf, a seaman asked me, boldly, 'Are you going to do the same in Tokyo, Sir?'

'Do you think I'm that stupid? You can behave normally now,' I said.

And he laughed in agreement.

21
Ship Handling

We were kept on our toes as we rejoined units of the scattered fleet after leaving Karatsu. Engaged in evolutions and station-keeping exercises at high speeds, *Voyager* was detached to serve as plane guard to HMS *Hermes*, a Royal Navy aircraft carrier of 28,000 tons and a maximum speed of 28 knots. She was big and fast, and wore the flag of Rear Admiral Jack Scatchard CB DSC, Second in Command Far East Fleet. Scatchard was well known for his explosive temper.

During a break from flying operations, the admiral on the carrier ordered *Voyager* to take *Hermes* in tow, a legitimate evolution but always daunting task for a destroyer to accept in open water. While the captain and navigator manoeuvred the ship into position, the chief boatswain's mate and his men assembled the required shackles and stoppers, together with hammer and pins. At the same time, Lieutenant Carpendale, the torpedo and anti-submarine officer, supervised his quarterdeck division, who were laying out the flexible steel wire rope, tying each flake (or loop) of rope to the next for control when it was veered (eased out) for towing. Chain stoppers were secured to the wire so that it could be held and let go safely. This is a complex and potentially dangerous operation. Everyone hastened, but with disciplined efficiency, as our ship closed on the carrier.

It is essential to this whole process that the gap between the two ships is minimal, short of hazarding either vessel. The towering bow overhang of a carrier is an obvious danger to the superstructure of the towing ship. This makes keeping a slow, steady speed critical, with just enough power to maintain steerage – but not enough to cause problems. Wind and sea affect each ship according to its hull shape, displacement and the area presented to the wind. With their huge topsides, carriers find windage critical. Destroyers are long and narrow and therefore more subject to rolling, especially while under the flight deck. On approach we narrowly avoided dismasting our own ship and were required to repeat the manoeuvre in order to avoid worsening the position. Things were getting tense. Looking up, I could see the gunnery officer's demeanour. It convinced me that the bridge, where he was standing as officer of the watch, was a very good place to avoid.

As the officer responsible for the seamanship of the evolution, I stood at the side of the quarterdeck with a microphone hailer to communicate both with the carrier's forecastle and our bridge. I had briefed the quarterdeck towing party, with the bosun, and we had already received the light cord heaving line thrown from the carrier across our quarter. This, in turn, was secured to the steel towing wire and hauled aboard *Hermes*. For their part, they were smart in shackling the anchor cable to the towrope and slowly veering a half shackle of cable over the bow to provide a dampener for towing. So far so good.

With such a large ship as a 28,000-ton aircraft carrier, the ability of the towing vessel to take up the strain of the tow safely is governed by the ship-handling skill and patience of the officer controlling the engine revolutions from the bridge. It requires a sensitivity bordering on stealth. We were going well, and the captain was managing to contain his seething anger at the humiliation of a near miss in our early manoeuvring. The tow began rising from the water as the ships separated. I placed a foot on the wire between the stern and the stopper to gauge the tension and monitor the potential for parting the tow. This is always a critical moment. Should the wire break under the strain, its weight does not cause it to drop straight into the water. The huge amounts of strain energy released make it recoil like a snapped elastic band, springing back and cutting to ribbons anything in its path. I had seen this happen as a midshipman in *King George V* when the forecastle officer came close to decapitation from a wire that whizzed over his head as he lay on the deck.

While the wire was taking the strain under revolutions for two knots on *Voyager*, the carrier began to show slight movement to follow in our wake. I felt relief because the job was basically done, and wondered for how much longer we would be required to continue the evolution. Then, without warning, there was a marked increase in revolutions and a surge of power through the ship. Martin told me later the order was for ten knots. Without hesitation I called, 'Clear the quarterdeck!' in the same instant as both Carpendale and the chief bosun's mate yelled an identical order. In my position, furthest aft, with my foot on the wire, I could see that everyone else was clear. But by then there was no time to run away so I dived flat on the deck. The parted wire flew over my inert body like a whip as it scythed across an otherwise deserted quarterdeck.

Duncan Stevens did not offer any explanation for his conduct (or express any regrets for the consequences), although it must have preyed on his mind. I gathered from Griffith and Martin that he had decided the process was 'taking too bloody long'. There was no order from the admiral to repeat the manoeuvre, although the evolution had not been completed. Admiral Scatchard's lack of respect for my captain at that moment most probably matched mine – and all of *Voyager*'s and *Hermes*' crews. No doubt the rest of the Far East fleet would soon get to hear about the debacle. My diminishing regard for Stevens and his inability to handle alcohol was now mingled with a growing concern for his capacity to behave rationally when sober. It seemed that a confrontation between us was inevitable.

The next day everything appeared to be proceeding normally as I was standing on the quarterdeck during a change of station in which *Voyager* was obliged to pass astern of *Rothesay*. Suddenly, a collision appeared to be almost inevitable as the distance between the two ships closed to mere yards. We discovered later that critical valves in the engine room had jammed open, preventing the execution of a change of speed and engine direction ordered from the bridge. Mechanical failure is a valid excuse for such a close call, but I was convinced the captain's reaction had been far too slow and that it was a reflection of his general inability to perform his duties properly following five days of alcoholic haze ashore.

That night I sat in my cabin and quietly tried to analyse the situation. A series of incidents had now occurred that were becoming more dangerous by the day. In my opinion, the captain should have formed an earlier appreciation of our situations, reacted promptly or taken swift evasive action. The towing incident, in particular, was a clear display of temperament. The captain was losing his grip, with almost criminal disregard for the consequences. I formed the conviction that if Duncan Stevens ever had a drink at sea he would lose the ship. At that moment

I believed, absolutely, that *Voyager* would be lost in collision if Stevens remained in command. It was not 'I think' but rather 'I know'. Could I prevent it? Only by having the matter out directly with the captain, a path that seemed impossible. If a collision were inevitable, could I minimise the consequences?

Perhaps it is a reflection of my personality (and twenty years of naval training) that my mind took me towards a purely practical response. I would reconstitute the damage control teams, each of which had been drilled to operate only in fixed areas of the ship. I would retrain them so that they would now be competent no matter where they were at the time of any impact. That seemed the most pragmatic approach to what now loomed as an inevitable crisis. For myself, if there were to be a collision, I would most probably die in it. I resolved to prepare myself so that I would be calm and self-possessed, not likely to be distracted from my duty.

The mind and heart interact in curious ways under intense pressures of this kind. I opened my safe and removed a jewelled bracelet that I had bought for Sue in Hong Kong, placing it on my bunk. I used it as a focus for clearing my mind while I made peace with myself, sitting quietly for some minutes until I was certain that I had total understanding of what I must do. I resolved to confront Captain Stevens when the first opportunity presented itself, without fear or concern for the consequences, as it was already certain that my naval career was virtually over. With complete peace of mind, I then lay on my bunk and immediately went to sleep.

22
Crisis in Tokyo

All fleet units visiting Tokyo and Yokohama assembled the next day, Wednesday, in high wind conditions caused by the fringe of Typhoon Polly. We were pleased to gain the safety of Tokyo Bay and hurried to secure our berth astern of *Vampire*. The officers were conscious of running late for an official function being hosted by the Commander in Chief Far East Fleet aboard the frigate HMS *Alert*, which was wearing his flag. *Alert* was alongside further ahead of us, decked with lights and bunting for a cocktail party, and guests were already arriving. Officers of both RAN ships were obliged to join the admiral and his staff as hosts, and we changed rapidly to white mess undress. Then we literally ran to *Alert* and joined the gathering on the quarterdeck under an awning.

Stewards served wine, spirits and cocktails to guests who were dressed in evening gowns and dinner suits, congregating in small groups around the deck. Noticing a very pregnant lady standing alone near the guardrail close to the stern, gazing at the night lights of the city, I approached her and asked, 'What sort of man would leave such a beautiful woman alone on a night like this?' She turned to look at me and replied, 'That sort of man!' pointing at a tall striking figure who was speaking to a group close by. We strolled up and joined them. Keith and Jenny Gale lived with their young children in Tokyo, where Keith was manager of the Japanese operations of an Australian company. Keith invited me to join him and a guest from New Zealand for dinner on the Saturday evening at the Mikado, a famous theatre restaurant. I accepted gratefully, while inviting them to lunch on board *Voyager* on the Sunday.

A reception was held at the Australian Embassy for crews of *Vampire* and *Voyager* on Thursday afternoon, followed by a Beer Party for the sailors in the Embassy grounds. The officers were then invited to a cocktail party at the Naval Attaché's residence, hosted by Captain and Mrs Dollard. I changed from uniform to dinner suit at Dollard's, by previous arrangement, and joined a Japanese business acquaintance of my father-in-law for a memorable dinner.

When back aboard in the wardroom I was chatting with Richard Carpendale (who was officer of the day) when Scott Griffith entered and informed me that the captain had returned and was unable to walk to his sea cabin, where he slept. Griffith and I carried Stevens to his bunk and put him to bed without him wakening. Things were obviously not improving. I was unaware that after the cocktail party, Stevens, Willis and the Dollards had been taken to the Gaslight Restaurant by an embassy counsellor and his wife. Their host, A. B. (Jim) Jamieson later gave compelling evidence of the occasion, describing Duncan as affected by alcohol, not eating his dinner and nodding off at the table. The captain had said, 'You'll look after me, won't you Jim?' addressing Willis. But Jamieson was confused for a moment, thinking that he was being addressed by his familiar nickname. By consensus among the party, Stevens was then placed in a car and returned to his ship.

The following morning, knowing that he was scheduled to lunch aboard *Alert* with Vice Admiral Dreyer, Commander in Chief Far East Fleet later that day, I suggested to Duncan that he and I visit a public steam bath. 'Good thinking, Number 1! You're a bloody genius!' he exclaimed, then ordered Leading Steward Freeman to 'Get the first lieutenant a coffee like mine!' I was brought a cup laced with a strong measure of brandy, and knew that Duncan was well on the way to getting himself drunk yet again. It was imperative that we embark on our therapeutic visit as soon as possible. We were at Tokyo Onzen by about 10.00 a.m. and, following steam baths and rinses, were allocated adjoining massage cubicles. I could hear his interchanges with the masseuse. The entire process was refreshing, invigorating and – provided you kept your mind free of sensuous thoughts – not embarrassing.

Stevens left the bath area a few minutes before me, and I was immediately anxious that he might be at the lounge bar before I could join him. My misgivings were well founded. He already had a brandy and ginger ale in his hand when I arrived. I accepted a similar drink as he admonished me, 'Drink up, I'm already one ahead of you.' The drinks, as with the earlier coffee, were doubles. I tactfully bought us another each and prevailed on my captain to return to the ship. He wouldn't leave until we'd downed another round.

In the late afternoon the captain attended a Queen's Birthday Garden Party at the British Embassy. Immediately after this function he joined a buffet dinner at the Dollards' home, in company with a large group of prominent expatriate Australians and Japanese guests. Keith Gale later described for me the salient features of Stevens' lapse during this function, as corroborated by both Farrelly and Dollard. Duncan had kept nodding off over his plate and was taken by car back to *Voyager*, accompanied by another officer, most probably Bill Money.

A restorative trip to the steam baths was on the agenda again for Saturday morning, but this time Stevens invited Money to join us. Essentially the same routine followed, but with three of us now buying rounds of drinks. A merchant navy officer was also at the bar as Duncan began slurring his words, and the conversation within our trio became increasingly bizarre. I turned to this stranger and said, 'Please listen carefully to what's being said! You may be a witness one day.' (Many years after the second royal commission I received a letter in which that officer identified himself and reminded me of the words spoken between us.)

A picnic in the countryside with Captain Willis and the Dollards was arranged for that day, but during the drive Captain Stevens felt ill and declined to eat when they arrived at the picnic area. He was due to attend an official reception with Admiral Nakayama and other Japanese naval officers in the evening, but instead was dropped off at the Dollard residence to sleep off his discomfort. When he awoke, he ordered the maid to give him a brandy, which he consumed. He then vomited and asked the Japanese servant to call a taxi, which returned him to the ship.

But I had a far more enjoyable night ahead of me. Keith Gale joined me in the wardroom for a drink before we were driven to the Mikado, then the finest theatre restaurant in the world. It was a truly magnificent establishment where even the reception area had solid transparent cast glass lounge chairs, each costing $10,000. We were seated immediately in front of the stage at a 'very special table', affording a privileged view of the whole performance. A diva sang an aria from *Madame Butterfly* while transported in an elevated gondola at least a hundred feet above and across the huge hall. She was utterly captivating. A chorus line of a hundred beautiful nude girls, dressed only in lavish headdresses and matching high-heeled shoes, performed on the stage. A water ballet was presented in a pool backed by a mirror fifty feet high, followed by a demonstration of Olympic-standard diving.

Any attempt at topping this extravaganza would seem to be a mistake, but Keith took us to a nightclub where we had coffee while witnessing a Tahitian troupe of totally nude men and women performing native dances. They were as spectacular as they were erotic – a fitting end to a night that I shall never forget.

Returning to the ship, I did not want the aura that seemed to cling to me to leave, so I showered, changed into uniform shirt and shorts and lay on my bunk to relive the events of the night while waiting for daybreak. My reverie was rudely broken when the leading steward knocked on my door at 6.30 a.m. and informed me that the captain wanted to see me. Going straight to his sea cabin, I found Stevens in his bunk, ashen faced, lying on a vomit-soaked pillow. 'You're sick, Sir, I'll get the doctor!' I said.

He raised his voice and barked, 'I don't want the doctor near me!' Then he ordered me to call on Captain Willis in *Vampire* at 8.00 a.m. and to apologise for him, saying that he was ill and to ask Willis to take the Sunday prayer service for both crews. When I returned to my cabin it did not take long for me to decide to share my situation with the doctor. I woke him to relay the captain's remarks and give him a description of Duncan's condition. Without preamble, I said, 'The captain's sick and he refuses to see you!'

Dr Tiller replied, 'I won't see him!'

His surprisingly negative response demanded that I ask what had led to this situation. Mick informed me that he had warned the captain that if he continued to ignore his advice to cease his drinking, he could no longer be responsible for his health and would not treat him. When I asked how serious the situation was, Tiller left me in no doubt. 'If he goes on like this he'll rupture his ulcer,' he declared, 'and if that happens at sea in the weather we're going into, there's no way I could operate on him, so he'd die.'

It was known that we were going out into a typhoon the next day. Even in calm weather the prospect of performing a major surgical procedure in the absence of a second medical officer, who could anaesthetise the patient and assist the surgeon, would create a dilemma. In the turmoil of a storm at sea, it would be disastrous. Common sense screamed that we should land the captain to a military hospital until the threat to his health had passed. But I knew Stevens would never countenance that, and Tiller agreed. Such an admission of illness would finish Duncan's prospects for any further sea appointments and promotion.

Stymied, I returned to my cabin, sat at my desk and tried to absorb the multiple ramifications of this crisis. As his senior executive officer, I must place the health and possibly life of Duncan Stevens before any selfish consideration. Do I follow his orders (which plainly involved a serious and continuing deception of the Navy), or do I follow my conscience and inform his superiors of his apparent unfitness to command? As I contemplated all this, I was also aware that should the captain die, I must accept the consequences of ignoring medical opinion. Whichever course I took, it seemed that any career prospects of my own that might have existed at this stage had evaporated. What to do? It needed no imagination to predict the reaction I would have from Stevens were I to confront him with the doctor's opinion and my private thoughts about landing him to hospital. I discarded that as an option. Duncan had ordered me to call on Captain Willis at 8.00 a.m. The only responsible action open to me was to use that opportunity and share all the information I had, giving Willis my assessment of the situation and alternatives. Alcohol itself need not be the issue. Willis was as aware as I was that Stevens had a history of ulcer problems on his medical record. To acknowledge now, officially, that Duncan was again suffering from a volatile duodenal condition would end his sea career.

At 8.05 a.m. I walked the few yards to *Vampire*. Jim Willis sat alone in his day cabin. He was a very big man, with a strong bovine face and serious demeanour, although he could certainly exhibit a sense of humour when amused. Although never slow in his movements, there was a sense of lumbering about everything he did. I conveyed my captain's message and received Willis's agreement to take the parade. On the point of leaving, I turned again and addressed him. 'Sir, may I speak to you in confidence about Captain Stevens' condition?'

'Yes, go ahead,' he told me, with evident concern.

As I embarked on a condensed account of events leading up to my interview with Mick Tiller, I was left in no doubt as to the gravity and impact on him of what Willis was hearing.

When I had finished, without interruption, he ordered, 'Send your doctor over to see me!'

'May I come with him, please?' I asked.

'No!' was the simple reply.

Surgeon Lieutenant Tiller was ordered to report to Willis as soon as I returned aboard. No more than fifteen minutes later the doctor was back aboard *Voyager*, with Willis. Willis instructed me to remain in my cabin while he and Tiller visited Stevens. The next forty minutes or so were like an eternity as I waited for the doctor to examine Stevens in Willis's presence, and then presumably for Willis to speak to Duncan alone. Willis came into my cabin and briefed me on the situation. 'When we go to sea tomorrow, as soon as *Voyager* clears Tokyo Harbour, Captain Stevens will hand command over to you. You will have command for five days. Tiller has said that your captain needs five days of absolute bed rest to make a complete recovery, and he is not to leave his cabin except for ablutions in that time. Do you understand?' I acknowledged, and he continued, 'I have told Captain Stevens that if he has another drink in the next three months he will be court-martialled.'

I asked what I should tell the other officers and was told, emphatically, that I should tell them that the captain was ill and that I would have command for the next five days. When I asked for permission to inform the commander in chief of my temporary command, he said, 'If you attempt to communicate the situation with anyone outside your ship, you will be arrested immediately and charged with mutiny. I have given Captain Stevens my absolute assurance on that!' With those words of decidedly cold comfort he left me, and we never discussed the situation again. I climbed the ladder to the captain's sea cabin with a terrible mixture of resolve and dread, both emotions that soon turned out to be appropriate.

'Livid' is a grossly inadequate word to describe the nearly insane man who confronted me. Stevens was consumed by rage and threatened me should I attempt to communicate the true position beyond the four who were now fully aware of it. With flecks of vomit around his mouth, he looked demented.

Inflamed by his language and unbridled hatred, I told him, 'If you ever have a drink at sea you will lose this ship! I am not going to allow you to kill this crew, and if I ever find you taking a drink at sea I shall draw a pistol from the armoury and shoot you!'

In response he threw a heavy glass ashtray, which I avoided narrowly, at my head. I left the cabin feeling that things could not get much worse.

Meanwhile, the expected social formalities of a naval visit to a foreign port had to be maintained. Lunchtime saw the influx of guests to the captain's cabin, including the Australian ambassador to Japan, Sir Laurence McIntyre, with his wife and other official guests. Somehow, Stevens was on hand to greet them as they came aboard. I entertained Jenny and Keith Gale to lunch in the wardroom, and listened attentively while Keith described the captain's projectile vomiting at an official function ashore in a room full of dignitaries, including senior Japanese naval officers and Captain Dollard. There was nothing for me to say, except that I was not surprised.

Both Captain Willis and Stevens dined at the Mikado that night. Amid this incredible theatre performance, Duncan Stevens fell asleep at the table and had to be revived to return to the ship. No normal man in reasonable command of his mind and body could possibly have dozed through such entertainment.

23
Five Days in Command

As we slipped our lines and proceeded towards Tokyo Bay, I remained on the port side of *Voyager's* bridge, seemingly ignored by the captain as he gave orders for the ship to follow *Vampire* away from harbour. The moment we entered the bay itself he turned to me, looked at his wristwatch and said, 'You have command until I relieve you at 1007 on Saturday!'

'Aye aye, Sir,' I responded, and with that, he left the bridge and went to his sea cabin. I was not to lay eyes on Duncan Stevens for the next five days – exactly to the minute. There had been so much malevolence in his eyes that I derived no pleasure from the situation, nor did I have the luxury of time to allow any emotions to come into play. The ship was mine, but the real test would be whether I could now employ my temporary command as the means of eventually bringing the crisis to a satisfactory conclusion.

Ensuring that we remained in station on *Vampire*, I stayed on the bridge and sent for my steward, asking him to procure a camp stretcher and stow it in the Asdic room at the back of the bridge. I would need to sleep there in order to be immediately available at night. My own cabin was too far away for the swift reaction times necessary in an emergency, and it was not equipped for adequate communication with the bridge. That accomplished, and when everything was sufficiently routine for me to leave, I summoned all officers who were not on watch to the wardroom. When they had assembled I addressed the officers exactly as Jim Willis had instructed, saying that the captain was ill and would be confined to his cabin for five days, during which time I had command. The captain was not to be disturbed for any matter, and all reports that would normally be made to him were now to be made to me. Dr Tiller was present, and I believe his presence was the reason not a single question was raised when I asked if there were any. I left the officers and returned to the bridge as the first effects of Typhoon Rose were being experienced in the open sea.

Any competent executive officer should be accustomed to spending brief periods in command. Having accepted my role, I was soon as comfortable with my surroundings as I had been on previous, albeit less dramatic, occasions. I enjoyed the unique feeling of being in control of a modern fighting ship and tried hard not to dwell on the latent situation that I knew still festered below me. The officers seemed to accept the status quo, and I received all of the usual reports that are part of the captain's domain.

A transfer from a Royal Navy destroyer was ordered, and as we moved into station on her port beam, her captain came to the wing of his bridge and, with a huge smile, called to me on his microphone hailer, 'Come a little closer and we'll pass it by hand!' We were markedly closer than Duncan Stevens had ever placed *Voyager* in transfers, for I was silently critical of this aspect of his ship handling. Although it is vital to be wary of the venturi effect when operating at speed close to other ships (a force created between the two hulls that can suck them together), it is equally important to be as close as safety permits in order to limit the strain on the men who were handling the ropes that carry the articles between ships. Too often, I had stood at the transfer site in *Voyager* and seen men in danger of being pulled overboard by the sudden movement of either ship, and seen the anxiety in their faces as they fought to retain their footing and grip.

During the following four days we were obliged to refuel twice, once from a Royal Fleet Auxiliary tanker and once from HMS *Lion*, in which the commander in chief was wearing his flag, having transferred from *Alert* after leaving Tokyo. Here was a precious opportunity to tacitly circumvent the order from Willis that his removal of Stevens from command of *Voyager* for five days remain secret! When we approached *Lion*, I was acutely conscious that both her captain and the admiral would be watching every ship that came close. In our case that meant they would be aware that Duncan Stevens was not on the bridge. We had an absolute obligation to be flying the flag hoist, which indicates that an officer other than the commanding officer is in command, but Willis's order had forbidden that action. I was craving some signal from the commander in chief querying our position on this, but for some reason it never came. Binoculars pressed to my eyes, I scanned the bridge of *Lion* while silently praying for some sign of recognition from either senior officer. Nothing. This chance to apprise them of the real situation passed.

But there was another way the damning fact of Stevens' unfitness could become known without my having to break the Willis secrecy order. All RAN ships are obliged to hold a weekly parade of captain's requestmen and defaulters. For *Voyager* this was scheduled for Tuesday, our second day out of Tokyo, and a significant number of each were due for appearance before the captain. The cox'n briefed me, and, with Lieutenant Martin acting in my usual place as prosecuting officer, I took the captain's role. There were men due for increase in their rating, to whom I granted their promotion. Some had misbehaved by overstaying their shore leave, and others had committed civil offences that merited punishment. This business was all transacted in the usual manner by Martin and me. When, on Wednesday, the paperwork was completed and brought to me for signature, I signed all documents as 'Lieutenant Commander for Captain (Sick)'. These few innocent-looking words represented the potential instruments of Duncan Stevens' exposure, and I knew it.

Two months earlier the captain had received an instruction that the Naval Board was to be informed immediately if he were too ill to command the ship. Stevens had then been explicit to me and his other senior officers that the notation 'For Captain (Sick)' must never be used again. But there was no way I was going to disobey the Board and be an accomplice to his and Willis's illegal cover-up. But it was now imperative that this documentation should leave the ship as soon as possible. Employing my usual authority as commander, I requested a helicopter be sent to us for mail collection. It duly arrived and lowered its hook for retrieval, but Typhoon Rose was at its worst. The violent pitching of the deck, combined with the extreme turbulence that was already making flying hazardous, prevented the transfer. Never did the weather gods play more fatefully with my personal fortunes. As the chopper flew back to *Hermes*, I saw any last hope of relief from my nightmare flying with it. With a heavy heart I resigned myself to whatever consequences would follow.

Meanwhile, Typhoon Rose continued to rage. Damage was sustained by one of the ship's sea boats, which could not be repaired until the weather improved. For three days the sea conditions were too hazardous for general movement on the upper deck, so it was restricted to emergency or essential traffic, such as going on watch or to the galley for the collection of food. These restrictions meant that most of the crew were confined in close quarters below decks. By contrast, I was able to experience the unique private thrill that comes from being on the open bridge of a small ship at sea in a storm. It was a feeling I had always savoured: the spectacle of nature in its unbridled, awesome, sometimes frightening fury. I found it to be one of the most mind-focusing aspects of life in the Navy, and perhaps the one I miss most, even today.

Every night, before turning in, the captain writes his night orders in the designated book, and each officer who takes over a watch must sign as having read and understood those orders. When I wrote the orders for my five nights as acting captain I carefully signed them 'Lieutenant Commander for Captain (Sick)' as I did the punishment returns and the personal papers of the requestmen.

During our final replenishment, when *Vampire* was in close company, I was conscious of Captain Willis scanning our bridge with his binoculars, as well as noting that several of his officers seemed clearly conscious of the unusual composition of our bridge team. I speculated to myself as to what response Willis might give to any questions that were asked.

As I stood on the bridge on the Saturday forenoon, with the weather moderating slightly against a clearing sky, I was conscious of every heavy minute that passed. Precisely at 10.07 a.m., Captain Stevens appeared alongside me, obviously having been waiting out of my sight for this exact moment to arrive. He just said, 'Get out of my sight!' and, without hesitation, I saluted and left. My five days in command were over; my nightmare was about to begin.

24
Subic Bay

Shortly after Stevens resumed command of *Voyager* we experienced engine room problems and were obliged to divert to nearby Subic Bay for shelter and to undertake repairs. Having been ordered from the bridge by the captain in such an ugly fashion I found it prudent to pursue duties that avoided his company. I had been checking the mess decks, and the upper deck as far as was safe in the still-stormy conditions, but returned to the bridge for the anchoring. We found a protected position in the lee of the land, near dense jungle. Our complete lack of electrical power resulting from the breakdown of the turbogenerator plunged the ship into total darkness and total silence. These eerie and unnatural conditions set the scene for the most traumatic single period I was to endure during the entire Far East cruise, and which was to change my entire life thereafter.

As soon as we were secure I went to my cabin, which was in complete darkness. On the previous night the fleet had been engaged in exercises which demanded that all ships were blacked out, so the dead light that covered my scuttle (port hole) was still in place. I sat in the silent darkness contemplating my situation. Without warning, the door was flung open and Captain Stevens exploded into my cabin like a Jack-in-the-box. With the punishment returns clutched in his hands he shouted at me, 'You're not going to get me like this!' He then ordered me to accompany him to his cabin. There he told me that he would have the genuine returns replaced by others, which would bear his signature as the officer awarding the punishment. He told me that I must sign as prosecuting officer, in lieu of Lieutenant Martin. Then he claimed that he had already spoken to every officer about the matter and that they all, except for Martin, would support his proposed action against me should I refuse to sign.

The retaliatory action he threatened was horrific. After being arrested and charged with mutiny, I was to be certified insane by two doctors (presumably those of *Vampire* and *Voyager*, although that was left unsaid). Rendered unconscious by injection, I would then be returned to Australia in a straitjacket for incarceration in the psychiatric ward of the Repatriation General Hospital, Concord. At the hospital I would be subjected to electroconvulsive shock treatment until my mind was destroyed. He had, he claimed, Captain Willis's absolute assurance of co-operation in this action should I attempt to disclose his period of forced absence from command. This I did not doubt for a moment, remembering Willis's warning to me in Tokyo. Stevens emphatically ended his tirade with, 'Don't think Martin can save you!'

Leaving his cabin, I can remember going to the now-deserted bridge where I gazed at the jungle while attempting to analyse and assess what had just transpired. Could this really be happening? My immediate thoughts were principally of the likelihood that even Martin's initial refusal to support this travesty would not be sufficient to protect me. If Stevens decided to make good his threat, I would have no way of communicating with anyone I could trust before I was identified as mentally ill and therefore out of reach. My wife and children would be devastated and would never enjoy my love and protection again. Perhaps it was paranoia, but by then I did not even trust the security of the ship's mail to be confident that any message I endeavoured to send to my family would not be intercepted and destroyed.

In the silent isolation in Subic Bay I tried to sift through my fears and form a rational plan of action. If I defied Captain Stevens, there was no doubt that he would immediately tell me that I was under arrest for mutiny and attempt to have me restrained and kept incommunicado from my fellow officers. I could not even approach David Martin, for fear of jeopardising him as well. Yet the situation at hand demanded that I make a decision. There could be no retreat.

In our position, detached from the fleet, it was impossible to get a message to another ship. In any case, if Stevens were to be believed, Willis's threat in his support meant that any relief in that direction was impossible. I was trapped by the consequences of my own cautious habit of not communicating the extent of my fears and observations to anyone else aboard. I had always assumed that at least David Martin shared my understanding of what the captain's alcoholic intake and habits were doing to him and their potential to jeopardise the ship. (We had certainly discussed the luncheon incident in Hong Kong as we were going to Repulse Bay for a swim afterwards.) But where else could there be convincing corroboration? I had even been silent about Stevens' drinking in tape recordings I sent to my wife, principally because I did not want to alarm or distress her. There could only be negative repercussions if my concerns prompted her to seek advice from elsewhere, but without the full picture. Trapped from all sides, I felt there was now no option but to yield to the captain's threats but secretly commit myself to leaving the Navy as early, and with as little fuss, as possible.

Later that day I signed the substituted documents at the captain's desk in his day cabin. Some little time after I had signed those retyped returns on Stevens' desk, Chief Petty Officer Jonathan Rogers DSM, the coxswain, came to my cabin. He had performed the usual role of presenting all requestmen and defaulters at the parade on the previous Tuesday. Now he was in distress. He pleaded, 'Please help me, Sir. The captain has given me an illegal order to sign false documents.'

I replied, 'I'll help you, Cox'n. I order you to comply. The consequences of refusal will be much worse for you, I assure you.'

He then left me and signed them in the captain's cabin. I believed that I had helped him avoid a similar fate to that which I now feared might await me. He was found later in tears on the upper deck by a petty officer, who gave evidence to the commission. Rogers never disclosed the reasons for his emotional state.

The turbogenerator was finally repaired and, with power restored, we weighed anchor and proceeded to the wharf at Subic Bay where the ship was secured overnight. I went ashore to visit the US Navy post exchange, mainly just to be free for a while from the oppressive atmosphere of *Voyager*. There were some souvenirs that appealed to me, and as I was taking them from their display, I became aware of Captain Stevens entering the store. In my haste to avoid him, I stumbled and almost brought the entire display case crashing down. He saw me, of course, and made a derogatory remark before moving away on his own business.

During the late evening, as I walked around the upper deck of *Voyager*, ensuring that all was in order and mulling over the events of the day, I heard the unmistakable sound of a fist striking flesh. Rounding a gun turret, I found two petty officers, clearly embarrassed to see me. 'Isn't this a beautiful night?' I asked.

'Yes, Sir!' both replied.

'Wouldn't it be a shame to spoil it by doing something stupid?' I asked.

They agreed, and returned to their mess with some relief. If only my own problems were so easy to resolve.

25
Singapore Finale

I was not sorry when *Voyager* rejoined the fleet at sea. Exercises were continuing as we headed in the direction of Singapore, and most things resumed their normal status. There was no indication from the officers that anything untoward had occurred and, for the moment at least, my troubles were largely subsumed within the day-to-day obligations of being second in command.

At about this time, a film was screened after dinner in the wardroom. During a reel change, Ian Blaikie, the supply officer, rose and poured a drink of spirits into a glass. 'I'm going to visit a sick friend,' he said as he walked out, closing the door. There was a stunned silence. The captain had told me, while we were in Hong Kong, that a complaint against my strict 'no drinking at sea' regimen had been made by some officers. I knew who they would be, but did not comment. 'It's your decision,' he said, 'but it is my wish that if they don't have a watch to keep, they should be able to have a sherry, if they wish, before dinner.'

'I shall tell them that, Sir,' I replied. 'And I shall also tell them that it is contrary to my wishes.' I did as I had said, emphasising my reasons that regardless of watches, any level of drinking at sea was a hazard if an emergency occurred.

But Blaikie was now going further than the captain's wishes, and his defiance could not go unchallenged. I told him that what he had declared he was about to do – taking alcohol for consumption below decks – constituted grounds for court martial. I allowed a couple of minutes to elapse before getting to my feet and saying, 'Continue without me,' then left.

In the cabin shared by Tiller and Terry Redman, I found Blaikie standing, drink in hand, alongside Redman who was turned in, suffering influenza. 'All right! You've got me, now you can court-martial me!' Blaikie said aggressively.

'Pour that down the sink,' I said, indicating the wash basin, 'and come with me.'

He did as I ordered and followed me back to the wardroom deck, where he said, 'Let's go to my cabin.' I declined, insisting on my cabin. When we entered, I directed him to sit, while I remained standing. On the attack, he immediately exclaimed, 'I know you hate my guts!'

'That's the first mistake you've made,' I replied calmly, and continued, 'I'm completely dispassionate about you. I don't care if you live or die, but I will not tolerate you having a detrimental effect on my officers and crew!' I went further, telling him that if he ever did anything that threatened the welfare and safety of my crew I would destroy him and his career, such as it might be. He was silent, and I dismissed him.

Our progress in completing an exhausting list of exercises aimed at defending the ship against exposure to nuclear attack was agonisingly slow, but we were getting there. The tropical heat made the exercises even more demanding, yet the sailors seemed to appreciate the necessity for thoroughness. When we had completed all of the build-up exercises, rigging hoses to wash nuclear fall-out from the ship, repeatedly erecting decontamination shelters, wearing anti-gas respirators in shockingly humid conditions and testing communications systems, we were ready for our major exercise. This required detailed planning, enthusiasm and discipline for success. Action stations were sounded – klaxon blowing – and every man leapt for his respirator and anti-flash gear while moving to designated posts. Each position reported when closed up and, very quickly, the captain was informed, 'Ship closed up at action stations, Sir!'

'It's yours, Number 1,' he said to me by sound-powered telephone, and I began to issue the requisite orders to progress the exercise. The ship steamed with all ventilation closed down and the entire crew enclosed, safe from fall-out, while the combined heat from the sea and engines raised the temperature in the ship to extremely uncomfortable levels. Simulated gas detection had everyone wearing respirators, just to add to our discomfort.

I was tolerably pleased with the reaction of the men, and we were more than half way through our two to three hours of torment when Duncan Stevens' voice, with undisguised venom, penetrated the entire ship. 'Jesus, Number 1! How much longer is this bloody thing going on?'

Not hesitating, I pressed my microphone button and said, 'Assume ABCD State 1', and 'Secure action stations!'

Then I stormed to the captain's sea cabin and confronted him. 'Sir, if you do that again, you accept responsibility, because I won't!' My fury did not abate quickly, but I had no further opposition in the nuclear exercises.

As we approached Singapore, Duncan directed me to take the ship, so that I handled it without interruption, to come alongside *Vampire* and secure. This generated much excited interest in *Vampire* as her officers watched in surprise, but I realised that Captain Stevens was establishing a scenario of training his senior seaman officers in ship handling, and our sister ship followed suit soon afterwards. We were also required to replenish ammunition before leaving, and Stevens directed me to take the ship out of the dockyard and to the remote wharf where the replenishment was undertaken. David Martin then took the ship on our return to secure alongside *Vampire* once more, with each of these activities carefully noted in the deck log as well as being mentioned in the report of proceedings.

When I was walking towards the quarterdeck during lunchtime one day, a discarded matchstick caught my attention. As I stooped to pick it up and flick it over the side, one of *Vampire*'s sailors addressed me. I had already noticed him and noted his dress, which included thongs (prohibited by me in *Voyager* for safety reasons when climbing vertical steel ladders) and a singlet (never allowed by me without a shirt). He was leaning on the guardrail (also an absolute 'no no' to my crew, again for safety reasons). I begged his pardon, and he repeated what he had just said. 'You wouldn't see one of our officers do that, Sir,' referring to picking up the match.

'Why not?' I was curious.

'Because they used to, and so did we,' he answered. 'That's why you have the best ship in the fleet!'

It seemed that my attitude – or maybe the warning from Willis in Tokyo – might also be having some effect on the captain's behaviour. Before our departure from Singapore a combined cocktail party was held by the two wardrooms on the forecastles, to which we invited the officers and wives of the liaison groups as well as many official guests of Royal Navy ships and establishments. A gangway linked *Vampire* and *Voyager* at the forecastles so that guests could visit either ship. Duncan attended, drinking only orange juice, which was a strange phenomenon. He looked decidedly unhappy, but none of my officers appeared to notice. Stevens had also lost so much weight that his clothes were starting to hang on him. He had some alterations made while the Chinese tailors were still aboard. As any competent medico will confirm, alcoholism is primarily a health problem, and the captain's body was now beginning to pay a serious price for his sustained drinking.

Our final night in Singapore remains vivid in my memory. I had a heated confrontation with Eddy Tapp, Scotty Griffith and Sub-Lieutenant Howland, all of whom were in the wardroom. Still fuming over the incident at Subic Bay, I demanded to know why Griffith and Tapp had consented to the captain's monstrous plan to have me charged with mutiny and then be transported to Concord should I not cooperate in changing the punishment returns. Tapp spoke sanctimoniously about loyalty to the captain, to which I replied in absolute fury, 'What about loyalty to the crew?' I repeated my conviction that Stevens would kill the crew if he continued drinking, but they obviously had different ethical standards and senses of propriety to mine. It was, and remains, my firm belief that officers are principally appointed to lead and care for the welfare of the men who follow them. Eddy had told me during the cruise that I was the best executive officer with whom he had served. So much for loyalty, because Stevens must surely have been the worst captain with whom he had served.

26
Sydney

───

Singapore could not fade out of sight fast enough as we proceeded
from the dockyard astern of *Vampire* and her splendid paintwork and
out into the Malacca Strait and towards Darwin. Every moment that we
were under the scrutiny of Admiral Dreyer presented an opportunity for
criticism of our shabby appearance. It was a situation of which I was
acutely conscious, but had never discussed with the captain. The trade
winds were blowing strongly, sending salt spray over the ship, so that
painting was going to be a heartbreaking task for the seamen after they
had first struggled to prepare all the surfaces. I reluctantly accepted that
there was no hope of being ready for the admiral's inspection, just nine
days away. It would have been good for the sailors' pride in the ship to be
reflected fairly by its outward appearance.

Then, a miraculous transformation. From nowhere, canvas shelters
began to spring up all around the upper deck, protecting the men and the
superstructure they were cleaning. The ship now looked like the branch
office of a local circus, but under their ingenious cover the men were
getting on with the job in grand style. I could only wonder how they had
obtained so much canvas, and how much planning had gone into this
covert enterprise. They had obviously purloined every scrap in the
dockyard that was not tied down or closely guarded and smuggled it on
board! As day turned into night, I was even more amazed to see light
coming from these makeshift shelters as the men worked on, snatching
quick meals and even a brief forty winks before returning to their tasks. I
had grossly underestimated their understanding of the importance of the
admiral's inspection for my career prospects.

While I watched in wonder and admiration, I was approached by the seaman officers. They requested permission to change into overalls and join the men in the mammoth task of preparing the ship for inspection. Although I understood their intentions perfectly, and appreciated the change in attitude towards me that had taken place gradually through the cruise, I refused the request with a sharp reminder of their role as officers. 'You have a much harder task. You have to lead your men and reassure them without patronising them. There is great dignity and pride in what they are doing, and for you to intrude would kill it!' They did as I told them.

After about forty-eight hours of unrelenting effort, one of the sailors spoke to me as I was making my way around the deck. 'A lot of money has changed hands over you in the last two days, Sir!'

'Oh, yes? Why's that?' I asked.

'We were betting on whether you would break down and ask us to work harder.'

'And if I had?' I asked.

'Oh, if you had, we'd have worked to rule, Sir.'

I had quite clearly been tested and had passed my exam. By the time we arrived in Darwin, five days out of Singapore, *Voyager* was looking much more as it should, but it still had a way to go.

Refuelling and stores replenishment were undertaken in the few hours we had alongside while the customs inspectors descended on both destroyers to carry out their task and collect all duty payments due on overseas acquisitions. I had briefed the crew to declare any items of conjecture in advance and to write to the collector of customs for guidance if they were in doubt. A team of three customs officers came aboard, but they soon all joined me in the wardroom for drinks. Eventually I suggested that they might wish to see the rest of the ship and the crew as we were becoming pressed for time. I was assured that they had no intention of doing either. 'No! We only wanted to see the captain and a chief petty officer for duty. We had a direction from Canberra. You impressed them so much by your honesty before leaving *Sydney* that they said we were not to take a penny from *Voyager*.'

'Oh God!' I replied, taking my hand from my pocket and showing them the bracelet I had been waiting to produce at the right time. 'What do I do about this?'

'It's not for sale, is it?' I was asked.

'No. It's for my wife,' I said.

'Miscellaneous jewellery, ten pounds. No duty required.'

Four days later, we anchored off Fitzroy Island for the inspection. When Rear Admiral McNicoll boarded, he asked me how much cable we had on each anchor and my mind went blank. I could not think! It was five shackles on the starboard anchor and four and a half on the port anchor, but I felt profoundly inferior for flubbing the question. At my request, he was generous and sincere in his praise of the sweeper who had tiled the concrete-covered deck of the ship's company heads and bathrooms, a selfless act that had raised the sailors' morale. At 3.00 p.m. we weighed anchor and steamed overnight to Edgecombe Bay in company with *Sydney*, *Vampire* and *Anzac*, anchoring for the day. Weighing again at 4.20 p.m., all ships proceeded towards Sydney, with the efficiency assessments conducted under way, and concluding with our annual full power trial. All of the records within the ship were inspected by the fleet staff officers who accompanied the admiral, including correspondence and ledgers, weapons firing results and routine returns. Many of these documents were taken back to the flagship for greater perusal before they were returned to us a week or so later.

Many happy families thronged the wharf to greet our Saturday morning arrival at Garden Island. I was thrilled to see Sue, who had spent the previous night with Susie Martin while the children were in Newcastle with their grandparents. I ushered Sue into my cabin for warm embraces. Then, from my safe, I removed the bracelet and other gifts I had for Sue and gave them to her. On opening the box and seeing her bracelet, she burst into tears. Meanwhile, Duncan Stevens had invited all of the officers and their wives into his day cabin where, to my utter dismay, they were eagerly drinking brandy and ginger ale and other alcoholic drinks as if it were already lunchtime, or later. Duncan had been sober for the previous two months. Now, with the assistance of Mrs Stevens, he was making up for lost time. I would have thought that this was a moment when a loving husband and wife might want to stay sober.

It was possible to enjoy overnight leave only until the pressing needs of *Voyager*'s pre-refit mode were determined. We needed to generate detailed lists of requirements for the dockyard divisions, the ammunition had to be removed to shore storage before the ship could be accepted into dry dock, and the post-refit work-up program had to be planned.

(Work-up is a crucial period for testing the effectiveness of major repairs and modifications to the ship's hull, equipment and weapons so that any deficiencies are identified and corrected. It entails a complex program of co-ordination between the ship and other units both ashore and afloat to simulate attacks and participate in evolutions and manoeuvres.) It fell to me to devise and organise that plan before eventually taking it to the captain's apartment in Darling Point for his approval and signature.

After spending Saturday night in Newcastle, I returned to Garden Island late on Sunday afternoon to attend an informal buffet dinner party in the wardroom with my aunt, Dad's sister, as my guest. The first minute in the wardroom was enough to gauge the prevailing morose atmosphere and trace its source. David Martin told me that a christening ceremony for the baby of Lieutenant Holmes, the ship's ordinance engineer, conducted on board that morning had been completely ruined by Stevens. He had arrived drunk and fallen full length on the deck from the top of the gangway, in front of the guests. Everyone had been appalled by this exhibition, which confirmed that the captain was back to his worst excesses. It was surprising to me, under the circumstances, that Duncan was himself in the wardroom, drinking slowly and evidently in a foul mood. Naturally, I refrained from introducing Aunty Marjorie.

But Stevens did not confine his exhibitions of inebriation to the Sabbath. He would arrive on board each morning showing every sign of being drunk, then make rapid recoveries. On the Monday morning, while the ship was being deammunitioned, he visited his civilian family physician. He returned in the afternoon to announce to me proudly that a 'knighted doctor' had pronounced him completely fit. His paranoia concerning me was transparent. (The titled medico turned out to be Sir William Morrow, a specialist in private practice. By circumventing the naval medical services Stevens was able to obtain a favourably potted version of his lifestyle and its effects on his health.)

By now I resolved to leave the Navy as soon as possible. After writing my formal resignation that evening I waited until the Tuesday afternoon before placing it on the captain's desk while he was sleeping off yet another overindulgence. He had been drunk arriving that morning but recovered to the extent of being able to attend the pre-refit conference at Fleet Headquarters. Lieutenant Ferrier, the deputy engineer, described him to me as 'incoherent' during that meeting.

When Stevens woke at about 5.00 p.m. he came to my cabin, completely sober, with my resignation in hand. The letter was simplicity itself. I had offered no reasons for resigning, which avoided any hostile recriminations among senior officers. Stevens asked me why I wished to leave the Navy. He said, 'You have a golden career ahead of you.' When I told him that I wanted to make a career as a management consultant and had already been assured of employment, he simply asked what he could do on my behalf. I asked him to expedite the acceptance of the resignation and my release from the service, pointing out that I had not waited until after the New Year selections for promotions, thereby allowing ample time for my successor to be nominated.

If Duncan Stevens did not realise that he and Willis had removed my last vestige of respect for the organisation that harboured them and their inhumanity, I would have been surprised. I was hell bent on fleeing from that milieu, which had been exposed to me in such stark and terrifying nakedness in Tokyo and Subic Bay. I now wanted to suppress those memories as quickly as I could. Both Dr McCaffrey in Newcastle and Bob Thomas of Perini Australia Ltd, a civil engineering company, had assured me of employment. I was a little daunted, wishing I shared their confidence in my abilities, but the die was now cast.

Meanwhile, the quotidian formalities of naval life ground on. Having won the fleet sporting competition for the year, *Voyager* was to receive the Pakistan Shield from the Pakistan high commissioner on the morning of Wednesday, 7 August. For some reason this rather banal little occasion was considered worthy of media coverage. Duncan had already boarded, helplessly drunk, so I told Martin to ensure that he was not seen by Captain Dovers, whom I expected would represent the admiral at the ceremony. I then went on board *Vampire*, the relinquishing holder, to obtain the actual trophy. To my horror, I was told the shield had been returned to the flagship, so I had to trek around the dockyard to *Melbourne*, retrieve the award and get back to *Voyager* before the high commissioner arrived. As the television footage showed, Duncan had made an astonishingly full recovery from incoherence and unsteadiness to apparent competence, in an hour or less. (This superhuman feat remained inexplicable to me until the second royal commission revealed the missing link. Stevens had access to a supply of strong amphetamines, a drug that can swiftly mask the visible effects of alcohol.)

I finally took the completed post-refit work-up plan to the Stevens apartment before lunch on the Thursday or Friday. Beatrice Stevens poured me a brandy and ginger ale while I waited for Duncan to study it. It was an extremely generous measure of brandy that took me some time to finish. When the captain returned to the ship, I had drafted the confidential reports on all of the seaman officers for his final approval and left them on the desk of his day cabin. He called me in specifically to discuss the report I had drafted for him on David Martin. There is a scale of assessment ranging from one to nine, denoting an officer's perceived performance under various aspects of professional and personal conduct. I had rated Martin as worthy of seven, eight or nine in all, notwithstanding the general reluctance of commanding officers to grade anyone at the eight and nine levels.

'I've never given anyone a nine in my life!' Duncan snarled at me.

'What does nine indicate, Sir?' I countered.

'Exceptional!' was his reply.

'Well, you have to have the courage to award him that if you agree with me that Martin is exceptional!' He endorsed my reports.

27
Final Sea Command

Voyager was secured for sea and ready for our passage to Williamstown when the captain arrived on board on Saturday, 10 August 1963. After changing into uniform he came directly to the bridge, where I reported to him. Without any preamble Stevens said, 'This is your last time going to sea. You have the ship, Number 1!' I was thrilled to be given this last precious opportunity, although I was suffering from a bad cold and felt like death warmed up. As I proceeded to give the orders leading to us slipping, David Martin came up to me at the pelorus (gyrocompass stand) and said quietly, 'He's as rotten as a fucking chop!' I realised with a sudden shock that Martin was right. The captain was drunk, and unfit to carry out any of his usual duties. (The fact that this had initially escaped my notice can only be explained by my elation at being handed the ship so unexpectedly. Perhaps my own state of health also prevented me from smelling the alcohol on his breath.)

Slipping from the fitting-out wharf we sailed out through Sydney Heads, into the Tasman Sea and down towards Port Phillip Bay for what would be *Voyager*'s last refit. When we were steady on course Duncan told me he was suffering from influenza and would be turning in. 'You have command. Call me when we're approaching Williamstown,' were his last words before retiring to his sea cabin. It was then a matter of routine for me to summon the heads of departments to the bridge and inform them of the captain's action in transferring command. They should now report to me until he resumed command in two days time. Everyone acknowledged my order and acceded to it over the following forty-eight hours. Mick Tiller had obtained the captain's permission to drive to Williamstown as he would soon be leaving the ship, which he did —

without replacement. The responsibility for medical care now fell on our newly arrived Petty Officer Sick Berth Attendant Wilson. Once the security of the ship at sea was certain I handed the bridge over to Martin and told him that I was also retiring to my cabin, succumbing to illness.

While in the Far East, I had drafted a letter that the captain sent ahead to the Naval Board, requesting that we be provided with accommodation throughout the period of refit aboard HMAS *Quickmatch*, which was mothballed in Williamstown. This was the first occasion on which such an arrangement had been considered, but it made sense to me that we should vacate the living and office compartments to allow the dockyard workers total and unhindered access to the ship. My view was that this would reduce the time and cost of the refit and yield enough savings to meet any additional expense associated with bringing *Quickmatch* into an adequate state of serviceability and comfort. It was agreed, and we berthed alongside the decommissioned destroyer when we arrived in the dockyard on the Monday morning.

This was a period of major changes in personnel, as a large number of the experienced officers left and men who had obtained higher rates through examination were promoted and drafted to new ships and establishments, or left to undertake specialist training. My appointment to *Voyager* 'additional on relief and then to shore, resignation accepted' was promulgated. David Martin, now promoted to lieutenant commander, was going to England to complete an advanced gunnery course.

Our welfare fund was embarrassed by the large amount of money raised from soft drink sales during the Far East cruise. The prospect of this handsome surplus passing undeservedly to a new crew was unthinkable. They should be responsible for creating their own means of financing welfare! I called a meeting to discuss the situation. The wives and sweethearts of the crew had been long-suffering during our absence and had not shared in the delights of the Far East. I proposed that they canvass their shipmates with the idea of hiring a hall, caterers and a fine dance band to have a memorable formal night of entertainment as thanks for the waiting. I also insisted that officers should not be invited, as it was the crew's money and the function should be just for them.

The dinner dance was held at HMAS *Lonsdale* on Friday, 27 September, and I attended in response to the insistence of the committee, although Sue was back in Newcastle. Tables were arranged for the occupants of the different messes in *Voyager*. Throughout the evening I was invited to join one table after another and enjoyed dancing with the young women who shared their husbands' and boyfriends' pleasure at being there. It was wonderfully managed, with obvious goodwill and companionship bolstered by a mutual feeling of a job well done. I was proud to be with them.

At one point the music stopped and the floor suddenly cleared. I was aware of a strange silence and looked up as a stoker approached the table at which I was seated. 'Would you like to join our table, Sir?' I thanked my most recent hosts and then started to follow him. As we reached the centre of the floor, a really lovely-looking young woman had joined us from the stokers' table and stood in front of me. 'Go on!' said the stoker, and she put her arms around my neck and kissed me very generously on the mouth. The whole assembly were on their feet applauding, as the stoker called out, 'That's from the crew, Sir!' That moment is my most lasting memory of the night, and still my most precious memory of *Voyager*.

During this period, the captain and I were able to alternate our on board duties and shore leave neatly. Stevens had four weeks off in October and Christmas at home. I took four weeks leave in November. While I was in charge, Sue and the children came down, and we stayed together for a week of relaxation.

While on leave I also had my first hands-on experience of the profession in which I would soon be earning my living. I spent three weeks working as management consultant to Perini in Sydney. Bob Thomas, who had assured me of employment there were I to leave the service, was more hard-nosed when I actually made that commitment and had burned my bridges. He proposed that I first demonstrate my worth in practice by spending time on his company's construction site at Redfern. The new Mail Exchange building was then the largest building project in the country in terms of floor area. It was a highly prestigious contract for the builders, but was running more than £200,000 over budget. My task was to identify means of stopping that haemorrhage.

Visiting the site for the first time, I was given a tour by a Perini staff member, and then shown to the site management office. It was all so new to me, with masses of timber formwork, piles of honey-coloured bricks and concrete in varying conditions all over the site. Different classifications

Captain A. E. (Toby) Cabban, my father, on home leave from Darwin in 1943.

Melva Cabban, my mother, at home in Newcastle in 1944.

My brother Laurie (aged five) and me (aged three) at home in Newcastle in 1931.

In Sydney, aged thirteen, on the day of my interview for entry into the Royal Australian Naval College.

Flinders House cadets of the 1941, '42 and '43 entries at the 1943 passing out parade. I am in the first row, second from the right.

John Matthew (who would later be my best man) and me at Naval College with George Lucas who is intructing us in the use of a sextant for navigation.

The 1943 passing out parade, at Flinders Naval Depot, of the 1940 entry.

Sue in the Jantzen swimming costume she was wearing on the beach at Newcastle when I first saw and fell in love with her.

Above: Sue with Mervin Cooper, the boy who formally introduced me to her in 1944 at a social game of tennis.

Right: David Leach, who would later become RAN Chief of Naval Staff, and me on leave in the Cotswolds, Gloucestershire (1947).

HMS *King George V*, the 48,000-ton battleship on which I did my initial sea time after graduation, in Sydney in 1945.

My first RAN ship, HMAS *Shoalhaven*, a River Class frigate with nine officers and about ninety petty officers and men, in port in Kure, Japan (1949). I was designated quarterdeck officer and am seated in the second row, second from right.

Above: Just engaged – Sue and me at Churchill's nightclub in London in 1951.

Left: Sir Robert and Lady Burrows who were not only dear and generous friends to me during my time in England, but also my virtual parents on my wedding day.

Above: Our wedding day at the Savoy Chapel. Sue looked more beautiful than ever that day in her full crinoline gown made from 150-year-old Brussels lace.

Right: Driving off on our honeymoon after our reception at the Pathfinder Club, 1 August 1951.

Sue and me at Huskisson on Jervis Bay where we bought our first home, a little fibro cottage, Mutmutbilly (1953).

Sue, David and me in Huskisson (1954).

Sue with Christopher (1958).

David, Christopher and me in Melbourne (1960).

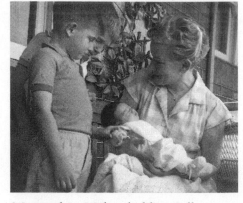

My mother, Melva, holding Sally while David and Christopher look on at their new baby sister (1961).

of builder were employed on the job, but there was no way for me to identify one from another. Nor was there any indication of authority to differentiate labourer from manager. The contrast with the overt displays of rank in the Navy could not have been greater.

While I reflected on what I had seen, I asked innocently, 'Do you have many injuries on the site?' When the answer confirmed my observations, I said that I would bet that most injuries would be nails in the feet. An incredulous manager asked me, 'How did you know that?'

'I did not see a thing on the site because I was so busy avoiding nails sticking out of broken formwork,' I replied. On my advice, work was stopped an hour early that day so that all broken formwork could be removed from the site.

Later, standing before a window in the office, I noticed a man sorting bricks from a jumbled mound and stacking them in two regular piles, watched by another man who leaned against a newly constructed wall. 'Who's that sorting the bricks?' I asked.

'That's the general foreman,' was the reply.

'And who's that watching him?' was my next question.

'A labourer,' was the response.

'Don't we have a role-reversal, here? What's a "general foreman"?' To my astonishment, I was told that he was the highest paid man on the job. My final query was, 'Where does he work?' Informed that he had an office on the site, without hesitation I said, 'Dismantle it!'

'He'll leave!' was the startled response.

'Dismantle it now!' was my heartfelt recommendation. They did, and he left.

Elsewhere, the temperature and humidity within the building made working conditions quite oppressive, and I suggested the use of large industrial fans to force air through constantly wet hessian sheets. All in all there were no more financial losses on the Mail Exchange project, and I believe the previous overages were recouped. My brief stint was effective enough to earn an assurance of full-time employment when I left the Navy, at least in the short term. More importantly, I had gained some precious self-confidence in my abilities as a management consultant.

At the end of November, Captain Bill Dovers, commanding officer of HMAS *Sydney*, was court-martialled for negligence concerning the deaths of five young officers during a sailing exercise in the Barrier Reef area. Captains Robertson (by then commanding *Melbourne*) and Stevens were members of that court, which found Dovers guilty and reprimanded him. The verdict and punishment were viewed as insufficient by some and harsh by others, including Stevens.

Not adequately aware of the circumstances, I have never attempted to make a judgement, although I liked and respected Dovers. Duncan returned to Melbourne from the court martial by train, accompanied by Commander B. H. Loxton, commanding officer of *Yarra*. Stevens was in a black mood as he returned to the ship and, to my relief, did not waste any time speaking with me after I caught up with him. I had missed him as I was on board *Voyager*. I paced the wharf, overseeing the crew, and then spoke for a few moments with Bruce Loxton, whom I liked. He said, 'Your captain won't be much good to you today, Peter. He drank a bottle of brandy on the train.'

On the following day the captain was desperately sick with a hangover and informed me that he was to spend the weekend with friends in Melbourne. He would also stay with them while undergoing a course at Flinders Naval Depot the following week. Petty Officer Wilson medicated him during this time, steadfastly refusing Stevens' requests for amphetamines. Duncan gave me details of his intended whereabouts and asked me to call his hostess with a message concerning his intended time of arrival. I was sorely tempted to alert her to his frail state of health but did not take that step. Perhaps my consideration was misplaced. Much later, at a pre-Christmas party at the home of Captain Robertson, I learned from the employer of Stevens' host that both Duncan and his host had been ejected from the Members Bar of the Melbourne Cricket Ground following disgraceful behaviour during that week. Stevens' host was then dismissed by his employer for his behaviour.

Late 1963 was a deeply difficult period for me. I struggled with feelings of mental confusion, self-doubt and guilt. With the approach of my transfer to civilian life, a deep-seated conviction that the ship and its crew's lives were in jeopardy continued to grow. Yet I was proposing to just walk away from this fraught situation! There was an increase in my alcohol intake of which I was largely unconscious. Maybe I was trying to stop myself thinking about my situation so negatively while, at the same time, seeking to separate the real reason for my resignation from a host of more plausible excuses. Was I actually going because I was past the date by which, logic told me, I needed promotion in order to justify my continuation? Was I fleeing the milieu in which a monster like Stevens, supported by an indulged bully such as Jim Willis, could threaten to strip a man of his humanity and render him a vegetable by shock treatment – without a voice being raised? Or, as I gradually convinced myself, was I simply honouring my promise to Sue that I would leave at that time if not promoted? Every day saw me trying to suppress the memory of the grotesque confrontation at Subic Bay. I must have been doing a good job of sublimation because I never once discussed it with Sue or any other living soul. The horror retreated deep into my memory, and the confrontation with Tapp, Griffith and Howland in Singapore is still the last distinctive recall of the false punishment returns that I can summon with clarity.

Among the new officers who joined during this time were our supply officer, Lieutenant Commander Bruce Carrington, the navigator Lieutenant Harry Cook and Lieutenant Price, a seaman officer on exchange from the Royal Navy. The new engineer was the only one of the incoming group with whom I was genuinely familiar, and I took him into my confidence. I repeatedly outlined my fears for the safety of the ship, including my absolute conviction that Stevens would lose *Voyager* if he had so much as a single drink at sea. He assured me that he took what I said seriously, and we seemed to be relatively close during that time. (Later, he was to deny – absolutely, and on oath – that these discussions ever took place.) Again, leaving nothing to chance, I repeated the same warning to Ian Macgregor, my successor as executive officer, after the formalities of handover had been completed. But his reaction was curt. 'You mind your own business and I'll mind mine!' That hackneyed riposte was a chilling reminder of precisely the attitudes that had prompted my resignation.

At noon on my final day aboard I went into the *Quickmatch* wardroom to share a last drink with the officers. Ordering a Scotch whisky and water from a steward, I was told by one of the officers, 'No! Have a beer, Number 1!' I insisted that I really wanted a Scotch but was howled down by several voices, all urging me to have a beer. Nonplussed, I reluctantly conceded. The beer was served immediately, in a beautiful new pewter tankard, inscribed 'To Lieutenant Commander P. T. Cabban RAN from the Captain and Officers, HMAS Voyager, 6-1-64'. It was a great thrill, and totally unexpected. I still treasure it, but sadly I was not able to have my last navy meal with those officers. Captain Stevens sent for me and insisted that I have lunch as his guest, despite my protestations that I would rather dine in the wardroom.

It was a dismal meal. There was nothing new for either of us to say to each other, and we talked in generalities for some time. Duncan gave me the unsolicited advice that I should avoid accepting any future invitations to naval vessels, as those who did under the same circumstances as mine were usually not respected for it. Then he said, 'What has surprised me most is that right until the last minute, you have conducted yourself like an officer who is striving for promotion. I take that as a compliment to myself.'

I could not let that go. I responded, 'Please don't make that mistake, Sir. I was never taught to behave differently.'

After that rather sour lunch I stepped ashore quietly, to be driven home to Newcastle by my father-in-law, who had been visiting Melbourne. During that long journey up the Hume Highway I remember mulling over what had been the first broad chapter of my life. This was not how I had imagined my naval career would end. But I thought that at least the door was now closed forever on my relationship with Stevens and the horrors of 1963. How wrong you can be.

PART 3

28

Out of the Navy

'I want you to go to Murray One and revise the critical path.' My new employer, the managing director of Perini Australia, Bob Thomas, did not beat about the bush.

My fragile confidence was severely shaken by the size of the task he had just dumped in my lap. 'I don't know a critical path from a garden path, Bob. Why me?'

'Because I trust you!' he retorted, and there's no good response to a comeback like that.

My decision to join Perini rather than accept Dr McCaffrey's offer to work in the health care industry had not been easy, but things now seemed to be settling down nicely. I had rented a comfortable four-bedroom house in Willoughby, and the family moved down from Newcastle almost immediately. We were soon happily established in Sydney suburbia. But now Bob wanted me to trek off into the engineering wilderness of the Snowy Mountains Scheme.

As we flew to Khancoban in a chartered Cessna I asked matter-of-factly, 'What's the manpower turnover rate on Murray One?'

'Why do you ask?' was Bob's response.

'It's an indicator of the quality of management,' I replied.

After landing and my introduction to the project manager, Bob posed the same question to him. 'The same as the rest of the Snowy. One hundred per cent,' was the reply.

Two hours later, as he boarded the aircraft for the return journey, Bob said to me quietly, 'Find out and let me know the turnover rate.'

'But he told you,' I protested.

'Find out and let me know!' he repeated firmly.

The real figures were 480 per cent for the highest paid and most critical group, the electricians; 350 per cent for the next most important group, the carpenters; and 120 per cent for the labourers. This gave a consolidated average on the site of 210 per cent a year, twice the average for the Snowy Scheme as a whole. That is the kind of challenge that faces a work study specialist.

On Monday, 10 February 1964, I began finalising my records before writing up a report. I had a meeting that day with senior Snowy Mountains Authority staff to share my conclusions and get their reaction to my initial recommendations. They endorsed all my major findings and agreed to support my suggested remedies, radical as they were. I hoped to fly back to Sydney on the Tuesday, but could not book a flight until early on Wednesday. At around seven on the Tuesday morning, just as I was about to call Sue, she called me instead with devastating news. An unidentified destroyer had been sunk in collision with the aircraft carrier *Melbourne*. We both agreed that it must be *Voyager*, as I had prepared her work-up exercise program and knew that she would be exercising with *Melbourne* at this time. The loss of life was said to be large, but there was no precise figure.

My feelings were indescribable. These were men who had served with me just a few months earlier. I could tell from her words and tone of voice that Sue's distress for the lost men, and for me, was powerful. Yet she was still unaware of the terrible drama I had endured in Tokyo and Subic Bay. The full picture of that would not emerge for another three years. In fact, those traumatic events were already flying into the deepest recesses of my mind. I reeled from confronting the fact that the unimaginable horror I had first foreseen in Japan's Inland Sea had now become reality. Isolated high in the Snowy Mountains, I was unable to react in any positive or constructive way. Instead, my demons were telling me that I was guilty of gross cowardice and responsible for untold loss of life and endless grief in the years to come.

There was no radio reception in the valley, and newspapers arrived at least a day old. As the day wore on and no news came through, I could only wait and become more irrational. I did not undress, go to bed or sleep for a minute that night. Alone in the VIP chalet, I sat and relived every moment of each ugly confrontation during the Far East cruise. My mind endlessly reviewed all the opportunities that I thought had existed for me to report Stevens' behaviour, and my fears, to a higher authority.

It might seem melodramatic, but I could find no forgiveness in myself and was merciless in my self-judgement. There was no escape from this torment except through the brain's bolthole, hysterical amnesia. I was saved from total insanity by the involuntary mental reflex that destroys critical memories at times of extreme stress. When the project manager arrived the next morning to pick me up and drive me to the airfield I was virtually incoherent, a condition he later described as 'gibbering'. During the timeless suspended animation of the flight back to Sydney I somehow marshalled my mental resources and had become outwardly rational once more. But a terrible black hole had been burned through my memory: I now had no recollection whatsoever of a single event in connection with the crucial false punishment returns and their consequences.

Following a quick stop to report to Bob Thomas, I visited Balmoral Naval Hospital where survivors of *Voyager* were being accommodated and assessed medically. As I went from one familiar face to another I expressed my remorse and sympathy and said how sad I felt that the captain had perished. The chief shipwright said, 'I suppose there were worse captains, but I didn't know any.' Disconcerted by this remark, I asked why he had felt the need to say something so disrespectful. 'He was drunk!' he said, turning to another survivor who freely confirmed it. I protested that Stevens would never drink at sea, but all of the men in the ward angrily rejected my statement, insisting that he was drunk on the night of the collision. I had always imagined that the captain was popular with the men, but not one would speak in his favour. They nominated as their source of information the new captain's steward, Officer's Steward Barry Hyland.

I wrote letters to the next of kin of every man who was lost and had served with me, with personal words of comfort based on my experience of each of them. It was sad work, but it also made me glad that I had taken time to know them all individually. To Beatrice Stevens I wrote as carefully and gently as I could. The mother of the new gunner, Lieutenant E. A. Brooks RN, wrote in reply that her son had written to her recently, 'Mother, I think this is going to be another *Battleaxe*'. HMS *Battleaxe*, a destroyer in which he had been serving at the time, was scrapped following a collision at night in the Clyde estuary in January 1961. Brooks' comment to his mother was sadly prophetic. Had he survived the collision his evidence would surely have been invaluable.

Around 12 February I telephoned Commander John Davidson, secretary to Admiral Becher, and offered my assistance in determining how Captain Stevens might have handled his ship in the circumstances. When it was announced in federal parliament that a royal commission, not a naval inquiry, would be convened to inquire into the circumstances of *Voyager*'s loss, I expected to be called to give evidence.

So it came as no surprise when I was informed, on 18 February, that two Commonwealth Police officers wished to speak with me. They were shown to my office where they asked me pertinent questions about usual procedures on the bridge during flying operations. (The collision had occurred shortly after *Melbourne* changed course during night flying exercises and ordered *Voyager* to take up plane guard station.) I explained that the officer of the watch was expected to act instantly on execution of the carrier's signals, ordering a change of station for the destroyer. Put simply, the plane guard destroyer was to change position relative to the carrier, from being clear of aircraft taking off, close on the starboard bow, to a position that was clear of landing aircraft, well to the left of the approach on the port quarter. From these positions, the destroyer could move rapidly to recover any aircrew who had to ditch or crashed into the sea during operations. I told the policemen that it was normal for the initial turn to be made sharply to starboard, reducing speed and relative bearing from the carrier as it continued on course, then turning with the wheel reversed to port while increasing speed when the carrier's relative bearing was 180 degrees, to pass astern of the carrier, slipping into the new position and then adopting the carrier's course. This manoeuvre – which sounds more complicated than the reality – is known as a 'fish tail' because the wake of the destroyer, seen from the air, resembled the movement of a fish tail on completion of the turns. I illustrated the whole process on a sheet of paper, signing it for the officers to take with them.

The captain's demeanour was discussed, and I told them of the accusations I had heard from some of the survivors in Balmoral hospital, at the same time reiterating the reasons for my conviction that Stevens would not drink at sea. My own demeanour must have seemed suspect, for I was extremely tired and my emotional state was desperate during the interview. In retrospect, I believe it could have been difficult to make rational sense of some of my statements. I just could not accept that Duncan had been drunk on duty, as described by the men. To my great relief the police finally left around 6.30 p.m. I felt emotionally drained.

Some days after the police interview in my office I was given notice that counsel for the Crown, preparing evidence for presentation to the royal commission, wished to interview me. John Smyth QC, a man with a formidable reputation at the Bar, was counsel assisting the royal commission. He led me over the statements I had made to the police officers and then probed deeply on the events of the previous year. It was a far from reassuring experience. Smyth did not tell me that Stevens had consumed a *triple* brandy before the collision. I was to learn this only when it was publicised after the inquiry opened. As our conference ended, Smyth remarked that they would be seeing a lot of me during the royal commission.

It must be difficult, with the knowledge that hindsight now allows us, to understand my concerns at the time. I was still convinced that Stevens could not have been drunk on the night of the collision. It was unthink-able to me that the commanding officer of a naval ship would drink while on duty at sea. My dominant anxiety was that some of the gratuitous information I had provided about the captain's conduct before his two months of sobriety would now be misrepresented in public. I determined to alert his legal representatives to the potential threat to his reputation. Frederick Osborne, a solicitor and former Liberal Party MHR, had briefed Laurence Street QC and John Sinclair to represent the Stevens family at the coming royal commission. Through my own solicitor I met Osborne in Sinclair's chambers. Sinclair had been fag master to John Matthew at the Naval College in 1942, so I knew him. I was comfortable relating to him my recall of the experiences of the previous year. I was thanked for my revelations, and John took me to lunch after the meeting. At this time Osborne was aware of Hyland's statement that he had served Stevens the brandy, although the post-mortem results were not available. Very shortly afterwards I received a call from Norman Jenkyn QC, counsel for the Navy, asking whether I would now share my observations with his team if Smyth called me to give evidence. Jenkyn seemed a trifle panicky. This made me decidedly uneasy about the likely thrust of Smyth's approach. Any mention of drunkenness would be appalling.

A few days afterwards I telephoned Scott Griffith, now a lieutenant commander, at his home and asked to see him. He told me that he had been interviewed by Smyth that day and invited me to join him and his wife for dinner. I went over all the events at Balmoral Naval Hospital and my interviews with the police, Smyth and Sinclair, desperately seeking confirmation of my contention that alcohol could not have played a part in the collision. Griffith must have concluded that I had lost my mind because I had totally forgotten our confrontation in Singapore over the falsified punishment returns. Now I was treating him as a friend I could rely on! He assured me that he had given unqualified support for my statement, except that he had forgotten my first day of command after we had left Sydney. Assuming that all was well, I drove home with a great load off my troubled mind. In fact, when called upon for corroboration Griffith had denied categorically most of what I had told Smyth. It would be some time before that duplicity was revealed.

29
The *Voyager* Inquiry

The Royal Commission of Inquiry into the Loss of HMAS *Voyager* first assembled on 25 February 1964 with the Honourable Sir John Armstrong Spicer as commissioner. True history (as we are often told) is much more than the simple recital of names, dates and places. But for me, the opening of that first *Voyager* royal commission became my 'hinge of fate' – Churchill's memorable phrase to describe the turning point of World War II. The orderly narrative of my life would now be broken by four years of intense personal anguish and trauma. Friendships would be tested to the limit, long-held convictions and ideals challenged. There is no doubt that I was permanently scarred by this ordeal, and perhaps some of those wounds were self-inflicted.

Spicer was a far from neutral choice as royal commissioner. He had been a Liberal politician and former federal Attorney-General in Sir Robert Menzies' cabinet. Now the chief judge of the Commonwealth Industrial Court, Spicer had little experience as a judge other than in industrial matters, and no knowledge of maritime affairs. His understanding of naval procedures would depend almost entirely on the selective evidence presented by a dozen partisan barristers and the 'assistance' of one serving officer appointed by the Naval Board.

When this large assemblage of legal firepower got down to the serious business of presenting evidence there were some immediate clues as to the government's desired approach to the *Voyager* disaster. The Crown would pay all the legal expenses of the Stevens family and the family of the late Lieutenant Price, yet no lawyers were provided to represent the interests of Captain Robertson or his officers. Norman Jenkyn QC appeared for the Navy as a whole, but not as the advocate of any individual serviceman.

Each QC had a junior barrister and instructing solicitor to assist in the preparation and conduct of their briefs. Captain Peek, who was seconded to advise Mr Smyth QC, counsel assisting the commission on naval matters, clearly knew both Stevens and Robertson, but at the time of my interview by Commonwealth Police I had no idea that he was involved. Robertson believed implicitly (and perhaps naïvely) in the honesty and fairness of the judicial system, and was given leave to sit at the bar table and to represent himself during the proceedings of the commission.

I was now working on Sydney projects for Perini, having reported on the Murray One Power Station. Louis Perini, the founder and president of the US parent company, visited Sydney and toured all the projects. I believed that my employment had become something of an embarrass-ment, almost an admission that there was a flaw in the ability of Bob Thomas and his senior executives. The Murray One project manager was Perini's son-in-law, and my report would have been anathema to him. I decided that I was wasting my time and Perini's money. With Bob's concurrence I wrapped up my work, collected my outstanding payment, bought the photographic equipment I had been using at cost price and left without rancour on either side.

Meanwhile, I followed every printed and spoken report on the hearings of the commission. As it progressed I became concerned that it was assuming the guise of a prosecution of the Navy in general and Captain Roberson in particular. I was expecting to be called as a witness at any time, for no one else living had more intimate knowledge of the seaman-ship and habits of Duncan Stevens while commanding officer of *Voyager* in the preceding year. Surely that had to be pertinent. I became more un-settled each night as the details of the day's hearing were broadcast.

Just six hours after the collision Captain Robertson's direct superior, Rear Admiral O. H. Becher, had comforted *Melbourne*'s captain by telling him, 'You could not have done anything.' Now, at the royal commission, Becher gave evidence that was plainly hostile to Robertson. In fact, the admiral's evidence seemed to have an adverse and lasting effect on the attitude of both Smyth and Spicer that was detrimental to a balanced inquiry and its findings. Sub-Lieutenant Bate, the officer of the watch in *Melbourne* on the tragic first watch, was then subjected to a ruthless and demeaning examination by Smyth and cross-examination by Street. They suggested that Bate was lying under the influence of Robertson. After this,

Jenkyn (counsel for the Navy) took Robertson aside and explained that the captain's ignorance of legal procedure was likely to place him in dire trouble. Jenkyn urged Robertson to retain his own senior counsel to represent him and to apply to the government to meet the costs.

At the time Robertson was facing this crisis I believed he was likely to be saddled with the entire blame for the collision as the Navy's price for saving Duncan Stevens' reputation. Every fibre of my being was crying out for me to keep well clear of the drama, yet I was driven by my sense of justice (and perhaps subconscious guilt) to intervene on Robertson's behalf. Then came the bombshell that Stevens had consumed a triple brandy ninety minutes before the collision. I was shattered, and believed that Steward Hyland was lying. I decided to seek him out and arranged to meet him for a beer in a city hotel. During our brief discussion he was adamant that he had served Duncan Stevens the triple brandy an hour and a half before the collision. A 'triple brandy' was not an accurate measure, but for Captain Stevens it was about half a tumbler. My whole thinking was now confused. I was unable to reconcile Hyland's statement with my memory of the captain's undertakings and conduct. But Hyland's memory was vivid, and it was abundantly clear that he was telling the truth as he remembered it. I asked him whether Stevens had consumed any other alcohol during that day and, to the best of his knowledge, he had not.

Picking up the telephone one evening, I called Robertson at home and outlined my analysis of the situation. I explained that I had been told I would be called to give evidence but was now concerned that I might not be. When I outlined the evidence I expected to give relating to Stevens, he rebuked me quite sternly. Robertson declared that he did not need evidence that might smear the reputation of a dead colleague and damage the good name of the Navy. Without thanking me for my offer the captain then said a curt 'Good-bye!' and hung up. I was shocked by this reaction, and it prompted conflicting feelings. On the one hand I felt dismay that Robertson could so sternly impugn my motives. On the other, I experienced a sense of relief that I had made the offer as my conscience directed and now need do nothing more. But these matters are never so simple.

Less than a week later, Robertson engaged David Hicks QC at his own expense, as the Crown had refused to meet his legal costs. Bear in mind that at this time Robertson was a serving naval officer with no reason to believe he would not soon be resuming his distinguished career. The secretary to the Naval Board had actually directed him to telegraph the Prime Minister, Sir Robert Menzies, requesting that the government should guarantee his costs for senior counsel. His approach was rebuffed by the then Commonwealth Attorney-General, Billy Snedden, although Stevens' family and Price's widow were being represented by senior counsel at taxpayers' expense. It seemed a blatant exhibition of prejudice on behalf of the government (and was later overturned after a deputation of Liberal backbenchers threatened to expose the issue in parliament). Through an unfortunate succession of incidents the Navy had caused Menzies considerable political embarrassment over the years, and I wondered whether the Prime Minister had decided to punish Robertson for the discomfort his government suffered when *Vendetta* drove into a dry dock in 1958. The sustained ill-will being directed towards the *Melbourne* bridge team during the commission hearings was palpable. Judge Spicer received no objection from Jenkyn to the hostile line of examination and cross-examination directed at the captain, navigator and officer of the watch.

Another facet to the persistent undermining of Robertson was the suggestion that as he had been in command of *Melbourne* for a relatively short time, he was therefore inexperienced in the handling of an aircraft carrier. This man had served as executive officer and second in command to Captain H. J. Buchanan in *Sydney* throughout the extended coronation cruise of 1953, and would have learned more than most officers about how to handle a carrier. As far as I know, he had at least as much experience as Becher and probably more than Peek when each of them assumed command of a carrier for the first time. Every captain's first command of a ship of significant size is given only after he has demonstrated his ability to control such a ship at sea and the Naval Board is confident of that ability. Jenkyn should – and might have – been made aware of this by both Becher and Peek. He had a clear responsibility to the Naval Board to leave no misunderstanding on the point. Why Robertson himself also failed to comment on the slur, or have his counsel address it, is another mystery.

After accepting that I would be no more than an interested spectator to the royal commission my confused emotions were stirred again by an unexpected phone call. Senior counsel for *Melbourne*'s captain now asked whether I would tell him what I had offered to make available to John

Left: About to fly solo in a Wirraway at the RAAF station at Point Cook.

Below: My Firefly in the steel wire crash barrier of HMAS *Sydney* after I had missed the arrestor wires. The captain was unimpressed.

In the CPO's mess with the recommissioning team during the refit of HMAS *Sydney*.

HMAS *Sydney* post-refit in its new role as a troop transport vessel.

HMAS *Voyager* in waiting position for refuelling while HMAS *Vampire* refuels.

HMAS *Voyager* at sea.

Above: Aerial view of the aircraft carrier HMAS *Melbourne* and the destroyers HMAS *Vendetta* and *Voyager*. (Photo: Australian War Memorial Negative Number 301014)

Left: Captain Duncan Stevens receiving the Pakistan Shield from the Pakistan High Commissioner after *Voyager* won the fleet sporting competition for the year. After having boarded the ship hopelessly drunk, Captain Stevens managed in a short time to make a full recovery. (Photo: Fairfaxphotos)

Survivors from HMAS *Voyager* being brought alongside HMAS *Melbourne* after the collision during night manoeuvres off the coast of New South Wales on 10 February 1964. (Photo: Australian War Memorial Negative Number 305438)

Above: The captain of HMAS *Melbourne*, John Robertson (left), and Rear Admiral O.H. Becher on the bridge as the aircraft carrier berths at Garden Island in Sydney after the collision with *Voyager*. (Photo: Newspix)

Right: The last formal portrait of Duncan Stevens – the strain of ill-health shows in his face.
(Photo: Newspix)

Sir John Spicer, Chairman of the first Royal Commission (1964). (Photo: Newspix)

Father and widow, Major General Sir Jack Stevens and Beatrice Stevens, arrive at a hearing of the second *Voyager* Royal Commission. (Photo: Newspix)

Jack Hiatt QC and me leaving the second *Voyager* Royal Commission in 1967 after another gruelling day of examination. (Photo: Newspix)

Justice K.W. Asprey, member of the second Royal Commission (1967–68). (Photo: Fairfaxphotos)

Justice Sir Stanley Burbury, Chairman of the second Royal Commission. (Photo: Newspix)

Justice George Lucas, who was excused from the second Royal Commission after illness. (Photo: Newspix)

Rear Admiral A.W.R. McNicoll, the Navy's key witness during the second Royal Commission. (Photo: Fairfaxphotos)

The Rev Dr Malcolm Mackay, one of the Liberal agitators for a new inquiry. (Photo: Fairfaxphotos)

Ted St John QC, my knight in shining armour. (Photo: Fairfaxphotos)

David Martin (later governor of NSW), who at the time of the 1967 Commission could only manage 'vague recollections' of his time on *Voyager*, but shortly before he died confessed to giving untruthful evidence to that inquiry. (Photo: Fairfaxphotos)

Robertson. The curious conflict behind this request did not escape me. Robertson had curtly cut me off when I had first offered to give evidence regarding Stevens' behaviour. Now, his own lawyers wanted that same information. I repeated everything I had told the Stevens legal team, adding only the detail of my meeting with Steward Hyland. Again, I awaited my call to the commission and the witness stand – with mounting dread. Again, it was not forthcoming. Robertson had categorically refused the appeals of his legal advisers to have my evidence heard. Before the commission began its hearings I had been advised not to leave Sydney, so I approached Smyth in Phillip Street and asked if I were to be called. He told me I would not be required.

In the event, Robertson was called as the final witness, having for weeks suffered the examination and cross-examination of others who had not the maturity, experience or training to form an opinion about the questions and propositions put to them by lawyers (who were themselves ignorant of the complex matters involved in manoeuvring large ships at high speed at night). Worse, Robertson had heard extended proclamations of Duncan Herbert Stevens' virtues go unchallenged by the counsel for the Navy while his own competence was held up to doubt and innuendo. He had instructed his hard-won team of representatives to maintain a gentlemanly silence on any questions of character.

The Spicer Report was tabled in the House of Representatives on 25 August 1964, and reported widely throughout Australia. Sir John had not directly blamed *Melbourne* or its officers for the loss of *Voyager*, nor did he specifically blame anyone on the bridge of *Voyager*, preferring to cast the majority of blame on *Voyager's* officer of the watch, Lieutenant Price, and the navigator, Lieutenant Cook, both of whom had perished in the collision. He found these officers at fault for not watching *Melbourne* at all times, and declared the ship's movements 'inexplicable'. But he did conclude that the collision might have been averted, or at least the damage reduced, if *Melbourne's* command team had kept a better watch and reacted sooner to the impending danger. Any naval officer with even minimal sea experience knew this conclusion to be nonsense, yet the implications of Spicer's suspiciously political finding blighted the lives and careers of three excellent officers.

The following morning Captain Robertson received a letter from the Chief of Naval Staff, Vice Admiral Sir Hastings Harrington (revealingly dated 23 August), informing *Melbourne's* commander of his appointment to the more junior captain's post of commanding officer of HMAS *Watson*, a shore training establishment in Sydney. For a man who had been in the most senior captain's posting in the RAN, virtually assured of promotion to rear admiral within eighteen months, being shunted down in this manner was an open insult. Although not technically a demotion, the reassignment signalled a clear verdict of 'guilty' by the Naval Board. Robertson decided that the only honourable course to follow was to tender his resignation. Writing in reply to the Chief of Naval Staff, he forewarned him of his intention and requested that consideration be given to the special circumstances of the case as it related to his pension entitlements. Resignation before official retirement risked the forfeit of all Commonwealth contributions to his superannuation scheme as part of his pension. But once he had received formal notification of the shore appointment Robertson immediately handed in his resignation, at midday on Thursday, 10 September. Admiral McNicoll, acting on orders from the Naval Board and pointing out the financial problems involved for the captain, unsuccessfully tried to persuade him to withdraw his resignation or defer it until he had taken up his appointment at *Watson*.

Robertson was now a national figure, and his resignation was front-page news. On Monday 14 September the press lauded his action, recognising the sacrifice for principle, while the Navy Minister, Fred Chaney, foolishly attempted to deny that the resignation had been received. Finally, in a meeting attended by Admirals Harrington and V. A. T. Smith, the minister told John Robertson that although he was not entitled to a pension, Chaney would try to get him one.

I watched this unseemly tragedy unfold with an overwhelming feeling of frustration, bewilderment and guilt. The obvious injustice now haunted me constantly. It seemed unconscionable that the Naval Board – which expected its officers and men to risk their lives in the service of this country – had failed in its duty to render justice and that same level of loyalty to the men under its command.

When the Spicer Report was tabled in parliament, John Jess MHR, a distant cousin by marriage of Robertson's wife Bettine, made an impassioned speech that foreshadowed backbench disquiet with the royal commission's conduct and findings. It was a courageous gesture by a member of the government party, and Jess put the treatment of

Melbourne's bridge officers by the commissioner and Smyth QC under public scrutiny. Meanwhile, nothing had come of the Navy minister's promise to seek a pension for Robertson. Jess approached Menzies and his successor, Harold Holt, attempting to secure a measure of fairness for Robertson in the matter of compensation for his loss of emoluments. The government was intractable, so Robertson was left to find work firstly as the 'Special Defence Correspondent' for *The Australian* and later at the Farmers and Graziers Company, with no pension.

In his New Zealand retirement, the Royal Navy Vice Admiral Harold Hickling CB CBE DSO had been closely following events. Hickling's interest was more than professional. He had been involved in a major naval collision during World War II and was so disturbed by the political handling of the affair that he decided to write a book about the disaster and its aftermath. Hickling, a stickler for preserving the separation of operational authority between the armed services and government, believed the Naval Board's complicity was symbolised by their failure to resign when the Spicer Report was published and the Prime Minister refused to make the Board's own report public. He contacted Robertson (by now working for *The Australian*) and asked if he would contribute to the book by telling him the details of the entire episode. Robertson flew to New Zealand, and during a week of trout fishing near Lake Taupo the ex-captain told his story and the book was hatched.

In September 1964 I was contacted by John Jess, who was then still unknown to me. He said that he believed the treatment of John Robertson was deplorable and asked whether I were prepared to do anything about it. Jess claimed he could do nothing himself unless I was prepared to help. I replied that if Robertson wished me to do anything, then I would, but it would depend entirely upon Robertson. I gave Jess next to no detail about Captain Stevens.

My phone call to Robertson revealed a changed man. He said that he had now lost his finer feelings about the affair and was anxious that the truth should be made known. I reminded him that I had offered to give the facts in the commission but that he had rejected my offer. To me, the central concern was to see some justice done and the captain's pension restored. No good purpose would be served by any further attacks on the reputations of individual officers or the Navy as a whole. I stressed to Robertson that under no circumstances was I prepared to make this matter a public scandal, or make a written statement. I would, if John Jess could arrange it, be prepared to give the information verbally to the Prime Minister or the cabinet on a confidential basis so they could review the commission's findings. Robertson said that this would be adequate and that he would call Jess, asking him to proceed on those lines. Soon afterwards, Captain Robertson told me that Jess was endeavouring to obtain an interview with the Prime Minister, but I was never called to Canberra.

Robertson wrote his own account of the *Voyager* disaster for *The Australian*, but without any significant new information the issue quickly faded from public view. In January 1965 I received a letter from Admiral Hickling, which Robertson had told me to expect. Hickling asked if I would write, for background use only, what I remembered about Stevens' conduct during 1963. I refused absolutely, not wishing to set down in words anything that might later damage my family or myself. The previous ten months had been traumatic enough. I was relieved not to have been called as a witness (although strangely concerned at the reasons as I imagined them). Having been so dismissive of my initial offer to assist, Robertson surely had no right to ask this of me now. But he was not to be denied. He asked if I would at least record my observations on a small tape recorder, on his strict undertaking that it would never be made available to any person other than Admiral Hickling. It would be restricted to background information only, so that I could not be identified as the source. Feeling that I could trust Robertson, I consented. He brought the recorder to my home and left it with me.

That night, without recourse to notes, diaries or any other form of *aide memoire*, I sat on the end of my bed and spoke into the microphone while the tape wound for almost an hour. In one long burst I exhausted whatever remained of my recollections of Stevens and the 1963 *Voyager* cruise. That, I thought, was that. I did not even bother to replay the tape after rewinding, just leaving the spool on the recorder for collection the next day. And that was the rather offhand origin of what would become the notorious 'Cabban Statement'.

A week or so later, Robertson came to the house and asked me to sign a transcribed copy of what I had dictated rather than written down. After a cursory reading of the typescript I signed it with minimal hesitation. Why did I go back on my earlier refusal to provide written material? I felt compelled to comply. Less than a year ago I had been a serving naval

officer, vastly subordinate to this man – a senior captain – whose personality remained dominant. Those who have never experienced a life of
unquestioning obedience from the age of thirteen to thirty-five can have
no inkling of the force with which disciplinary influence continues long
into civilian life.

Admiral Hickling wrote and published his book, titled *One Minute of
Time*, and for a few days it caused a mild sensation. Although he made his
case well, the book did not stir the Australian public into action on behalf
of the wronged captain of *Melbourne*. Hickling had kept his promise not
to include any direct quotations from my background statement or information that might identify me as a source. On the day of publication, Sue
and I were invited to the Robertson home for dinner. Admiral Hickling
and his partner, Mrs Anstruther, were also guests. She wore a magnificent
diamond and ruby brooch in the shape of a vice admiral's flag, a Cross of
St George on a white background with one red ball in the upper
quadrant next to the mast. The publisher's Australian manager, John
Reed, and his wife, were also present. Reed felt very strongly that an
injustice had been done to Captain Robertson and pressed me to agree
to be interviewed on radio and television. I explained that I was not
prepared, under any circumstances, to discuss publicly the information I
had shared with Admiral Hickling in confidence. Reed accepted my
position, but not everyone feels equally bound to honour the integrity of
assurances they have given. A sequence of small betrayals would soon
catapult me from careful anonymity on to every front page in the land.

Captain Robertson, in breach of his word to me, had already shown
the transcript of my statement to John Jess. I was next prevailed upon to
allow Jess to show it to the Prime Minister. What good would it now do
to protest? I agreed that if circulation of the statement were restricted to
the Prime Minister and Minister for the Navy, then Jess could go ahead.
I even volunteered to be interviewed by them if they wished. Sir Robert
Menzies eventually read my statement in the company of Jess early in
1965 and, after speaking by phone to Minister Chaney, he said that
although I had not been interviewed, all other reports confirmed that
Stevens was a competent officer. Jess insisted that not withstanding his
competence when sober, he was unfit to command. Jess continued to
campaign behind closed doors in Canberra on Robertson's behalf but
received no acknowledgement of letters he wrote to Harold Holt (who

had replaced Menzies as Prime Minister in early 1966) on the matter. Finally he obtained a personal appointment with the new Prime Minister and showed him my statement, emphasising that neither Robertson nor I wanted the contents made public. Through friends, I also attempted to meet Holt and David Fairhall, Minister for Defence, but to no avail.

Time passed slowly. Despite his best efforts, Jess had failed to stimulate any political action. Meanwhile, I agonised about my dilemma. Was it really worth challenging the injustice done to Robertson and his bridge officers? Would the Royal Australian Navy be permanently stained by the revelation that one of its senior commanders was a drunkard? These doubts were amplified by the terrible pain I still felt over the loss of my shipmates on *Voyager*. They were not just an anonymous alphabetical list of names on a death notice. They were faces I had known for years, friends, comrades, smiles I would never see again. My conscience could not free itself from the agonising thought that maybe they would still be alive if I had had the courage to act earlier and formally report on Duncan Stevens' behaviour in 1963. It was not so much my career that I was afraid to risk but my own sanity and my family's security. My career was already at risk, if not destroyed by my actions. But would the burden of guilt be somehow lightened if I had the courage to speak out now?

In early August, Sue and I were invited to a dinner party with John Jess, held at the Robertson home in Neutral Bay. After the meal, the ladies withdrew to allow the men to discuss the lack of progress with the Prime Minister and cabinet. Jess urged me to write a strong letter to him, to be passed on to Holt. By the end of the evening, almost every word and punctuation mark had been agreed. I awoke the following morning without any recollection of the letter! Whether my short-term memory loss was the result of hysterical amnesia or vintage port was beside the point. It was not going to be so easy to avoid writing that letter as Jess was on the phone early, reminding me of my undertaking and repeating, word for word, the content that had been agreed. I admitted to myself that the phrases sounded very much like me, so I sat down, typed it out and mailed it immediately. There was no reply.

Two years later that letter was finally aired at the second royal commission. When challenged as to its forceful tone and content I said that the extreme language expressed my only hope of provoking some political response. Calm, rational approaches had, so far, achieved nothing.

30

The *Voyager* Debate

An intemperate letter intended for the Prime Minister's eyes only
might be played with a dismissively dead bat, but an electrifying
headline in a popular tabloid newspaper could not. 'DRUNKEN
DUNCAN – *Voyager* Scandal: This is what it's all about,' screamed the
front page of the Melbourne *Truth* on 9 May 1967. The cat was well and
truly out of the bag.

Attributed to an anonymous source, the article described an incident
in which the late Captain D. H. Stevens was carried aboard *Voyager* after
having been found lying unconscious in the gutter in Hong Kong. Curi-
ously, this was not one of the damning incidents I had outlined in my
recorded statement for Hickling. Indeed, I had no immediate recollection
of the event. Only years later did I recall that I had related it to John
Robertson during the first royal commission. Then, when he was urging
me to sign the transcript of my statement for Hickling, he had said, 'You
haven't mentioned everything.' I can only speculate now that either Jess
(probably) or Robertson himself leaked the Hong Kong incident to the
press, but we will never know. In any case, the source was irrelevant. The
unspeakable had now been yelled from the rooftops, and a reluctant
government could no longer avoid the issue.

While I was standing with my wife in our kitchen the morning after
the gist of the sensational *Truth* article had been republished in the
national press, the telephone rang. As I moved to the phone, Sue said,
'Don't answer that yet. It's about *Voyager* and it's dangerous! I'm going to
record it.' She immediately attached to the phone a suction-cup recording device I had bought in England. Sue was dead right! It was John Jess,
proclaiming – without seeking my permission – that he intended to 'go

public' with my statement. He would first reveal its content in the party room that day and then if necessary to the press. I attempted to prevail on him to keep to his word on the matter, saying that what he proposed to do jeopardised my career and my family's welfare. Jess was an excitable man, given to declamatory outbursts. 'I don't care about you and your family. I only care about justice for John Robertson,' he said. He hung up shortly afterwards, and we were left in despair. There was nothing we could now do to stop him dishonouring his promise of confidentiality. The die had been cast.

In a perverse way, that betrayal forced upon me a resolution of the dilemma that had become such a personal agony during the two and a half years since the terrible night of 10 February 1964. I had been experiencing increasing feelings of compulsion to fight for the truth, no matter at what cost, together with counter feelings of desire to accept the status quo and get on with my life. Several times I had spoken with Chris McCaffrey, seeking his counsel and reassurance. Each time, with logical argument, he advised me to 'drop it, Peter, or they'll destroy you!' And each time I would agree and thank him, then call again a few months later.

There was no peace of mind for me as I could only watch on from the sidelines while working hard to build up my practice as a work study consultant to a range of health care institutions. I was now retained by several bodies, including the Benevolent Society of New South Wales, The Women's Hospital Crown Street, ten other New South Wales hospitals and the Hospitals Commission. Sophia Leung, a brilliant young economics (honours) graduate, joined me as an associate. But the pressure of our mounting workload (and the unconscious burden of guilt, which I failed to recognise) was building within me. I told Sue that if I did not have a break immediately, I feared a breakdown. She called a friend who was prepared to look after the children, and on the following day we drove to the Blue Mountains for a week of relaxation. Acting on impulse one morning, I stopped the car outside a TAB agency and placed two bets and a 'daily double' wager. The winning result, of which we were unaware until that evening, paid for the whole week's expenses. We celebrated our luck with champagne.

Meanwhile, the combined impact of the *Truth* revelations and the persistent agitation of John Jess within the party room forced the Prime Minister to agree that the whole matter should now be debated in parliament. Holt wanted to kill the issue once and for all. Dates for this debate were promulgated, and all of my worst fears of being transformed into a public figure were about to be confirmed.

But what seemed like an impending disaster also carried the seeds of salvation. My 'three wise men' were all Liberal MHRs, each acting with commendable courage and independence. Harry Turner, the Member for Bradfield, telephoned for an appointment, then knocked on my front door and introduced himself. (We had recently left our rented house in Willoughby and moved into a comfortable old home in Cremorne.) Not in so many words, Turner announced his intention to question my integrity about the events in *Voyager* in 1963. I was, at first, disinclined to be friendly and questioned his right to presume to doubt my word. But he was very forgiving and understanding of my attitude, so we slowly settled down to detailed discussion and explanation. In the end, he was convinced of my veracity and would later join John Jess to speak in my support during the debate.

My next white knight appeared in the person of Edward St John QC, the recently elected Liberal Member for Warringah. St John's credentials are widely known. He had been a senior member of the New South Wales Bar and an acting justice of the Supreme Court of New South Wales, and was chairman of the International Commission of Jurists. It was Ted's comfort and guidance, more than anything else, that carried me through the traumatic weeks to come. St John asked me to visit him at his home in nearby Clifton Gardens, where he wished to interview me in the company of the Reverend Malcolm Mackay MHR (later, with some irony, to be Minister for the Navy). For more than three hours I was questioned by these two men. Ted employed his impressive skills as a barrister to cross-examine me on every point of my statement and every other issue that I had raised. At the end of this session, St John informed me that he would make his maiden speech in the House in support of Jess's submission and described me as 'a witness of truth'.

Further meetings followed, including one with two psychiatrists who were experts on alcoholism. After questioning me in detail these doctors declared their opinions categorically that Stevens was an alcoholic. They also quizzed me about Beatrice Stevens, and when I described her pouring the drinks and the strength of them, they laughed. 'You obviously don't know!' one said.

'What?' I asked.

'There are always two!'

St John insisted that Sue's and my presence in the House of Representatives during the debate was of paramount importance. 'They are cowards and will attack you unmercifully unless they can see your face in the House,' he told me. I was soon left in no doubt as to the bare-knuckle ways of Canberra. Ted met Sue and me on our arrival at Parliament House and took us to his office, where I was briefed on an agreement he had made with Channel Seven for an interview with me. The deal was that, in Ted's presence, I would speak informally with them in the first instance, and all the questions that I would be asked on camera were from a straightforward list that I was given. Only the agreed questions would be asked.

The interview was held as planned, but at the very end a further question was asked. In the confusion, I replied. Channel Seven had violated their agreement, and the only segment of the interview that was screened that night was, of course, the last question and my response. Chester Porter, as my junior counsel, was to comment later, 'It's just as well that you answered as you did, because no one could understand what you were talking about!'

Ted then took us to the King's Hall, where we were joined by John Jess and introduced to other parliamentarians from both sides. We were escorted to the Public Gallery, overlooking the chamber of the House of Representatives. As we watched avidly we were conscious of the presence of two friends, Ron Golsby, the CEO of Crown Street Hospital, and his wife Barney, who had driven down to provide us with moral support. This heartfelt gesture meant a great deal as many so-called friends had now vanished from our small circle.

The Attorney-General, Nigel Bowen, Member for Parramatta, opened the debate on the *Voyager* inquiry on Tuesday, 16 May 1967 with a ministerial statement. He began with an overview of the circumstances of the collision, saying, 'It was essential that a full and searching public inquiry should be held.' He went on to mention that Captain Robertson had chosen to appear for himself in the early stages of the inquiry, as if he had been offered and declined legal representation (which, in truth, the government had denied him). The attorney sought to remind members that 'the commission was a public inquiry and, I believe, the most searching public inquiry ever conducted into the operations of one of the services in this country'. Admiral Becher was mentioned as supporting, in evidence, the commissioner's findings regarding Robertson that he should have done more to avoid the collision. (Becher, remember, was the flag officer who had assured Robertson, his flag captain, 'You couldn't have done anything' just hours after the collision.)

Dealing with my statement, Bowen asserted that counsel assisting the inquiry was entirely correct in concluding that evidence that Captain Stevens was intoxicated on past occasions was not relevant. It was interesting to note, he said, that other parties before the commission were aware of my allegations yet none of them saw fit to call that evidence. That struck me as a remarkable understatement, or at least a patently disingenuous oversimplification. Bowen said, '. . . the fact that Captain Stevens was not intoxicated at the critical time was positively established by scientific evidence.' Later, he made the remarkable claim,

> Even if, contrary to the views that I have expressed, evidence was available to establish that Captain Stevens was intoxicated on the night in question, that evidence would not affect the findings of the commissioner that responsibility lay with *Voyager*. Nor could it affect the finding of the commissioner that Captain Robertson should have given a warning when he realised a collision was imminent, or the findings that Commander Kelly and Sub-Lieutenant Bate did not keep an efficient watch.

The lengthy statement concluded with the plea that, '. . . we must be on our guard against reopening matters which are merely likely to provide sensationalism or which will in no way advance the interests of the nation.'

John Jess, Member for Latrobe, was granted leave to exceed the standing orders time limit to complete his speech, the transcript of which occupies thirteen full pages of Hansard. After outlining his unsuccessful attempts to achieve a review of the facts, he pointedly observed that he had yet to be acquainted with any of the refutations of my statement from serving officers that the attorney claimed to have. Jess stressed his concerns in forthright manner. In order of importance, they were:

> Whether the things that the former Prime Minister said should be done were done; whether the Naval Board and the government

acted to suppress evidence that could be considered relevant, and, if this evidence was relevant, whether the Government or the Naval Board allowed an officer to be promoted to the rank of captain while knowing his condition or his weakness; and whether it allowed him to remain in command of a ship the result of which could have been – I am not saying it was – a collision involving the loss not only of the ship but also of eighty-two lives. Thirdly, and this is the least important point, if the suggestions inherent in those two questions are proved to be fact, it must follow that Captain Robertson, Commander Kelly and Lieutenant Bate were unjustly treated because in my view it is not sufficient to argue that although a large percentage of a trial was incorrectly carried out the results in respect of one or more persons would have been the same anyway.

Jess then read out sections of a letter from Robertson that stressed his desire, and mine, to keep the matter private and my agreement for Jess to 'give everything to the Prime Minister or the full cabinet or anyone else you think would like to hear it'. Speaking of the affect on the morale of the Navy, he asked members 'whether they consider that it is kept at a high state when men know that if they are involved in an accident or circumstances under which they may be put on trial or may be the subject of a royal commission, they cannot expect the full facts of the case to be brought out and may indeed find that their senior officers, far from supporting them, desert them'. In reference to the statement that Admiral Becher supported the finding against Robertson, Jess said that counsel for the Navy

> . . . is not an admiral or a technical person; his advice must come from the department and be paid for by the Commonwealth. At this hearing counsel for the Navy contended that what Mr Smyth had put forward about bells, alarms, signals, rattles, or whatever else it was, would bring the Royal Australian Navy into contempt and would make it the laughing stock of the navies of the world. He argued that the things that had been said not only about Robertson but also about Kelly and Bate were unjust and unfair and were not a reasonable criticism to bring against these officers. Now we find the Navy has done a switch, and it is a case of 'We would have shot

him anyway.' The government may say he must have been a log as counsel for the Navy. If he was a log and if Smyth is perfect, I do not know what sort of commission it was.

John Jess then indulged his talent for rhetorical sarcasm to ridicule the scientific evidence upon which the commissioner had placed so much reliance. He pointed out that the transcript of evidence ran to 4,380 pages, of which 'the investigation on the subject of alcohol aspect covers approximately three pages. It is the sweetest investigation that I have ever seen. I only hope that if at some stage I am charged with drunken driving I have opposing counsel as considerate as were these counsel.'

When dealing with an attack on me, Jess noted that it had been said in another place that I was a vindictive officer and an alcoholic, and he would like anybody who wished to make that assertion to see me and say it to my face. He said, 'Let me say this. Lieutenant Commander Cabban went through his own solicitor and at his own expense because he felt that in fairness to the Stevens family he must let their solicitor know what he had said. If this is vindictive, I do not know what the word means.' And on the second charge he said that a minister had shown him a report by Sergeant Turner of the Commonwealth Police, who interviewed me at Perini, saying that I was blind drunk. Jess then said to the minister, 'How could a blind drunk man make a technical statement like the one on page 1 of the three you showed me? If he were blind drunk, why is there no mention whatsoever in the police sergeant's report of his interview? Further, if he were blind drunk he should have gone back on another day.'

Part of this long speech contained a revealing insight into the veracity of the recently appointed First Naval Member, Vice Admiral McNicoll. He had been questioned in relation to the triple brandy served to Stevens one and a half hours before the collision. Tackled by Jess about the precise measure of a 'triple brandy', the Minister for the Navy, Don Chipp, stated that it was only equal to a single brandy in the Navy. When asked, by telephone, by the minister in Jess's presence, McNicoll had confirmed that 'a triple brandy is equal to one brandy'.

'From when?' asked Jess.

'From the end of the war,' was the good admiral's reply. How amazing that no one else, to my knowledge, was ever aware of that unique volumetric equivalence. I had been wine caterer in a frigate, *Shoalhaven*, commanded by the same A. W. McNicoll, and even I did not know.

The most prophetic part of the Jess speech was his stinging challenge to the government and the RAN. 'Bring the seamen who were there, bring the sick bay attendants, but do not bring the serving officers of the Navy who may wish or have no alternative but to not remember or to answer "I cannot recall" or "It is not in my recollection". Statements of this kind will not convince me.'

Don Chipp spoke next. He artfully sought to reduce the 'nub of the problem' to just one aspect of Jess's speech. 'His case rests or falls on the validity or otherwise of the allegations of an officer he named, former Lieutenant Commander Cabban.' Referring to Captain Robertson being appointed to *Watson*, he offered the ignorant and naïve proposition that it was justified because while Robertson was engaged in the inquiry, Melbourne 'was worked up to a most efficient ship. I would challenge any man in this House or any man outside this House who had any sort of naval experience to suggest that at a time when we had a totally or almost totally worked up ship, the flagship of the Royal Australian Navy, it was thinkable to change captains. It was unthinkable and it was not regarded at the time to be a proposition.' The minister should have been informed that Commander Alan Willis had worked up *Voyager*, completely, and then handed the ship to Duncan Stevens after four months in command, having demonstrated total competence. Also, Captain Robertson had more than adequate qualification to say that it was not only thinkable, it was also what should (and would) have happened without political interference.

Chipp then unveiled what he probably believed was a tactical master-stroke. He had directed the secretary of the Navy to collect responses from every serving officer I had named in my statement for Hickling. None of these men were given access to the entirety of my statement, just the few lines that specifically related to them. They were being asked to comment without context, and in the clear but unspoken knowledge that those responses could affect their careers. In the House, Chipp quoted selectively from these unsworn statements to refute my claims. They were tabled after his speech and published in handy pamphlet form the following day. Chipp's stratagem at first looked like a body blow to the Jess–St John cause. In fact, its flaws soon helped to discredit both the Navy and its overly loyal minister.

I was shocked to read part of Captain G. J. Willis's statement, in which he said, 'If the alleged state of affairs had existed I should have been aware of it. Had it existed as suggested it would have been Cabban's duty to report it to me. The report in Tokyo was made at Stevens' direction.' This from the man who had threatened me with court martial for mutiny if I tried to inform anyone outside *Voyager* of the command that he had ordered Stevens to give me.

Griffith was also quoted as saying, 'Captain Stevens was very keen to train his officers in ship handling and did so on many occasions, including replenishment at sea evolutions. It was therefore normal that I as navigating officer should receive more than an average number of chances to handle the ship.' This was absolute rubbish. I never saw or was aware of Griffith or any other officer than the captain handling *Voyager* in a replenishment. He certainly allowed Martin to take the ship alongside, and from alongside, after I had done this twice in Singapore during our final visit.

The Navy's desperation to cover its own tracks often reached farcical proportions in the statements collected for the minister. For example, the Chief of Naval Staff, Alan McNicoll, said of Stevens, 'In his whole career there was no mention in his confidential reports of alcohol. If my word cannot be taken for this I am prepared to sign a statutory declaration to that effect.' How extraordinary that the most senior officer in the service should believe that if his word were not good enough, then it would be accepted if he signed a declaration. It would be difficult to imagine a more telling indication that he was concealing the same reports he wished to deny. (On the second day of the debate, Clyde Cameron, Member for Hindmarsh, went to this very point, saying that on the strength of that statement alone, McNicoll should resign. In any case, I already knew this claim by McNicoll was wide of the truth. I had received a letter from a retired officer who, as Duncan's commanding officer, had written to Sir Jack Stevens years before, warning of the excesses of his son's drinking.)

Edward St John's maiden speech commenced about half an hour before the dinner adjournment and would instantly become the most celebrated first speech by any new member in the parliament's history. The proceedings were being broadcast on ABC radio, and the sheer drama of the moment electrified the audience across the nation. St John took as his starting point the royal commissioner's report, in reference to the primary cause of the collision. He acknowledged Captain Robertson as a fine man and a great loss to the Navy, but then startled everyone by saying that he was not concerned with any possible injustice to him. 'I am concerned with much more important matters – the safety of the Navy and the men in the Navy, and the safety of this country.' This was a brilliant tactical approach to adopt. At a stroke, Ted lifted the debate from the mundane level of seeking compensation for a wronged individual to the much more profound issues of national security and ethical standards of our armed services. It also allowed him to go straight to the core of the *Voyager* scandal: alcohol, and the failure of the royal commission to face the possibility that Duncan Stevens might have been unfit to command.

With a lawyer's instinct for explosive detail, St John reminded parliament that there had been alcohol in the blood of the only three bodies recovered from *Voyager*, including that of Duncan Stevens. He pointed out that the press had never known of these alcohol content levels because the post-mortem reports were only tendered as documents to the commission, not read aloud to the courtroom. As his speech continued after the dinner adjournment, Ted began to amass a formidable critique of the performance of the commission and Judge Spicer's findings. He raised Smyth's failure to challenge my evidence regarding Stevens given in his chambers and his subsequent failure to recall me to say that I was uncorroborated.

St John went on to question the expert evidence about Stevens' blood sample.

> What about Professor Blackburn's evidence that, having regard to Captain Stevens' drinking habits, 25 milligrams of liquor did not matter all that much? If it was desired to place reliance upon Captain Stevens' drinking habits, to show that 25 milligrams did not affect him, then those drinking habits should have been established by evidence and not referred to at second hand by Professor Blackburn. The whole of the evidence of that gentleman is based on . . . autopsy reports and blood samples which were not proven in evidence.

Soon afterwards, in the same passage of his speech, Ted made the point that after the samples were tendered, Spicer had butted in to say, '"Very well. As I understand it – and I think this should be made clear early in the piece – there is no suggestion that the captain . . ." Mr Smyth then takes him up by saying, "No. Neither the captain nor the navigator was in any way affected by liquor . . ." Then comes the evidence of Professor Blackburn who was uncertain of his qualifications, and his opinion that 25 milligrams of alcohol was insufficient to affect Captain Stevens.' St John underlined the point that 'every man on a destroyer has a vital function to perform or he would not be there', which was precisely why I had prohibited officers from drinking at sea.

The most celebrated moment of theatre that night was when the Prime Minister broke with longstanding convention to make an inter-jection during St John's maiden speech. Referring to the comment by Smyth QC that he did not consider my evidence relevant, Ted asked the House:'Is this not one of the facts and circumstances leading up to the *Voyager* disaster? Or have I lost the meaning of the word "irrelevant"? Are we playing a battle of semantics? What is the meaning of the word "irrelevant"?'

At which point Holt called out, 'What is the meaning of the word evidence?'

Quick as a flash, St John shot back, 'I did not expect to be interrupted by the Prime Minister.'

Ted was merciless with Admiral Gatacre, the man who had promoted Stevens to captain, and who had described Duncan to the commission as 'the paragon of all virtues'. St John brought *Voyager*'s commander and his protectors down a peg or two.

> Captain Stevens is pictured as the model of all qualities of which the Navy could be proud. The fact is that this man had been court-martialled and convicted for hazarding his ship. It may be that there was a lot of sympathy for him in the Navy and that a lot of things could be said in extenuation, but would it not be right to mention it? Was it withheld from Mr Smyth? If so, by whom was it withheld and for what purpose?

The *Vendetta* incident had been mentioned as a slight against Robertson, while his Distinguished Service Cross and three Mentions in Despatches had been conveniently overlooked.

Don Chipp was roused to fury by St John's devastating oratory and could not let the new member's speech close without making himself an actor in the play. When Ted said that the substance of my statement for Hickling could be verified, Chipp leapt to his feet, shouting, 'Who verifies them?' He had to be physically restrained by his ministerial colleagues. Ted was careful to respond to the interjection, thereby ensuring that Chipp's outburst would be recorded in Hansard. 'Let a proper tribunal determine it,' he said, then he moved: 'That the following words be added to the motion: ". . . and is of the opinion that a select committee should be appointed to inquire into and report on this whole matter." '

When my name had first been introduced in his speech Ted drew the House's attention to my presence with Sue in the public gallery. Of me he said,

> Lieutenant Commander Cabban is a man who has the highest reputation in the Navy. I have seen and heard from his so-called flimsies [the Navy's personal performance assessments] nothing but praise. He is loyal, industrious, able, intelligent, efficient; a man of high moral character . . . On all sides I hear nothing but praise for this man.

These glowing words made a stark (and welcome) contrast to the barrage of slurs and innuendo I had had to endure over the preceding few weeks.

The next speaker in the debate was Harry Turner, supporting both John Jess and Ted St John. He emphasised what I believed was closer to the most important issue that had troubled me so deeply. 'For what purpose should we reopen this matter? If an alcoholic can be in charge of an Australian ship and Australian lives – eighty-two have already been lost – then the same thing could happen tomorrow, next week or next month.' He spoke of his three-hour meeting with me, describing me as an honest and sensible man prepared to speak the truth. He was to be the last of the government speakers to support the motion for a select committee on the first day.

James Killen, the Member for Morton, followed in support of the government against the motion. Quite understandably, he sought to repudiate the statements of Jess, St John and Turner and attempted to gain emotional mileage from the notion that an attack was being made on a dead man and would only bring added grief to his family. Jess foresaw this line of argument and had already given examples of support from among the grieving relatives of the other eighty-one victims of *Voyager*'s bridge team. On the subject of blood alcohol, Killen supported the assessment of Professor Blackburn that the quantity could in no way affect any man. Killen was essentially trying to get the government off the hook by avoiding a public hearing and all the possibilities that it would provide for harm to the government. He moved 'That Captain Robertson should be offered reinstatement with seniority restored as from the date of his resignation, and if this is not acceptable to Captain Robertson the government should make an *ex gratia* payment of the amount of any entitlement denied him by his premature retirement.' His speech concluded: 'Thereby we would be helping a man who acted honourably throughout the commission and who has acted in a most honourable way since.'

The debate resumed at 3.30 p.m. the following day with Fred Chaney, the former Acting Minister for the Navy, continuing the government's line without adding anything meaningful to it. He attempted to prop up the damning evidence of Admiral Becher, which Robertson believed had heavily influenced Spicer's adverse finding. Events in the coming months would show how naïve the former minister was to contradict St John's contention that he would not care if Chipp produced 'a stack of statements from serving officers saying that they could not corroborate the evidence'. Chaney claimed, 'From my own experience of officers of every level I believe I can accept their word when they are asked to give it and believe that this House also can do so.'

Sam Benson, the Independent Member for Batman, then made some interesting (and extremely uninformed) statements concerning records of alcohol consumption aboard naval ships. He stated, 'One can see how much every officer . . . drinks day by day, week by week, and month by month.' All that can be discerned from the wardroom wine books is how much an officer signed for, not how much he actually drank. Liquor purchased for the entertainment of others is not recorded separately. The amount of entertaining on board ship depends on the social attitude and habits of individual officers. Also, Benson had the mistaken impression that each drink the captain consumed would be recorded. Captains purchase their drinks in bulk and either pour for themselves or have a steward pour, from their own bottles. In those circumstances it is impossible to track actual levels of consumption. Benson was another who hammered the theme that I 'had a duty to perform on behalf of all the

people subordinate to him' and to report my concerns to a higher authority. He somehow managed to overlook my report to Captain Willis, in
Tokyo, which gave Willis the opportunity (and the duty) to take the
matter further. Willis had threatened me, and then denied it. We were to
hear widely conflicting opinions in the months ahead by Admiral
McNicoll and the now-promoted Admiral Peek about what would have
happened had I attempted to speak confidentially about Stevens.

The first opposition member to join the debate was Clyde Cameron.
He seemed a crafty man of outstanding intellect, well chosen for the
opening attack on the government's case. Needing no invitation to drive
a wedge between the government and its dissident backbenchers,
Cameron immediately supported Edward St John's motion. He identified
the central issue: '. . . that is, whether the Naval Board suppressed or was
responsible for suppressing or withholding vital evidence concerning the
character and drinking habits of Captain Stevens.' I believed that he was
absolutely correct in asserting that somebody must have withheld
evidence concerning drinking. That could have been at the instigation of
one or more members of the board, with or without the knowledge and
connivance of the government. Cameron continued by rejecting the
claim of the minister, Don Chipp, that members who now raised the
subject were pursuing the dead. 'Nothing is improper which leads, or
which may lead, to the discovery of the persons or the methods responsible for the deaths of others.'

It seemed that every politician who could claim even the most
tenuous connection with naval affairs wished to be part of the debate. For
me, it was a surreal, almost out-of-body experience looking down on the
nation's elected representatives as they bandied my name and reputation
about in a tableau of political point-scoring.

William McMahon, the Treasurer, was next to rise and address the
House. McMahon had served as Minister for the Navy at the time of the
Korean War and was not held in much respect by officers with whom I
served on board *Sydney* after she returned. They were less than impressed
when he addressed the crew as 'Ladies and Gentlemen' and then entreated
them to appreciate that he had sacrificed Christmas with his family to be
able to visit them in the war zone. Getting quickly into stride, McMahon
was pleased to reiterate that Smyth had considered me an unreliable and
uncorroborated witness. He then proceeded to a direct attack on me,

saying that I had been twice grounded for crashing my aircraft and twice resigned because I was dissatisfied and disenchanted with the Navy. 'All this shows the attitude of the man whose evidence is now substantially relied upon.'

McMahon soon shifted the focus of his assault on to Ted St John's speech, claiming to deplore it. Singling out Ted's reference to the blood alcohol reading from the body of Able Seaman Parker, McMahon illustrated his total ignorance of its significance by highlighting the fact that Parker had no duty on the night of the accident. Those who serve at sea do not clock off and go home at the end of their watch. Every man on board a warship in emergency circumstances is immediately on duty for damage control purposes. That was the entire reasoning behind my strict control of alcohol consumption at sea and Commander Willis's support for it. What was left unsaid was that if Stevens had shared our view, maybe none of this drama would have happened.

The debate was adjourned, yet again, at 5.20 p.m. Sue and I met Jess, St John and Cameron in the King's Hall to discuss progress, knowing that the Prime Minister was scheduled to speak during the evening session. We were suddenly interrupted by a man with whom I was not familiar, who said, 'Mr Cabban, you've won! There is going to be a royal commission.' I begged his pardon but he went on, 'I have just spoken to Sir Frank Packer, and he has told the Prime Minister that if he does not hold a royal commission, he will bring the government down.' Ted St John identified this prophet as Alan Reid, doyen of the parliamentary press gallery. Reid was the chief political correspondent of the *Daily Telegraph*, which was then owned by Packer.

'There's just one catch,' Reid continued. 'McMahon's going to drop a bucket on you after dinner, and if you break down, the deal's off!' The bottom fell out of my world as I tried to face the implications of what had just been said. Experience had shown me that absolutely anything could be said in the House under privilege. A person's reputation may be shamelessly traduced without recourse to right of reply. I had heard myself being praised and vilified as if I were not there, and had heard the lies of Sir Alan McNicoll, Captain Willis and Lieutenant Commander Griffith repeated to my detriment. I cannot recall speaking a word after Reid's casual revelation, but vividly recall being unable to eat when taken by John Jess to the Hotel Canberra for dinner. I excused myself and asked

Sue to walk me back around Parliament House so that I could pull myself together. My imagination ranged feverishly over a horror list of false accusations to be levelled at me and the damage they would do to me and the family.

Returning to King's Hall, Sue and I found that Ted had secured us seats in the Speaker's Gallery, on the floor of the chamber, directly behind the cabinet benches. As we were moving towards the gallery, we were passed by a large group of uniformed naval officers led by McNicoll and including Captain John Goble, previously my commanding officer of 817 Squadron, and Bruce Loxton, promoted to captain since I had left *Voyager*. I greeted them by name but was treated to scowls of disapproval. They were obviously there as visible support for the Prime Minister, but I doubted whether anyone was impressed or intimidated by their presence.

At 8.45 p.m. Harold Holt entered the debate, first in praise of the Navy and then in support of Sir Robert Menzies' conduct in regard to the inquiry and its attitude to both captains. The Prime Minister then punctiliously supported Spicer, Smyth and former ministers for the Navy before starting in on me.

> I have no wish to make a personal attack upon Lieutenant Commander Cabban. I believe him to be a conscientious man with a sense of duty, which he has demonstrated with some courage by the way in which he has brought these matters forward. But as my colleague the Treasurer pointed out earlier today, if we are to rely on this statement and build this structure upon that single statement then we cannot ignore some of the elements in the past record or the personal history of the man who makes the statement.

Clyde Cameron interjected, 'So now the Prime Minister will drop the bucket.'

Holt continued:

> Here is a man who, having as a member of the Naval Air Arm, failed to make the grade and, having been twice removed from that posting, sought twice to resign from the Navy; and who in the course of the first application said that he was disillusioned with

the Navy. I think these are relevant facts. I do not wish to over-emphasise them but they are relevant when, I repeat, the basis of the allegations is the statement coming from this man.

That was 'the bucket'. Ancient history, most of which had been ventilated previously. I was relieved that there seemed to be no more.

The Prime Minister then adopted an approach that struck me as both curious and questionable. He read into the record a long and irrelevant sequence of confidential report summaries relating to Stevens and his naval career. A very telling report from his appointment as executive officer of *Melbourne* described him as 'finding it a little difficult being second in command. He is a forceful character with only average brain power, and because of this he is inclined to rush his fences. At present he makes too much noise too frequently to inspire quiet confidence in a carrier.' The next, during the same appointment, said, 'He is inclined to brood over problems.' In January 1964, just weeks before the collision, it was written of him that he was of average intelligence, but 'does not strike me as having great abilities and has probably reached his ceiling'. Towards the conclusion of his speech, the Prime Minister asked, referring to twenty reports on Stevens by senior officers:

Is it reasonable for anybody seriously to believe that the charge could be made that any one of these men, let alone all twenty of them, could be so lacking in a sense of duty and so lacking in a sense of responsibility to seamen under the command of such an officer and going on operational duty with their lives at hazard, that the officers concerned would fail to report some blemish in the character of this man that made him unfit to control a ship or made him a hazard to the lives of the men under his command?

The temptation to shout a resounding 'Yes!' to that was well-nigh irresistible. And all those who have had to serve under alcoholic captains and admirals in the RAN during my years of service would have joined in with a hearty 'Hear, hear!', had they the integrity to stand and be counted. Holt repeated Benson's false suggestion that I did not make a report to a superior officer. He cited the case of an unnamed officer who had done that and subsequently risen to become Chief of Naval Staff.

Holt did not live to appreciate the irony that I had, in fact, reported Stevens to a superior officer who chose to lie about it and not report it further. He, too, became Chief of Naval Staff!

In closing, the Prime Minister conceded that he had yet to have meetings with his colleagues on the matter and was not rejecting a further judicial inquiry or select committee. He said that he expected to report the government's position the following day. The debate was adjourned at 9.35 p.m., and Sue and I were relieved that we could retire for the night, both feeling emotionally and physically drained.

The government's bluster had not been enough to sway public opinion. Jess, St John and Turner demonstrated that there was something rotten in the state of the Royal Australian Navy, and Harold Holt knew that any further attempts at political resistance would be counter-productive. The following day the Prime Minister advised the House that a judicial inquiry would be conducted, probably by three judges, and outlined the probable terms of reference. The Leader of the Opposition, E. G. Whitlam, welcomed the proposed inquiry, but 'only if its terms of reference were wide enough to cover the matters contained in this document [the Cabban Statement]'. Holt agreed. The debate had concluded, and I was now the central figure in a royal commission.

31
Preparing for an Ordeal

What had I done? Against all my better instincts and intentions, former Lieutenant Commander P. T. Cabban would, within a few weeks, be confronting the juggernaut of a royal commission. Me. A minor, self-employed management consultant with a young family, a mortgage and absolutely nothing to gain from the months of gruelling public exposure that lay ahead. I certainly had no desire for either celebrity or martyrdom. My new situation was not of my own making – it was largely the actions of others that had betrayed me into breaking ranks. But there could be no turning back. I believed that all the significant information I had provided to Hickling in the so-called Cabban Statement was fundamentally solid. Duncan Stevens had been palpably unfit to command a vessel at sea. The Royal Australian Navy must have known of his incapacity, yet did nothing to remedy the situation. Eighty-two men were dead. My conscience told me that whatever personal discomfort I might now have to endure, this was the best opportunity we would ever have of getting to the truth of the *Voyager* disaster.

What I did not fully understand, as Sue and I returned to Sydney, was the mountain of work in front of me. Royal commissions are not trials – there are no charges, no plaintiffs or defendants – but they are conducted by judges and barristers, employ the lumbering machinery of the court system and so, inevitably, take on the intensity of adversarial advocacy. As our preparations began, it soon dawned on me that my position would be chillingly similar to that of a person charged with a major crime. Every last detail of the statement I had dictated without notes or references more than two years earlier would now be challenged by a small army of lawyers. It seemed to me rather like the reverse of the normal presumption of innocence: as the principal witness, I would need to prove the truth of my recollections. But corroboration for many of my accounts of key incidents would be hard to obtain. In some, with Stevens dead, I was now the only eyewitness. In others, involving *Voyager*'s officers or other serving RAN personnel, it would be a 'your word against mine' standoff. I was more than grateful to have Ted St John's guidance before the upcoming legal brawl. As a serving parliamentarian Ted could not, of course, appear himself as counsel at the royal commission, but his knowledge, contacts and forensic skills proved invaluable. Meanwhile, I still had to earn a living and meet my clients' needs. They showed an enormous amount of goodwill to me at the time and, assisted by Sophia Leung's growing understanding of the practice, I was able to partly fulfil my obligations.

It is tempting to view all courtroom sagas through the prism of Hollywood cliché: flashy cross-examination, tearful witnesses and astonishing last-minute breakthroughs. The reality is much slower, but far more interesting. The months of the second royal commission became perhaps the dominant chapter of my life, so it is useful here to offer some insights into our preparation for those long days of hearings. From the outset, the need for more compelling evidence in support of my allegations was urgent. Ted was delighted when Sue produced two personal tape recordings that I had sent to her from *Voyager*, soon after the Subic Bay incident in June 1963. We played them back, and Ted exclaimed, 'These are pure gold!' On my return from the Snowy after the collision, with total irrationality, I had collected every one of the message tapes that Sue had saved and set about wiping them all clean on the tape recorder. Alarmed by my behaviour, Sue had secretly taken two of the tapes while I was distracted and hidden them. Her instinctive action was nothing short of inspired, and was destined to be of vital importance to us in the coming months.

The choice of my legal representatives during the royal commission was crucial, and again Ted St John's advice proved to be invaluable. He explained that the accepted sequence of events in complex legal matters is first to engage the services of a solicitor who, in turn, would advise a barrister who, in turn again, would brief senior counsel if appropriate. There was no doubt that my role as the central witness required representation by a 'silk' (as QCs are known), but Ted was adamant that my survival would principally be determined by our choice of junior counsel. Chester Porter was, without question, the barrister-at-law whom he wanted to represent me. The youngest lawyer to be called to the New South Wales Bar at the time of his entry into the profession, Chester had earned spectacular early acclaim when he proved to the McDermott royal commission, as junior counsel to Jack Shand KC, that an innocent man was serving time for murder, and secured his release. It would be left to Chester to confer with Ted in the selection of which silk to approach, and then the two barristers would choose a solicitor.

My first interview with Chester Porter in St John's chambers in Phillip Street, Sydney, was brief and to the point. Asking me only one question, he was satisfied by my instant response and agreed to represent me. A range of possible QCs was nominated and discussed on the basis of availability and suitability. My advisers now knew the likely composition of the opposing legal teams and the identities of the government's nominated judges and counsel assisting them. I was told that J.T. Hiatt QC had agreed to an interview. If we liked each other, he would represent me.

Jack Hiatt seemed a very imposing figure when I met him in his chambers with Chester and Ted. Again, I was asked only one question, and as quickly as I responded he said, 'I'll take you!' We shook hands, and the choice of solicitor was then made: the firm of Gordon L. Beard & McDonald. This provided me with a four-man team, as Gordon Beard and Tony McDonald could alternate daily in court attendance while attending to their other clients without detriment to my needs. I felt that my legal fortunes were in good hands. Chester was described by Ted as 'the best tactician at the Bar', and they both agreed that Jack was 'the best strategist at the Bar'. The greatest compliment I have ever been paid was the faith shown in me by this team of advisers when they assured me that they would undertake my representation without charging me a fee, despite the fact that they estimated the commission would occupy them full-time for six months. This undertaking was a considerable sacrifice on their part. It was also the only way I could have been properly represented, as I had no resources to meet the fees.

Jack and Chester planned the underlying approach – the strategy that was to be adopted and then relentlessly pursued on my behalf throughout the proceedings. Fundamental to their position was the acceptance that we could never hope to match the resources at the government's disposal. We assumed that there would be considerable sharing of information between the Navy legal team and those representing the Stevens family. The situation in relation to the Robertson camp was more problematic. Our interests did not precisely coincide when considered against the terms of the inquiry. Whereas our overriding concern was to establish the truth of the Cabban Statement, Robertson's lawyers only sought a variation of the findings of the first royal commission to the extent that *Melbourne*'s captain would be cleared of any fault in the collision. Put bluntly, Robertson – having done everything in his power to force the new inquiry – could now sit back and let others do the hazardous work of proving that Stevens had been unfit to command *Voyager*.

The terms of reference for the Royal Commission of Inquiry into the Allegations of Lieutenant Commander Cabban and Matters Incidental Thereto had been promulgated as:

1 Whether any of the allegations made by Lieutenant Commander P. T. Cabban in the document attached to the Letters Patent regarding the drinking habits and seamanship of Captain D. H. Stevens were true and being true established that Captain Stevens was unfit to retain command of HMAS *Voyager*?
2 If it is found in answer to question 1 that Captain Stevens was unfit to retain command of HMAS *Voyager*
   (a) Did the Naval Board know or ought they to have known of such unfitness to retain command and were they at fault in failing to relieve him of command?
   (b) Should the findings made in the report of the royal commission relating to the loss of HMAS *Voyager* be varied, and if so, in what respect?
3 Whether the allegations in the document disclosed evidence which was available to counsel assisting the royal commission and was improperly withheld from the royal commission?

Three commissioners were appointed by the same letters patent, of which the terms constitute a part. They were Sir Stanley Charles Burbury, chief justice of the Supreme Court of Tasmania, chairman; Kenneth William Asprey, a judge of the Supreme Court of New South Wales; and Geoffrey George Lucas, a judge of the Supreme Court of Queensland. Leading counsel assisting the commission was F. T. P. Burt QC, assisted by

Philip Jeffrey. Others appearing were W. P. Ash QC, with John Sinclair for the Stevens family; Peter Murphy QC, with Humphrey Henchman for the Navy; R. G. Reynolds QC and E. P. T. Raine for Captain Robertson; and W. H. Gregory for Lieutenant Price. Secretary to the commission was R. H. Wineberg.

The three royal commissioners each had 'form' that was notorious around the Bar. Sir Stanley Burbury was famous as Solicitor-General in the prosecution of Professor Orr for his affair with Suzanne Kemp at the University of Tasmania. Justice George Lucas was the judge in the case against Nancy Young, a woman wrongly convicted (and later pardoned) for the manslaughter of her daughter, Evelyn. Justice Kenneth Asprey was well known to all of my legal advisers, and they assured me I could expect him to attend closely to the government's interests in the case.

Suffice it to say we did not look to the bench for much comfort, but in the counsel for the Crown we had total faith. Francis 'Red' Burt was a well-credentialled and successful criminal prosecutor in Western Australia. Both Jack Hiatt and Chester spoke highly of his ability and integrity. That confidence in his sense of justice led us to the most critical decision taken by our team: we agreed to share with the Crown every piece of information we had, or would uncover, during the inquiry – whether it helped our position or not. We handed over my correspondence with Admiral Hickling, including a letter in which he asked how a man, as I had described him, could be promoted captain in the RAN. In reply, I assured Hickling that I could name admirals and other senior officers who were notoriously in the same category. We also gave Burt a letter I had received from my former Hong Kong friends, then living in the Netherlands, responding to my request for a written account of their recollections of the party aboard *Voyager* just before we left. In the reply I was asked what incidents I would like them to address, as their memories were not perhaps sufficiently sharp to satisfy my needs. I wrote back saying I required only their most accurate and detailed first-hand descriptions of anything that they could recall without my prompting. It was later left to me to nominate one of the four witnesses to be offered passage to Sydney to testify. We chose Piet Liebenschutz.

As soon as he was established in an office, counsel assisting the commission contacted Jack Hiatt asking for us to meet for an initial conference and briefing. Mr Burt, as I always thought and spoke of him, impressed me with his forthright and friendly manner. He gave not the slightest hint of intimidation, and I had no trouble telling him the genesis of my statement and the history of my service career. I had been told that he served with distinction as an RAAF pilot in World War II, and this fitted his impeccable demeanour and bearing. It was a long conference, and I was asked to repeat in detail my descriptions of many of the crucial incidents described in my original statement. The lawyers pressed me repeatedly for any leads they could follow to help corroborate my assertions. At the end of the meeting I was asked, through Jack and Chester, to make a formal statement, witnessed by my solicitor. The extended interview had helped order my memory, and I was eventually able to produce a coherent sequence of events and conversations that I could recall with clarity and confidence. This statement was then dissected minutely to ensure there were no contradictions, omissions or errors in fact that might be established before submission. The eventual precision of this statement underlined for me the huge difference between a properly prepared legal document and the improvised account of events I had dictated for Admiral Hickling back in January 1965. Eventually a statement of forty-seven pages was presented to Mr Burt, and at the end of the inquiry it was tendered as exhibit 182.

Any and all evidence to which I might have access was noted, and plans were made to obtain it. This involved attempting to locate witnesses and arrange interviews. I was enlisted to approach those I knew and could contact directly. Disappointment was frequent as many who knew the truth found compelling and personal reasons to lie or dissemble. I listened with mounting anger to blatant denials of the events of 1963. It was difficult to believe that so many husbands had never discussed *Voyager* in letters home or face to face with their families on leave. The apparent destruction of correspondence from that period seemed to verge on the hysterical – much like my irrational wiping of tapes.

During the early days of preparation my input was central to the entire activity. We generally worked very long hours, and many evenings saw us still poring over documents well after midnight. Chester, whose home was on the northern beaches peninsula of Sydney, had another forty-minute drive each way beyond my home, yet never once complained. The lawyers were quite skilful at avoiding the attentions of the media, but our home address and telephone number were, however, in the public domain. Cabban is not a common surname, and I received many un-solicited letters of both support and abuse, as well as occasional phone calls. One distressing call came from the anonymous wife of an alcoholic, sobbing as she spoke, telling me that I had described her husband in my statement.

Children have little or no defence against the cowardly attacks of other children, reflecting the views and fibre of their parents, and my sons suffered physical and verbal abuse from bullies at school and while travel-ling. To their credit they did not make me aware of this until years later, but it seems they usually gave as good as they got in defending my name. Sue protected Sally, who was only seven, by walking her to and from school daily. Ted St John alerted me quite early during this period that there was a tap on our telephone line.

Early one morning during the inquiry I received a call from a switch-board operator at Navy Office. The young woman was distressed and weeping as she told me that she had been unable to reach Jack Hiatt and was desperate to inform us of a conversation she had overheard between Admiral McNicoll and an officer identified by nickname. She claimed that officer was instructed to convey instructions to counsel for the Navy to effectively corrupt the judges. I wrote down every detail in duplicate, gave a copy to Sue in case I had a mishap, and drove to the city and gave my copy to Jack, who in turn gave it to Mr Burt. He was told that my information was correct. Counsel for the Navy, Peter Murphy QC, had refused his instructions from that officer and informed the judges.

Our solicitor, Tony McDonald, was tireless in seeking evidence throughout the period before and during the inquiry, particularly in locating potential witnesses and obtaining their statements. The state-ments of survivors of *Voyager* were made available to us, and a thorough perusal of them by Chester provided valuable background material. Although there were only two surviving men who had been on the bridge of *Voyager* at the time of collision, it was important to be prepared for anything that might arise. While I provided background on potential witnesses with whom I had served, Hiatt and Porter commenced inter-viewing and evaluating those who were produced by the solicitors, but I was never present.

Throughout this period it was hard to avoid being concerned that four highly trained lawyers were expending an enormous amount of time and effort on my behalf, but with little prospect of payment. Finally, the Attorney-General informed the commission that the Crown, at a standard daily rate, would reimburse the fees and associated costs of all who were approved to represent parties to the inquiry. My legal team could face the coming months without worrying about their bank managers.

Although I was now scrupulously avoiding any contact with the media, it was inevitable, as the start of the commission's hearings drew nearer, that 'Peter Cabban' had become a public figure. There was no doubt my state of emotional tension was worsening. When I presented a paper to the annual conference of the Australian Hospitals Association, I felt nervous and had difficulty concentrating. I caught myself wondering whether the audience would have preferred to hear me describe the events of 1963 rather than the operational patterns of the Crown Street Hospital's Outpatient Department. Underlying this unease was the growing conviction that I did not have a sufficiently detailed and reliable recall of events to carry me through the royal commission hearings. I might let everyone down.

With now only days to go, Jack and Chester made it abundantly clear to me that I must be prepared, both mentally and physically, for a real ordeal as a witness. The challenge was not just the exhaustive examination and cross-examination but also the sheer length of the sittings. They predicted that the hearings would stretch to four months or more. No date for reporting had been specified by the government. I was touched by the lawyers' concern, but was not motivated to begin an exercise program. My worries were all about my memory.

Dr Bernie Amos, the Director of Medical Services at the Royal North Shore Hospital, offered me advice for which I have always remained grateful. Dr Amos said that many doctors spend a great deal of time in court as witnesses and understand the most important aspects of the role. 'When you are asked a question, think carefully of the answer to that question, then reply, only answering that precise question, nothing more or less. Don't attempt to answer until you are ready. If you need more time, ask for the question to be repeated.' My advisers in Phillip Street had already tutored me on answering only the question being asked, and not to give a 'free kick' to examiners by anticipating the following question or going into unnecessary detail. A worse mistake was trying to answer a question that had not actually been asked but might have been implied. Bernie's advice rounded off my understanding of what I had been told by Jack and Chester. It would be of critical importance when I was under cross-examination by Peter Murphy QC, representing the Navy.

When the final day of preparation had ended, I lay awake and faced the fact that I must confront my fears for my memory once and for all. The coming days would see me required to respond accurately to untold questions covering every minute of a period of more than twelve months, three to four years ago. They would be posed in a hostile atmosphere, in a carefully contrived manner, designed to catch me out in the slightest falsehood or inaccuracy. Looking through the bedroom window at the moonlit sky, I began to analyse the situation and consider what I could do to control it. A dependable memory is at the core of sanity itself, and I had to look at my own memory in a clinically detached way. Veracity can be established only when memory is tested and found to be reliable. A person might have a general memory of something, but without the recollection of specific supporting details that memory is next to useless. The value of the whole royal commission would substantially hinge on my capacity for accurate recall. If the human brain operates as a computer, it should logically be possible to retrieve every experience. All that I needed to establish was the correct recall mechanism. What should I do next? Perhaps a first step might be to identify some significant experience or fact associated with *Voyager* of which I was generally aware but could no longer recall in specific terms.

To begin the experiment, I cast my mind back to very recent times. While working with Perini I had been asked to devise a means of cleaning a multistorey crane support, which was smeared with oil and grease. Proposing a solution required the nomination of a suitable detergent agent. The detergent I wanted to propose had been commonly used in the RAN for oil spills and grease removal, yet only weeks after leaving the Navy I could not remember its name. A quick call to Naval Stores soon elicited the brand, but after procuring a quantity in 1964, I had forgotten the name again and could not recall it in 1967. That lapse was to be my focus for trying to establish a recall mechanism. Closing my eyes to assist concentration seemed a good starting point, but immediately I became aware of distracting light through my eyelids, even tightly closed. I needed to 'project black', or create a total absence of light. How to do this? Concentration was out of the question. The moment I began concentrating, a myriad of unanswered questions and confusing thoughts would flood into my mind. What was needed was the antithesis of concentration. I had to divorce my body and mind from all sensation and allow my brain alone to be receptive. I relaxed each limb in turn and banished awareness of it, then my body, then everything.

At the instant that I was totally detached from sensation, utter black was at the centre of my awareness, and simultaneously I felt and heard a distinct popping as if tiny valves had sprung up in my brain. Right across my vision in large flaming, solid gold, three-dimensional block letters was the word GAMLEN – the forgotten brand of detergent. I opened my eyes and said very softly, 'Thank God!' and fell into a deep sleep. At no time after that did I question my memory. Years later, and with some trepidation, I made one or two feeble attempts to repeat this 'projecting black' process but abandoned them as my reason told me to let it go. Do not interfere with something that was given when it was most needed.

PART 4

32

The Cabban Statement

The first working day of the royal commission – proceedings that would swiftly come to dominate my every waking hour – was almost entirely devoted to a long opening address by Counsel Assisting the Commission, Francis Burt QC. It was his job to clarify the format of the inquiry and how the hearings would differ from the normal adversarial patterns of a courtroom trial. He also outlined what he considered the appropriate scope of the commission in relation to its terms of reference and the general approach he intended to take to witnesses and written evidence. More than 150 witnesses had already been interviewed by commission officers and that number would inevitably grow as the proceedings continued. The truth or otherwise of my statement was to be the centre of enquiries. I was to be examined first, followed by witnesses to my position regarding the original inquiry. Medical evidence concerning Captain Stevens would then be called. To short-cut the task of reviewing 5,000 pages of transcripts, a condensed volume of extracts from the most obviously pertinent evidence heard by the Spicer Commission in 1964 was circulated to all parties.

As his detailed four-hour exposition unfolded, I formed the view that 'Red' Burt was clearly a dedicated, conscientious and fair-minded man resolved to extract the truth of the matter as far as it could be determined within the legal constraints of the inquiry. Despite all his customary deference to the bench, Burt was nevertheless quite forcefully staking out the precise dimensions of the battlefield on which he intended the coming war of words to be conducted. It was an impressive opening stanza and my confidence in counsel assisting grew by the minute. He demonstrated that his review of the first commission had been thorough and incisive. He went directly to the key issues and questions now to be resolved, and showed an awareness of the unique circumstances the inquiry would have to explore. And, if I had any doubt that this might not become a real 'gloves off' fight, then Burt allayed those fears within minutes.

Counsel assisting had a bombshell. He told the commission that all six copies of the report of proceedings of *Voyager* for March 1963 – the crucial Navy documents that would corroborate many of my assertions – had disappeared. Every RAN ship submitted its monthly report of proceedings (and multiple copies) to fleet headquarters and, ultimately, to the Naval Board for review and filing. These reports contained a detailed record of all official calls made by the captain, exercises conducted, movements of the ship from place to place, names of ships in company and any other details considered important as an account of the ship's activities. Burt allowed himself a subtle touch of sarcasm when he told the judges, 'It may seem to be surprising that all copies of the report of proceedings of HMAS *Voyager* for the somewhat critical month of March 1963 have been mislaid.' Surprising indeed, especially alongside the equally remarkable loss of *Voyager*'s deck log for the month of June 1963, also by the Navy Office. It remains my opinion that these unprecedented disappearances were the result of deliberate action.

As if to gently underline this unspoken theme of convenient omissions, Burt then moved to an outline of the circumstances under which I had not been called as a witness at the first royal commission, despite being interviewed by both the police and Smyth QC. Viewed in hindsight, Burt conceded that his brother counsel had clearly been in error and that the decision not to examine me publicly before Spicer was either negligent or incompetent. Nevertheless, he did not believe it likely that this commission would find my evidence had been improperly withheld. I was being introduced to the law's seemingly endless capacity to find fine distinctions not immediately apparent to the layman.

In relation to the absolutely key question of what actually constituted 'fitness to command', counsel assisting turned to a less-than-useful precedent involving fraud and crime, and made the revealing comment that he was not implying that Stevens was guilty of 'any matter that can be described as conveying any degree of moral turpitude'. Instead, Burt dwelt on the known medical history of the captain and linked the combined effects of liquor and an ulcer condition on performance. He was foreshadowing the argument that illness alone could reflect on fitness to command, and that the extent to which illness may have been covered up fell within the terms of the inquiry.

Burt took considerable pains to emphasise my various endeavours (at my own expense) to protect Duncan Stevens' name and reputation, at least until the time that evidence of the triple brandy and blood alcohol findings had been publicly reported. His intention was clearly to pre-emptively undermine any suggestion that I was conducting a 'vendetta' against the Navy and the dead captain, as had been suggested by the minister and others in parliament. Regrettably, this honourable action of Burt's on the opening day of proceedings did nothing to dissuade the Navy and the Stevens interests from repeatedly pursuing the 'revenge' line in the months to come. He also patiently led the three judges through his approach to hearsay evidence, much of which would lead directly to many of my assertions in the Cabban Statement. He argued that the general trial-law test of hearsay (that it required corroboration from at least one other independent source to be considered reliable or relevant) should generally apply, but that the special circumstances of the *Voyager* disaster might entail some relaxation of this rule. The sad truth was that many of those who did, or could, corroborate my statement had perished in the collision.

Which led us to the statement itself, the very core of this new inquiry. Up to now, the transcription of my recollections recorded on John Robertson's machine for Vice Admiral Hickling had been suppressed by an order prohibiting publication. The chairman had already announced his decision to lift that prohibition. It was clearly ludicrous to deny public access to the material which had prompted the royal commission. At Burt's invitation, Junior Counsel Assisting the Commission, Philip Jeffrey, rose and read onto the record every one of the thirty-six numbered paragraphs of my statement. The words that I'd dictated late at night without any recourse to a diary or notes would now become our 'text for the day' for the next four months.

CONFIDENTIAL

1. My name is Cabban. I joined *Voyager* in September 1962, as Executive Officer, three days after Commander A.A. Willis took

command and soon after we commenced the work-up. There were several new officers including the Navigating Officer, the Gunnery Officer, the Captain and myself and the Engineer Officer. At the end of the work-up we were a reasonably well-knit team although Captain Stevens described the wardroom team subsequently as the most depressed group of officers he had ever seen. And the reason for this is important. When I joined *Voyager*, the day I joined, my predecessor carried on drinking with the officers until 3 in the afternoon. I had just left *Sydney* where I served as Executive Officer from the time of standing by till the conversion to troop carrier and I had insisted in *Sydney* that there would be no drinking at sea. Subsequently with Commander Willis's complete support, I insisted that there should be no drinking at sea in *Voyager*, and I also revised the bar hours in harbour and insisted on 100% adherence to these hours except with Captain's or my direct permission and in our presence. These were not popular orders and they required firm discipline to maintain. However, shortly after Captain Stevens joining, two protests were lodged by the Engineer Officer, who was an Acting Commander, and the Supply Officer, a Lieutenant Commander, and I represented these protests to the Captain and he supported them to the extent of saying that he saw no objection to officers who had no watch and who had no direct contact with the ship's company having 'a beer' in the evening. I should mention here that it was customary for the ship's company to be allowed to purchase a 26-ounce can of beer on most nights when no exercises took place. This didn't in any way affect my attitude towards officers drinking. I made it quite clear in the wardroom that this was the Captain's ruling and officers were free to abide by it as far as they wished but I still disapproved of any seaman officer drinking under any circumstances.

2. Subsequently, none of the seaman officers drank at any time at sea with the exception of a Gunner who joined the other two, and although they were quite open with me that they disagreed, the remainder were very loyal officers and supported me to the end. They were also kind enough when I left the ship to say that although they had disagreed with me at the beginning, they thought I had been right.

3. During the work–up, Commander Willis had expressed the opinion quite strongly, that the Navigating Officer was a poor ship handler. This is important because Captain Stevens on the first occasion that he took *Voyager* alongside collided with *Vampire* and subsequently rarely, if ever, handled the ship personally again, in my time onboard, entering or leaving harbour, leaving it to Lieutenant Griffith on almost every occasion. On two occasions I handled it leaving harbour and entering harbour in the Far East. And on the last occasion that I left harbour in a ship, which was from Sydney to Melbourne I was given command. At that time I thought of it as a very generous gesture although the Captain was visibly affected by alcohol, on this occasion the time being 0800.

4. In his other ship handling, Captain Stevens was inconsistent. His station keeping ability was extremely good and most officers would have been proud of it. But his handling was inclined to be affected by his temperament. On one notable occasion *Voyager* was taking *Ark Royal* in tow and almost collided by passing under the flight deck of *Ark Royal* just clearing our main mast, and then in a fit of pique when the tow took too long to take up he rang on revolutions for 10 knots with disastrous effects; parting the tow at the risk of all on the quarterdeck. This was a rather ugly piece of seamanship in the face of the Fleet.

5. On another occasion, when taking station on *Rothesay* for a transfer, we overshot and roared in between her and the ship behind, which was at standard distance, missing them by the narrowest of margins with no credit.

6. He was subject to violent outbursts at the Officer of the Watch if he was either slow to react or if he made a mistake. Towards the end of the cruise the Officers of the Watch were able to cope with this but they were a little disconcerted earlier on. This extended even to abuse of Officers of the Watch over the armament broadcast from the operations room.

7. In defence of Captain Stevens, he didn't consider that this should be taken seriously by officers after the event. He expected them to

learn and then forget the tone in which he spoke. This took quite a bit of learning.

8. His temperament could range from buoyant good humour to depression when sober. He showed flashes of very fine leadership ability and I had the impression most of the time that the ship's company thought he was a very good captain. I may have been naïve in this, for subsequently, after the loss of the ship, there was none of this respect reflected in the survivors to whom I spoke, to my great surprise.

9. Captain Stevens was a good athlete, particularly for his age; opening the bowling for the ship's company. The ship was the cricket champion of the Fleet (he was also a reasonable bat and a good fielder) and he was a good squash player, again, for his age.

10. I will now deal with the factors concerning Captain Stevens' drinking habits during the time that I served with him.

11. The first real flash I had of understanding Captain Stevens' drinking ability or habits was in our farewell party in Sydney where it was necessary for his wife to tell him publicly that it was time to leave.

12. When the ship proceeded to sea, the Captain told me that he was ill, not having been to sea for some time, so I had command for the first twenty four hours, *Vampire*, who was the senior ship present, being informed by signal at the Captain's instructions.

13. During the period in the Far East the situation became more than trying, it was quite desperate, as he drank for very long periods in harbour until he became violently ill and then would spend days in bed being treated by the doctor and his steward until he was fit to again start drinking.

14. Captain Stevens drank brandy almost exclusively, but he was at times known to drink beer or whiskey.

15. I became very anxious about the way things were developing and uncertain where to turn for advice. The Captain of the flagship was Captain R.I. Peek, who had been my captain when I was

Executive Officer of HMAS *Sydney*. Captain Peek received me when I called on him with my Captain's permission in Hong Kong, and most strange for him, he required me to remain standing. He was pleasant, formal, he asked me very briefly how the ship was and then I left. I had lost any opportunity I might have had to seek his advice simply because I felt instinctively that he knew and didn't want me to put myself into an impossible position.

16. It was an extremely trying period and this stage was climaxed by the Captain's birthday on which he was invited to a mess dinner as the guest of the mess. This was the first time on which he was invited in this manner and he arrived, although I had been warned ten minutes before that he had been drinking, completely under the influence but able to walk. It was obviously necessary for us to proceed with the dinner as quickly as possible if he was to last it, but unfortunately, before anything else could be done, he got on his hands and knees and crawled across the mess to the table. Before soup had finished, I had to stand, make a brief speech, and take him from the mess, with the present the mess had bought him, to his cabin. The officers and stewards were outstandingly loyal on this occasion and a word of this incident never reached the Fleet to my knowledge.

17. This pattern continued but it reached a climax during the visit to Tokyo. In Tokyo, the Captain became worse to a degree we hadn't seen before and on two occasions I took him (one accompanied by the Engineer Officer) to steam baths to get him fit to deal with his social engagements at lunch time. One, a lunch with a Japanese Admiral. But to little avail. He was carried from Captain Dollard's home after he had disgraced himself there. I've learned subsequently from Captain Robertson that he had in fact been sick all over the place on this occasion at Captain Dollard's home. And on the Sunday, which was the fourth day in Tokyo, he sent for me at 0630 to inform me that he would be unable to attend the church service that morning and I was to inform Captain Willis to this effect. The Captain when I saw him had his head on a pillow with a towel over it. The towel was soaked in vomit. I asked if I should get the doctor because he looked wretchedly sick, and he said 'no'.

I saw the doctor and the doctor said he wouldn't treat him – that he had warned the Captain that this would happen – and that it was his opinion that should the Captain rupture his ulcer at sea the Captain would die.

18. I went on board *Vampire* and informed Captain Willis of the Captain's condition and his message and of the doctor's opinion and explained my worry on the Captain's behalf. Captain Willis asked me to send the doctor to him, which I did, and he then went on board *Voyager* and went to the Captain's cabin where he spoke to him. Nobody else was present when Captain Willis spoke to Captain Stevens but during the next two months Captain Stevens did not have a single drink, and that covered the period between Tokyo and Sydney, which was quite a remarkable feat.

19. There was one other incident, which I should mention in this period, of which Mr. Smyth was informed. It was a Captain's lunch in Hong Kong to which Captain Stevens was invited, attended by the Captains of all RN ships present at the time. On this occasion a signal arrived in *Voyager* during the lunch hour, to say, 'YOUR CAPTAIN HAS PASSED OUT AND WILL BE RETURNED TO YOU WHEN HE IS FIT'. I replied, asking was a doctor required and the reply came back, 'NO'. The captain did subsequently come back, said nothing and went straight to his cabin. I learned from Commander T.P. Irwin RN the Engineer Officer of *Rothesay* that the Captain had passed out on the wardroom deck of *Rothesay*, and the Captains present wanted to send him back to his ship in the condition he was, immediately. They were absolutely disgusted and considered that he was unfit to be there. Commander Irwin prevailed on them to allow him to place Captain Stevens in his cabin until he was fit to go back and they reluctantly allowed him to do this but offered no assistance. This indicated the feeling of the Fleet at this time.

20. Following the return to Sydney, Captain Stevens arrived on board every morning that I was there at approximately 0800 very heavily under the influence of alcohol, told me that I had command and went to his cabin and retired for the day. He was wakened by

his steward at 1600. He commenced drinking again and carried on ashore as soon as he had sufficient to get going. I submitted my resignation at this time and he was genuinely distressed at this and was surprised. My decision was not as a direct result of his conduct nor do I think it was greatly influenced by it, although any last temptation I may have had to remain in the service at this stage was dispelled by this performance. Captain Stevens did not come onto the bridge after the ship left Sydney Harbour until it was ready to enter Port Phillip Bay. I had command of the ship for that stretch as well, while he lay in his bunk.

21. I'm sorry, I completely omitted the fact that immediately following our departure from Tokyo, Captain Stevens told me that I had command of the ship for the next five days. That he wouldn't be coming from his cabin and my command was complete, and I was to inform all the officers but not to send any signals indicating my command. He directed me that he was not to be disturbed on any account by anybody and this is exactly what happened. We were with the British Far East Fleet and running before a typhoon carrying out exercises.

22. During this period the ship was engaged in an intensive exercise program which included no fewer than five refuellings or transfers and was under the close eye of the RN flagship, *Lion*. The ship's company, and the officers for that matter, were informed by me that the Captain was ill and were given no inkling of any other reason for the Captain's absence. The ship performed well and I was exceptionally proud of the conduct of the officers during this period. As I have said earlier, they were sympathetic to the Captain, considering him a sick man, and incredibly loyal.

23. Following the ship's arrival in Williamstown, the Captain spent very little time on board with me, our leaves being taken at different times. However, he returned to the ship after the court-martial of Captain Dovers of HMAS *Sydney*, on which he had been a court member together with Captain Robertson. And he travelled by train from Sydney with Commander B.H. Loxton RAN, Captain of HMAS *Parramatta* at that time. (Correction, he was Captain of *Yarra*,

which was on the opposite side of the dock from us). Commander Loxton informed me that Captain Stevens had drunk a bottle of brandy on the train on the way down. This statement didn't surprise me in the least. When I saw the Captain in his cabin, having missed him on the gangway, he expressed regret that I hadn't met him and was obviously well advanced on a bottle of brandy. At 1600, his steward came into the mess and asked for another bottle of brandy for the Captain. I knew that the first bottle had been full and asked if he had finished that, and the steward said, 'Yes'. At 1900, I called into the Captain's cabin to see if he was all right and he had half consumed this, which would have been his third bottle of brandy since leaving Sydney on the previous night. The next morning the steward came for me from the Captain to say that he was sick and I found the Captain in the usual condition with a very vomit-soaked towel under his head, looking dreadful. He said that he was very sick and to send the Leading Sick Berth Attendant to him as it would be about a week before he was on deck again. This was a fairly accurate assessment as he was in fact inside his cabin for the next seven days, although he was able to start drinking brandy again on the fourth day, taking it very gently. At this stage we had a new ship's company of recruits and it was important that they shouldn't have this knowledge of their Captain. Unfortunately, the stewards were new and I didn't know if I could rely entirely on their discretion and loyalty. However, at the time I had no indication that this didn't prevail.

24. Mr. Smyth asked me in his chambers in Phillip Street, in the office near where the inquiry was held, at what time Captain Stevens started drinking and I replied that if he was having one of his periods of drinking he would have brandy in his coffee at breakfast time and go steadily on from then. This is not an exaggeration but it is applied, as I say, to the periods when he was drinking. On these occasions when he drank he was inclined to become under the influence very quickly and he drank very large glasses of alcohol. His standard brandy on these occasions would be almost half a tumbler full of brandy topped up with water.

25. I was called to Mr. Smyth's rooms, after I had been interviewed by Commonwealth Police, as I was the senior officer who had

served in *Voyager* in the previous twelve months surrounding and in Australian waters. I was asked almost exclusively questions concerning the drinking habits of Captain Stevens and I replied to the questions I was asked, giving most of the story eventually that I have just outlined, perhaps even adding more instances which don't help at this stage. I was very anxious at this stage because I knew Captain Stevens didn't drink at sea, only in harbour, while I served with him. And I repeatedly stressed this to Mr. Smyth, who assured me that all was well and he understood this. I didn't want any slur on Captain Stevens' name. I was quite convinced that under no circumstances would he ever drink at sea. I had taken the precaution even of informing my successor, Lieutenant Commander Macgregor, of the Captain's drinking habit and also stressing to him most strongly, the necessity for the officers in the wardroom not to drink at sea because of the Captain's habit. He replied that he was capable of making his own decision and I have good reason to believe that all the officers in fact drank at sea following my succession. Perhaps this was a perfectly healthy reaction following my autocratic rule. However, I would stress that of the officers in the wardroom when I left, only one seaman officer, Lieutenant Dowling, who was killed, and the Electrical Officer, Commander Tapp, who was killed, had served in the ship in the Far East under Captain Stevens.

26. The work-up was planned under my co-ordination by the Staff Officers who left the ship, so that Captain Stevens, while approving the work-up had not planned it and had not carried out a work-up with these officers, or in the ship at all.

27. To come back to Mr. Smyth. When Mr. Smyth was questioning me, I asked him straight out if he was trying to infer that Captain Stevens was drunk at the time of the collision. He asked why I questioned this; I said I had heard rumours to this effect, which I had from unexpected sources, and I said I wanted to make it quite clear that Captain Stevens would not drink at sea. Mr. Smyth said that was clearly understood. When I was leaving Mr. Smyth's office, which was after an interview lasting almost an hour, he said, 'We'll be seeing a lot of you at the inquiry.'

28. Now, subsequent to this, I thought it was important that, if Mr. Smyth was going to call me and wanted me to give this kind of evidence, and believing that Captain Stevens wouldn't drink at sea, that it was in the interest of his relatives that my statement should be known equally to them as well as Mr. Smyth. So through my own solicitor, I arranged to meet Mr. Osborne, who was the solicitor briefing Captain Stevens' relatives' counsel. Mr. Osborne heard me and discussed it with me and came to the conclusion in fact that I did like Captain Stevens, which I don't dispute for a moment; he was a very likeable person, but I had no respect for him, only pity. Very soon after this I received a telephone call from the solicitor briefing the counsel representing the RAN, Mr. Jenkyn QC. He sounded rather panicky and said that he understood that I had some information that I had offered to Mr. Osborne and that were I to be called by Mr. Smyth would I please see them, that is Mr. Jenkyn's solicitors, and also allow them the knowledge that I had passed on. Some time after the Commission had started and I had been careful not to leave the Sydney area in case I was called, I started to wonder if I were going to be called and went to see Mr. Smyth and asked him. He said, 'No'. He had decided to reduce the other witnesses and I would no longer be required. Very shortly after this, it became patently clear that I had been misled by Mr. Smyth and others when the evidence was given that Captain Stevens had had a triple brandy on the bridge of *Voyager*.

29. It is very important at this stage that I mention that although Mr. Smyth didn't deny that Captain Stevens had drunk anything, in fact Mr. Osborne did, in saying that all Captain Stevens had had before the collision was a glass of brandy at lunch time on the day before the collision. This I think is most important to understand, because they at the time knew the truth. All the signs were then quite apparent that Captain Robertson was being taken, as the Americans say, for a ride, and was going to be saddled with the entire responsibility. In some alarm of this injustice, I rang Captain Robertson and offered to give evidence on his behalf although this was the last thing, I can assure you, that I wished to do in my

own interest. I considered it a duty in the interest of justice to him. At this stage of my now civilian career, the last thing I wanted was to be associated with anything smacking of a smear, but the injustice in this case was so glaring that it couldn't be avoided.

30. I received a letter from the mother of the RN Gunner who died on board *Voyager*, following a letter that I wrote to her expressing my sympathy. This officer had been court-martialled the previous year as Officer of the Watch of *Battleaxe* during her collision, and she said that she had received a letter shortly before my own, from her son, written before he died but received by her subsequently, in which he said, 'Mother, I think this is going to be another *Battleaxe*'. This is interesting, particularly as during the previous year, *Voyager* had been in at least five near collisions to my knowledge and in none of these do I think that *Voyager* was in any way to blame. This illustrates a factor that isn't appreciated by the general public that near collisions in an active fleet are very common things. On three of these occasions the officer who was *Voyager*'s navigator at the time of the collision had been the navigator of the ship with which *Voyager* was in trouble, that is *HMS Caesar*, so that his influence in the ultimate collision may have been more significant than evidence can prove. I'll give you more detail of one of these instances if you are in any way interested.

31. *Caesar* ordered *Voyager* to cross the screen from the starboard wing to the port wing at night having detached a SAU. The relative track was straight through *Caesar*, so I asked the Captain to inform *Caesar* that he would pass astern of her. As we approached *Caesar* and were just about to pass astern, *Caesar* turned 180° to starboard, that is towards us, and was suddenly on a collision course. It would have been impossible to turn to starboard to avoid it so I was obliged to go hard-a-port and full astern both engines, stopping dead in the water in front of the advancing convoy, very close to it and no further than 50 feet from *Caesar*. Both ships stopped dead in the water. I switched all my lights on, needless to say, at this time, having been blacked out at the beginning of the manoeuvre. There was never any explanation asked for or offered for this incident. My

memory is hazy on the other incident so I shan't attempt to remember it.

32. Another personality incident that may be of interest is that the Officer of the Watch of *Voyager* at the time of the collision had just completed a long period, I think probably 12 months, at HMAS *Watson* as instructor in the tactical floor, so that his ship handling knowledge, although he may not have served in destroyers, should have been as good as any officer on board.

33. Finally, I'd just like to say that I can envisage very clearly the situation on the bridge of *Voyager* at this time, and if the Officer of the Watch had put the wheel in a direction which the Captain thought was wrong, it wouldn't have been unlikely for the Captain to have shouted at the Officer of the Watch to put the wheel the other way. And for the Officer of the Watch to become rattled because the violence in the Captain's voice could have rattled him, put the wheel the other way and waited for the Captain who, in his opinion, had command, to give him another order. And that would be the last thing that happened until the collision was inevitable, with the officer of the Watch dithering, not knowing whether he should do anything or not.

34. The size and complication of the bridge is such, that the number of officers there was excessive. And I have discussed this with other officers who have served in *Voyager* with me and they all said the same thing – how often they have known a situation on those bridges where the Officer of the Watch didn't know what was happening, simply because there were too many experts around. This too, could well have been a factor in the situation. The navigator, the First Lieutenant, the Officer of the Watch, about two midshipmen and the Captain, the yeoman and two signalmen crowded into the wretched bridge with so many levels, it is not surprising that people weren't paying attention to what they should have been.

35. I think that concludes what I have to say. If any remarks are required on the personalities of some of the very good officers and men who lived and died I would be very happy to supply them.

36. The main facts outlined above were substantiated by Lieutenant Commander Griffith RAN, Navigating Officer of *Voyager* during the period in which I served in her, when interviewed by Mr. Smyth QC.

Signed: [P. T. Cabban]

33
Witness

When the hearings of the royal commission finally began I was as mentally prepared as my own personality and state of fitness would let me be. If, in Shakespeare's memorable phrase, I was now to be 'wedded to calamity', then so be it. As we walked into the small Sydney courtroom my mind was fully focused on the day's proceedings. The atmosphere was tense with expectation, but I felt quite relaxed, confident that my preparation was adequate to meet whatever lay ahead. I was still naïvely confident that the truth would soon be discovered and that the commission would not become the exhausting, drawn-out affair my advisers predicted.

The three commissioners sat together in the elevated central dais on the northern wall with their assisting counsel to the right and front of them. The witness box stood to their left. Other counsel sat in a row set back from the witness box, separated by a small passageway, with my representatives on the judges' right and those for the Navy and Stevens family on their left. The press enclosure was behind the witness box on the eastern wall, with an access door between it and the opposing counsel. Public benches were arranged in rows behind the legal teams. I sat immediately behind my lawyers, on a bench, and remember watching while Sir Jack and Lady Stevens, accompanying Duncan's widow Beatrice and their legal team, took their seats. Captain Jeff Britten, my old shipmate from *Warramunga*, accompanied Murphy and Henchman (for the Navy), but I knew that Jeff was not there as my friend. Mr Burt had referred to me as Lieutenant Commander Cabban, although Jack Hiatt stated that I did not use my former rank as a form of address, preferring to be called Mister. Throughout the inquiry, Ash called me 'Commander', as did the bench, while Murphy and Hiatt called me 'Mr Cabban'.

The first mild shock after being sworn in was the dimensions of the witness box. It was extremely compact and uncomfortable, with just a small wooden bench seat and a short counter on which documents could be rested. The commission was then led by Mr Burt through a record of my education and career in the Navy. Particular attention was given to my resignations, my attitude to the Navy and my impression of my own promotion prospects at various times. The file on the Benevolent Society's approach to the Naval Board to secure my release from the Navy was also produced and discussed in some detail. The fact that I had six commanding officers reporting on my fitness for promotion without sufficient knowledge of my abilities was highlighted in the questions and answers, as was my above-average assessment as a pilot following my grounding. The questions quite clearly pointed to the way the Navy's attacks on my attitude would be formulated, but in doing so they also helped us prepare the ground for my rebuttal of the inferences they sought to draw.

The extended meetings in Hiatt's chambers saw us go over almost every aspect of my career, with those most significant to the inquiry dissected in great detail. At any show of emotion from me, Chester and Jack enforced reason and rationality to ensure that I viewed aspects of my past in a better perspective and would remain calm under pressure. Every word of my statement for Admiral Hickling – the words that sat at the very core of the whole royal commission – had been analysed exhaustively. To their everlasting credit, not once did Jack or Chester ever make me feel regret or inadequacy about the content or tone of that document. They understood, perhaps better than I, the circumstances in which the statement had been made and how it had then been exploited. I was comfortable with counsel assisting, Mr Burt, as his examination led me through the incidents I had described, and I had no difficulty in responding. There was never any temptation to try to anticipate a line of questioning, to go beyond the answer to a question or to reply before I was ready. This first day was a good introduction to what was to come in cross-examination.

Although the Crown team had required Sue to make a statement for the commission, I insisted that she would not attend the courtroom or be called by us as a witness. She was under enormous pressure of concern for me and for our children, and she did not need to bear the strain of observing me and the parade of false witnesses we knew would be produced to counter claims of mine that she knew to be true. My confidence in Susie Martin's spontaneous assurance about David's evidence was so complete that, when it was canvassed by Jack or Chester that he might let me down, I stated unequivocally that I would walk out of the court and face jail rather than return if he did not tell the truth. Seasoned barristers are accustomed to such heroic leaps of faith from their clients. While I remained unaware of their disquiet at the time, they awaited his testimony with some trepidation because they already understood the significance of the fact that he had not been asked, before the parliamentary debates, for corroboration of my statement.

The examination methodically followed the sequence of events in my statement, until we came to Subic Bay. At that point Mr Burt noted that I had made tape recordings for keeping in touch with Sue. He directed me not to mention the content of the critical tape, but secured my acknowledgement that I still had the one I had sent at the end of June 1963. After a brief submission to alert the judges to the approach that he was recommending as to the admissibility of the tape, he moved on to the return to Sydney. When Burt enlarged on his very considered remarks concerning the tape the next morning, there was exactly the type of legal ruckus that he had foretold. Counsel for the Navy and the Stevens family both wanted access to the transcript in advance of any decision being made as to its admissibility. Hiatt and Burt were adamant that it should not be distributed because of its potential to encourage the adoption of adversarial positions by the parties. The commissioners ruled, contrary to their assisting counsel's advice, that they and all counsel should see the transcript or hear the tape before a decision would be made.

Returning to a line of questioning that had begun the previous day, I was asked to enunciate my analysis of my promotion prospects on our return from the Far East and I confirmed my view that when I was not listed for promotion at the end of June 1963, I believed that I should resign and seek another career. Consequently, my resignation was submitted on 5 August. The rest of my opening evidence dealt principally with the ship's movements, my interaction with the captain and a detailed explanation of the correspondence between Admiral Hickling and me and the making of the Cabban Statement.

W. P. Ash (for the Stevens family) built the early part of his cross-examination on an attempt to make me agree with Hickling's fanciful notion that all captains lived 'in a goldfish bowl' where their every word and movement were public knowledge. Life in the modern Navy is not like that. The captains in each ship that I served in were discreet in their own cabins. Nothing they said to their guests or other officers in the confines of their cabins ever reached the wardroom or the rest of the ship, except when they wanted it to be known. Ash went on at length about my evidence that the ship was the happiest in which I had served and, particularly, that I had described my twelve months under Duncan to Beatrice Stevens as my best year in the Navy. Ash attempted to persuade me that these terms demanded that the captain must be an outstanding leader. That, of course, was the last thing I would concède, and I held the confident expectation that David Martin would disabuse everyone of that misconception when he gave evidence. Then Ash tried to build up a picture of a captain bowed down by the sheer pressure of work related to correspondence and official duties. These, presumably, were the reasons for Stevens' fatigue and drinking. Yet throughout his attempt to paint this picture of a poor man under the strain of official functions and heavy duty, Ash failed to recognise that Captain Willis – commanding the other destroyer at the same time, and with equal duties – somehow did not resort to the bottle or fail to appear on duty when he should. I continued to answer each question, and that question only. The repeated tactic of proposing situations for me to agree or disagree with was sustained throughout the morning.

At times, the lines of questioning pursued were quite bizarre, and it was a challenge not to display the slightest degree of emotion in my responses. When Ash picked over the first visit to the steam baths, I was asked a series of questions about Stevens' drinking in the morning. He asked whether I might agree with the suggestion that I was of the belief that he had 'been up drinking in the morning'. I replied, 'I would not have been surprised.'

Ash continued, 'Drinking before breakfast – that is the suggestion, is it?'

I answered, 'I did not suggest it; you asked me.'

'You would not have been surprised?'

'No, Sir.'

But Ash still had one utterly unforeseen – and, for me, traumatic – shot in his locker. After finishing with the Tokyo visit he almost casually referred to counsel for the Navy making some documents available to him. To my utter amazement, Ash then handed me a file that I identified aloud as of punishment returns for June 1963. He directed me to read out the dates and the signatures of the officers who were recorded as rendering the punishments on each return. Stunned, I read out my name and the captain's with dates that fell within the five-day period during which I had already given sworn evidence of my command! It was evident that Ash and Murphy believed they had absolute proof of Captain Stevens being in active command on the first and second days out of Tokyo. I could not, and would not, concede that. I agreed that the documents were dated on those days and signed to represent that the captain had awarded the punishments on those days, but I was adamant that they did not represent the facts. I knew he had not awarded them on those days. He had been sick and confined to his cabin.

This impasse presented exactly the complex type of can of worms that lawyers delight in opening. Ash and the judges vied with each other in attempting to understand my position. Ash tried to persuade me that Stevens would not have willingly signed these documents if they were not a true account of the facts of the punishment parades. I offered the obvious alternative that they had been ante-dated to hide his medical condition. That was received with hostility, with the word 'fraud' unwisely being used by Ash, who was swiftly corrected by the chairman. Whatever was suggested, I would not resile from the absolute position that Captain Stevens did not award any punishments on the dates that were typed on the returns. Leaving the matter unresolved, Ash sought to tender the documents as an exhibit, but as Jack Hiatt requested that they be left available for his study, and Mr Burt also stated that he also had been unaware of them until they were produced, the chairman ruled that they be left available until the following Monday.

The interaction between Ash, Burt, Hiatt, Murphy and the chairman occupied only a few minutes, but I had been transfixed by the documents sitting on the ledge of the witness box. They were incomprehensible to me. They simply could not be what they purported to be. My mind would not function properly as I attempted to reconcile them with everything I could recall, and I knew for the first time in my life what the expression 'mind in turmoil' truly meant. Without warning, with the commission hearing still going on around me, I had a vision so vivid and startling it seemed like a memory coming to life before my eyes. Captain Duncan Stevens, dressed in white shirt and shorts, walked straight out of the wall of the courtroom with the documents in his hand, his face florid, shouting, 'You're not going to get me like this!' I was on the point of collapse with shock and turned to the bench. 'Excuse me, Your Honour, am I permitted to speak to my counsel?'

Sir Stanley replied, 'Not at this stage, no.'

I answered the next two questions by Ash before the commission was adjourned at 3.55 p.m. for the weekend. Jack came to me immediately as the judges retired, and I told him, 'They are forgeries, Jack. Please get Mr Burt.' I described my illusion to them both, to which Mr Burt said, 'I believe you.' Turning to Jack he said, 'He will have to remember it all or they will crucify him on Monday!' It was agreed between them that Jack would lead me on Monday morning, but then it would be open slather! The worst weekend of my life had just begun.

In both the Sydney evening newspapers on that Friday night, and in the *Sydney Morning Herald* on Saturday, the reports of the inquiry were headlined as a '*Caine Mutiny* Situation'. Those journalists could have had no idea how apt their words were. While Jack, Chester and I were unwinding over a beer after the day's hearing, our thoughts were dominated by the epic problem that faced us on Monday. One of the most significant passages in my statement confirming Stevens' incapacity to command his own ship had been directly contradicted by documents supplied to the commission by the Navy. If I were unable to satisfy the judges with a detailed and credible version of those events, then my value as a witness at the inquiry would be undermined. We agreed that I would meet Jack in his chambers on Saturday morning so that we could work together to fill the gaps in my memory and develop a comprehensive account of the incident I had recalled so dramatically in the theatre of my mind.

At home, a tiny trickle of clarity began to intrude into my turmoil, and I asked Sue to write down on a note pad everything that I managed to remember. When recalling any aspect of *Voyager* I would instantly 're-enter' the place in the ship, or ashore, and the people who were present and just listen to what was being said. This had become increasingly difficult as time since the collision had increased. When we retired for the night, there was no question of switching off the light. Sue had the pad in one hand and pen in the other. While we dozed, I would wake up suddenly and say, 'Write down so-and-so,' and she would write whatever it was. Then we might sleep for a few more minutes until my next flash of recall. It went on like that throughout the night, and I took the pad to Phillip Street after breakfast, to piece it all together with my long-suffering counsel.

Jack and I decided that the most therapeutic atmosphere for continuing this saga would be in the Leagues Club across the street, and that is where we repaired. By the time we had exhausted my memory bank for the day, many of the gaps in the sequence had been bridged, but there was still a long way to go. Most annoyingly, I could not identify the ship's location when the incident occurred, a worrying memory lapse for any naval officer. The remainder of the weekend was dominated by this relentless pressure to recall anything I could about those fateful five days out of Tokyo. Sue quietly supported me through what was the greatest ordeal of my life until then. We were acutely conscious that my survival hinged on the state of my memory when Jack rose to examine me on Monday morning.

Hiatt, Chester Porter and Tony McDonald were all sitting in a circle with me in Jack's anteroom at 7.00 a.m. as I recounted the details of the defaulters' parades and punishment returns. After a weekend of agonising effort I could now recall them with certainty. My lawyers questioned me with great deliberation to ensure that I had missed nothing and that my account fitted all the previously sworn facts. But there was still the one glaring omission: I had not been able to remember the ship's position at the moment when Duncan had stormed into my cabin. The room was silent while I endeavoured to project myself back into my cabin to find a clue. It was imperative that I be able to confirm where the confrontation had occurred. Breaking my concentration, an impatient voice, probably Chester's, shouted, 'For Christ's sake, think!'

'For Christ's sake, shut up!' I replied, equally vehemently. Then suddenly I was back in *Voyager*. 'That's funny, it's dark. I can't see anything. And there's no noise. It's as quiet as a tomb. Oh, Jesus! We're in Subic Bay!'

'How do you know?'

'We've just had a turbogenerator breakdown – the only time in my career.'

'Why is it dark?'

'I haven't had time to remove the deadlights from my scuttle after night exercises,' I replied.

'Why couldn't you have done that in the witness box? No one could disbelieve you!' said Chester. We barely had time to get to the hearing where Jack led me through the incident – complete with the key corroboration we had established just in the nick of time.

One of the most unpleasant periods for me early in the commission proceedings was the cross-examination on aspects of my statement concerning the week in Sydney after our return from the cruise. Many of the more crucial details had faded from my memory. In particular, I failed to recall that I had instructed Martin to hide Stevens as long as possible from the admiral's representative before the Pakistan Shield presentation. I had also forgotten Ferrier's description of Duncan's drunken performance at the pre-refit conference and Martin's graphic account of the Holmes baby's christening. All of these incidents did not come back to me until much later as my damaged memory was slowly restored. Similarly, the significance of Stevens' abrupt recovery from semi-stupor to sobriety was not explicable to me until his access to amphetamines became known many months later. Nevertheless, I was still confident that my general recollections expressed to Hickling had been accurate. Stevens did, indeed, arrive each morning the worse for wear and was able to recover dramatically to attend to vital activities. He had then returned to sleeping and drinking.

When the cross-examination went on to cover the period of *Voyager*'s refit at Williamstown (where the periods of time when both Stevens and I were in the ship together were brief), Ash again used punishment returns in an attempt to prove that Duncan was on the ball. Unfortunately for that premise, the paperwork was in even more of a mess than the falsified June returns. There was clear evidence of different pens being used by the captain on the same documents, different dates and even signatures with dates that did not correspond to the times when that signatory was in the ship. These inconsistencies were never sorted out, but I believe that the refit returns were also falsified to give the impression that Stevens attended parades that he did not. His signature was always prominent. The confusion over my assertion to Hickling that I had command in this period for a week was clarified when it was maintained that Stevens was on board for five days, had two days with friends in Melbourne and then two at Flinders without returning to the ship in between times. There is no doubt that any period when he was on deck was brief, and he would have been very shaky. I had felt for him in his extremely ill state during that time, even to the extent of considering warning his hostess. I still do not believe that he took defaulters parades during this period. What convinced me was that all punishment returns for the period were typed and signed, with Griffith signing over my rank and appointment after I had left the Navy (and a full month after the first punishments were awarded). No RAN ship, even when alongside for a refit, allows itself to slip that far behind in its formal paperwork.

At one stage during his questioning of me Ash suddenly referred back to my letter of condolence to Beatrice Stevens. He asked how I could have said that 1963 was my happiest year in the Navy when I was prepared to make such denigrating accusations about her late husband. Once again, Ash proved himself rather careless when quoting the purported words of others. I had not said that it was my 'happiest' year. I had written that it was my best year, and I had chosen every word with care, so as not to hurt while also being truthful. It was left to Jack Hiatt, in his re-examination, to give me the opportunity to explain the apparent contradiction. But in its report of the day's proceedings, the *Daily Telegraph* front-page headline proclaimed, "'Happiest" year spent on *Voyager*', illustrating just how easy it is to assume in error when not listening intently. Perhaps the most remarkable aspect of all this was that Beatrice Stevens claimed, under oath, to have destroyed all of Duncan's letters written to her from *Voyager*, yet she had retained my letter for more than three years after her husband's death. These seemed curious priorities for a loving wife.

There were some improbable moments of light relief amid the drama of cross-examination. In response to a question, I had described my actual observation of Duncan having been sick, standing dressed only in his underpants after he had vomited. Ash repeatedly referred to this incident as 'the captain being sick in his underpants' to the great entertainment of the spectators. I struggled to retain a stolid demeanour while correcting him, saying, 'in his underpants, being sick'.

When Ash was making light of my concerns over the captain ruining the long exercise that required the ship being sealed in stifling conditions, simulating atomic fall-out, he suggested that even in the inquiry one might expect someone to ask, 'How long is this thing going on?'

I asked, 'By whom to whom, Mr Ash?'

This raised peals of laughter, and Ash conceded that he had asked for that. I was not even smiling and assured him that I did not mean to be funny.

Both Ash and the bench laboured the fact that I had signed the transcript of my dictated statement for Captain Robertson, thereby validating it. Burbury entered this aspect forcibly by asking what Robertson said to me when asking me to sign. I said that I thought that he had asked me if it were true that I knew that Griffith had substantiated my statement and the facts, to which I replied, 'Yes', as I understood from Griffith. Then I had been asked to note that on the document and sign it. I was uncertain of whether that was immediately after it was returned from New Zealand or later when it was to be submitted to the Prime Minister. When asked what had induced me to sign it, I said that it was in response to a request from a responsible person. The chairman also questioned my opinion, in retrospect, of my representation of Stevens' character in the statement. I conceded that it appeared to be out of balance as the captain was a very likeable man when sober. Perhaps I should have placed more emphasis on that, but would it have mattered in the end? The ship was lost after he had been drinking at sea, so, even if he had been the most popular man in the Navy, any assessment of his character when sober and happy was, in truth, irrelevant.

Peter Murphy QC, for the Navy, opened his attack by questioning my sphere of work in the field of management consulting, with emphasis on psychological analysis. In spite of my denying any recourse to this aspect of consulting, he tried to tempt me into self-assessment, suggesting that I might define myself as introverted. I declined, and suggested that self-analysis is always a mistake. The commissioners, however, seized on the idea that I was an introvert and Duncan an extrovert, and I believe that synthetic contrast coloured their attitudes henceforth. Murphy hammered away at the genesis of the Cabban Statement, its authentication and my beliefs concerning the treatment of Robertson at the hands of Smyth, Osborne, Spicer and the Navy. Counsel for the Navy displayed more venom in this cross-examination, more skill and ruthless quoting (and misquoting) of my evidence – in and out of context. Returning to my statement, he asked whether I considered that it portrayed fair background character material of Stevens. When I conceded that it probably did not, the chairman jumped in again. I explained that I did not think that character had anything to do with the collision – intake of alcohol did. Whether through ignorance or intent, Murphy implied that Duncan had 'a brandy with his dinner' on the night of the collision, which I am certain Steward Hyland did not say. It was left to me to query that, and to reiterate the size of the drink: a *triple* brandy.

As predicted by my legal team, an enormous amount of time and energy was expended playing the man and not the ball. Long hours were consumed in efforts to question my character, abilities and motives. It was as if counsel for the Navy and the Stevens family believed that by destroying my standing at the commission, the scandal behind the tragic loss of *Voyager* would somehow just evaporate. The accident in the Gannet Trainer was the subject of protracted questioning, all aimed squarely at unsettling me emotionally and establishing that I had a deep-seated grudge against the Navy. This followed an attack on my flying ability while in HMAS *Sydney*, in which the facts were distorted and manipulated by Murphy's advisers. Mr Burt, who objected to this entire line of questioning (and was supported reluctantly by the chairman), pointed out the irrelevancy of the tirade, and it ceased. It was promptly replaced by questions directed to my experiences in *Warramunga*. Again, innuendo was used in attempts to induce me to anticipate hostility towards the Naval Board and witnesses to be called later.

My level of emotional distress rose under the relentlessness of these attacks, and I felt that I was on the verge of breaking. But luckily, just at that moment, I had a clear realisation of what was happening to me. Instead of answering the current question, I took a deep silent breath, looked into Murphy's eyes, smiled, and asked him to repeat his question. We both knew from then on that I was not going to break down.

The cross-examination by counsel for the Navy occupied close to two days before Jack Hiatt's re-examination provided an opportunity to clear all of the contentious matters raised by Ash and Murphy over the previous five days. Hiatt began by confirming that I had not been reading any transcripts of evidence over the course of the inquiry, nor had I read any RAN reports of proceedings in order to refresh my memory. Next, Jack elicited from me details of my two meetings with Scott Griffith, first in Subic Bay and then in Singapore. Griffith, in the first instance, had claimed that Stevens was a sick man and that he owed total loyalty to him, and advised me to support the captain. In the second meeting I had beseeched him with Tapp and Howland to put the welfare of the ship's company and the Navy before any other interest.

My counsel led me so that I was able to counter the barrage of criticism of my flying ability. Most of this had misrepresented incidents beyond the pilot's control as accidents attributable to me. But the chairman, having allowed Murphy to parade these falsehoods, now rebuked Jack, cutting him short as if these matters were irrelevant. Before the interruption, Jack had established that not one of the four recorded incidents that occurred in my test flying was an accident, as had been portrayed by Murphy. Early in his re-examination, Hiatt crucially asked if I had anything to add concerning the incident in Hong Kong when Stevens whistled at stewards. I replied that it was the first occasion at which I had seen him drunk in front of civilians. Burbury was upset by this use of the word 'drunk'. I confirmed that I meant it as commonly understood and that my guests had used the same expression to describe the captain's condition. Ash objected, and asked that my reply be struck out as hearsay. Both judges Asprey and Burbury flagged their attitudes by saying that they would not be taking 'the slightest notice' of that evidence.

Following a review of the reasons for describing 1963 as my best year in the Navy, the circumstances in which I became aware of the collision and my immediate reactions were examined. Responding to questions from the bench, I told of an overwhelming feeling of guilt deriving from my failure to take action. I was asked a loaded hypothetical question: did I believe that had I not resigned I would have been on the bridge of *Voyager* on the night of the collision? I replied that Alan Willis had told me that if I were on the list for promotion I would be reappointed to another ship, or shore duty, and that Duncan had said I would be on the next list. Then Burbury asked what more could I have done after reporting to G. J. Willis in Tokyo, to which I responded that I believed I should have reported the Subic Bay incident. I now remember being conscious of that in Sydney yet still fearing the threat of psychiatric incarceration if I reported to a more senior officer. With the conflict boiling down to Willis's and Stevens' words against mine, I had settled for briefing those

I believed I could trust about the critical importance of not drinking at sea.

After Jack had finished with me, Mr Burt rose to conclude the process of my initial examination. At this point there was a further embarrassment in RAN record-keeping to explore. The deck log of *Voyager* for June 1963 was missing from Navy Office, the only such deck log ever to have been mislaid. Murphy offered the preposterous claim that it had gone down with the ship – seven long months after it was last in use. Captain Britten had apparently assured him of that, but Mr Burt assured us that it was the only *Voyager* deck log that was missing. All deck logs are forwarded to Navy Office for reference and safe storage each month. The June log would be at Navy Office by August at the latest. Why was it crucial to locate this piece of evidence? Because the June log would have recorded the extended period of bad weather that struck *Voyager* while Stevens had been stood down from command for five days after we had left Tokyo. During his cross-examination, Murphy had shown me the June deck log of *Vampire*, purporting to confirm that the sea was calm during the period of my command when I had insisted that typhoon conditions prevailed. When Burt produced the *Voyager* report of proceedings for June to compare with *Vampire*'s log, the tempestuous state of the weather was confirmed, leaving only two possibilities: either the ships were not operating together or *Vampire*'s log had been subject to tampering. Mr Burt was later to tender a cable that he had received from the US Navy's Guam weather station that confirmed my evidence. The conditions at the times in question were described simply as 'typhoon'.

I can only surmise that there must have been too many entries in *Voyager*'s deck log that corroborated my evidence for it to see the light of the commission and close examination. It was obvious to any reasonable observer that the crucial log had either been deliberately concealed or destroyed. (No suggestion of that was contained in the report of the commissioners, nor did they comment on the *Vampire* entries or the irrefutable weather evidence from Guam.)

I could not help beginning to form the impression that Mr Burt was trying hard to balance the negative impression generated by counsel for the Navy, the Stevens family and even the commissioners themselves. His questioning brought out that Duncan Stevens had told me that he had seen the fleet medical officer, McNeill, so that no record of his illness would reach Navy Office to threaten his career. He also produced a copy of *Navy News* with a description of a cricket match between the Hong Kong Wanderers and *Voyager*, described by Ash as a good hard match, won by the ship's team 152 to 37. Stevens was clearly not in the team, as had been claimed by Ash as evidence that he was well and active.

Adding to these inconsistencies, Mr Burt had done brilliantly to detect that the punishment returns for the period after Tokyo while I was in command were out of serial number sequence and out of date order. The associated returns to Navy Office showing the financial implications of punishments were also out of sequence. That alone should have helped corroborate my evidence against the decidedly suspicious records tabled by the Navy. Someone in the flagship and at Navy Office had obviously failed to notice this anomaly in 1963. Again, in 1967, they should have noticed the discrepancies and ensured that they disappeared along with *Voyager*'s deck log and report of proceedings! In later examination of the coxswain's writer, Able Seaman Ennor, Burt ascertained that the punishment returns signed by Stevens had been typed on another typewriter, not his. Ennor could, of course, not explain this as they were clearly prepared by another typist. Interestingly, I could not recall that I had awarded promotions that were due to requestmen at the same times. (This was later established by the evidence of ratings who were no longer serving in the Navy. Those still serving denied it.)

At the end of October, Burt was to call as a witness Sergeant B. J. Fitzgerald of the Commonwealth Police. As officer in charge of the Document Examination Bureau, he gave evidence on the typewriters and pens used in the preparation of the punishment returns for February and March 1963. He testified that on only one set of returns – those in the June batch ex-Tokyo – a black biro had been used by both Captain Stevens and the cox'n, Jonathan Rogers. For some reason I was directed to leave the court during the taking of this evidence. My absence while this testimony unfolded was crucial. I knew that the captain had the only black biro in the ship. When I returned, the only question I was asked was, 'Did you use your own or the captain's pen to sign the returns?', and I could not remember. Had I known of the black biro – which had to be Duncan's – that apparently trivial detail would have changed the course of the entire proceedings.

My volatile letter to John Jess of 10 August 1966 was read by Mr Burt and tendered after I confirmed that I had declined endeavours to persuade me to appear on radio and television in support of John Robertson. The text of that letter was as much a guide to my state of mind as the marshalling of a convincing case. I wrote:

I am more concerned at this time over the conduct of matters relating to the MELBOURNE/VOYAGER collision than when I first spoke with you. In the face of written opinion and published facts, the opportunity to act honourably has been spurned by the government, either deliberately in violation of democratic obligation, or from ignorance of the depth of principle involved.

There must be points of emphasis taken from such a wide issue, to provide a basis for review, and I shall amplify those which demand satisfaction as a matter of the greatest urgency.

The impartiality of the Judicial System was outraged in the proceedings of the royal commission, with evidence which was obtained by the counsel assisting the commissioner in chambers, and which he considered aloud at the time to be sufficiently important to require me to be available to attend as a witness, suppressed so a true background evaluation of Captain Stevens' conduct could not be made in public. The only conclusion which can be reached on this point in the proceedings, when seen in relationship to the manner in which Captain Robertson was persecuted by presentation of a false picture of the other key figure in the collision, is that a commission was used as an instrument of political expediency. Is any Australian citizen guaranteed better hope under comparable conditions?

While the previous point raised emphatically the involvement of the commissioner and other counsel who were aware of and a party to impartiality, it is evident that there was connivance of the government to procure a false report, for how else would such an attitude develop? It is inconceivable that any outside agency could exert that kind of pressure on such powerful men.

The silence of the Naval Board subsequent upon the announcement by the Prime Minister that a royal commission was to be the means of enquiry was itself a shock to most naval officers, but their acceptance of the report to the House of Representatives can never

be condoned. The Naval Board as a body is responsible to, as well as
for, the officers and men who are prepared to give their lives when
necessary as a result of Naval Board policy or direction. The
survivors of *Voyager* looked for confirmation of their belief in their
leaders and none was forthcoming in the evidence of the Board's
conduct.

There has been no reaction to the very general knowledge of
the influence which alcohol played in the command of *Voyager*, and
the fact that the ship was in collision only five weeks following my
relief as Executive Officer, and the total removal of the restrictions
placed by me on drinking at sea by officers. This indicates a blind
fear of any encroachment on privilege regardless of danger to life
and cost, without consideration of the simple issues involved and
ease of finding an intelligent solution. Do we have to go through it
all again before the public will bring down the Board and the
government for its failure to act?

Please write to me of your intentions in this matter, for I am
reluctant to submit to the pressures which are on me to publicise
the facts in my own possession if I can be assured that positive
action is possible without a repugnant ventilation of dirty linen. I
believe the time is suitable for much credit and honour to be
obtained by the government by an honest and open reappraisal of
the situation.

Burbury appeared to put great store by my letter to Jess, asking how I
could claim that suppression of my evidence as to Stevens' conduct
constituted an injustice to John Robertson since Spicer had attributed
blame to *Voyager*. He added, '. . . and some criticism of Captain Robertson for failure to warn'. I expressed my belief that any captain of
Melbourne would, in the circumstances prevailing, have expected *Voyager*
to be commanded by a competent destroyer captain who would know
better than *Melbourne*'s captain how to execute the change of station he
had ordered. He would not consider making any alteration to his course
or speed, or even to query *Voyager*'s actions. He would accept that there
would be competence and a degree of boldness in ship handling from a
captain who had been working with carriers for twelve months. But had
Judge Spicer known that Stevens was possibly under the influence of

alcohol, and that Robertson could not have even guessed that, then surely he would have taken a different view. The rigid conditions under which any officer on *Voyager*'s bridge other than the captain can give a wheel or engine order while the captain is present on the bridge were also reviewed. The commissioners were assured that once the captain gives a wheel or engine order, he has absolute command until he gives another order relinquishing command to his nominee, generally the officer of the watch or the navigator.

In order to leave no doubt about my authority for command out of Tokyo, Mr Burt asked if it were derived from Willis or Stevens. Willis had directed it, and informed me in the first instance that Stevens was going to give me command. Stevens actually handed over to me when we cleared Tokyo Harbour. When asked what I would have done had Stevens refused Willis's order, I said that I would have consulted the doctor. If the doctor confirmed that Duncan Stevens was unfit to command, then I would have arrested the captain and assumed command. In the ensuing examination of details of Stevens' threat to me and my reaction to that threat, I described the conditions that convinced me of its reality. He claimed that two doctors had assured him of their willingness to certify me. (Burbury instructed the press that those details were not to be published.) Various scenarios were canvassed to find my attitude to seeking out other officers to determine their positions and the possibility of my suggesting to them that the captain was sick and I should take over. These were, of course, impossible to contemplate in the situation of Subic Bay, totally detached from any senior unit. Here was a man who, in making his threat, was ordering me to commit a criminal act in signing false documents. He had given illegal orders to the doctor to hide his medical condition, and conspired with a more senior captain to conceal his unfitness to command. If the truth leaked out he'd be facing court martial, dismissal from the service, disgrace and possibly jail. And I was being asked whether I could have said, 'Sir, you are sick. Give me command.'

At the beginning of the tenth day of the inquiry I was called upon to explain a remark I had made to the Commonwealth officer, Sergeant Turner, which he had in turn reported to Smyth. I had told Turner that I was glad that it was the officer of the watch who had piped 'Hands to collision stations', adding that 'if it had been the captain, it would stink'.

Turner knew that Able Seaman Webster, in his survivor's statement, had insisted that he was certain Stevens' voice had called 'Hands to collision stations' a moment before the collision. The sergeant asked me why I said that, not sharing his knowledge of Webster's statement with me. I had replied that something would have been wrong on the bridge in that event, owing to the relative positions of those who should have been present on duty. Mr Burt now asked me the significance of that state-ment. I described the bridge layout with the captain's chair on the starboard side of the bridge on the right of the pelorus, which was, alternating with the wings of the bridge, the officer of the watch's prin-cipal position. If the OOW were on a wing, then he would have been aware of the impending danger at all times. The captain must have climbed about four steps to reach the pelorus in order to assess the situa-tion, then used the broadcast and the voice pipe to the wheelhouse, thereby extending the delay of action.

Mr Justice Lucas then put the proposition to me that I had, in fact, never forgotten the events of Subic Bay, but through shame or some similar consideration had chosen not to introduce them into my evidence until Friday afternoon. He told me to take time to consider his proposi-tion before answering. I could not believe that he was asking this. I rejected it out of hand and said, 'Surely you saw that I was in a state of shock on Friday when I asked to speak to my counsel?' He acknowledged that, and Jack Hiatt was on his feet saying, 'My client is willing to submit to a psychiatric examination to establish this, your Honour, if the commission wishes.' That was news to me! But Burbury responded instantly with, 'Mr Hiatt, we don't have to be told about hysterical amnesia!' That was the first time that I became aware that my condition was well known and had a name. No one thought to advise me that I might require help to get over it.

I felt relief that I was finally out of the witness box, but it was to be short-lived. I was to be recalled on three more occasions, with little or no notice, and the prospect kept me in a state of constant apprehension. For more than a week I found myself unable to transport myself instantly back into *Voyager*, and the thought of being recalled during that period was petrifying. The crisis passed and, as my obvious distress lifted, Jack Hiatt said, 'You're back in *Voyager*, aren't you?'

34

Sir John Spicer's Assistants

The twists and turns of my long tenancy in the witness box might have yielded some seemingly confusing evidence, but one impression remained inescapably clear: the Royal Australian Navy had, at various times, done its best to cover up material that might have reflected badly on Duncan Stevens and their own conduct. Now, the three wise judges of the second commission would have to consider a far more subtle and uncomfortable question. Did the lawyers who conducted the original inquiry themselves keep from public scrutiny information that should have been made known? The third term of reference charged the new royal commission to investigate 'Whether the allegations in the document [the Cabban Statement] disclosed evidence which was available to counsel assisting the royal commission and was improperly withheld from the commission'.

In effect, we were about to embark on an inquiry into an inquiry. Just dealing with the volatile proposition that evidence could have been 'improperly withheld' was to wander into a potential minefield. The commissioners, the press and the public would all now be treated to the unique spectacle of eminent lawyers putting each other in the witness box.

The dominant (if unwritten) heft of reference 3 was the notion that the decision not to call me as a witness before Judge Spicer had resulted in the first commission not having the benefit of the type of information I was able to outline in the Cabban Statement. The lawyer who briefed John Smyth QC to assist as counsel to the original *Voyager* inquiry was J. C. Braund, from the Crown Solicitor's office in Canberra. Considering that he was involved in the taking of more than a hundred statements, it is understandable that he now told the commission he could not recall much of what was said during my interview. But his evidence concerning the general handling of statements was both interesting and pertinent.

Mr Burt led him through the normal processes for taking, recording and signing the statements of witnesses and the filing processes that followed. There were three types of bound volumes of statements, classified according to the origin of the witnesses: *Melbourne*, *Voyager* and *Albatross* (the Fleet Air Arm base at Nowra). Later statements from servicemen that had not been taken in time for binding were stored in one envelope. The statements of miscellaneous civilian witnesses were generally filed together in another envelope. Burt seemed at his most effective when dealing with such dense hedges of legal paperwork. Having already established that a formal statement of my evidence was not taken (although Braund saw Sergeant Turner's notes and my statement given to him), he simply asked what had happened to these documents. They had been placed in an envelope, which bore the number '78' and the words 'Cabban Statement'. No other statement had been filed individually in that manner. Why? Braund replied that for no other reason than that he would then be able to find it if it was wanted! But it had not been distributed. By contrast, Braund said he was unaware that Professor Blackburn's statement had been distributed to other counsel.

Jack Hiatt saw fertile ground for investigation into the interviewing process. He asked Braund about the specific duties that the solicitor undertook during the *Voyager* conferences, only to be interrupted while all three commissioners fell over each other to put words into Braund's mouth. Not surprisingly, his eventual reply was a simple agreement with what they had said and a convenient reason for him not to recall much detail. He did, however, manage to remember that Griffith had been identified as an ex-*Voyager* officer to be called for interview and that a statement was not taken from him at the time. That process might or might not have applied to other witnesses, but Braund could not recall. When asked by Reynolds, for Captain Robertson, whether there were another seventy-seven envelopes (as logic might have suggested), Braund said that there were not. He could think of no reason – at least that he could recall – for numbering my statement '78'. Then, apparently contradicting all this, he said that he had registered all the statements in a book, by number.

Senior Constable G. E. Wright of the Commonwealth Police, who had accompanied Sergeant Turner when I had been interviewed in February 1964, was next. Led by Mr Burt, he confirmed that I had appeared 'bright and intelligent' and calm at the time of interview, but that he had smelled alcohol on two occasions. As I remember drinking wine with my lunch that day, I have no argument with his recollection, and in any case he was adamant that it did not affect my responses or behaviour. It was useful to have this clear refutation of the widely circulated slur that I had been under the weather during the police interview, but the issue was relatively minor. Much more significant, to my mind, would be the evidence of the instructing solicitor for the family of the late Duncan Stevens. If anyone held the key to unlocking the 'improperly withheld' puzzle, it would be Frederick Meares Osborne.

Osborne had instructed Laurence Street QC and John Sinclair in their appearances before Justice Spicer in the first royal commission. Now in the witness box himself, he agreed that he and I had met for an hour and a quarter before meeting with Sinclair. While maintaining that he did not know why I had wished to see them, he acknowledged that he had not only read Hyland's statement about the triple brandy but had also interviewed the steward before meeting me. Patient questioning confirmed that it was Osborne who had approached Stevens' 'knighted doctor', Sir William Morrow, and contacted Professor Blackburn after receiving the post-mortem report of alcohol in the three bodies recovered after the collision. Thus, key expert witnesses to the first commission had actually been selected by the solicitor for the Stevens family – an interested party – and not by the Crown.

The examination of this extremely experienced solicitor then moved on to more contentious ground. My statement had quoted him as maintaining that Stevens only had a brandy with lunch on the day *before* the collision. His response to this was crafted brilliantly. Osborne now claimed that he had been referring to the day before the *night* of the collision; that is, the day *of* the collision. He said that he knew the ship had been in harbour the day before and that it would have been 'irrelevant' to mention that Stevens had a drink on that day. I had, of course, been emphasising that Duncan never drank at sea, so Osborne must have known the crucial relevance of the timing of that drink. My entire attitude would have changed if he had told me that Stevens had consumed spirits on the same day as he would be taking *Voyager* to sea. Osborne must have known that, yet he had been careful not to deny me.

Osborne went on to concede that he had probably discussed my evidence with counsel for the Navy, claiming that he believed they were very largely of the same interest in that respect. This was a deeply revealing observation in the context of the first inquiry. The presumption that the interests of the Navy and the Stevens family would coincide after the loss of eighty-two lives is breathtaking. Osborne denied that Street had been present during the interview in Sinclair's room.

Peter Murphy then extracted from Osborne a complete denial of any influence on him by the Naval Board during the Spicer inquiry, at least on the issue of my being called to give evidence. I can only imagine that the implication Murphy was seeking to refute was that McNicoll or others might have tried to persuade Osborne to exert influence on Smyth or Spicer to suppress any negative source of evidence as to Duncan's fitness to command. That had not occurred to me. I believed that it was sufficiently in the interests of the Stevens family to do this without the need for any additional pressure from the Navy.

Jack Hiatt was far more forthright in his cross-examination of the solicitor for the Stevens family. My counsel tried to get Osborne to concede that he understood that I was, back in 1964, actually defending his client from any accusation that he was drinking at sea. But when, at last, Jack extracted a 'Yes' from Osborne, it was overlaid with the remarkable qualification that he had meant to convey to me that Duncan had, in fact, had a drink at sea! Why had he not said that outright when I was hammering the point that Stevens would not drink at sea? He would have known the terrible import of what I was saying. Osborne was adamant that he had not misled me into thinking Stevens had not ever had a drink at sea. But he did admit to knowing that on the evening before the collision Duncan had been drinking at the home of Dacre Smyth, captain of the Naval College at Jervis Bay. Now he claimed to be unsure whether he had known this while speaking with me in 1964. Nor could he remember whether he had been aware that Stevens had had a drink on board *Melbourne* at lunchtime the day before in Jervis Bay. The most telling question asked by Jack Hiatt was: what was the purpose of Osborne telling me anything about when Stevens last had a drink if I had not emphasised to him that the captain did not drink at sea? The improbable reply was that he was not sure. Indeed, he thought it possible that I had asked him!

No doubt Fred Osborne was confident that his long experience of the legal process made him impregnable behind a wall of intricate sophistry and hair-splitting. Fortunately, a good barrister can blast holes through those defences with just a few direct questions. Mr Burt asked Osborne to concede that whatever my motive for seeing him, he, as solicitor for the Stevens family, was in an adversary situation and, as such, had formed the opinion that my evidence would be adverse to his interest. Osborne had to agree that it was obviously adverse. Then, to make the facts completely clear, Burt had him confirm that it did not require the Navy, or anyone else, to convince Osborne that it would best serve his interests if my evidence were not called. Game, set and match.

John Bowditch Sinclair, who had been junior counsel for the Stevens family in 1964, had heard all of Osborne's evidence while waiting to appear as a witness. He confirmed that Laurence Street QC was his leader in the Spicer commission and stated that Street did not attend the meeting with me on 26 March 1964. He had a copy of Hyland's statement on that day, along with the post-mortem report. Sinclair also had a good idea of what Dr Morrow and Professor Blackburn were likely to say about the blood alcohol levels in the bodies. Sinclair's transcribed notes of our meeting were authenticated by him, although he claimed to have no independent recollection of their substance. Under questioning by Reynolds, Sinclair confirmed his notation that I had said I had had command of *Voyager* for a period of four or five days out of Tokyo. This important corroboration was both in his draft notes and in the final typed account of our interview.

During these early days of the commission I was beginning to suffer financially from the lack of opportunity to earn any income. Our costs of living continued at home, plus the obligation to keep my professional practice running at even a minimal level. Now there were new expenses associated with travel and parking during the inquiry hearings and private legal conferences. With little capital (having long since exhausted my paltry deferred pay from the RAN), I faced the prospect of going broke with equanimity. At the lunch adjournment one day I excused myself from attending our routine discussion of the morning's proceedings and made a quick visit to a jewellery store in the city. On my return, clutching a small black velvet box, I was asked if I were celebrating something – a birthday or anniversary, perhaps? Showing the pair of sapphire and diamond earrings that I would give to Sue, I replied that I was celebrating going broke but was determined to 'go out on a high note'. I was selling my car, my only saleable asset, the following day.

In retrospect this all seems rather melodramatic, but it had the unintended consequence of prompting my friends to embark on a course of action to rectify the situation. Until then, they had overlooked the fact that I was the only full-time participant in the commission whose income was not being met by the Federal Government. A uniform scale of remuneration for solicitors, barristers and senior counsel had been established when the inquiry opened, but the key witness and author of the Cabban Statement had been appearing *pro bono*. After an approach to Mr Burt to explain my situation and a telephone conversation between him and the Attorney-General, I was asked what I would accept as reasonable compensation (while at the same time being warned not to be 'silly'). I said that I had two alternatives: I would accept half of my verifiable, normal income, or nothing. I pointed out that I was paying my associate, Sophia, and that my wife was my secretary. It was essential that both be retained on their existing conditions. Half of my normal income was agreed, and paid retrospectively from the commencement of my full-time commitment to the inquiry, for which I am grateful to both the Crown and my legal team. I was in considerable debt by the conclusion of the commission, but it could have been much worse.

John William Smyth QC, counsel assisting Justice Spicer, was called after Captain Robertson had given his evidence. Smyth had been the relentless interlocutor whose personal dominance of the first royal commission allowed Spicer to ignore any question of Stevens' fitness to command and deflect some of the blame for the collision on to *Melbourne*. His appearance in the witness box was greatly anticipated by all parties, and the Sydney legal community in particular. If evidence had in fact been 'improperly withheld' in 1964, then someone would now have to extract those details from Smyth. For my part, Smyth's testimony lay at the absolute centre of my claims that the Navy and the Crown had participated in a cover-up. Smyth's last words to me after our interview – 'We'll be seeing a lot of you at the commission' – were the bitter epitaph to my original faith in the inquiry process. I had not been called, so my testimony to the health problems of Duncan Stevens was never heard.

The examination and cross-examination of major witnesses rarely proceeds in a logical, straightforward manner. Judges take little notice of the order in which facts are elucidated. They are often diverted by the need to satisfy tangential legal questions not apparent to the layman. As a consequence, even key evidence can be led in a frustratingly random manner. The pattern of the mosaic emerges slowly. Mr Burt examined Smyth rigorously about his interview with me and the impression that it had created in him. Smyth's memory was not precise, but he believed I had told him that I had command for either five days or ten days during the Far East cruise, and that I had said that I had to carry the captain to bed nearly every night in Tokyo. (Hiatt was later to quote Braund's recollection of the same interview and established that I had not said this at all.) But Smyth was certain that I claimed to have had command for a finite number of days. Specifically, he referred to a period when the ship left North Queensland (apparently confused with Darwin) and thought that I had said the transfer of command covered the entire passage to Singapore.

In terms of the drinking incidents, Smyth said that Griffith had denied them. Further, Smyth said that Griffith had maintained that Stevens was in active command throughout the cruise, and that he had never seen him intoxicated or ill. Smyth maintained that he was told consistently, except by me, that Stevens was a man who could hold his liquor. The description I had given of the near collision with *Caesar* had seemed to him to be too colourful, which determined his attitude that I was unreliable. Bearing in mind that the interview took place quite soon after the collision and that my memory and my mind were still being buffeted by trauma, I cannot honestly blame him for doubting me at that point.

Taken through my statement paragraph by paragraph, Smyth said that during our interview in 1964 I had not brought up many incidents described in it, which I am sure is true. When asked if he knew that *Voyager* carried a doctor, he said, 'No', and he had not enquired of that. In relation to the triple brandy (which had been qualified by naval witnesses right down to an ounce and a half), Smyth agreed that Hyland had told him the measure of spirits he had given Stevens was level with his three fingers around the bottom of a glass. Mr Burt promptly pointed out that this was very close to what I had described as about half a tumbler. Smyth asserted that he had asked me whether I thought that Stevens was drunk at the time of the collision, rather than me asking whether he were trying to suggest that he was. He denied that I had said I had heard rumours, but I am absolutely certain that I did, and that we had even discussed the source of them. When Smyth's attention was drawn to the description in my statement of the *Caesar* incident, he acknowledged the consistency with what I had described to him but could not remember me linking the *Caesar* navigator to the *Voyager* collision. Asked about the selection of Professor Blackburn as the expert on blood alcohol, he claimed not to know whose choice the professor had been, but when it was confirmed that the Stevens interests had nominated Blackburn, Smyth had no comment. He conceded that had he been aware of Stevens' ulcer condition, he would have drawn the professor's attention to it.

Burt had certainly traversed most of the terrain. Now it was the turn of my own counsel to draw this patchwork quilt of guarded recollections into focus. In his cross-examination, Jack Hiatt did not waste any time in taking Smyth to the crux of the matter: whether, as counsel assisting the first inquiry, he had allowed his subjective judgements to unfairly limit or distort the evidence that was presented for consideration. Jack soon had Smyth agreeing that he had concluded in 1964 that I was grossly exaggerating. He thought that if what I had said about Duncan's drinking were true, then it would be known throughout the length and breadth of the Navy. ('Known' and officially acknowledged are, of course, two entirely different things in a large institution such as the RAN. Even recently I have been told by two more officers who served with Stevens in other ships that he was turned in sick from drink for days on end.) Smyth conceded that if what I were saying was true – the sustained drinking and loss of command out of Tokyo – then he would have thought it was serious enough to enquire further. But he had called for Stevens' flimsies and spoken to several officers about Duncan's drinking. No adverse reports were forthcoming. The Navy cover-up was, of course, already in full swing, and it seemed remarkable to me that a barrister of Smyth's great experience had so unquestioningly accepted the uncorroborated denials of an interested party.

When specifically asked whether he discussed Captain Stevens with Captain Peek, Smyth was sure that he had, yet was uncertain if he had also discussed me with Peek. Nor had he called for my flimsies. If it had been necessary to review Stevens' personal records to establish character, why not mine? When Hiatt referred him to Braund's recollection of the interview (in which I had mentioned Stevens returning to *Voyager* one night in Tokyo in a state that required his being carried on board), he could not recall that being said. Most remarkably, Smyth said that he did not take any notes of persons interviewed during the inquiry, nor did he require anyone else to do so. There is no record of who was seen or in what context they were interviewed. Finally, to Hiatt, he said that Scott Griffith had denied absolutely everything that I had said about sickness, drinking, command and near collisions. The body-blow of that denial to my assertions in the Cabban Statement was a powerful shock. I can still see Griffith, at his home in the presence of his wife, assuring me that he had corroborated me in every detail!

Yet, after all this, Smyth still denied that his decision not to call me as a witness was based on the question of my reliability, but was rather prompted by his assessment of the relevance of the evidence he understood I would offer. But when cross-examined by Reynolds, for Robertson, Smyth claimed that he had decided that I was unreliable and exaggerating before the meeting with Griffith confirmed this view. Nonetheless, he maintained that if he had considered my evidence relevant he would have called me. Smyth QC was so skilful at juggling these fine distinctions and apparent contradictions that he was rarely pressed on the more fundamental issue of whether he was recalling events in a reliable manner. Then, in response to a direct question asking whether he had formed the view that I was 'psychiatric', he conceded that he had. The evening newspapers delighted in the headline 'Cabban Psychiatric'. In London, the tabloids played with the words 'Cabban Mad', which did not do much for the confidence of my relatives and friends in the UK.

Meanwhile, Reynolds, again quite understandably, was most interested in the aspects that affected the Spicer findings concerning *Melbourne*, and particularly John Robertson. He framed his questions in such a way as to highlight Smyth's appreciation and understanding of *Voyager*'s movements before the collision as indicators of who was in command on the destroyer's bridge. Smyth had accepted that a 'fishtail' manoeuvre, as described by me and confirmed by Becher, was usual for Stevens. Should the captain not have been alert to the potential danger when his ship departed from that pattern? Smyth did not think so. This area of speculation was certainly interesting, and might have even been legitimate under the 'seamanship of Captain D. H. Stevens' term of the inquiry, but it strayed a long way from the commission's essential purpose.

Mr Burt soon brought us back to the main highway when he rose to re-examine Smyth. He introduced matters relating to knowledge of my statement, of which Smyth had been made aware in mid-1965. Samuel Landau, secretary of the Department of the Navy, met individually with Sheppard (junior counsel assisting the commission) to review and make notes of my statement. These notes were subsequently proofread and amended by Smyth, and they specifically contradicted his contention that I had not told him much about the drinking habits of Captain Stevens during the 1963 cruise. This threw into clear doubt the counsel assisting's position on irrelevance. Burt had earlier secured an agreement from Smyth that he had approached the first inquiry as a 'running down' collision, similar to a motor vehicle accident. Yet, at the same time, he had not wanted to investigate and determine Captain Stevens' drinking habits! Instead, Smyth had accepted Blackburn's untested evidence, coupled with the accounts of the two survivors from the bridge of *Voyager* who had said the captain was not intoxicated. He also concluded that Stevens would not be hung over from a previous drinking bout, but never bothered to explain the basis of that conclusion. Nor was he convincing when revealing that he did not require notes of interview and statements to be taken when he did not intend to call a potential witness. Burt saw his opportunity and grabbed it. He asked Smyth whether this meant that he had already decided not to call me. The trap had snapped shut, but Smyth simply denied it. Nevertheless, it was secretly comforting to watch this very senior QC get a thorough – but ever-so-polite – mauling from one of his peers. There was more to come when the juniors crossed swords.

Chester Porter cross-examined Ian Fitzharding Sheppard, who had been Smyth's junior counsel at the Spicer commission. Sheppard struck me as an honourable man, and he testified that he had been present together with Braund throughout my interview by Smyth. He had already confirmed that it was his habit to make only sketchy notes during interviews. Now, Porter established beyond doubt that the three senior legal members of the Crown team interviewed together only if the potential witness was deemed, in advance, to be very important to the inquiry.

Sheppard also referred to my disclosure of matters related to the captain's drinking as being 'sensational' and leaving a much greater impression than other witness interviews. Chester then extended his probing to ask what the Crown team had done to follow up the potential evidence I had offered for the first commission. Sheppard said that after interviewing Griffith, when Hyland's statement came to hand, he had sent for Lieutenant Tuke, the captain's secretary at the time, to seek any corroboration of my allegations. Also, Signalman Evans from *Voyager* was recalled to the counsel's office by Sheppard to give a statement, of which a record was kept, regarding the captain and alcohol at the time of the collision. Evans' second statement disclaimed any knowledge of Stevens' drinking that night, but no record was ever made of Tuke's statement. Remarkably, Evans' account was therefore the only record retained in respect of Duncan's sobriety or otherwise on the bridge.

Steward Barry Hyland had been interviewed alone by Sheppard. In cross-examination it emerged that the statement attributed during the debates to Landau, secretary of the Navy, was wrong and grossly misleading. It claimed Hyland had said that Stevens did not have anything else to drink that day. In fact, the steward had come on duty only at 6 p.m. and said that he had no *knowledge* of any previous alcohol being consumed by Duncan Stevens that day. Hyland was not cross-examined during the Spicer royal commission and was not asked whether the captain had drunk any other alcohol during that day. When Chester Porter then queried the selection of Professor Blackburn as an expert witness, and the decision not to use established specialists in the field of the effects of alcohol on performance, there was open hostility from the bench. Sheppard told the inquiry that the professor had made it clear to the Crown that he was not a coroner's witness, and then Chester made the telling point that Blackburn's evidence was never tested at the first royal commission.

Sheppard offered a frank insight into the early attitudes of those who had been charged by the Crown with the responsibility of establishing the truth in 1964. He said that on reading Robertson's first report of the collision he and Smyth had formed the opinion that they would be in an adversarial situation with him. In that light, Smyth had decided not to call Robertson as a witness and had advised him to seek legal representation. Later, Sheppard revealed to Reynolds that immediately after reading

Robertson's report to the Naval Board, Smyth had decided that he would be making substantial criticism of *Melbourne*'s captain. How naïve of John Robertson to believe that he could represent himself, without understanding the vast difference between a naval inquiry and a royal commission!

The legal representatives of Captain Robertson had been slowly building their case for the reopening of the first commission's findings. Astute cross-examination was establishing prejudice, ignorance of the technical details involved and the unbalanced selection of expert witnesses. I felt that some of these points were making an impact on the commission, and at the conclusion of Sheppard's session Judge Burbury declaimed at some length on the use of the word 'adversary'. This gave Sheppard the opportunity to say that the word had been put into his mouth. Reynolds agreed, no doubt grateful that the crucial word had been accepted so readily as appropriate.

35
Medical Evidence

The detail of each day's evidence in the commission was now being scrutinised with such intensity that it was easy to lose focus on the principal object of the whole exercise. The first term of reference asked the fundamental question: if any of the allegations in my statement were true, did that establish 'that Captain Stevens was unfit to retain command of HMAS *Voyager*'? The apparently simple word 'unfit' was the crux of the matter. As far as the inquiry was concerned, its meaning was largely confined to the sense of physical incapacity – medically unfit. Not surprisingly, we would now hear exhaustive evidence from members of the medical profession, both naval and civilian. The phalanx of lawyers who crowded into the courtroom each morning had the task of un-tangling not just conflicting versions of events but also conflicting medical opinions. Everyone was aware that the commissioners were likely to seize on any subtle shade of meaning in the evidence of expert witnesses that might suit their purpose. A procession of doctors would be called to outline their views of Duncan Stevens' medical condition. Stripped of all its medical jargon, legal euphemisms and tactical distrac-tions, the job of this section of the inquiry was to determine whether Stevens was a drunk, seriously ill or perhaps both.

The first medical witness called was Surgeon Commander J. R. McNeill. He was an old friend of Duncan Stevens and fleet medical officer on board *Melbourne* during the 1963 cruise. McNeill testified that he had called aboard *Voyager* two or three times without informing her medical officer, Michael Tiller, of either his presence or that he had consulted with the captain, who was Tiller's patient. I had not been aware of McNeill's visits to *Voyager*, either. He had also seen Stevens aboard

Melbourne, again unbeknown to Tiller, and had diagnosed Stevens as fit before I visited Captain Peek in Hong Kong. (That was when I had been informed of the outcome of the diagnostic visit immediately before my leaving for *Melbourne* – a deliberate attempt to undermine any intention I might have had to discuss Duncan's health with Peek.)

The commissioners could not have escaped the conclusion that McNeill's friendship with Stevens led him to ignore, or circumvent, standard medical and naval practice. Worse was to come. He acknowledged that Stevens had informed him that he had been vomiting and suffered pain, but described this as 'mentioning' rather than as complaining. He insisted that his friend was not suffering a recurrence of his ulcer, but that these symptoms were only signs of a 'pre-ulcer condition'. Hiatt's cross-examination centred on the telephone call McNeill had made to the Member of Parliament, Sam Benson, during the *Voyager* debate on 17 May. In that curious conversation McNeill volunteered that Stevens had come to him privately with a serious stomach condition. Now, in the courtroom, he struggled to resile from his words as quoted in Hansard. When each of the commissioners intervened, he admitted that Stevens had suffered very intense pain. The failure to have this condition investigated further by X-ray examination in Hong Kong was queried, but McNeill could offer no credible reason.

In a written statement he had prepared more than three weeks before appearing, McNeill recalled that at Manus Island in 1954, Stevens had complained of pain and vomiting. Now, in the witness box, his memory was not as certain about the vomiting. He said that on the hypothetical set of symptoms put to him of a recurrence, about six weeks bed rest would be recommended for a patient. When challenged as to his reasons for not reporting the obvious ulcer condition while at Manus, McNeill declared that he honestly did not consider it serious enough. He was even prepared to deny the necessity to report pain and vomiting in a medical record. Yet these same records noted an itchy scalp, bruised fingers and mild attacks of dermatitis.

Burt drew from McNeill that a duodenal ulcer had symptoms of severe pain and vomiting and that these could require bed treatment. With little or no warning the ulcer could perforate and haemorrhage, causing a life-threatening crisis at sea. McNeill claimed that he judged the severity of the condition as his criterion for reporting – despite the fact that the Department of Veterans' Affairs decides pension eligibility on those records, and naval regulations required them to be complete and comprehensive. The inescapable conclusion was that this failure to report a serious and debilitating medical condition could have been prompted by Stevens' need to conceal that unfitness from the Navy.

On the subject of this duty to report fully on Stevens' health (and the likely outcomes if his ulcer perforated), McNeill tied himself in knots under the skilful cross-examination of both Burt and Hiatt. He disclosed that he had visited Duncan when he was hospitalised in Balmoral Naval Hospital for a period after being diagnosed with a duodenal ulcer in 1959. He conceded that he was certainly aware that a confirmed recurrence would jeopardise Stevens' career, but he was firm that Duncan never asked him not to report his illness.

The evidence of Dr Kerry Goulston, a consultant physician at the Royal Prince Alfred Hospital in Sydney, was specific and differed from McNeill's opinion. Goulston stated that the appropriate treatment for a duodenal ulcer patient was that they should not be exposed to too much stress and should have long periods of rest. They should be put to bed or hospitalised if symptoms are severe. His belief, shared by many others, was that diet was not as important as thought previously, as long as spicy food was avoided. Ulcer sufferers should drink alcohol only if necessary, and then in very small amounts with food. If they had to drink then it should not be to excess. Asked for examples, the doctor described 'large amounts' as two middies of beer a day or one or two glasses of sherry, depending on a person's habits. He said that there was no scientific proof that spirits eased the symptoms of ulcers. Finally, he said that if the patient were engaged in work that would deprive him of the possibility of avoiding stressful situations and taking regular meals, then he would ask him to change his lifestyle. Goulston left the commission in little doubt that Stevens should not have been commanding a destroyer, and was flouting all the normal precautions associated with a proven ulcer history.

Surgeon Commander Tim Haughton was in charge of the surgical section of Flinders Naval Hospital at the time of his evidence. Haughton had served with Stevens on Manus Island, but during that time Duncan had shared his stomach problems with McNeill rather than with Haughton. McNeill, or his predecessor, had presumably prescribed Amphogel, a non-stock antacid preparation for gastric problems, and this had been noted in his records. Only the removal of a wart had been recorded by Haughton, who was emphatic that he was meticulous about record-keeping and could therefore conclude that he knew nothing of Stevens' gastritis.

But Haughton's evidence was profoundly revealing in non-medical areas. He told the inquiry that Duncan would often drop in to Haughton's home late in the evening and confide his worries in his host. The theme was usually Stevens' ambition and his deep concern that he was in a backwater at Manus from which he could not gain adequate reports of recommendation for promotion. Haughton said that he spoke infrequently during these times, preferring to listen. Duncan would tell his life story, and of his fears, ambitions and family troubles. He said that when Beatrice Stevens joined her husband at Manus, these confessional visits abated.

Sir William Morrow – the anonymous 'knighted doctor' whose positive opinion Stevens had confronted me with at the climax of our crisis on *Voyager* – was seriously compromised as an expert witness. Morrow, a prominent gastroenterologist, had examined Stevens as a private patient without the customary referral from the Navy and could reasonably be expected to frame his evidence in a manner that reflected well on his own treatment. More significantly, Judge Asprey (one of the three royal commissioners) was a long-standing friend of Morrow and had also been treated by the 'knighted doctor' for an ulcer condition. Worse, Sir William was a consultant specialist to the Navy, yet he had failed to report Stevens' condition to the RAN after he had examined the captain in 1963. Morrow was also the Stevens' family physician. At no stage during the commission hearings, or in the ultimate report, did Justice Asprey disclose his intimate personal relationship with Sir William Morrow, the 'expert' medical witness. Asprey had attended the elite Sydney private school Newington College with Morrow, and they both then studied at the University of Sydney. They were close friends. All of this was known to Hiatt QC, and I believe (from Hiatt) to Burt, and very probably by other counsel at the inquiry.

Asprey's failure to disclose this close personal relationship was a major breach of judicial ethics, and would help to explain his strenuous attempt to exclude every genuinely independent expert witness on alcoholism. It would be difficult to imagine a more serious subversion of the strict fairness and impartiality expected of a senior judge. Why this has not emerged before now I am at a complete loss to understand. Hiatt had incorrectly believed that I was aware of this relationship, and told me of it only when I asked why he always referred to Asprey as 'utterly corrupt'.

Morrow produced his clinical notes and reports concerning the late Captain Stevens to Burt QC, who tendered them as an exhibit. These notes indicated that Duncan's ulcer had been diagnosed at the Naval Hospital in Hong Kong and that he had been hospitalised for a period from May to June 1959. Morrow confirmed making a note that one of the features causing aggravation to his ulcer was Stevens' drinking 'too much' on shore. A barium meal X-ray had been completed, and this showed that the ulcer had produced deformity but was inactive. Replying to Burt, Sir William stated that bed rest would be appropriate if a patient were in pain and vomiting some years after an ulcer was confirmed. Responsibility should be removed from him for at least four or five days, with complete bed rest. To me, that seemed to confirm Tiller's diagnosis in Tokyo precisely.

Ash QC, for the Stevens family, expended considerable effort ensuring that Morrow agreed that the captain had consumed large volumes of Amphogel, obtained from McNeill after exhausting *Voyager's* normal stocks. In a veiled reference to the Sunday morning in Tokyo, Ash hypothesised Stevens in bed sick at six-thirty, slyly continuing '. . . and you can assume that he had been stone cold sober for the whole of the previous day'. I could not believe that the commissioners would allow this fairy-tale scenario to proceed, but Ash seemed desperate to secure any support for his fantasy of a fit man beset with stomach problems brought on by overwork and spicy food. Morrow duly complied. In response to Hiatt's probing, in obvious reference to the 'captains' lunch' episode, Sir William said it was difficult to imagine the pain of an ulcer causing a man to lose consciousness. Morrow told Burt that Duncan had been reticent in providing information on his experiences in the Far East, and that as his doctor he had been obliged to extract it from him.

As a tailpiece to his evidence Morrow revealed that at the time of the 1964 royal commission the instructing solicitor for the Stevens family, Fred Osborne, had approached him for information concerning Duncan's health and also asked for a recommendation for an expert on blood alcohol analysis. He had recommended Professor Blackburn.

Following Sir William's evidence, there was a hiatus while all counsel (except Murphy QC) and the commissioners debated the suitability and veracity of that evidence on the basis of Morrow's own admission of his limited expertise.

As the medical evidence continued it became clear that one of the most significant areas of inquiry for the commission would be the apparent failure of the Navy's reporting systems to ensure that Stevens' health problems were properly recorded and known. The RAN medical director general, Surgeon Rear Admiral Coplans, was called to explain the naval requirements for recording patient histories. He left no doubt as to the inadequacy of Roger McNeill's records relating to Captain Stevens. The lack of reference to Stevens' ulcer condition in naval medical reports during 1963 could not be explained other than by systematic and deliberate cover-up to the level of captain's rank in the seaman branch and at least to surgeon commander in the medical branch. This was no surprise to me, nor to any past or serving naval officer at the time. Burt wished to know to whom a ship's (junior) medical officer could report if his captain ordered him not to report a condition that he wished to conceal. Coplans gave the obvious, simple and correct answer. He would have to protest in writing to the captain, who must then forward it to the administrative authority.

In his written statement read into the transcript, Surgeon Rear Admiral Coplans said that if my recollections were accepted as far as vomiting was concerned, then in his opinion Stevens was suffering a recurrence of his duodenal ulcer and would not be fit for sea service. A perforation of the ulcer at sea would completely incapacitate him, requiring major surgery. The captain of a destroyer in that condition would be immediately relieved of his command. In cross-examination, Ash proposed that I, as second in command while relieving Duncan when he was on leave, could be expected to have added something to the periodic medical report from the ship in my own writing. Presumably he was implying that I should have noted that the captain appeared to have an acute ulcer and was concealing it with the assistance of medical practitioners ashore and afloat!

While Hiatt was cross-examining Coplans, the chairman put to him a hypothetical scene that approximated the facts I had related of the passage from Tokyo. Coplans obliged by saying that in those circumstances the captain should be discharged to hospital for six weeks of treatment. He would then have been clinically down-graded for shore service for about twelve months, and might not go to sea again. The implications this carried for Stevens' further ambitions in the Navy were obvious.

The doctor closest to the situation had been Michael Tiller, whose evidence was anticipated with varying degrees of emotion and apprehension by the different parties. Mick Tiller was a big, bluff, confident fellow who had been *Voyager*'s doctor during the 1963 cruise and went on to a distinguished career as an orthopaedic surgeon. He was not called until 16 August when he had returned from Edinburgh where he was undertaking final studies towards a fellowship of surgery. Tiller was technically still in the Navy while finishing a ninety-day refresher period on completion of service. In later life Mick was happy to concede that his years in the RAN were largely a means to securing his qualifications. This might have been reflected in the rather curt, unvarnished style of the responses he had originally provided to the Navy when shown those passages of my statement in which he had been named.

Having first said that he had not been aware of any abnormality in the captain's health before the birthday dinner, Tiller was then asked what was the captain's condition when he entered the wardroom. He replied that he looked confused and was drunk. He described Stevens at the table looking dull, unaware of what was happening and moving his head slowly. Tiller told Burt that the captain was incoherent when he tried to speak after being given his present, and then described me assisting Stevens from the mess. He remembered seeing Duncan in his sea cabin afterwards and satisfying himself that his condition was solely related to alcohol.

When asked to describe his crucial meeting with Captain Willis on board *Vampire*, the doctor's recollection was very hazy, and he definitely could not remember any specific advice that he gave. He did recall that they had discussed the captain's health, and that Willis was a 'sincere sort of man' who was worried about Stevens. Surprisingly, he could not recall my involvement in Willis's decision to send for him, but he did remember an occasion when I had asked him about the possible consequences of an ulcer. This supposedly had occurred on the quarterdeck, in the afternoon. The only time that I recalled discussing this question was when he was in his cabin in Tokyo, before I saw Willis. Probed about Stevens' temperament, Tiller described an incident when the captain had bellowed from the bridge, 'What the fucking hell are you doing down there?' He confirmed my evidence that Stevens tended to flare up quickly, and then often forgot all about the incident.

Tiller's time in the witness box provided more than medical evidence. He revealed much about the way in which the Department of the Navy had strived to marshal a counter-attack against the substance of the Cabban Statement. In London, Tiller had received a message asking him to call Commodore Dacre Smyth, the naval representative at Australia House. He went to see him on 27 April 1967, just two days before completing his naval service, and Dacre Smyth handed him three papers. Each contained a brief extract from my statement at the head of the page, and left space below where Tiller's comments were presumably to be noted. Burt produced these papers in the courtroom and, one by one, directed Mick to say, to the best of his memory, what his comments had been. Tiller told him that he had corroborated the general thrust of what I had said, but felt that I had overstated some aspects.

Then, a bombshell. Dr Tiller disclosed that about a week later he had received a telephone call from the secretary of the Navy Department, Samuel Landau, who discussed his responses. He was asked by Landau, having told him that he had been given little time in Dacre Smyth's office to consider his replies, whether he would mind if they were destroyed. He said that he did not mind if Landau destroyed those initial responses – statements that had confirmed the crucial thrust of my outline of Stevens' health problems. (Tiller's original replies were duly destroyed, eventually to be replaced by a more considered statement that became an exhibit of the commission. It contained the memorable description of Captain Stevens being 'full as a boot'.)

Burt questioned Tiller on statements made by the dental officer, Allan Kyd, who had not yet been called, contradicting Tiller's earlier evidence in which he had denied the captain ever appeared in the sick bay other than on his normal rounds. Kyd had said that Stevens often came for a bottle of medicine, and that Tiller had described Stevens' symptoms to him. Tiller denied both these statements emphatically. Again, when shown part of David Martin's statement, he denied that he had ever told Martin that the captain was not co-operating with him on the question of diet. *Voyager*'s doctor was then confronted with evidence, given by the captain's cabin hand, that Stevens had been turned in for three or four days in

Hong Kong and was too ill to see the shoemaker when he called. Again, Tiller denied any recollection of Stevens' illness.

The incidents in Tokyo and the following week were fundamental to the Cabban Statement, and Tiller faced a long series of questions concerning that period. Some of his responses bordered on the bizarre. He could not agree that Willis was present in Stevens' cabin when he spoke to him about diet and the deleterious effect of alcohol. He went so far as to say that the first time he had seen Stevens after the meeting with Willis in *Vampire* was when *Voyager* was at sea. In answer to Burt's query of what he had told him when he eventually saw Stevens in his sea cabin, he said Duncan was in bed and that his condition had been brought on by alcohol. According to Tiller, until he had seen Willis, he had believed the captain was fit and well, and he did not know what had made Willis think otherwise.

The situation was in danger of descending into farce when the chairman intervened, asking if Stevens had told the doctor anything about wining and dining unwisely in Tokyo. This blatant invitation for Tiller to get the captain off the hook either went unnoticed or was deliberately declined. Tiller denied any such recollection. Not to be denied, Burbury went on, 'People are apt to get a little stomach upset in the East, are they not?' At this early stage of the inquiry the chairman had already signalled the intended tone of the commission's final report. The judges would do all in their power to ascribe Stevens' fitness problems to his duodenal ulcer while downplaying the role of alcohol. All the bench needed to do was encourage enough compliant (even if memory-deficient) testimony to support them in this pre-judgment.

But the doctor was an awkward witness. Although he no longer held any particular affection for the Navy, he also seemed to believe that it might not reflect well on his career prospects if he were to emerge from the inquiry as too strident a whistle-blower. It was a narrow path to tread, yet some of Tiller's more disarming responses in the witness box exposed the strained atmosphere in *Voyager* during the 1963 cruise. Under cross-examination by Hiatt, the doctor made his opinion of naval officers clear following the now-notorious birthday dinner. He said that he had previously been in dispute with some colleagues as to whether he was a naval officer first and a doctor second, but now thought, 'Well, that blows that up!' Tiller also described Commander Tapp, *Voyager*'s electrical officer, as a bit of a sycophant, or 'yes-man', when giving his reason for discounting Tapp's suggestion that the captain's obvious drunkenness was in fact only a stomach upset.

The procession of medical evidence was interrupted by a witness whose thoughts must have been dominated by the commission for months. The small, bespectacled figure of Samuel Landau, secretary to the Department of the Navy, was called to the box and sworn. Landau was a most senior public servant and, as such, answerable first to his political masters in cabinet (and Don Chipp, the Navy Minister, in particular). But he was also secretary to the Naval Board, where his department provided administrative support for the admirals who were in operational charge of the service. It was, in a way, fortunate for Landau that the interests of the government and the Navy clearly coincided as they closed ranks to protect each other from the impact of *Voyager*.

Landau cannot have been surprised when his initial examination covered the missing March report of proceedings, all six copies of which had mysteriously disappeared from his department's files. He could throw no light on this matter. Next came questions concerning his actions in respect of the responses he had collected to extracts from the Cabban Statement. He had passed some of these to the minister, but others – including the statements from Tiller and Alan Willis – were kept in his safe. He did not think the fact that Willis had completely corroborated my comments about his opinion of Griffith was relevant, and had excluded it from the material contained in the parliamentary paper tabled by Chipp. This appeared to indicate that the Naval Board had colluded with the minister to discredit me, and to exclude anything that might support the substance of my statement. (The commission had, of course, already heard evidence that Landau destroyed Tiller's original comments, which broadly agreed with my descriptions of events involving Stevens and alcohol.) That had neatly cleared everything away for the minister to claim in parliament – quite wrongly – that there was no corroboration for my statement.

Hiatt's cross-examination of Landau was measured, but throughout this session he was repeatedly interrupted by each of the commissioners, as well as by Murphy (for the Navy) and Ash (for the Stevens family). Jack Hiatt obviously knew more than Landau was prepared to tell. The judges were equally determined to preserve politically sensitive material from public exposure. There were objections to the line of questioning that proved that Landau had in his possession a revised statement by Lieutenant Commander Griffith, substantially corroborating me, while he was actually in the House of Representatives, before and during the minister's speech on 16 May. Landau sat in parliament and did nothing to intervene while his minister claimed, at the despatch box, that Griffith had not corroborated me. There was further damning evidence that Landau had knowingly allowed his minister to mislead parliament. He confirmed that although he had actually received Tiller's comments before the party room meeting in Canberra, he had not provided them to the minister before that meeting. He had discussed with the minister his intention of calling Tiller after the party room meeting, but there was never a possibility of receiving his revised statements before the debates, so in the end none were received. Many months later Gough Whitlam, as opposition leader, referred in parliament to 'this creature Landau'. Whitlam had to withdraw the remark, but anyone who had watched the performance of the Navy secretary during this period could only agree with that insult.

The dentist, Surgeon Lieutenant Allan Kyd, followed Landau to the witness box. His initial statement had been supportive so I looked forward to a straightforward and honest disclosure of his observations. Sadly, Kyd was soon resiling from what he had said when interviewed before being called as a witness. Where originally he had stated that the captain appeared in the sick bay regularly to pick up medication, now he claimed he had meant only once or twice. Similarly, 'often present in person' now meant no more than twice. But the dentist acknowledged, after some prevarication, that he recalled Tiller telling him that Stevens suffered severe discomfort from stomach pains and a stomach disorder, and had bouts of illness. (Tiller was adamant in his denial of this.)

Chester Porter cross-examined Kyd, and his questioning prised open a sensational door that had until then been kept firmly shut. He raised the possibility that alcohol might not have been the sole cause of Stevens' erratic behaviour. Covering the wardroom dinner, Chester asked whether Kyd had formed the opinion that when the captain entered the mess he had consumed a few drinks on top of a powerful drug. Kyd said, 'Yes.' To confirm this reply, Porter asked a supplementary question about high-powered pills, and received another 'Yes'. The genie was, quite literally, out of the bottle. It was probable that Duncan Stevens had been taking a significant drug other than Amphogel, and in pill form. Burbury, Asprey and Ash all exhibited immediate alarm over this suggestion, and Kyd eventually back-pedalled. But the suggestion of Stevens using a powerful drug in combination with alcohol was discussed for long enough to be noticed.

In his autobiography, published in 1978, Don Chipp refers to a 'secret session' of the commission, held close to this time. The former Navy minister claims that the alleged hearing was with an unnamed doctor who disclosed that Stevens was supplied with, and was taking, amphetamines. All three commissioners later denied this to Lieutenant Tom Frame, who was then researching his PhD thesis on the *Voyager* tragedy. In spite of those denials, I have always believed Don Chipp on this, for why on earth would he need to invent such a specific allegation? It might be unrelated, but following the closing of the sittings the secretary to the commission, R. H. Wineberg, approached Jack Hiatt in an obviously disturbed frame of mind, saying that he wished to see him at a later date. His subsequent accidental death prevented this tantalising meeting from ever taking place.

Notwithstanding the surprise emergence of amphetamines as a medical side issue, the central question of alcohol remained. The evidence that *Voyager*'s captain had occasionally consumed prodigious amounts of spirits was overwhelming, but did he consistently drink to excess? During the debate in parliament that had prompted the inquiry, Ted St John described Duncan Stevens as a chronic alcoholic. There was now an undisguised eagerness by the commissioners to avoid any suggestion that this description could be accurately applied to him. They wrote to Dr John Birrell, Victorian police surgeon and a specialist in matters relating to alcoholism, and to Sir William Morrow, requesting them both to respond with their assessment of the condition of Captain Stevens, given the set of circumstances in the birthday dinner, the *Rothesay* lunch and the 'lost in *Yarra*' incident. Birrell replied, stating unequivocally that he and two extremely well-credentialled colleagues had reached the conclusion that Duncan was an alcoholic. In his letter to the commission dated 20 September 1967 (exhibit 183) Birrell states, 'It is perhaps worth mentioning that the taking or action of tranquilizers or barbiturates such as Amytal or phenobarb together with a level of 25mgms per cent [blood alcohol] could produce quite marked effects.'

But the commissioners decided that they would not call Dr Birrell as a witness. Instead, they preferred to recall Sir William Morrow, who took a much more benign attitude to 'unwise drinking' by a man with an ulcer history. Morrow pleased the judges with evidence that was not considered by either Hiatt or Samuels QC to be expert in the field of alcoholism. Fortunately, both Hiatt and Samuels fought strongly for Birrell to be called. They were supported by Burt, who stated the case with total impartiality and a persuasive exposition of the special factors involved. The commissioners finally gave way, and Dr Birrell journeyed up from Melbourne for his turn in the witness box.

Birrell's particular area of expertise was the behavioural effects of alcohol. Long before the introduction of random breath testing his role, with Victoria Police, gave him abundant opportunities to study inebriation and the distinctive characteristics of drunkards. He was cross-examined superbly by Hiatt and had no reticence in describing Stevens' behaviour patterns as those of an alcoholic. This led to perhaps the most famous quote of the whole inquiry. Jack was rather labouring the point, asking Dr Birrell questions that elicited the same response, confirming his conclusion that Stevens was an alcoholic. Hiatt was finally interrupted by an exasperated Justice Asprey. 'It is like asking a question in these circumstances: if you see a man outside an hotel clutching an armful of broken bottles of beer, lying in the gutter, reeking of alcohol, you ask him if he's drunk.'

Not missing a beat, Hiatt replied, 'In this commission one gets the impression that it would be an ulcer.'

Birrell's evidence was certainly encouraging, but the most incisive expert material put before the commission on the question of alcoholism and Stevens' behaviour was contained in a written statement whose author was, incredibly, never called as a witness. A consultant pathologist, Dr F. S. Hansman MB, ChM MRCP (London), FRACP, MCPA prepared a scientifically precise document of sixteen pages after reviewing the transcripts of both inquiries, thus far, including the evidence of Professor Blackburn and Sir William Morrow. In the first part of his report, Hansman concluded that although the validity of the blood analysis from the recovered bodies could be accepted, the validity of the actual material on which those analyses were made could not. Indeed, he stated that they were open to grave doubt. Dr Hansman wrote that Professor Blackburn could not be held to have been qualified to give expert evidence in the matter before the commission, and that Blackburn's calculations were based on 'an intake of alcohol' that was never assessed or specified in a court procedure. Instead, those figures were derived from information provided by Smyth QC (as counsel assisting the first commission) and before Steward Hyland's sworn evidence was heard. Blackburn had been at pains to stress the unsatisfactory manner in which the post-mortem specimens were obtained, but then drew deductions on the basis that these samples were valid. This left the distinct probability that some of the complement of *Voyager* might have been affected by alcohol they had consumed shortly before the disaster.

Part II of the Hansman statement, 'The Significance of the Triple Brandy and its Relation to an Unknown Factor X', is critical to our understanding of the likely factors leading to the collision. The pathologist first gave a thorough discourse on the difficulty of detecting liver damage, even by liver function tests, despite the fact that Morrow had found the liver palpable. Then he asked: why did Stevens not give his private consultant (Morrow) a straightforward account of his medical history, including his recurring attacks of so-called alcoholic gastritis, his bed confinement after Tokyo, the shrunken appearance and marked loss of weight, which all provided considerable evidence of a damaged liver? Hansman used the evidence of Dollard in the restaurant on the Sunday evening before our departure from Tokyo to illustrate an episode when a situation evoking stress might lead Stevens to take an 'incitant drug' where alcohol was also taken. The events of Sunday morning provide the most telling evidence: 'Too sick to attend Church Service and apologies sent. Then a remarkable recovery by lunchtime. The most feasible explanation is that he took an excitant drug to prepare himself for the important and stressful occasion of meeting and entertaining the Australian Ambassador to Japan on board the *Voyager*.' Then, in the evening at about nine o'clock, he had the episode described by Dollard as 'half asleep. From being quite alive and alert in his behaviour and appearance he was suddenly and quite suddenly – I think this is the same sort of thing that happened at the buffet party in my house – his head dropped and he was half asleep.' Dollard reported three comparable episodes, and there was another in *Rothesay*.

What caused these extraordinary changes? Hansman noted:

Stevens never apologised, made excuses or gave any explanation of his behaviour relating to these episodes. If there had been nothing

he wished to conceal, nothing on which he feared to be questioned, it would be expected that he would have made an effort to
re-establish himself in the respect of his fellow officers and seek
medical advice as to their cause. Neither Surgeon Commander
McNeill or Surgeon Lieutenant Tiller gave evidence that he sought
their advice on this matter.

He continues, 'Obviously these could not have been isolated incidents
where he took excitant drugs but in other cases the circumstances, and
therefore the end results, varied.'

I believe the reason this eminently qualified and appropriate expert
witness was never called for the purpose of testing his evidence was the
conclusion that he reached:

We can finally return to the fateful night on the *Voyager* to suggest
that a rational explanation of events preceding the collision would
be as follows:

On the evening Captain Stevens became increasingly affected by
the responsibilities he was faced with, and so again he resorted to an
excitant drug and then after the supper he felt the need of further
stimulation and took his triple brandy, at a period of time closely
related to 8.56 p.m. he had a sudden episode over the chart table
and the rest of the officers on the bridge were in a confused state at
that critical time.

Even if the hypothesis of an excitant drug can be definitely
excluded, the fact still remains that whatsoever the causes of the
previous episodes that these same causes apparently operated once
again on that evening.

This statement had been signed two months after Kyd's evidence was
given, so it had no influence on Chester Porter's awareness that Kyd was
referring to the captain taking amphetamines, the 'excitant drug'
probably responsible for all of these episodes. Hansman was explaining
precisely why I had observed that Stevens could sometimes drink
for long periods without effect while, on other occasions, he would
'fold' very quickly. More than that, he might have explained the true
wellsprings of the collision: a fatal mixture of alcohol and amphetamines.
That was hardly what the commissioners, the government, the Naval

Board or the Stevens interests wanted. Is it any wonder the judges declined to have this analysis aired at the commission? It would also explain a secret session being convened to verify that Duncan Stevens had, in fact, been taking unprescribed and unrecorded amphetamines. By any measure the failure to call Dr Hansman as a witness was an extraordinary omission.

36

Admirals' Hypotheticals

From the outside, the Royal Australian Navy might seem like a vast, impersonal institution. In truth, at least at the officer level, it is remarkably small. The paths of the professional senior cohort cross and recross many times between the time they complete their college training and the time when a select few achieve flag rank. A disaster such as the *Voyager* collision brings those inter-relationships into sharp focus; the scandal that followed placed loyalty, friendship and respect under sometimes unbearable pressure. Embedded in these conflicts was the ancient moral dilemma of having to choose between personal conscience and the common cause: the expendable individual against the greater good. For the Navy – indeed any segment of our armed services – the means to resolving any doubts in that context always lies in the rigid machinery of rank. The institution can function only if everyone within it accepts the unbroken chain of absolute authority that descends from the Naval Board to the lowliest ordinary seaman. But while command cascades down each finely graduated rung of the promotional ladder, responsibility refers upward. That is the price of rank. It was inevitable that the admirals who ran our Navy during the mid-1960s would be spending time in the commission's witness box.

Rear Admiral R. I. Peek, who had been commanding officer of *Melbourne* in 1963 before Robertson, had now succeeded Rear Admiral Becher as Flag Officer Commanding Australian Fleet (FOCAF). Peek was familiar with most aspects of the first commission, having been attached as its 'naval adviser'. He was my captain in *Sydney* in 1962.

At the commencement of his examination, questions were led concerning his role in the first inquiry, and the admiral said, 'I believe I was there as a so-called naval expert to assist counsel.' But during the

Spicer hearing Peek had also given evidence as an expert witness. His statement regarding the moment before the collision raised the possibility that Stevens could have taken control of the ship out of the hands of the OOW. Burt now pressed Peek for an explanation of the conditions under which command on the bridge passes from the OOW to the captain and back. The admiral was specific, confirming my contention that when the captain gives a wheel or engine order to the officer of the watch, the captain then has the ship until he transfers it back to the OOW.

Inevitably, the questioning turned to alcohol, and Burt laid his groundwork very carefully. The terms of reference of this second commission allowed the judges to vary the Spicer findings on the loss of *Voyager*, but only if they had first satisfied themselves that Stevens had been unfit to command. That, in turn, would depend on their acceptance of specific incidents as described in the Cabban Statement. Burt began by suggesting that the commission might conclude that Stevens had a brandy occasionally for pain relief, leading to vomiting. This might have distracted him from the running of the ship at the crucial time. If this were true, and Spicer had not considered it, then the findings of Spicer might have to be varied. It was a clever use of hypothetical argument. The artful device of having witnesses consider a hypothesis that closely followed the scenarios described in my statement would emerge as a consistent theme while the admirals were giving their evidence.

Burt secured agreement that 'drunkenness' is when the subject is so affected by alcohol that he is unable to perform a duty that he might be called upon to do. Peek tried to draw a distinction between being drunk at home and on board, but this difference foundered without the circumstance being specified (as with captains who lived aboard). Collecting himself, the admiral was firm that a captain should never be incapable of carrying out his duties on board, and on any notice. As FOCAF he would be concerned if a captain were drunk on board in any circumstances. The chairman intervened to ask about a captain in civilian clothes ashore being affected by alcohol while not representing his ship. Peek said he would look on one instance with disfavour, but when put as a repeated action, he would propose that the board remove that captain administratively. He regarded the hypothesis that was, in effect, the Hong Kong Army party as much more serious, leading probably to court martial.

To Burbury's suggestion that to be drunk in uniform at an official function ashore would be more serious, the admiral responded that he would regard it as less serious than being drunk at a social function on board his own ship. 'On board his own ship he is personally in command; when he is ashore there is somebody else personally in command in his own ship.' To a stranger wandering into the commission these courtly debates about varying degrees of gravity would have seemed bizarre. Outside, a person found to be drunk was routinely locked up for a day by the police – for both their own and society's protection. Yet in the RAN it seemed there were important distinctions to be drawn between whether the drunk was ashore or on board, and whether he was in uniform representing his ship or in mufti just having a good time as a private individual. I found it difficult to reconcile the weight given to these issues with the loss of eighty-two lives.

Reynolds QC, for Captain Robertson, adopted the hypothetical technique to probe Peek's view of Stevens' conduct at the birthday dinner. Did the captain's behaviour indicate a lack of responsibility? Peek replied that he would issue a very serious warning to the captain and, 'I think I would go further than that in fact. I think I would have a formal inquiry made as to whether the condition was due to alcohol or sickness: I would not let it rest on gossip, in fact.' Then, to the proposition that 'You would give grave consideration to immediately relieving that officer of his command, would you not?' Peek responded, 'If the facts were established as you have given them.' Following an objection by Ash, Burbury from the bench rephrased the proposition in unequivocal terms, 'That the captain was very much under the influence of liquor at the beginning of the dinner, that he went down on his hands and knees over to the table, did not survive the second course and then collapsed and retired?' Peek saw where this was leading and asked, 'Could I correct the previous answer? I think I agreed with you I would consider relieving [him] of his command. I do not believe that is, in fact, what I would do. I would, if there was a *prima facie* case as you suggest, I would allow a court martial to adjudicate on the matter, which is one of the purposes of a court, of course, to see whether the facts are true or not.'

No doubt the bench was meant to be flattered by this testimonial to the process of justice, but Judge Lucas seized on the unpleasant practical implications. 'You would be content to leave him in command until the determination of that court martial was made?'

Peek: 'That is true.'

Here was bitter confirmation of my ever-present fear in 1963. How could I expect a fair consideration of any complaint against Stevens while the captain still retained his position? What would my access to potential witnesses have been? Duncan would have made hay with all the officers depending on him for promotion. The captain's day cabin door was opposite mine. He was aware of anyone seeing me, for whatever reason, and vice versa. Meanwhile, both of us would have had to continue the essential communication required for the routine running of the ship. What a nightmare, and fiasco, it would have been!

Returning to the debacle of the birthday dinner Ash QC, for the Stevens family, suggested that horseplay was quite common at mess dinners, which was acknowledged. When he suggested it was not unusual before the meal, he was told, 'I think most unusual. I believe I would have been horrified had my captain behaved in the way that has been suggested, before the dinner.' And that was exactly the effect on me when Duncan dropped to his knees. Peek then related the conduct to 'his lack of sensitivity towards his officers'. Sadly, I believe that Duncan was too drunk at the time to realise that he was being insensitive.

Going further along the hypothetical track, Reynolds (for Robertson) then expanded his questioning to include Tokyo and the concealment of the handover of command. After a long passage of objections and legal argument, he was eventually able to ask Peek directly whether a captain in that situation would be a man unfit for command. 'I think that would be going too far. He may, on your hypothesis, be unfit for medical reasons.' But could he accept the concealment of the handover? 'If I accept that, I would agree that this showed the characteristics [unfitness to command] you have outlined. It still might be explicable on medical grounds.'

The chairman asked, 'Do you mean unfitness to command at that point of time, or in a general sense that you think he would be unfit to command generally and should be relieved of his command?'

Peek: 'I believe if it came to my notice that a captain had deliberately concealed such a state of affairs from his senior officer he should be relieved of his command by administrative action of the senior officer or FOCAF.' The admiral acknowledged that a captain with an illness he could cope with (and from which he would recover) might not reveal it, but that deliberate concealment as opposed to mere 'failure to report' was objectionable. In relation to the requirement to inform senior officers of a captain's absence from the bridge owing to illness at sea, Peek said that the officer in tactical command should know if it were for twelve to twenty-four hours, and that FOCAF and the Naval Board should be informed of two or more days.

With his customary patience, my counsel Jack Hiatt now extracted a sequence of concessions from Admiral Peek that did much to make real for the commission the difficulties of my position as executive officer in *Voyager* while grappling with what should be done about the captain's health problems. Peek agreed that, 'It would put him in an impossible position. They could not go on being the captain and executive officer of the same ship. One would have to go, and if the complaint were unjustified one would assume it would be the executive officer. The moment of truth comes when it becomes official.' Had I made a report, would I be completely in the hands of the other officers in my ship as to what judgement they made between the conflict of loyalty to their captain and loyalty to the Navy generally? Peek said that while he could conceive of one or two officers giving false evidence, he 'could not conceive of a whole wardroom giving false evidence at a formal board of inquiry'. From what we had already heard at the royal commission that proposition held little comfort for me, or for my legal team.

After outlining the 'Lost in *Yarra*' incident, Hiatt put to Peek: 'And it would then inevitably lead to a court martial, would it?'

'I would think so.'

And to leave no doubt as to the seriousness of the breach, Jack pressed for confirmation. 'Even if there was nothing else at all, this would be the only thing – even with a captain of impeccable character?'

'That would be my view.'

Events as I had described earlier in the cruise, including the departures from Sydney and Darwin, were put to Peek. Would he expect the executive officer to be desperately worried by that stage? He said that if he had been in my shoes he certainly would have been worried. Turning to the crucial defaulters' parade after Tokyo, the admiral confirmed that it was not permitted by regulation for me to exercise the powers of captain's rank in any circumstances. I knew this, but had deliberately gone ahead out of my desperation to obtain some hard evidence of the illegal situation in which Willis and Stevens had placed me. That implication was, of course, obvious to Stevens when he resumed command and had the paperwork retyped.

On the subject of this concealment of the situation by falsifying the punishment returns, Peek said, 'This goes beyond concealment: this goes to falsification of public documents, which I think is an offence under the Naval Discipline Act.' Hiatt put it directly to Peek that the captain must have had a tremendously compelling reason to do this, saying that there was only one answer, if the facts were established. Burbury intervened twice from the bench to derail this conclusion, but the point had been made. Jack asked Peek to consider the situation in which senior officers had declared that their loyalty to the captain required them to support him, regardless of what had been done by way of destruction of documents. 'I find this difficult to imagine,' was the reply. Indeed, I would have found it impossible to imagine – until it actually happened. On balance, Peek had been a fair and open witness. Now it was time to hear from his ultimate superior.

Vice Admiral Sir Hastings Harrington, who had been Chief of Naval Staff at the time of the collision, died not long after the initial inquiry and was superseded by Vice Admiral Sir Alan McNicoll. Through his earlier appointment as Flag Officer Commanding Australian Fleet, McNicoll was the officer most likely to have relevant knowledge of Stevens' conduct and *Voyager*'s operations in 1963. Together with Samuel Landau, he was also the most likely to have been the recipient of reports from Dollard, Willis and Ambassador McIntyre, either directly or via the Department of Foreign Affairs. I had served with McNicoll as my captain in *Shoalhaven* in 1949. His evidence occupies almost 150 pages of transcript and was taken over a period of three days – days that I did not enjoy, one iota. He had earlier submitted a twenty-six-page statement that concluded by stating the obvious: there were abundant opportunities for any of *Voyager*'s officers to submit complaints about their captain to higher authority if they had wished to do so. What he neglected to mention was that those complaints would have to be submitted through the captain himself.

Burt began with the paperwork. Could Sir Alan shed any light on the disappearance of the six copies of the report of proceedings for the month of March, as yet unexplained by either Landau or Peek? Regrettably, he could not. Meanwhile, the Navy insisted on maintaining the integrity of the AS206 confidential reports on officers – with which I had no disagreement – but when the admiral was in the box, counsel entered into hearty debate over their admissibility. Burt initially wished to raise questions relating to McNicoll's comments on Stevens' ship-handling abilities, while Jack Hiatt wanted to establish whether Duncan had recommended me for promotion. The report on Stevens, dated 6 January 1946, expressed McNicoll's view that he 'handles his ship well but his movements in company sometimes show more impetuosity than judgement'. Straining to give credence to the theory that some senior officers often considered impetuosity a virtue, the admiral eventually said that on qualities such as speed of reaction and dash he rated Stevens high, but on the more reflective ones of judgement he rated him lower.

McNicoll rather fancied his abilities at character assessment. In the first paragraph of his vitriolic submission to the Minister for the Navy on the eve of the *Voyager* debates, he had described me, from his memory of *Shoalhaven*, as being immature and foolish. On reflection I believe he was most probably not far off the mark then, but I do not believe his arrogance lessened whereas I matured and became more responsible. Burt scored a subtle direct hit during a sequence of questions relating to the difficulty or otherwise of me seeking advice informally in Hong Kong. McNicoll said that the first lieutenant would be in a very difficult position *vis-à-vis* his captain when required to canvass the views of other officers in the ship. 'I can see a very considerable difficulty; it is a very unenviable position.' Burt added, 'In a case like the present one, it really involves a very large area of judgement?'

McNicoll replied, 'I am not sure what actual case you are referring to.' I took some small, secret pleasure from seeing the vice admiral's real persona peep out briefly from behind his ice-calm demeanour.

When giving a reply relating to his view on a captain's concealment of his condition when ill and unable to attend the bridge, McNicoll gave a particularly long-winded response. He concluded that it would be a very distressing situation if it occurred, but he would find great difficulty in believing that it had actually happened. What was routine in *Voyager* during 1963 was clearly incredible to the vice admiral! Expanding this hypothesis to include falsifying documents, Burt proposed that investigation had established the falsification. This drew from the admiral, 'I think it would be a court martial offence.' It was revealing that all three commissioners, as well as Murphy and Ash, kept interrupting Burt as he then attempted to invite McNicoll to express an opinion as to whether such behaviour would constitute unfitness to command.

Murphy QC, for the Navy, gave McNicoll the opportunity to avow that, to his certain knowledge, no documents of the Naval Board contained any reference to any matter that in any way touched upon matters set out in the Cabban Statement. It seemed a case of 'methinks the Chief of the Naval Staff doth protest too much'. Hiatt resisted pressure by the chairman to cross-examine McNicoll on factors of fitness to command that had been put to Admiral Peek. Burbury joined in, describing certain propositions put to Peek as self-evident. But Jack argued that Ash, if anyone, should put these hypothetical cases to McNicoll. This was argued back and forth until Hiatt, in a faintly exasperated reply to Justice Lucas, said, 'I would have to agree with Your Honour, to an extent, because something which is accepted as self-evident with Admiral Peek is by no means self-evident with Admiral McNicoll.' How prophetic that was.

Much of this verbal sparring was atmospheric – the type of exchange that lawyers hope will provoke some apparently inconsequential lapse from the witness that eventually leads to a major concession. We were on far more substantial ground when my counsel began to pick through the way the Naval Board had gone about attempting to discredit the statement I had dictated for Hickling. Just three weeks before the commission began hearing evidence, the deputy Crown solicitor wrote to eight officers who were then serving overseas to ask whether they could corroborate the Cabban Statement. (The letter had, in fact, been drafted by Murphy QC in his capacity as counsel for the Navy.) Hiatt now asked the vice admiral of his personal knowledge of that letter, written on 26 June 1967. It included extracts of my statement and an outrageously leading paragraph: 'For your information, it is alleged that Captain Stevens during the period *Voyager* was in port during her tour of duty in the Far East between 31st January 1963 and 3rd August 1963 drank to excess. I might add that I have not been able to obtain any corroboration of these allegations from witnesses already interviewed in Australia.'

McNicoll claimed only very recent knowledge of the letter. Hiatt mercilessly pursued the vice admiral, querying the intent and veracity of the last sentence, given that the board had by then substantial knowledge of corroboration of my claims. He sailed close to the wind, referring to the Naval Board as 'that inchoate entity'. Judge Lucas suggested that any reply could only be comment. The paragraph, Jack countered, was either untrue or misleading; untrue if, at the date it was written, people had been interviewed, and misleading if they had not. In the end, McNicoll avoided committing himself to any opinion of the construction to be fairly placed on the paragraph, suggesting that it was new to him and that he would require time to think about it.

A similar haziness attached to the vice admiral's recall of the telephone conversation between Landau and Tiller during which the doctor was pressured to agree to the destruction of his original comments on my allegations. McNicoll agreed he had 'some knowledge' of the call, but could not remember whether Landau had told him the details of his actions, which were now on the record in the transcript of the commission. The most senior officer in the RAN could not even remember that his conversation with Landau was before the parliamentary debate, only that it was soon after Landau and Tiller had spoken.

The Naval Board maintained pressure on its officers and men during the period of the inquiry in some less obvious ways. *Navy News*, the free newspaper available to all personnel, contained daily bulletins of the commission, including the names of witnesses and detail of their evidence on each incident. Hiatt cited this as a source of influence and coercion on as-yet-uncalled witnesses. McNicoll, always quick to laud the newspaper for its informative value and impact on morale, was nevertheless able to dismiss this proposition. He also denied knowledge of any directive or bulletin issued to serving personnel advising them that the Naval Board expected those who were witnesses to tell the truth without qualification or reserve.

The vice admiral's unctuous manner as a witness almost invited attack. Jack asked him whether he had noticed any undue difficulty in memory, bearing in mind that the events under examination were four years back. Murphy immediately rose to suggest that Jack was being unnecessarily offensive, but the chairman interposed that the suggestion had some arguable basis and was therefore not objectionable as comment. There was more fun to be had taking McNicoll over advice he had apparently given the Navy Minister. During the *Voyager* debate Don Chipp cited the vice admiral as confirming that a 'triple brandy in the Navy' was equivalent to 'one' brandy. McNicoll now told the inquiry he thought he had said that a triple brandy was equal to one 'tot' – of which there are thirty to a bottle. That was news to me. Whenever I had been the recipient of a tot of rum as a midshipman, I was treated far more generously.

Coming to a more serious aspect of my situation, McNicoll was asked whether he conceded that I had done my duty to the Navy in reporting to Jim Willis in Tokyo. The vice admiral first claimed that he had been overseas when Willis gave his evidence, then said that he had read the transcript – 'rather hurriedly'. McNicoll asserted that my conversation with Willis would not be considered as a formal report. It had perhaps the elements of an informal report, being more in the nature of just going to a senior officer for advice. Hiatt then put the facts directly of my evidence as to the discussion with Willis. McNicoll at last conceded that it was a report. From that point he agreed that an investigation should be commenced, first with the doctor. Then, if the doctor confirmed the seriousness of the medical condition, would it be proper to see the captain? 'Not necessarily,' said McNicoll. 'If you were convinced of the gravity of the situation I would get him to the nearest naval hospital for a thorough overhaul so I would have the opinion of a competent medical board and prognosis.' This was the Chief of Naval Staff at his obfuscating best: happy to invoke formal steps of procedure, irrespective of any personal considerations or consequences.

On his second day in the witness box, Vice Admiral McNicoll was asked by Hiatt whether he had received any advice, as far as the interests of the Naval Board were concerned, that it would be unwise to deal with hypothetical questions. He replied, 'This is an opinion which I reached myself very readily having heard some of the hypothetical questions put to earlier witnesses.' When challenged to substantiate his written submission that my statement contained deliberate falsehoods, he could only cite Bruce Loxton's denial of having told me that Duncan had drunk a bottle of brandy on the train. (Note that the denial was of having told me, not that the incident itself had not occurred.) Hiatt later challenged McNicoll's response to the letter of Dr Malcolm Mackay in which that member of parliament had praised my personal qualifications and character. The vice admiral's response underlined the determination of the Naval

Board to diminish the impact of the Cabban Statement by denigrating my motives. 'I do not agree with Dr Mackay that he had no grudge against the Navy and no antipathy towards Stevens.' McNicoll acknowledged having seen Duncan's final report on me, dated 30 September 1963, in which he recommended me for immediate promotion for the second time in six months. Nevertheless, the Chief of Naval Staff could then write: 'It is baffling that Dr Mackay and his associates are prepared to accept the unsworn testimony of a man who failed to make the grade in the Navy against the word of serving officers, however senior.'

Admirals should be very careful before using such loaded phrases as 'failed to make the grade'. Their words might come back to haunt them. Just four years earlier McNicoll, as FOCAF, had himself forwarded to the Naval Board my 206 from Stevens. It read:

> *Departmental Report:* Cabban has carried out his duties as Executive Officer with zeal and energy. His planning has usually been good and the results of his efforts better than average. He has run the wardroom with tact and firmness and handled welfare matters thoroughly and conscientiously. As his experience as an Executive Officer increased he gained more confidence. He would have enjoyed greater success if he had developed a more positive approach.
>
> *General Report:* Despite the submission of his resignation Cabban has continued to work conscientiously and well. He has a good knowledge of welfare and morale problems and has done very well in this aspect of his work. He is, above all, intensely loyal. He is normally cheerful and possesses a quiet sense of humour. He keeps himself fit and his appearance is good.

But the Chief of Naval Staff was in the witness box to play the man and not the ball. Although he confirmed he had first seen my statement for Hickling as early as August 1965, he acknowledged that he never attempted to see me to determine whether it were true or whether the Navy should 'put its house in order'. McNicoll counter-attacked, 'We have become so accustomed to the document that one forgets what a cruel and pitiless document it is. One knows it is not the product of a wicked man, but it seemed a purposeless document. And in so far as the Navy putting its house in order, the first thing, and the step which is lacking, is to convince anyone to whom the document is shown that it is a true document.' The vice admiral could not have staked out the Naval Board's battleground more bluntly: to them, the entire royal commission was a waste of time because, they believed, the Cabban Statement was untrue. Well, we would see.

37

Conflicting Evidence of Japan

As the exhausting days of hearings ground on and on there seemed to be no obvious end to the inquiry. It was easy to slip into the delusion that this was now my normal life. Every morning I would take a place behind the lawyers and watch as an endless procession of witnesses trooped in and out of the courtroom, each to be examined and cross-examined at length. This vast assemblage of human resources was entirely dedicated to sifting through the minute detail of just a few short months of naval life. Often, the real purpose of the whole exercise tended to drift out of view. Why were we all here? A quick glance at the terms of reference soon brought us back to reality.

The primary task of the commission was to establish 'Whether any of the allegations made by Lieutenant Commander P. T. Cabban in the documents attached to the Letters Patent regarding the drinking habits and seamanship of Captain D. H. Stevens were true.' Absolutely fundamental to the Cabban Statement was my account of events in Tokyo. The inquiry now turned to the rather unsavoury task of testing the veracity of reports I had given of incidents in Tokyo when Stevens had been seen – by most observers – to be clearly affected by his drinking. These had been social occasions, some of them formal, so securing witnesses would not be a problem. Establishing the truth was quite another matter. The conflicts that soon emerged over even simple matters of fact underlined the huge unspoken forces at play behind the daily public hearings of the commission. A pattern for these clear divisions rapidly became apparent. The witnesses in Tokyo of high rank or standing now struggled to recall anything that might have confirmed Stevens' excessive use of alcohol; those on lower rungs of the status ladder could remember these incidents with little difficulty. As the senior counsel assisting the inquiry would eventually submit, the conflict between these two versions of events was so profound that it constituted the 'breaking point' of the whole inquiry.

Captain Alan N. Dollard DSC RAN had been the Australian services attaché to the Australian Embassy in Tokyo in 1963. It fell to Dollard to arrange the program for *Voyager*'s visit to Karatsu during the Far East cruise, and ten days later he met the two ships when we arrived in Tokyo. In keeping with standard diplomatic practice he had organised a generous social program ashore for senior officers. We, in turn, were expected to reciprocate with hospitality on board for our various hosts. Dollard might not have known it at the time but, in Captain Stevens, he would encounter the proverbial guest from hell. Four years later, standing in a witness box in Sydney, those memories had faded with remarkable speed. He had no clear recollection of Karatsu except that Captain Stevens was quite normal while he was there. Nor did Captain Dollard notice anything unusual in Tokyo until, at a buffet dinner in his home, he looked into the room where Stevens was dining and noticed that Duncan's head was nodding and he seemed to be half asleep. He thought Duncan had been overtaken by fatigue and probably drink. Dollard admitted some concern, but could not remember whether he had spoken to Stevens at once or whether he first went outside to arrange transport to take Stevens back to his ship. He eventually managed this with a friend of his who offered his chauffeur. As Dollard re-entered the house, a *Voyager* officer met him and said that he would take the captain home. Dollard believed he spoke to Duncan and said, 'Duncan, I think you've had it' [or something of that kind] 'and it's time you went home.' He identified this officer as Commander Money. (When questioned earlier, Money denied he was involved in the incident at Dollard's home and said that he had left early with Blaikie. But, on being recalled after Dollard's evidence, Money conceded some recollection of the incident but not actual involvement. Blaikie could not remember anything about the party.)

On the Saturday, Dollard and his wife drove Willis, Stevens and a Royal New Zealand Navy officer to a picnic at which Duncan was too ill to leave the car, eat or drink. Returning home, the Dollards suggested that Duncan should go to bed at their house, which he did. This entailed

Stevens missing the scheduled dinner that night, hosted by the Japanese admiral, head of the Maritime Self-Defence Force. In the report of proceedings, it was claimed that Stevens had attended this dinner, but the commissioners treated that obvious falsehood as unimportant. On arriving home at 11.00 p.m., the Dollards were told by their maid that Stevens had got up and ordered a brandy. He had immediately been sick and then asked for a taxi, which took him back to *Voyager*.

The following day, Willis and Stevens met the Dollards and the Australian ambassador, Sir Laurence McIntyre, for lunch on board *Vampire*. Dollard was surprised to see Stevens looking very well. The meal finished without incident at about 2.00 p.m. In the evening, the Dollards met Stevens and Willis at a restaurant, as guests of Arthur Jamieson, the counsellor of the embassy. Dollard noticed nothing unusual in Duncan's appearance or demeanour, but shortly after sitting down to dinner, one or two of them noticed that Stevens was half asleep. He described the captain as 'from being quite alive and alert, and quite normal in his behaviour and appearance, he was suddenly, and quite suddenly – I think this probably was the same sort of thing that happened at the buffet party at my house – his head dropped and he was half asleep'. Dollard took Stevens out to his car and sent him back to the ship. When he returned to the table he spoke with Willis about the incident, and concluded that Stevens' ulcer had, on those two occasions, been aggravated by some drinks. Captain and Mrs Dollard thought Stevens was unwise to be drinking at all, but he wondered whether Willis, as senior officer of the two ships, was at all concerned. Questioned by Burt about his own opinion of Duncan's fitness to proceed to sea in that condition, Dollard expressed his conclusion as 'the sooner he got to sea, the better'.

Pressed by Jack Hiatt, Dollard was certain that he had discussed Stevens' health with Willis, but he was just as certain that Willis had not told him anything about Duncan being unwell in the morning. Jack questioned the lack of any contact with Tiller or attempts to obtain medical attention for Stevens on either occasion of his obvious illness. Dollard was adamant that the action he had taken was adequate in the circumstances. When asked whether his concern and actions would have been different had he known of the captains' disastrous lunch in *Rothesay* while in Hong Kong, and of the birthday dinner, Dollard said that if it were known, as fact, then he would take action. And if that information came to him as rumour, he would be 'on guard'.

Dollard's evidence gave the impression of a man struggling to preserve a thin veneer of social equilibrium despite the distressing behaviour of one of his most prominent guests. Captain G. J. Willis, during that same period, seemed to have been playing a solo game of blind man's bluff. Hear no evil, see no evil. In the witness box, Willis could not remember very much about any function in Tokyo. He did recall that *Voyager*'s captain felt unwell at the picnic and subsequently missed the Japanese admiral's dinner, but he did not know where Duncan had gone: back to his ship, or to the Dollards' home. Stevens was ill on the Sunday, Willis recalled, but Tiller did not tell him that the captain's ulcer was the cause, just a stomach upset or gastritis, and he certainly denied threatening Stevens. When Dollard's evidence of the dinner on Sunday night at the Gaslight restaurant was read to him, Willis could not remember the Jamiesons at all but did associate that event with his recollection of a meal earlier in the week. He was clearly confused, recalling an act from *Madame Butterfly* and placing it at the Mikado nightclub. It was little wonder that he also failed to remember anything about Duncan Stevens on the night. Strangely, he conceded that he must have discussed Duncan's health with Dollard, either on Saturday or Sunday, but not, of course, in relation to drinking. For me, it would be difficult to imagine a more comprehensive *volte-face* than that managed by Willis at the commission. His flat denial of events and conversations to which other witnesses could attest was stark proof of the willingness among the most senior RAN officers to perjure themselves in the cause of the cover-up.

Evidence given by more neutral individuals soon contradicted Dollard and Willis. Flight Lieutenant Maurice Farrelly was attached to the Department of External Affairs and employed as an interpreter at the Australian Embassy in Tokyo in 1963, when *Voyager* visited Karatsu and Tokyo. By the time he was called to give evidence Farrelly was a squadron leader. Burt asked him whether he had formed any opinion as to the captain's health or as to the amount, if any, that he was drinking during our stay in Karatsu. Farrelly said that Stevens never looked well to him at any stage and, although not intoxicated, was drinking fairly heavily and consistently. Significantly, when questioned as to whether drink appeared to affect the captain to a greater or lesser extent than he might have anticipated, Farrelly said that at times he seemed to be affected more quickly than expected, but at other times, not.

It was established that Farrelly and I had spent some time together in Japan, and he was asked whether I had discussed the captain with him. Towards the end of the visit he recalled that when we were alone I had told him I was worried about the captain's condition and thought that he was drinking more than was good for his health. Asked by Burt to be more specific, Farrelly replied that I was worried that the amount that Duncan was drinking was having an adverse effect on his health. He thought he could remember me saying that I would be pleased when the ship got back to Australia so that it would no longer be my worry. Nevertheless, he felt that the relationship between Stevens and me was good.

Farrelly and his wife had attended the dinner at Dollard's home on the Friday night after we arrived in Tokyo. He described Stevens as being 'pretty well under the weather' and 'the worst I had seen him'. He went to Dollard and said that Stevens looked as though he might have difficulty seeing the evening through. About half an hour after they had sat down to dinner, Farrelly noticed that Stevens, who was sitting close by him, had slumped in his chair and looked to be half asleep. He was having difficulty even getting his glass back on to the table and missed the table a couple of times. (This reminded me immediately of Duncan missing his mouth with the sweet corn during the birthday dinner.) Farrelly went to Dollard and suggested that they should do something to minimise further embarrassment. He saw Dollard speak to an officer, whom he thought was Bill Money, who soon after went to Stevens and asked if he would like to leave. At that point Farrelly joined them and helped Stevens out of the room to a stairway where they were met by Dollard. The two captains went upstairs.

Some time later Dollard requested that a car be arranged for the transfer of Duncan back to *Voyager*. Farrelly remembered prevailing on an Australian guest to permit his chauffeur to do so. He said that Dollard and, he believed, Money, helped Stevens into the car. Farrelly then gave the driver directions. The Japanese guests appeared to accept the explanation that the captain was unwell, and Mrs Farrelly had not even noticed him leaving. During the dinner the captain had invited the Farrellys to join him for lunch on the Sunday. However, when they arrived at *Voyager* Duncan was waiting for his guests at the gangway but was obviously not expecting the Farrellys. He looked very drawn and apparently had no recollection of inviting them, so they lunched in the wardroom instead (after Stevens had taken his other guests to his cabin).

Keith Gale was called late in the inquiry. He attested to the fact that he and his wife Jenny had seen and spoken with me on three or four occasions during our stay in Japan, including meals and sightseeing. Keith recalled that I had expressed my concerns to him, primarily for the safety of the ship, and that I had discussed the conflicting loyalties I had for the captain and the crew of *Voyager*. He also recalled seeing Duncan on the Sunday at lunchtime and that his appearance was flushed and very tired, which accorded with what he understood I had described to him earlier. Regrettably, he did not recall having seen Duncan at Dollard's home, as he had described him to me during lunch, although he did remember being there for the buffet dinner.

The counsellor to the Australian Embassy was Arthur Barclay Jamieson, a most impressive witness. In the 1930s he had won a scholarship in Japanese, graduating from Melbourne University. He was still serving in Japan, the last of three appointments there that had begun in 1947. Philip Jeffrey, junior counsel assisting the commission, led Jamieson through an outline of his contacts with officers of *Vampire* and *Voyager*, and particularly their captains. Between 100 and 150 guests had been invited to the Dollards' cocktail reception, including senior diplomatic staff and officers from the Maritime Self-Defence Force of Japan. All serving personnel were in uniform. Dollard had explained that the social program for most RAN officers was already full that night, but that the two RAN captains were not engaged for the evening. Jamieson invited them both and the Dollards to dinner at the Gaslight restaurant. Jamieson said that at the beginning of the cocktail party Stevens was fresh and alert, but by the time he and his wife left Stevens looked 'a little the worse for wear. He looked as though he had had more drinks than other people at the party.' Asked to describe Stevens' personality, he said he had a gay, outgoing and quite charming nature.

When the main course was served at the restaurant, Duncan did not touch his food. Jamieson — embarrassed that a guest was not eating — asked him if there was anything wrong with the meal. Stevens said 'no', but he did not feel like eating it at the time. Jamieson told the commission 'he began to look a little more tired, and I suppose he may have had a drink or two that had some cumulative effect'. A few moments later, as Jamieson was busy talking to somebody at the table, he heard Duncan say, 'You'll look after me, won't you, Jim?' As his nickname was Jim, the host thought he was being addressed and turned to see that Duncan was in fact speaking to Captain Willis. At that stage Stevens' head was nodding and he was slumped in his chair. There was no word or sign that the captain was suffering any stomach complaint. This happened almost three hours after arriving, so Jamieson was able to call for the bill and pay it before joining his guests as they all left the restaurant together. Stevens was definitely with them, and Jamieson remembered sitting in the front seat of the hire car that the embassy provided, with the three captains in the back. Mrs Jamieson and Mrs Dollard travelled to the ships in Jamieson's car. Jamieson noted the date on his receipts record as Thursday, 6 June – D Day. On the Sunday, the Jamiesons visited *Vampire* at lunchtime for drinks and did not see Duncan. They never received a letter or message of thanks for their hospitality, or heard from Captain Stevens again.

My knowledge of Stevens' ulcer and his frequent bouts of 'crook stomach' was probed at length by Asprey, who wanted to know how soon I had become aware of the problem. He seemed to be pursuing some private line of argument intended to subsume the effects of excessive drinking into the aggravations of a duodenal problem. Asprey effectively challenged me as to whether I would have been able to differentiate between the two. I responded that I had been in absolutely no doubt after Tokyo because before that Tiller had insisted that the ulcer was under control, saying that if Stevens left the grog alone he would be all right. Whether I was dealing with a sick man or something else I did not know. The commissioner finally asked, 'But when you got that information in Tokyo, you then realised that the ulcer was playing an important part?'

'Yes. If it had not been for that I do not think I would have made the report to Captain Willis at that time. I just felt there was a risk to his life that I could not afford to be responsible for.'

In cross-examination, Hiatt asked Jamieson whether he attributed Stevens' behaviour to an excessive consumption of alcohol, and the reply was, 'That is correct, yes.' Particularly telling was a passage on the theme of rumours within the Australian community in Tokyo of Duncan's drinking. Jamieson confirmed that '. . . one did hear that he drank a little more than most people would at some functions'. In re-examination, the chairman intruded when Philip Jeffrey mentioned the change in Stevens' demeanour at the restaurant being 'sudden'. Jamieson explained this rate through the illustrative device of a graph: he indicated a gradual downward trend with a sudden acceleration. Diplomatic duties demanded Jamieson's return to Tokyo the following day, a disclosure that caused Burt to express deep regret. He now intended recalling Dollard as a witness because of the vast contrasts that had emerged between his evidence and that of other witnesses. But this was a royal commission, not a criminal trial, so reluctantly Burt conceded that Jamieson should be allowed to go.

Sir Laurence McIntyre was Australia's ambassador in Japan during 1963. He had lunch, accompanied by his wife, in *Voyager* on the Sunday. The ambassador was adamant in his sworn evidence that he had heard no rumours of, nor was he aware of, any of the incidents of which every other witness had comprehensive knowledge. McIntyre stuck rigidly to his patently false evidence that Stevens was bright, cheerful and of healthy appearance at lunch, even when pressed by Hiatt (over the chairman's determined interruptions) to acknowledge the graphic accounts of the morning's illness and indisposition. Not one other person had thought the captain was looking well at the time. (Years later, this credibility gulf was the basis for my application, under the freedom of information laws, for the correspondence between the embassy in Tokyo and the Department of Foreign Affairs. It yielded acknowledgement that I had a legitimate interest but regretted that the department's copy had been shredded and the Tokyo copy could not be found. Why was I not surprised?)

In view of the strong, confident and compelling evidence given by Farrelly, Dollard was recalled to the witness box. This was not entirely without precedent in similar inquiries, but the decision seemed to underline serious doubts as to the veracity of his original testimony (or at least a recognition that there were other credible versions of the events he had described). Not surprisingly, Dollard adhered to his earlier sworn evidence. He had no recollection of anything untoward, and could not agree with either Farrelly or Jamieson in their accounts.

Captain Robertson had told me that Dollard, an old and good friend, described to him incidents of Stevens being hopelessly drunk and vomiting. Yet we could not persuade John Robertson to give evidence of this, and he even refused to attend the courtroom while Dollard was denying all knowledge of Stevens' intoxication in Tokyo. It was extraordinary that *Melbourne*'s captain – the only man who stood to gain from this royal commission – refused to provide it with the simple testimony that would have corroborated so much of my statement. Robertson knew that the navigational aspects of Spicer's original negative findings could be revisited only once Stevens' unfitness to command had been established. But still he persisted with this ridiculous affectation of gentlemanly 'honour' that restrained him from even being present while the drinking habits of a brother officer were being examined. There was an infuriating odour of hypocrisy about all this. The captain was happy to let others do the difficult and sometimes dirty work of restoring his reputation, so long as his own hands were not soiled in the process. In the event, Robertson sent his loyal wife Bettine to attend the inquiry in his stead, an inadequate and meaningless gesture.

What remained for the commissioners to contemplate after Dollard had completed his second stint in the witness box was a classic evidentiary stand-off. Who should be believed? In his summary, Burt said:

> There is a very fundamental and important conflict of evidence, not between individual witnesses, but among a number of witnesses. With respect, it would seem to be necessary to make a finding at this point as to who one believes. Does one believe the evidence, broadly speaking, of Dollard and Willis, or does one believe the evidence of Jamieson and Farrelly? Because to believe Jamieson and Farrelly would be destructive to the credit of the two serving naval officers, Dollard and Willis, and perhaps also, to a very substantial extent, of Commander Money.

Burt did not hesitate to go on to point out the apparent consequences of accepting Farrelly and Jamieson. His relentless logic put the two senior naval men in a distinctly unflattering light:

> It fixes Captain Dollard with knowledge of a state of affairs upon which surely he should have made a report to the Naval Board. Also it fixes Willis with a knowledge of a state of affairs upon which he, too, should have made some report. But even more than that, if you reach the stage of being able to say that each of the captains was possessed of knowledge of a kind which should have placed upon

them a duty to report, and it appearing quite clearly that they did not report, then it lays the foundation for the acceptance of the Cabban evidence as to command out of Tokyo. It then renders it more likely that Willis would have made the type of arrangement with Cabban that Cabban says he made. Particularly, it renders it more likely that the command out of Tokyo would have been, as described, unofficial – meaning no more or less than no signal would have been made.

Burt then continued by developing an outline of how significant this issue now was to the entire function of the inquiry:

It would seem impossible to reconcile the two sets of evidence on the basis of defective memory or opportunity for observation or upon any other basis. One must come out boldly and say that one or other of the two sets of witnesses is not telling the truth. If one recalls the evidence of Farrelly, not only did he play a significant part in the events as they happened at the Dollard party, but he played a significant part with Captain Dollard. He spoke to Captain Dollard. He made arrangements with him and so on. This is his evidence. So it is not the same as two observers at the same scene moving independently. They are in fact co-operating. Once one believes Farrelly and Jamieson then of course the overall finding is inevitable, namely that the captain was drinking too much in Tokyo, too much in the sense that it caused some objective signs of intoxication.

But perhaps the most crucial observation in Burt's address concerned me: 'So a prior finding on these matters as they occurred in Tokyo might, in one sense, be described as the breaking point in the inquiry. Whatever findings the commission makes at this point, they do not significantly depend on the evidence of Cabban at all. Cabban plays no part, really, in the Tokyo events until the Sunday.'

It was a telling conclusion. For once, it was not my veracity that the judges would have to consider.

38
Variations on a Theme

By now I considered myself to have become something of a court-room veteran, attuned to the subtle daily undercurrents of a process that was attempting to grapple with huge issues through the patient accretion of seemingly unrelated and often irrelevant detail. The funda-mental veracity of the major assertions in the 'Cabban Statement' were rarely reduced to simple black/white, true/false terms. Instead, faintly contradictory shades of meaning were compared and contrasted. Ambiguous evidence was picked over with the detached interest of a botanist examining some rare species through a magnifying glass. By this time I had gradually become inured to the discomfort of evidence given with an artful haziness designed to obscure, rather than deny, the truth of my claims regarding Stevens' health and behaviour. All that changed when serving naval officers still with promising careers ahead of them took the witness stand. Many had already foreshadowed their evasions and false responses in the material Don Chipp published as a parliamentary paper during the *Voyager* debates. But nothing prepared me for the shock of sitting just feet away from former friends and colleagues as they blatantly lied on oath. I learned a painful lesson in what ambition can do to a man's principles, and how loose a grasp of the truth can be.

David Martin had arrived from the UK only shortly before being called as a witness. He had returned to assume his new appointment as commander of HMAS *Creswell*, the naval college at Jervis Bay. It has been suggested at senior naval level that he was advised not to 'rock the boat' – not to lie, but to avoid specific recollection. If that is true, and I have no reason to believe otherwise, then he stuck to the script brilliantly. The rewards he soon reaped were far greater than mere pieces of silver. His career certainly outstripped others who were even more cavalier with the truth and gave as little consideration to how their conduct might affect the safety and welfare of men at sea. I was not bitter, but I was bitterly disappointed and devastated by the evasive testimony of a man whom I had considered both a good friend and a professional colleague.

Burt, as the patient counsel assisting, was not taken in by Martin's performance, but the only opinions that really mattered were those held on the bench. It was clear that the commissioners were captivated by Martin, and with good reason. His artful inability to recall specific details of the most crucial incidents largely absolved the judges from having to make any definitive findings as to Stevens' behaviour. At the same time, Martin's deliberate haziness allowed later witnesses enough latitude to be similarly careless with the truth. It is difficult to either debunk or confirm a vague recollection, and its impact diminishes along with its lack of corroborative detail. This tactic of always putting key events into the softest possible focus was a tactical masterstroke. It simultaneously got the commission, the Navy and Martin himself off the hook.

The evidence of *Voyager*'s gunnery officer during 1963 occupied a little under a day and a half, but it is no exaggeration to say that his words changed my life. Martin was on the very threshold of corroborating me so often, but just could not be quite certain of time, person or place on each occasion. No other witness approached him for stealth in avoiding commitment to fact. It was impossible to pin him down. How an officer with a memory as demonstrably unreliable as this could possibly have been entrusted to command ships singly, and as a fleet, defies reason. The term 'vague recollection' assumed the dimensions of a *leitmotiv* in the transcript through Martin's repeated use of the phrase. How he could have only a vague recollection of his comment on Stevens in Hong Kong ('the ignorant bastard') or his angry outburst ('he's as rotten as a fucking chop') as we left Sydney, or his prosecution of defaulters out of Tokyo, I do not know. This was the same man who protected him before the Pakistan Shield fiasco, and told me about the captain's appalling lapse at the Holmes christening. David Martin was privy not only to these events but also to a shared intimate opinion of them. His disgust with the captain was even deeper than mine. Now, all of this was reduced to 'vague recollection'.

At the same time, Martin was careful to damn me with occasional faint praise. But there was no trace or pretence of the admiration and respect he had conveyed in his letter of thanks to me following his promotion. (That he could blithely write to me as a friend afterwards and invite me to call and meet defies belief.) Jack Hiatt later told me of 'Red' Burt saying, 'If David Martin had told the truth today, the royal commission would be finished in two weeks and the Cabban family saved an ordeal.' Chester Porter expressed the view that if Martin had told the complete truth the commissioners would not have believed him, and that his minor corroborations did me more good than harm. I disagreed strongly at the time. More recently, after a wealth of supporting evidence has slowly emerged from independent sources, Chester told me that while he had always thought I tended to exaggerate, he now concedes that my original descriptions of proceedings on board *Voyager* were accurate. Martin must obviously have felt some pangs of conscience after he returned to Jervis Bay. He came back to the commission voluntarily, claiming further memory of events and even elaborated on his previous evidence some-what to my advantage. But it was much too little, much too late.

The final blow from Martin's perfidy at the commission came many years later. In 1994 the author and naval historian Tom Frame gave an inter-view to the ABC's *Four Corners* program on the thirtieth anniversary of the *Voyager* disaster. Frame had recently spoken with Martin, who was then just a few weeks from death. He quoted Martin as telling him that his evidence during the commission was 'bullshit'. He had said that Duncan Stevens was 'hopeless' (although he had written to Beatrice Stevens crediting her husband with teaching him everything he knew). Frame later added that Martin had derided Stevens' ship handling and also asserted that *Voyager's* wardroom was 'the most dysfunctional' he had seen. These extraordinary admissions – the truth at last – were of little comfort to me. In a meeting with Peter Collins (the former New South Wales Treasurer and Leader of the Opposition) in 2004, Collins assured me that he would never have recommended Rear Admiral David Martin to fill the vacant post of Governor of New South Wales if he had had any inkling of Martin's conduct as disclosed by Tom Frame. There is bitter irony in the knowledge that my insistence, back in 1963, that Duncan Stevens must report on him as 'exceptional' undoubtedly kick-started his rapid career rise.

Whereas Martin had been the virtuoso of vagueness, Captain G. J. Willis was first and foremost of the absolute liars. He denied every aspect of his discussion with me in my cabin in Tokyo and any knowledge of my command out of Tokyo. It was obvious that Willis needed to deny these truths in order to preserve his career. But bald-faced defiance in the witness box would not, of itself, have been enough to sustain these false-hoods. On reflection, I believe that the action he had taken in Tokyo was carefully premeditated to accomplish specific goals. There were three good reasons for adopting this course:

First, although not wanting Captain Stevens' life jeopardised by a perforated ulcer, he was determined to avoid his being hospitalised ashore in Tokyo. To have acted otherwise would have entailed a formal report being made to the ambassador, the Commander in Chief Far East, Flag Officer Commanding Australian Fleet and the Naval Board. With the number of witnesses to Duncan's intoxication in public situations, it would have become difficult, if not impossible, to conceal the real cause of the captain's illness and the wider reflection it cast on the Navy.

Second, Willis did not wish to have a court martial on his hands. Had FOCAF and the Naval Board received open confirmation of his real actions, rather than a discreet report claiming the subterfuge of ill health brought on by Asian conditions etc, then the regulations allowed no other path than a formal charge. Willis's action would at least save the remain-der of Stevens' career, even at the cost of any future sea commands. I feel certain that Willis must have forwarded a confidential report at some stage, as insurance for his own career if nothing else. No doubt his discre-tion was noted – and mutely applauded – by the Naval Board. (Also implicit in the assumption that Stevens' public vomiting and collapses in Tokyo would not be officially confirmed was the belief that no report would emanate from our embassy.)

Third, Willis wished to avoid the practical difficulties involved in finding a replacement captain for *Voyager* at such short notice. It would be impossible to avoid appointing a stand-in commander as a period of two months still remained of the attachment to the Far East Fleet. He would be unlikely to have entertained the practicality of my being officially endorsed as provisional captain. Protecting Stevens saved Willis from an administrative nightmare.

One of the most deliberate lies told by Willis was that Stevens contin-ued drinking 'in moderation' for the remainder of our time in the Far East after Tokyo. He had told me that he promised Duncan he would face a court martial if he drank at all in that period! It was unfortunate that

Jack Hiatt was feeling ill at the time Willis was called so that the sharp edge was off his normal cross-examination style.

I was fascinated to learn what would come from the evidence of Lieutenant Commander Scott Griffith. At the time he was called, Griffith was serving in HMAS *Parramatta*, commanded by my brother-in-law, Commander John Matthew. There was no reliable indication of just where his testimony might lead. At his home Griffith had assured me that he had corroborated my evidence to Smyth QC. But from the material circulated in his name at the time of the parliamentary debates it seemed obvious Scott had done no such thing. In fact, had he supported me at that early date it is highly doubtful that a second inquiry would ever have been needed.

I was surprised at the extent to which Griffith first corroborated me on minor points of my statement. The first twenty-four hours out of Sydney presented him with no trouble, nor did my description of Stevens' temperament (but he never heard him swear, of course). The captain, to his knowledge, was never sick in the Far East and certainly not after Tokyo. Griffith had him being transferred to *Lion* by helicopter for a conference around that time – something that happened much earlier in the cruise – when I was taking defaulters and the captain was confined to his cabin. Scott made a significant concession when he acknowledged that, at the birthday dinner, he had a vague recollection of seeing the captain on his hands and knees and had formed the impression that he had too much to drink. But, rather remarkably, he did not know what made him form that impression. He remembered that Stevens was quite normal at Dollard's party, but not well when he went to the steam baths, and had missed one engagement in Tokyo owing to illness, turning in early.

Griffith was able to say that I had 'limited command' for two days after leaving Tokyo Bay on the Monday, giving the start time as after 12.00 noon (as opposed to the actual time of 10.07 a.m.). In 1964 he told Smyth that Stevens had been fully in command at all times. I would have thought that as the responsible navigator he should have had a clear re-collection of the elapsed time leaving a major harbour. In his earlier statement Griffith made the preposterous suggestion that as this was a weekend period there was nothing for the captain to do, so he had taken two days rest! He had, however, noticed that Stevens was looking tired and slightly flushed in Sydney, but had no impression that he was affected by alcohol, either on the bridge when leaving or at any other time. But there was no dispute that Duncan handed over to me leaving Sydney and then disappeared for two days.

Some of the detail that emerged during this examination was highly intriguing, especially as it related to the secretary to the Naval Board's propensity for tampering with evidence. Mr Burt led Griffith on his visit to Sam Landau's office, an appointment that had been made in order to 'correct' an earlier statement. After some reflection Scott specifically denied Landau's assertion that he, Griffith, had torn the original statement before he left. Landau had sworn that it was torn and so he had it destroyed. In fact, it was left in an envelope with a line drawn through it.

Murphy, for the Navy (and with the strenuous support of counsel for the Stevens family), endeavoured to have the Navy's plan of the typhoons tendered as an exhibit, supported as it was by *Vampire*'s deck log. In reply, Mr Burt explained that he had not put in the plan 'for a reason that perhaps is better not stated because it may embarrass the Navy'. But Murphy pressed the point, saying, 'I want to be clear as to whether it is being suggested it is a wrong plan.' It was an unwise flourish. Mr Burt responded, 'I am getting a proper plan drawn. If one takes the positions of *Vampire* out of its log book and plots them, it is a ship that never got back to Australia; at one point of time it was inland of Tokyo. That is the reason for the delay.' Murphy must have regretted the gratuitous opening he had given counsel assisting to underline naval incompetence publicly before the commissioners.

In re-examination, Griffith prevaricated when he could not give an adequate explanation for having said in his statement that shipping was 'sparse' during the passage to Williamstown. (This comment was presumably intended to soften any impression that the captain's turning in and absence from command might have endangered the ship.) The report of proceedings, which Griffith himself had written, disclosed that *Voyager* exchanged identities with eighteen merchant vessels during the two-day trip. In a similar vein, Scott had claimed that as the captain had nothing to do for two days out of Tokyo, he had turned in for a rest while the fleet reconstituted and there were no exercises. Burt patiently produced factual evidence of the presence of a cruiser, four destroyers and a frigate, attended by four fleet auxiliary tankers and supply vessels, beginning from the Monday morning. Clearly, there would have been plenty 'to do'.

Further, Burt showed the number of replenishments undertaken by me to be four as I had stated, not 'one or two' as stated by Griffith. Again, this was verified by the June report of proceedings, written by Griffith and signed by Stevens. It gave me little pleasure to see this man's shameless lies and exaggerations so systematically demolished.

When it came to the weather, getting Griffith to acknowledge that it was not calm for the first few days out of Tokyo was like pulling teeth. Even according to *Vampire*'s log it was a moderate gale. The truth inevitably surfaced when Chief Petty Officer Barker attested that the weather was so bad *Voyager* was battened down – which it was. Further corroboration came from Able Seaman Mead and several others. It seemed that only the destroyer's bridge officers had any difficulty recalling the extreme weather that week. On the matter of the punishment parade, Griffith was told that a sailor from his division would give sworn evidence that it was I, not Stevens, who had punished him for being absent without leave in Tokyo, and that Griffith had actually represented him at that parade. Nevertheless, he denied any memory of the incident, but conceded I might have issued the punishment.

The succession of witnesses called after Scott Griffith were all examined on various aspects of the Cabban Statement. After weeks of courtroom labour we were still trying to establish whether my allegations were 'true and being true established that Captain Stevens was unfit to retain command of HMAS *Voyager*'. Bill Money, the engineer officer, gave evidence that was directly in conflict with me, Captain Dollard and Squadron Leader Farrelly. I had outlined my specific recollections of Karatsu and the smuggling ashore of Black Bottle brandy, a court-martial offence that I attributed to Bill Money. Hiatt overheard an angry and disgusted Justice Asprey describing Money's evidence in very colourful language outside the courtroom, but the commissioners eventually chose to take no action. Ian Blaikie, the supply officer in *Voyager*, did not surprise me with his denials of almost every situation in which I had described meetings and conversations with him. The single exception was the occasion of his taking a drink to Redman's cabin, which he described as stupid. The commissioners mentioned him unfavourably as a witness.

Among the seamen who gave evidence, the most compelling was Able Seaman Peter Mead. A tall and cheerful larrikin, Mead was disarmingly straightforward. He was clearly believed by Burt, who described him in his final address as honest. But the judges finally had to reject the bulk of Mead's evidence because his corroboration of the 'Lost in *Yarra*' farce was too damning for them to tolerate beyond a basic finding that the incident had indeed occurred. Steward Eddy, who testified to his dislike of me personally, nevertheless gave a word-for-word account of my encounter with Money and Blaikie in the wardroom before Duncan had gone ashore and been returned to *Voyager* by the four sailors who had rescued him from *Yarra*.

Of the stewards, Desmond Menkins was the most memorable. Although still serving, he told the absolute truth in a most extraordinary passage of testimony. Led by Phil Jeffrey, junior counsel for the commission, Menkins agreed that his initial statement to Burt denied any memory of the birthday dinner. But then he had turned at the door of Burt's office and said that he wished to say more. He not only described the captain on his hands and knees crawling to his seat, he also mimicked Duncan trying to find his mouth with corn on the cob, and missing it – giggling while he did so. It was a very funny account, and no one in the courtroom could doubt that a clear picture of that bizarre tableau was still present in his mind.

The next witness gave evidence that made me sick at heart. Lieutenant Commander Barry Tuke was Duncan Stevens' last captain's secretary. Sue and I accommodated him in our home for some days immediately after the loss of *Voyager* and we considered him a friend. He testified to the constant sober presence of Stevens in Williamstown after the Dovers court martial and at all other times. This conflicted with so much other earlier evidence to the contrary that it was only a matter of time before Tuke's evidence would be questioned.

A civilian accountant and reserve officer, Lieutenant Keith Cleland, had served for two weeks aboard *Sydney* after the collision, at the same time Tuke was serving in her. He had read the evening newspaper reports of the day's proceedings, then telephoned Jack Hiatt in the morning. Acting on Hiatt's advice, Cleland called the Crown Solicitor's office and came to court to make a statement. Cleland, whom I did not know, had formed a close association with Tuke during their short time together in *Sydney* and ashore. Hiatt was directed to lead Cleland's evidence on just the one point: Tuke's sworn evidence that Duncan Stevens preferred to fly between Sydney and Melbourne. Cleland now told the commission that Tuke had told him his captain's preference was 'to travel to Sydney by train so that he would be able to consume a bottle on the train'. Tuke was then recalled and confronted with this evidence. Unaware of Cleland's presence in court, he first denied that he knew him at all, and acknowledged the friendship only when Cleland was asked by Burt to stand up and be recognised. It was a classic moment of old-fashioned courtroom theatrics. But when told of Cleland's statement, Tuke now claimed that he would have only been quoting hearsay evidence, from me! For a man appearing to be caught out in a blatant lie, this was an ingenious – if incredible – response.

There was more drama to come. Outside the courtroom Jack Hiatt observed a suspicious-looking financial transaction of some kind taking place between Captain Jeff Britten, the Navy Office representative briefing Murphy QC, and two serving naval witnesses yet to give their evidence. Petty Officer W. S. Strachan and Leading Seaman A. B. Matthews had both been granted promotion by me ex-Tokyo in June 1963 and were being called to give evidence of the circumstances of the requestmen's parade. Strachan made a statement on 5 July and signed it on 12 July, in which he disclosed that he had attended the parade five days after leaving Tokyo because the captain had been turned in. But, in the witness box, those five days now changed to 'about' five days. When pressed by Hiatt, Strachan admitted that on the previous afternoon Britten had suggested to him that it might not be exactly five days. Yet only a week before he gave evidence, the petty officer admitted he had been certain it was five days. Clearly affronted by this apparent subversion of the commission process, Sir Stanley Burbury indicated that Captain Britten should be called to the witness box.

Britten was first directed to leave the court while Leading Seaman Matthews gave his evidence. Matthews was one of the ratings nominated by Mead as possibly being involved in returning the inebriated Duncan from *Yarra* in Hong Kong. He lost no time in denying any knowledge of the incident. He agreed that he did not like me, for he had been subject to punishment by me for repeated offences and I had warned him of extreme punishment if it continued. His recollection of Britten's intervention was distinctly lacking in substance after only a twenty-four-hour lapse in time, although he did recall the conversation's quarter-hour duration. When Britten was finally called he rebutted all aspects of the conversation to which Strachan had sworn. Hiatt pushed him hard on the question of how many other witnesses he had been speaking with, but Britten was careful to deny that any of those discussions were related to their evidence. He was a far from convincing witness, and was extremely careful in his behaviour after his unexpected appearance in the box.

The contrast with the next major witness could not have been greater. Piet Liebenschutz was the sole witness to represent the Dutch guests who'd seen Stevens' unkempt appearance and condition at the Hong Kong farewell party. His evidence was compelling and vital to me because he could testify that Stevens had been drunk in the presence of civilians. He also placed Martin and Griffith in the immediate proximity, a fact that highlighted their own, less frank, recall of those events. Both Ash and Murphy savaged Liebenschutz in cross-examination, with benign support from the bench. It appeared that the judges did not wish to credit this testimony. But the following morning Jack Hiatt was able to recall Piet and establish that he had an honour from his government similar to a knighthood. This now weighed critically in his favour with the commissioners. His new-found credibility was underlined when Ash blundered on with his attacks but was sternly rebuked from a suddenly supportive bench.

Lieutenant Richard Carpendale was torpedo and anti-submarine officer in *Voyager* during the 1963 Far East cruise. The letters he wrote home to his wife Jenny, whom he had married only a year before, were pivotal in helping to clarify his uncertain memory of events. With charm and diplomacy, Burt had prevailed on Jenny to despatch all the letters written in the June–July period of the cruise. After the judges had tactfully censored them (sparing the Carpendales any embarrassment), excerpts were read into evidence with great effect. At one point Richard commented on my period of command ex-Tokyo:

Actually it's quite a relief to have a change of Captain – even if only for a short period – and things have gone very smoothly in Captain Stevens' absence. I know he has had an ulcer but he continues to knock hell out of it at every port and just has no capacity for liquor at all. As a consequence he is in a pretty dreadful state for days after, on this occasion he also had a bad tummy – or perhaps it was the same thing. Anyhow he got up again this evening and doesn't look at all good. I'm afraid I haven't all that much sympathy for him but

I suppose it's possibly because he is not an easy person to work for and the change to Cabban was like cool water on a thirsty tongue – (very poetical).

Fortuitously, Carpendale also wrote of the typhoon and heavy weather overnight on 12/13 June. This had prevented us transferring mail to HMS *Barossa* and, on 14 June, from landing mail at Okinawa. That was the helicopter I had hoped would take from *Voyager* the punishment returns that confirmed Stevens was not in command at the time. Of the wardroom, Richard said in evidence, 'It had its disagreements in it, but generally speaking it was a very happy one, yes.' The morale of the ship was as high as that of any ship in which he had served. Describing his leaving the ship in Williamstown, Richard recalled that I had prevented him from saying goodbye to the captain. Stevens had called for another bottle of brandy, and Carpendale correctly assumed that I did not wish to see them both embarrassed.

One nagging question was still unresolved. If, as I believed, the punishment returns after Tokyo had been retyped for Stevens' signature, who had done that work? The identity of this presumably coerced forger has never been satisfactorily established. Able Seaman Ennor, the cox'n's writer, did not type the returns, and it was shown that his typewriter had not been used. It was illogical to assume that some rating was given such a clandestine task, so suspicion fell on the two sub-lieutenants, Forrest and Howland. Howland caused a flutter of apprehension among the legal teams when he entered the witness box carrying a briefcase. What was inside? Could he have kept the incriminating original returns bearing my signature to absolve himself from any charge of falsification? It was well within the compass of the commissioners and the counsel assisting them to seek to know the contents of his briefcase, but not a voice was raised to enquire. I could only assume that Burt and his team had good and valid reasons to let the matter pass. This was one of those peculiar passages of tension during the commission of which there's no hint in the transcript.

The final witness to be called was Commander Errol Stevens, former executive officer of *Vampire*, who had only recently returned from an overseas appointment. He testified that as 'opposite numbers' he and I had a good, co-operative relationship in which we got together on most days in harbour to discuss mutual ships' activities. Stressing that I was extremely loyal to Duncan Stevens, Errol had nevertheless formed a picture from my informal reports of my concern for my captain's health. He confirmed that I attributed these health problems to his level of drinking, and that this had involved me having to take the ship after leaving harbour. Errol was positive that there were occasions in harbour when he had noted that Captain Stevens failed to attend colours and that he had been told that Duncan was ill.

Vampire's old XO also provided useful confirmation of key incidents outlined in my statement. He remembered that my concerns climaxed in Tokyo, where I had repeated to him a report from my officers of Duncan vomiting at Captain Dollard's home during a party and having to be taken back aboard. I had also told him about having to take Stevens to a steam bath on two occasions to get him into shape for functions. Additionally, from his own observation after I had mentioned it to him, he had confirmed that Griffith always handled *Voyager* berthing and slipping in harbour. This was opposed to the practice of most captains, and specifically of Willis, who always handled *Vampire* except after the final visit to Singapore, when he had allowed other officers to do it. Errol had also observed me handling the ship during replenishments. He remembered that when we were speaking together in Singapore, I told him that I had been in command for 'several days' out of Tokyo while Duncan was ill.

Throughout the conduct of the inquiry some interesting and very reassuring spectators took time to show their support. Vice Admiral Sir John Collins KBE CB sat alongside me without comment through an entire session, wordlessly demonstrating his opinion. Many other dear friends also demonstrated their solidarity. They all came and went without a murmur, but their unvoiced messages of support spoke loudly to me.

Each evening, when we received a list of possible witnesses for the following sitting day, I then wrote out at least twenty questions and the answers to be anticipated, based on my knowledge of the character, habits, misdemeanours and/or triumphs of each individual. Some were extremely successful in shaking the confidence of a reluctant witness and drew the required response, as they wondered what else might be exposed. It was like a dark game, but there were no winners, and no one was keeping score.

39
Recalled to the Witness Box

The sheer bulk of evidence taken by the commission, plus the written exhibits, was now so daunting as to be almost beyond the capacity of any competent individual to retain. We had been sitting for four months and produced a mountain of transcripts. The various concluding addresses of counsel were still to come, then the long wait as the judges considered their findings, wrote a detailed report and finally presented it to the government. The whole process was slow, cumbersome and exhausting.

After giving my initial evidence, I could not just sit back and watch on as an interested spectator while the inquiry unfolded. Throughout the commission I was liable to be recalled at any time to face further examination and cross-examination on new evidence raised, or to clarify parts of my own previous evidence in the light of new material introduced by other witnesses. This, in itself, created a permanent sense of apprehension. Technically it was not so much my personal credibility that was under examination but the truthfulness of the specific claims I had made in the so-called 'Cabban Statement'. My name was in the formal title of the commission. While no person could reasonably hope to recall the totality of events more than four years past with absolute accuracy, the essential truth of particular incidents as described was certainly verifiable. For the seventeen weeks of hearings I sat poised, expecting to be confronted at every turn.

In the end I spent a total of eleven days in the witness box. That I managed to emerge from the experience with my credibility intact can largely be explained by a decision taken at the beginning of the hearings. I had decided not to rely on my memory of what I had said previously, or to qualify answers in terms of my earlier statements. Rather, I would always treat each question on its immediate and obvious meaning. From that starting point I could instantly clear my mind and enter the environment of the ship or relevant place to 'see' the situation before answering. I also tried to avoid giving the commissioners the impression that I believed my memory of these events to be complete and infallible. I readily acknowledged each new piece of information that fitted in with my recollections, either to enhance it or to correct a flaw, and was thereby able to answer questions from the perspective of this fresher and more detailed picture of what had occurred. The moments at which I was recalled to the witness box were spread throughout the duration of the hearings, but I think it useful, at this point, to summarise some of the more crucial instances. With the benefit of hindsight many of these *ad hoc* examinations seem diversionary and almost trivial. At the time, however, each had to be met as a direct challenge to my reliability as a witness.

At my first recall to the witness box I was responding to the commissioners' direction that I produce a record of the occasions to which I had referred during the first two months out of Sydney when Stevens was ill, or recovering from illness. With the assistance of the *Voyager* reports of proceedings and *Vampire*'s March report I was able to recall the Darwin episode, and also recalled that on the Friday we departed Darwin I had conducted simple replenishment approaches with *Vampire*. Duncan conducted more complex replenishment practices on the Monday. In relation to the replenishments out of Tokyo, I was able to confirm that it was Tuesday 11 June, and that our evolutions had included a refuelling, two token provision replenishments and a transfer with HMS *Lincoln*. There was also the refuelling from the flagship, *Lion*, two days later. That was the level of detail required of me by the inquiry.

Sir Stanley Burbury questioned me about the condition of Stevens when he gave me command, leaving Sydney for Williamstown. I said that I was not asserting that he was incapable of controlling the ship, but rather that, 'Had he been a junior officer I would not have permitted him to carry out his duty'. This was because I would have considered anyone less capable of holding his drink – anyone whom I had known less than I had known the captain at that time – should not have been allowed in a responsible position. Asked what it was about Stevens that made me conclude he was under the influence of alcohol, I referred to his mood changing from cheerful to dull, his unsteadiness and the smell of alcohol.

Burbury then switched to my taped message to Sue in which I had said, 'Captain Stevens told me that I had command for the next five days.' He questioned whether it was Willis or Stevens who had actually put me in command. I said that Willis told me that he had instructed the captain and that the captain then told me, in his cabin and later on the bridge.

Months later I was recalled following the testimony of Landau and Dollard. The judges were satisfied with the chronology that had been produced in the meantime and allowed Jack Hiatt to lead me through the incidents that the commissioners required to be subject of further examination. My conversation with Farrelly was raised, and I was able to confirm the substance of some of his recollection. This examination continued on an incident-by-incident sequence with isolated questions that were intended to fill gaps and clarify previous evidence. It was a test of my composure to have this long sequence of unrelated questions fired at me for most of a day. There was detailed coverage of the confrontation between Money, Blaikie and myself as witnessed by Carpendale. I was able to quote the specific conversation that I had already recorded in my long statement to Burt before the inquiry hearings began. That conversation had been repeated by Steward Eddy, but denied by my protagonists.

The *Rothesay* lunch incident and Commander Irwin's evidence were revisited, and I said that the message from the Royal Navy ship was clearly on signal pad paper and delivered by boat to *Voyager*'s officer of the day. I had a very clear recollection of the conversation with Irwin and his description of the events. I was also asked why I had left my letter of resignation on the captain's desk, rather than taking it to him personally. (Mrs Stevens gave evidence that this had upset Duncan.) My response was that after the captain had returned from the pre-refit conference at Garden Island, immediately after lunch his leading steward had given me the message that Stevens had turned in and that I 'had the ship'. I had wanted to be sure that he read my letter before proceeding ashore.

A procession of seemingly secondary particulars were put to me in the box. My evidence concerning Loxton speaking of the bottle of brandy on the train was raised in light of Loxton's denial (although he had conceded that Stevens consumed ten brandies during the journey – and Loxton could not recall the exact size of those ten drinks). Carpendale had described being prevented by me from seeing the captain when leaving *Voyager*, although I could not verify the date from memory. But, when the subsequent supper party at Carpendale's flat in Point Piper was also reviewed, I recalled the circumstances and dates of the Sydney meeting with Griffith. The fact that Griffith had invited me to see him was re-inforced when I remembered that it was my birthday and that Sue was upset because this interfered with her plans to celebrate with a party for the children. I recalled a good deal of my conversation with Griffith and his anxiety to assure me that he had corroborated me generally. Ash QC, for the Stevens family, cross-examined me on my long statement – proof of evidence – to Burt, which had been only marked for identification and not sworn to. Jack Hiatt objected strongly when Ash misquoted and appeared to bully me, although I thought myself quite capable of coping with the attacks. Judge Asprey encouraged Ash to continue, while the chairman urged him to confine himself. This was more proof (if any were needed) that the three judges were far from united in their view of the proper course of the inquiry.

As observed earlier, the inquiry was, in many ways, a royal commission into a royal commission. Much of the three judges' time was spent re-examining the conduct and content of an inquiry conducted by another judge three years earlier. They were, in effect, sitting as an appellate court. The third term of reference – that dealing with the possibility of evidence being 'improperly withheld' from the Spicer commission – further broad-ened their task. It was a unique invitation to delve into the behind-the-scenes mechanics of the first inquiry's legal processes. For example, the new inquiry had to consider an affidavit in which David Hicks QC, formerly senior counsel for Captain Robertson, wrote of a conversation he had had with Laurence Street QC (counsel for the Stevens family) during the first commission. Hicks, now a judge, claimed that Street had approached him to offer a deal whereby neither counsel would attack the other's client during the inquiry. He went on to say that while Robertson had refused to sanction any attack on Stevens, Street QC nevertheless attacked Robertson during the sitting and in his summary. Street, by then also a judge, informed the commissioners that he denied the conversation. The chairman of the second commission now deftly closed judicial ranks by ruling that the conversation had absolutely no relevance. The Hicks affidavit was never tested in court.

Murphy, for the Navy, examined me at length on the letter that I wrote to Jess. He was joined in this questioning by the chairman. I was asked whether the letter was my own composition and replied that I could not claim that it was entirely mine because you cannot avoid refining your thinking during a discussion of the kind that led to the letter. To the suggestion that I was imploring Jess to do something, or else I would have to publish all the facts set out in the tape, I said, 'No, I was not.' The final paragraph expressed my conviction that I was now under pressure to speak publicly, but also believed that the government was still able to behave with discretion and correct the situation. I mentioned that I had given a copy to Alan Fairhall, then Minister for Defence. Reminded that Burt had said that I was emotionally involved in the issue at this time, I was asked to describe the nature of that involvement. 'I felt that through some neglect of mine, through a very profound feeling of guilt which persisted from the time of the collision onwards, that the Navy was still in a position where another ship could be lost with a similar or greater loss of life.'

The chairman asked, 'Why do you think that?'

My rather intense reply still reads as a fair summation of the complex emotions with which I had grappled:

> I do feel that my failure – in fact not only my failure but my reluc-tance to give evidence at the first royal commission – was somehow something discreditable. I had not wanted to come forward and I was very reluctant to give the kind of evidence I felt Mr Smyth was going to call me to give, and I was a little ashamed of my feeling. I hoped at that time that the Naval Board might correct whatever situation they may have found existed, as I thought it did, and I then would be off the hook. When this was not done I felt that I had failed in an over-riding duty that was more important than me or the issues that were affecting me at the time.

Burt, counsel assisting the commission, also revisited my letter to Jess and wondered what action I believed the Naval Board could have taken. I said that I thought, perhaps naïvely, that a review of the evidence would not be drawn out and that there would be complete agreement as to the appropriate response. First, the board would abolish drinking at sea. They would then look closely at my description of events and formulate a reporting system to cover such a contingency. There was, at the time, no device by which I could have sought advice without committing my captain and myself. Had there been a ready answer to this dilemma then

I would have adopted it, rather than write the letter of frustration to Jess.

I wondered whether Judge Burbury had been comprehending anything that I had said when he asked if I was reluctant to give evidence about the captain's drinking at the first inquiry. I directed his attention to the evidence of Braund and Sheppard in that respect. Murphy QC wanted to know how I imagined the public would 'bring down the Board and the government for its failure to act'. I maintained that had another ship been lost for the same reason, not having corrected the deficiencies, then the public would throw the government out. 'What deficiencies were they?' asked the chairman, with presumably feigned innocence.

'I considered that there was a captain who was not – certainly not well – who was in command of *Voyager* at the time it was lost.'

Later, the chairman read back my response to his earlier questioning when I had said I could not dispute the evidence of Smyth and Sheppard, in that I only told them about two isolated drinking bouts. He could not understand why I was complaining and how I thought those would have any relevance to the inquiry. Once again, my response revealed just how much difficulty I had had in resolving the conflicting issues at stake:

I do not want to appear devious in this answer, but the answer I gave you in relation to Mr Smyth's evidence was a very carefully considered one. I am not going to accuse either Mr Smyth or Mr Sheppard of being incorrect in their statement. When I made my statement to Admiral Hickling it was my belief at that time that I had told Mr Smyth what it contained. The interview occupied about an hour, and the part of it that dominated my memory was the part concerning drinking. Mr Smyth said to me in a manner which was the fact that first made me decide to go to the Stevens interests, 'We will be seeing a lot of you at the royal commission', and he was obviously pleased at what he had uncovered and it was obvious he believed I was not going to enjoy anything to do with the hearing of this kind of evidence if this kind of evidence was what he wanted, and it was definitely concerning the drinking aspect that he was indicating I would be called.

Asprey then took over, raising the recently presented evidence of Keith Gale concerning my discussion with him on *Voyager*'s upper deck on the Sunday in Tokyo, after I had seen Willis. I confirmed that Gale's statement was correct and that it did reflect the concerns I felt at the time regarding the captain's drinking and the safety of the ship. In particular, the captain's condition following the second steam bath led me to feel that he had lost all discretion and did not seem to care how he was presenting himself or his responsibilities. I agreed that I had felt he was close to completely losing control of himself. The chairman then interposed, asking if I were concerned about the consequences to his health of Stevens' drinking ashore. When I explained that, immediately on leaving harbour, I had ordered Steward Freeman to inform me immediately if the captain had a drink at sea, Judge Lucas asked, 'You thought he was likely to break away from his life-long habit?'

'Yes.'

Burt concluded my re-examination, taking me through a long list of incidents, clarifying details where my memory might have been prompted by other witnesses' evidence. He queried my meaning of terms such as 'heavily under the influence', 'intoxicated' and 'heavily intoxicated'. I described any man heavily under the influence of intoxicating liquor as being incapable of carrying out his duties. He has been drinking, he has lost his sense of responsibility and you could not give him any responsible duties to perform. Asked how objectively discernible the condition I described would be, I said you would see tiredness, a drawn face or, on some occasions, a completely unnatural expression that is at the excited, 'highlight' period of intoxication. I believed that even a naval officer of modest experience could identify a person in this condition as being drunk, or having drunk so much that they needed to rest before commencing any work. I would use that description of a man who can walk normally, converse with people and so on, if my experience indicated that this was not going to last long. As to how I would describe one who was so intoxicated that he could hardly walk and was staggering, the phrase 'dead drunk' clearly applied. 'I am referring to the fact that he is heavily influenced by drink, and his duty and activities just cannot be trusted. Somebody like that, I think, is somebody you want to get out of sight as quickly as possible.'

Burt asked me to respond to the suggestion that I had a very strong attitude of disapproval towards people who drink in connection with their work. I disagreed, and outlined circumstances where in civil employment it is expedient to entertain, but that I would never drink at lunchtime in my capacity as a consultant in a hospital. The last questions I faced concerned a series of letters signed by the captain and by me for the captain. Judging by the date stamps that they bore, there was no apparent relationship between the dates on which they had been written and when they were signed. It was even difficult to discern who had written them. Some were signed by the captain, but on a stamped date when he was in fact on leave. It was clear that there was no adequate system of monitoring outgoing correspondence, and it would be dangerous to assume that the dates established by the correspondence were in any sense a reliable indication of what the captain had been doing on any nominated day.

It was with a sense of enormous relief that I left the witness box for what would be the last time. It seemed as if I had spent my entire life in that uncomfortable little cubicle. The summaries of evidence and submissions of counsel were prepared while the court was in recess at the beginning of November. Then, almost immediately after it resumed, another bombshell. Justice Lucas suffered a mild heart attack.

I was devastated by this news. Lucas, I felt, was my only hope throughout the torment of open hostility coming from Asprey and the more benign Chairman Burbury over the four gruelling months of hearings. Lucas was admitted to St Luke's Hospital, Paddington, for a brief period of assessment, then returned to the inquiry so that a decision could be made as to whether he should continue in his task or be excused for convalescence. Incredibly, the judge left that decision to me! I was, in reality, being asked whether I would accept the two openly hostile commissioners to decide my fate or insist on the continued involvement of the third – a man whose health was now an unknown factor. With a sad sense of *déjà vu* – this was a virtual mirror of my moral predicament in Tokyo – I gave the obvious consent to Lucas withdrawing from the inquiry. What a relief this must have been for the Navy, the Stevens family and the two remaining commissioners. The health scare turned out to be minor, and Justice Lucas returned to the Supreme Court bench in Queensland soon afterwards.

While Burt commenced his address, Gordon Samuels QC settled to the mammoth task of reviewing the transcript and familiarising himself with the intricacies of navigation. Samuels, appearing for Robertson, had the job of persuading the commissioners that they should revisit the navigational findings of the first inquiry. In bald terms, Samuels was there solely to clear Robertson's name. *Melbourne*'s captain and his bridge officers had certainly been criticised by Spicer, and the unfairness of this blame became a significant factor in the decision to make public my experiences with Stevens during 1963. For days on end the commissioners were led by Samuels, using models and diagrams, as they attempted to make sense of what had happened in a matter of minutes and seconds off Jervis Bay nearly four years earlier. To make their task even more difficult, they were obliged to understand how Judge Spicer had previously arrived at his damning conclusions without the benefit of first-hand evidence from the principal participants. It is probably reasonable to comment that they seemed much more motivated to take a contrary view of Sir John's reasoning on the navigational aspects of the tragedy than they were inclined to favour my position. But the terms of reference were constructed in such a way that the commissioners were not free to make isolated judgements. To overturn Spicer they would first need to find – on the basis of the allegations in the Cabban Statement – that Stevens had indeed been unfit to retain command of HMAS *Voyager*. Ted St John had observed that the terms of reference 'were arranged like so many Chinese boxes'. He was right, and it was the very ingenuity of their construction that gave me hope that the inquiry might yet approach the truth.

40

Melbourne's Case

There is a general mistaken perception that the second royal commission was all about obtaining justice, if not retribution, for John Robertson. That was indeed a fortuitous outcome. He and his bridge officers were undoubtedly wronged in the Spicer inquiry, and were subsequently vindicated by the inquiry's findings. But the fact is that the question of *Melbourne*'s role was, as the title of the second commission rightly proclaimed, 'incidental' to the major questions contained in the first term of reference. Simply, the judges had to determine whether my account of the proceedings aboard HMAS *Voyager* in 1963, and the picture it painted of Captain D. H. Stevens, was correct. Everything else hinged on the answer to that question. There could be little doubt that if I were telling the truth, Stevens was unfit to command, and I could surely not be the only serving officer in the RAN who was aware of that sad fact.

Melbourne's Captain Ronald John Robertson DSC entered the witness box on 28 July 1967. Throughout the inquiry he was able to maintain the pose of the gentleman officer who remained aloof from making personal judgements and would never stoop to the dishonour of denigrating a colleague. I watched as this mystique of high rank worked its magic on the commissioners, and bit my lip.

Robertson was almost fifty-one when he began his evidence. He told the courtroom that he had known the late Captain Stevens since 1950, but not served in the same ship or establishment. He considered him to be a competent destroyer captain and a friend. Led by Philip Jeffrey, Robertson confirmed my account of our contacts and his instructions to Hicks QC not to attack the reputation of Captain Stevens during the first commission. When asked if he still held the view that the material within the Cabban Statement could have assisted Sir John Spicer, Robertson replied, 'The material in the Cabban document was not available to me at the time Cabban rang me. It first came to me in full on the occasion when Cabban and I talked after dinner. It was at that time, or shortly afterwards, that I realised that it was certainly relevant, in my opinion to the *Voyager* royal commission.' Further, he felt certain that 'it would throw such a different emphasis on the whole collision that practically every paragraph of the commission's report would need revision'. By this he said he meant, 'The atmosphere in the court room – which I am certain must have been communicated to Sir John Spicer – was constantly one of attack against *Melbourne* and attack against all my efforts at producing the sort of navigational information that was designed to be helpful to the commissioner.'

This was, of course, the nub of the Robertson camp's wedge to reopen the Spicer findings. It gave the commissioners a path to revisiting Spicer's navigational conclusions without having to make any painfully derogatory findings about the behaviour of *Voyager*'s captain. Captain Robertson was clear that the inference that Stevens was under the influence of alcohol on the night of the collision need not be drawn, but rather, if my statement were accepted in whole or in part, 'he should have left the ship before the collision occurred: in fact he should not have been left in the ship to bring it back to Australia from Japan'. Robertson also agreed that my statement disclosed that Stevens' remarks to his officers had the effect of unsettling them until they knew him better and that *Voyager* had a fairly new team in February 1964.

Much of Robertson's time in the witness box was devoted to preparing the ground for an inevitable review of the navigational aspects of the Spicer findings. The chairman insisted that Robertson be expansive in his explanations. Always careful not to insult Spicer by innuendo or direct criticism, Robertson said that even with his own counsel he had to spend days going over and over the points related to courses, speeds, relative bearings and the like. Street QC (for the Stevens family at the first commission) had further complicated matters for Spicer by throwing confusion into these issues, while Smyth was openly hostile. Robertson maintained that Sir John had made an error of fact in his findings because he was confused and could not get at the facts correctly during the hearings. The atmosphere in the courtroom, he contended, was that the actions of a fine competent man, then dead, were being considered against three present living officers who had got together to drum up a defence. Robertson believed that Sir John had done remarkably well in a super-human task, but that the circumstances in which he had formed his judgements were totally adverse to *Melbourne's* bridge officers.

Judge Asprey returned to the specific criticisms levelled at *Melbourne*, particularly in relation to the lack of any warning signal to *Voyager*. Robertson reiterated that he would not, in any normal circumstances, have considered warning *Voyager* that she was in a dangerous situation. It was apparent from the report that Spicer concluded that *Voyager* was on a steady course towards *Melbourne*, when in fact all the evidence indicated that she was on a continuous turn until twenty seconds before impact. The implication was that *Melbourne's* team was not watching and that Stevens could not be assumed to not be watching, because he was a competent and experienced destroyer captain. To my mind, this was the inherent inconsistency behind the original finding: the Naval Board and the government could doggedly maintain that *Voyager's* captain was completely fit and competent, yet the ship's movements immediately before the collision remained inexplicable. This yawning gap between the official 'line' and reality was, of course, spanned by the cover-up. Sir John said, '. . . the primary cause of the collision was the final course followed by *Voyager*', but qualified this conclusion with 'I cannot understand . . .' and 'I cannot conceive . . .'. These were hardly helpful findings at the end of a process whose primary purpose was to determine the causes of the collision. Robertson also submitted that if it were found that Stevens was not suitable to be left in command of *Voyager*, 'that throughout 1963 he had been carried along by a very efficient and dedicated bunch of officers, and he was left in 1964 with a brand new crew, I am quite certain he [Spicer] could not have written that and would have thought differently about the whole collision'.

On 5 October, Reynolds QC (for Robertson) was given the opportunity to develop his position. He acknowledged that there was difficulty, as a matter of logic, in seeing how findings of unfitness to command would have any bearing on the Spicer findings if the respective courses of the two vessels were not in dispute. The main issue, he said, was the course of *Voyager* in the few minutes before impact, with a secondary question of how long *Melbourne* had been on a steady course before impact. The Robertson submission was that the criticism of those on the bridge of *Melbourne* must be considered in the light of the course of *Voyager* and not otherwise, as it was ultimately found. Reynolds reminded the commissioners that Robertson conceded that he would not have a case had *Voyager* been on a steady course for a minute more or less, as had been found by Spicer. But if it were established, as they intended to show, that *Voyager* was on a turning course until twenty seconds before the collision then matters would stand entirely differently.

After citing the lengthy statement by Sir John Spicer regarding the failure by Captain Robertson to indicate that his engines were going astern, Reynolds QC said this was lesser criticism than urged by Smyth, based on 'the considerable experience and competency of the late Captain Stevens'. He continued, 'A perusal of the entire transcript of the first commission relating to the navigational problem and the events of that night does not disclose any suggestion that the late Captain Stevens was other than first-class quality in every possible respect.' But counsel for Robertson then went into the reasons why the Spicer finding relied on witnesses to a steady course who were not in a position to know the facts, not having been on the upper deck or in the wheelhouse. Again, the chairman queried the underlying premise that the commission's terms of reference permitted the inquiry to go so far in relation to challenging the basis of Spicer's conclusions. Reynolds concluded his reply with, 'I would concede that the mere "might have come to a different conclusion" is not good enough for my purposes.' This left the chairman in no doubt. Reynolds required a conclusion that Sir John Spicer should have concluded differently.

By November 22 Samuels had replaced Reynolds, but Murphy QC was now arguing on behalf of the Naval Board that the case for any review of Spicer's original navigational findings foundered. He presumably based this argument on his and Ash QC's submissions in refutation of my claims. It was an audacious attempt to scuttle the whole inquiry. Commissioner Burbury understood his difficulty but signalled by subtle hint that the judges were unlikely to support such a sweeping conclusion. He told Murphy that he thought the only course was 'to let Mr Samuels develop his argument and to hear you at a later stage with some possible reply by Mr Samuels'. Samuels duly addressed the commission for five days and succeeded in demonstrating Captain Robertson's well-researched reconstruction of the events preceding the collision as far as the two ships' courses, speeds, wheel movements and engine orders were concerned. Then Murphy QC spent more than a day in putting the Naval Board's position of criticising Robertson's inaction from the moment they judged him to have sufficient doubt of *Voyager*'s intentions. Nobody in the courtroom was left in any doubt that the Navy and the government were determined to hold the line that had so successfully been established at the first inquiry.

All of this might have been fascinating for anyone with an interest in the problems of manoeuvring large fast ships at close quarters, but it had very little to do with me. It was left to my own counsel, Jack Hiatt, to bring the inquiry back to its primary function. He made the assertion in his address, 'So that we submit that throughout these proceedings that the Naval Board has set out to discourage the uncovering of the truth of the issues posed in Question 1.' Murphy, on the other hand, claimed that the board was anxious to seek the truth at all times. Burt, assisting the commission, suggested that 'the truth lies somewhere in between'. In his summary of the evidence presented by those counsel who were advancing theories, supporting or disputing Sir John Spicer's findings, Burt was incisive. He showed that the former commissioner had criticised *Melbourne*'s captain on the basis of his own report, but that this report could not be correct as the times that relied on Captain Robertson's flawed recollection and reconstruction of events that were demonstrably wrong. Sir John had then applied his own determination of the times to a theory that was based on different times. The Spicer chronology was a hopeless muddle. In fact, there had been no time for Robertson to react in any manner other than as he did.

Much has been written and argued since then as to the cause of the collision, including confusion over signals, courses, minutes and seconds. There are now scores of brilliant and obscure solutions to the problem. In a letter to Vice Admiral Hickling, I described the most likely scenario based on my experience of the captain's established reactions and knowledge of the others involved. Only one ingredient was absent in the evidence available to me at the time: that of Stevens' abuse of amphetamines to recover from the worst effects of alcohol, as disclosed by Don Chipp.

The answer to the mystery of this 'inconceivable' collision is, to my mind, simple and grotesquely obvious. Until the night of the collision Stevens did not, on *Voyager*, drink at sea. His outbursts of intemperate abusive criticism hurled at officers of the watch were also established, and may well have made a collision inevitable. When *Melbourne* executed the signal that required *Voyager* to change station, Lieutenant Price, who was officer of the watch, turned the ship to starboard to commence the expected fishtail manoeuvre to take up the appropriate station on *Melbourne*'s port quarter. Stevens, who had consumed a triple brandy, and was by this time affected to an undetermined extent (and perhaps exacerbated by amphetamines), was confused because *Melbourne* had also commenced turning. He shouted an expletive at Price and countermanded his OOW's order, ordering a turn to port. Price – who disliked Stevens and, more significantly, was afraid of him – was shaken, humiliated and totally disheartened. Having repeated his captain's order to the wheelhouse, acknowledging that Duncan was in direct command, Price would have simply stared ahead as he awaited the next wheel order from his captain. None came. He did not even consider looking at *Melbourne* before being startled from his introspection by the confused lookout's alarm cry. By then it was too late. Meanwhile, the command team of Stevens, Macgregor and the navigator, Cook, were all three feet or more below and in front of the OOW, with their heads behind the blackout screen of the chart table and 'their arses sticking out of the radar' (as described so pungently by Captain Becher after the Suez Canal incident of *Vengeance* in 1955).

When the alarm call came, the captain, with his night vision destroyed by peering at charts and the radar, then had to turn and mount three staggered levels of the badly designed bridge to join Price at the pelorus. This action lost him critical seconds before he could even attempt to appreciate the situation through the disadvantage of an alcohol-affected brain. This is, of course, my own speculation, but I have visualised it as if I were standing at the pelorus, in Price's shoes. Sadly, it makes perfect sense to me.

41
A Question of Loyalty

When I began writing this book I was still confused and angry, with a great deal of guilt and emotion coursing through me. The writing, particularly after the broadcast of the ABC's *Unfit to Command* documentary, acted as a form of catharsis and enabled me to revisit many dark and hidden compartments of my memory and confront the reality of events that I would rather remained buried. I have also read, for the first time, the transcript of proceedings at the royal commission, much of which is etched in my memory and some of which I would challenge as to its veracity. Fortunately, I have been able to call on Chester Porter, who has a wonderful way of getting me to come back to earth and accept that my powers of recall are not infallible.

And I am also more than grateful as I read the transcript of 'Red' Burt's final address. The grand summings up of counsel assisting the commissioners can be long, detailed and tedious. At the time he delivered it I was so wrung out by the months of hearings that I instantly put his words into the far recesses of my mind. The transcript is a precious record. Burt spoke to the commissioners in terms I am certain they did not wish to hear, but could not dismiss:

> In our view, one cannot assess loyalty without first making primary findings of fact, any more than you can assess motive without making the primary findings of fact.
>
> If one supposes that what Cabban said in his statement is true, or more accurately, I think, as it is in Cabban's mind that we are now dealing with, if one supposes that he believed what he said in his statement to be substantially true, then one makes a reasonable

assessment of his loyalty to the captain by seeing just what it was that he was saying to Liebenschutz, Farrelly and Gale.

Burt went on to say:

This is evidence I wish to read Your Honours because it has another important significance. Cabban says that his state of mind was one of increasing apprehension from the period in Singapore up to the period of Tokyo, and it might be a rather interesting exercise to see whether one gets any reflection of this state of mind, one of increasing apprehension, from what Cabban is saying to these named people.

What he expresses to Liebenschutz, and I am paraphrasing, is loyalty to the ship, concern for the ship, attachment to the ship and attachment to the Navy. Later at Karatsu to Farrelly he expresses worry about the captain's health, a worry that was compounded by the fact that he personally liked Stevens, and then to Gale in Tokyo, and this at a time at which Cabban says the position became quite desperate, he expresses concern for the captain and a personal crisis involving concern for the safety of the ship.

One sees at these points, if one accepts the evidence, that there is by this time a very critical conflict of loyalties in the mind of Cabban. It is not a question of being disloyal, it is a question of loyalties coming into conflict. The conflict is between a loyalty that he had to his captain and a loyalty, not so much to the Navy as an abstraction, but a loyalty that he had to other people serving in *Voyager*.

This is stated to be the substance of the matter by Gale. Then to complete the picture prior to coming back to Sydney he subsequently gave the impression to Commander Stevens that he, Cabban, was trying to cover up for the captain. To keep things as quiet as possible. It struck Commander Stevens Cabban was very loyal to the captain. Finally, and again prior to coming back to Sydney, Your Honours will remember the evidence of Howland and the conversations that took place after Subic Bay in the wardroom where Cabban was speaking quite overtly of the conflict of loyalty he had with being loyal to the captain and loyal to the Navy. This discussion took place as to how the conflict was going to be resolved.

Quite incidental to this conversation this has another significance. If there was nothing at all in the Cabban Statement it is
difficult to see how a conversation of this type could get under way
at all. It would simply lack in subject matter. Be that as it may . . . it
is very difficult to spell out from this evidence any conclusion of
disloyalty, and to assume disloyalty in our view is to throw away the
key to understanding and it is a very important key. It is this conflict
of loyalties it would seem to us to explain so much and the way in
which the conflict was in the end resolved, explained so much
because in the end the conflict was resolved, if one can say that, by
Cabban turning his back upon it and walking away. He did this
very shortly after his experience at Williamstown. He speaks to
Holmes about this and . . . it is a key to the understanding of this
facet of the inquiry because it explained why Cabban assumed such
a high degree of personal responsibility for the disaster.

You may think this was an extravagant thing to do but you do
not begin to understand why he did it unless you assume that he
was loyal to the captain and resolved his conflict in a way which to
him in the end was not satisfactory and that he felt that he had
really walked out on the problem. One can see that a recognition
by him that he had, in fact, turned his back on the problem and left
it unresolved appears to have been still operating at the time of the
first commission. This might explain why he gave Wright the
impression that he could say a great deal more but that he was
reluctant to say it . . . or that he seemed hesitant about bringing
forward matters detrimental to other people.

I am not in this saying necessarily Cabban was justified in
believing anything. All I am saying is this may well be a very important key to the understanding of what appears to be a complex
problem. To say simply that Cabban was a malicious troublemaker
is surely to miss the essential point. It may be the story is a very
sensitive one, perhaps a little too sensitive for advocacy. But if you
assume subjective disloyalty I think one does immediately disqual-
ify one from understanding the story.

My learned friend Mr Ash criticises an observation which I
made to the effect that primarily the attack on Cabban was directed
to judgement and only to a limited extent to his veracity. I did not

mean to suggest by that no other attack had been made in the course of this hearing. I was, rather, suggesting this is where the attack lay at the end of the day. I thought this would be understood because in the course of the hearing everything personal about the man had been attacked, his competence as an airman, his competence as a hospital planner, his veracity, his loyalty, his emotional stability, sense of humour. Outside the commission his sobriety and within it his motivation and his judgement. There are very few other things that could be attacked.

But most of the attacks threw more light upon the mind of the attacker than they did on the mind of Cabban and by and large we would observe that the attacks did not succeed and in the end it is true to say that the primary question which controls Your Honours' judgement really rotates around Cabban's judgement rather than any other personal matter going to his credit.

In conclusion, Burt said of me,

Cabban was criticised in the addresses for exaggeration and so on, and in many instances counsel were referring to hearsay information that appears in the Cabban statement, or making use of it to show he was exaggerating . . . It was made clear there and agreed to by all counsel, that no attack could be made on his credit for the inaccuracies of the hearsay information, which was of course never investigated.

One might have expected such words from one's own counsel. To know they were spoken by the scrupulously impartial QC assisting the commission is now a special memory of what was otherwise a deeply harrowing experience.

PART 5

42

The Royal Commissioners' Report

The *Report of Royal Commissioners on the Statement of Lieutenant-Commander Cabban and Matters Incidental Thereto* (also known as the Burbury Report) was issued on 1 February 1968. With appendices, it comprised 253 pages. At the time it seemed as if my whole life from that point forward would be qualified by what the report contained. I collected a copy as soon as it was available and skipped straight through to find the main conclusions. Then I embarked on a more deliberate reading to get an impression of what the commissioners had found in relation to my evidence. It was, to my mixed dismay and relief, a dog's breakfast. While I accepted that there could never be total vindication of the Cabban Statement, the core finding of the inquiry was still profoundly disappointing: Duncan Stevens was unfit to command – no surprises there – but because of an ulcer exacerbated by unwise drinking. The judges held that he was not an alcoholic, and I was said to have presented a highly coloured account of Captain Stevens' drinking habits.

The royal commissioners' detailed findings of fact in relation to Captain Stevens' excessive drinking were ridiculously merciful. Where the first inquiry had simply covered up any suggestion that Duncan was a drunkard, the second pretended that the primary cause of his incapacity was duodenal malfunction rather than his obvious addiction to the effects of brandy. Specifically, the commissioners stated that there were only three occasions on which there was evidence that he was intoxicated – 'mildly', 'moderately' and 'slightly' – whereas I had attested to five. (I can now recall clearly at least eleven incidents of the captain's alcohol abuse during 1963.)

The commissioners' apparent desire to protect whatever shreds were left of Stevens' reputation required their report to contain some peculiar contortions of logic. On other points the judges simply decided to reject matters of fact that did not suit their position. I had stated that I had had command for two days after departure from Darwin, but they found this to be untrue. Yet Stevens had been drinking all night before we left, and Lieutenant Wright could not have forgotten Freeman reporting to him that Stevens did not know where he was. The commissioners record the captain, on an assumption from the *Vampire* report of proceedings, as having drinks on board *Lion* on Sunday, 3 March, the day following Duncan having been drunk in *Caesar* and vomiting in his bathroom. I had taken the church service and gone to *Lion* and gave evidence of my sense of unease and of avoiding the admiral. They also found that he was not affected by alcohol in Trincomalee.

The incident, reported in *Truth*, when Stevens was found unconscious in the gutter after the China Fleet Club party was not in evidence, as I had not recalled it in time for it to be introduced during the hearings. Stevens' condition during the 'Lost in *Yarra*' fiasco was described as 'being unwell rather than drunk' – in the face of all of the evidence of the confrontation in the wardroom and the 'What do I do when you're drunk, Sir?' exchange. The firm evidence of this incident from one honest sailor, Mead, was dismissed. Martin said there was an occasion in Hong Kong when the captain was affected by alcohol, but the report concluded, 'It is not established that Captain Stevens was intoxicated at any time during this visit, but it is established that his stomach trouble intensified and that on occasions he was seen by Cabban and Surgeon-Commander McNeill doubled up with pain.' So why did the judges imagine that I went to see Peek at all? What matters of substance did they conclude I had in mind to lay before this superior officer?

At the Army party, they found Stevens was 'mildly intoxicated'. He was a patent disgrace to his uniform, yet as far as the two wise commissioners were concerned this shameful display was of only 'mild' intoxication. I wondered what sort of wild parties these men must attend. On board *Rothesay*, they found that Duncan 'was not intoxicated at the luncheon, but had to leave early because he was unwell'. This conclusion refreshed my dismay that Commander Irwin had not supported me, and that the letter from Captain Place VC, advising him not to tell what happened, was not marked as an exhibit. In Karatsu, I had given evidence of having to attend the tea-drinking ceremony because of Stevens' condition, but could not specify the precise dates on which he was drunk. This allowed the commissioners to conclude, 'We find that at no time during this visit was Captain Stevens intoxicated: but we find that he was drinking unwisely . . .'

I became sick at heart reading on through the judges' repeated denials of the captain's appalling state during the Far East cruise. Their account of Tokyo, where there was the most damning evidence that did not rely on me, was classic Burbury and Asprey. On Thursday 6 June, 'Captain Stevens suddenly nodded off at dinner but was not intoxicated.' The following morning, 'At breakfast he had a coffee royale and after the steam baths several brandies and ginger ale.' (But no mention of intoxication.) Then that evening, 'We find that Captain Stevens had been drinking consistently but was not intoxicated and that he suddenly nodded off at the dinner table and arrangements were made for him to leave.' On Saturday, no reference is made of the coffee royales that were consumed, and, 'After the steam bath they each had five brandies and ginger ale.' (But again, no intoxication.) Yet, on the way to the Dollard picnic, 'Captain Stevens became unwell during the car trip. He returned to Captain Dollard's home and lay down. Arrangements were made for someone else to substitute for him at a Japanese admiral's dinner party. After sleeping for some time, he woke up and had a brandy and vomited.' (Presumably not as the result of intoxication.) Then, that evening, 'Captain Stevens vomited in Captain Dollard's home.' We can only assume that the commissioners were describing the same incident, although it is described as another. Finally, on the Sunday, at lunchtime, 'Captain Stevens made a remarkable recovery.' Recovery from what? Surely not intoxication?

When *Voyager* returned to Sydney the judges were of the view that: 'The evidence does not establish that Captain Stevens was intoxicated on any occasion during the week in Sydney and we find that the allegations . . . are untrue.' Incredibly, this was the same week when he tripped on the gangway before the Holmes christening, the same week in which Martin told me Stevens had been drunk and Martin had kept Captain Dovers out of his way while he pulled himself together (presumably with amphetamines) for the Pakistani Shield, the same week when Ferrier told me of his incoherence at the refit meeting, the same week I had put my resignation on his desk while he slept, the same week when he was not fit to see defaulters until after three o'clock on Friday afternoon, and was then drunk as we were leaving harbour. The report notes, 'Cabban maintained . . . that Captain Stevens was affected by alcohol when *Voyager* left Sydney at 0900 hours was true. We do not accept this evidence but we find that Captain Stevens was unwell and that he did retire to his cabin after *Voyager* cleared Sydney Heads until she reached Port Phillip Bay.' If only David Martin had told the truth of those hours, which he could never have forgotten! On Duncan's arrival in Williamstown, returning from the Dovers court martial, the commissioners agreed, 'Captain Stevens drank eight to ten brandies and water during the train journey.' (But clearly, he was not intoxicated, even 'mildly'.) Then 'Captain Stevens was confined to his cabin, ill, at least from Monday, 2 December, until Thursday, 5 December, but had recovered by Friday, 6 December'. It was during this period that I had given evidence of him consuming more than a bottle of brandy in a day.

The report used Sir William Morrow's uncorroborated assumption that Stevens drank brandy to relieve his ulcer pain to twist the truth as to his chronic alcoholism. In contrast, Burbury and Asprey refused to acknowledge any hearsay evidence from me unless it was supported by direct testimony from other witnesses. This position conveniently relieved them of any obligation to refer to Stevens' horrific threat to have me certified before any defender of my rights could intervene – the cause of my hysterical amnesia. (This evidence was given in closed court and at the discretion of the Commissioners was not included in the transcript.) Nevertheless, they recognised me as an honest person, intensely loyal to my captain, 'as he thought he should be', and rejected the allegations that I held a grudge against the Navy. Their character assessment of me was, in fact, a curious blend of formal praise and gratuitous psychobabble. First, the judges said there could be no doubt that I was, at all times, a thoroughly competent and efficient executive officer and an enthusiastic and dedicated naval officer with an almost overwhelming ambition to reach the top. They said I tended to dramatise events and to exaggerate, yet for some reason then decided that I was an 'introvert' whereas Stevens was an 'extrovert'. The evidence all indicated the opposite. Duncan was as introverted as any man I ever saw, and sought solace in drink. Surgeon Commander Tim Haughton told the inquiry of Stevens' ulcer history and the evidence of his anxiety that led to it. This served to underline Duncan's inward-looking frame of mind, as did my evidence of him confiding in me, and his seeking out the relatively junior Money and Blaikie as drinking companions rather than Jim Willis, his fellow destroyer captain.

But perhaps the most extraordinary example of the commissioners' deliberate contrariness was their insistence on painting me as seeing myself as Captain Robertson's champion. This was in total contradiction to my firm denials in evidence. The judges were desperate, as were Ash and Murphy, to ascribe this motive to me despite the fact that I had stated clearly (and they acknowledged in the report) my reluctance to adopt this imagined role as Robertson's 'White Knight'. Rather, the inner compulsion that I was unable to resist – my entire purpose – was to ensure that no sailor ever died at sea through any neglect of mine. But, carried away on their flight of fantasy, the commissioners seized on the casual comparison of my position in *Voyager* with that of Maryk in *The Caine Mutiny*. Obviously desperate to condemn me with ridicule, this conceit allowed them to attribute to me delusions of casting myself in a dramatic situation that did not exist.

There were tidings of great joy for the *Melbourne* interests in the report, but this vindication came too late. Any implication by Spicer of fault on their part in the collision was totally reversed, with each of them, collectively and individually, cleared of blame. Regrettably, there could be no question of reinstatement for Captain Robertson, who would have been a rear admiral by this time, almost certainly to be promoted to Chief of Naval Staff and ultimately knighted, if not for Duncan Stevens. Commander Kelly's career was already blighted and Sub-Lieutenant Bate's life was destroyed emotionally. There was little personal comfort for either of them in the findings.

On the potentially explosive third term of reference, Smyth QC was cleared of improperly withholding evidence from the first inquiry because he had had the concurrence of Sir John Spicer in finding it irrelevant. With a single legal side-step, this conclusion neatly avoided having to address the damning fact that Stevens' excessive drinking would have been of crucial relevance to the first inquiry but had been covered up.

Instead of Lord Nelson putting a telescope to his blind eye we had Sir John Spicer refusing to acknowledge primary evidence.

And what of that great institution that had laboured so mightily over the preceding four years to hide the true wellsprings of the *Voyager* disaster from public view? The Naval Board itself was largely white-washed in the Burbury Report, but the basis of that exoneration was frail to anyone with a practical grasp of the working relationship between seagoing officers and the shore admirals who command them. On the issue of Stevens' unsatisfactory health, the commissioners found that Tiller and McNeill had failed to report the captain's medical unfitness, thereby denying the board the knowledge that they would otherwise have obtained – or should have received. Willis and Dollard were believed in their entirety while the blame fell conveniently on Tiller and McNeill, neither of whom were now serving naval officers.

Although both Captains Dollard and Willis had a duty to report Captain Stevens' unfitness to the Naval Board and the immediate admin-istrative authority in the Far East, and were liable to court martial for not doing so, they were not criticised. Burt had made it clear to the commis-sioners that they had either to accept the evidence of the two senior serving officers or to accept Farrelly and Jamieson (who had nothing to gain by concealing the truth). Not surprisingly, the judges chose to believe the evidence that best fitted the picture they were painting. They accepted Captain Willis's false evidence as to what happened between himself and Stevens and what he told me. This obviously came as a great relief to the Naval Board. It was all very well for the service to exert every effort to protect the reputation of a deceased captain and the reputations of the senior officers who had failed to supervise that captain. But the Naval Board also owed a duty of loyalty to the men of lesser rank who were imperilled by that captain. Instead, they betrayed those men to save the senior officers. They dodged the very issue of Stevens' gross deception of the Naval Board, aided and abetted as it was by medical and executive officers, and its incalculable cost in the lives of eighty-one other innocent men.

Willis was eventually promoted vice admiral and knighted, instead of being investigated and punished. Commodore Dollard, who was deco-rated in the Korean War, missed out on further accolades from a grateful Naval Board, but Captain Britten was promoted commodore and honoured by Her Majesty with a CBE, presumably for his attention to witnesses. David Martin was promoted to rear admiral, became Governor of New South Wales on retirement and had a charitable foundation named in his honour when he died (shortly after confessing to his untruthful evidence at the inquiry). Sir Stanley Burbury was appointed Governor of Tasmania. In my view, as the findings of the second royal commission began slowly to sink in, the pattern of cover-up established under Sir John Spicer had been seamlessly continued. Later, the expression, 'Punish the innocent and reward the guilty' sprang to mind.

43

Parliamentary Post-mortem

It was Australia's system of parliamentary democracy that had prompted the second *Voyager* royal commission. Now it was time for our elected representatives to consider the findings of the inquiry to which they had given such reluctant birth. While the tragedy of the collision and its aftermath were always legitimate political concerns, a parliamentary debate over the Burbury Report had implications that went far beyond the normal battle for advantage between government and opposition. The protection of privilege would allow each speaker the freedom to canvass virtually any aspect of the inquiry and to take the debate well beyond the guarded wording of the published report.

Three distinct areas of interest in the report were immediately obvious to even a casual observer of this saga. The first was simply personal: where would a fair reading of the commission's findings leave the careers and reputations of its principal *dramatis personae*? Next, at the institutional level, what were the implications for the government, the Naval Board and the conduct of its senior staff? Finally, taking a broader view, was the royal commission process itself the most appropriate method for handling such complex matters? Each of these questions would inevitably be raised during the parliamentary debate that traditionally follows the government's formal motion that the report of a royal commission be 'noted'. In the great arena of public opinion, these speeches in the House of Representatives were the opportunity for the Westminster system to test the findings of Burbury and Asprey. Analysis, interpretation, comment, criticism and speculation would abound. Sue and I had a huge interest in what would be said, but we decided not to attend parliament to hear the debate when it commenced on Tuesday, 2 April 1968. There had been too much emotion during our previous Canberra experience, so we preferred to listen to the ABC broadcasts and to read Hansard.

The Hon. E. G. Whitlam QC opened as Leader of the Opposition. His introductory remarks were an astute attempt to spike the guns of those who had already enlisted synthetic patriotism to promote their claims that any further examination of the disaster would harm Navy morale. He quoted Rear Admiral Crabb, Flag Officer Commanding Australian Fleet, who had said, 'the Navy had absorbed and taken enough kicking around', and Rear Admiral Peek, by then Second Naval Member, who protested that the Navy had 'suffered over the last six months from press headlines and a lot of stupid questions from legal people at the royal commission'. These were transparent attempts to hurriedly close an open wound, but Whitlam hoped that none of this fear-mongering would mar a searching debate. Laying aside the description of the royal commission as 'a lot of stupid questions from legal people', I do not believe Admiral Peek's view reflected the opinion that I later heard attributed to Admiral Sir Victor Smith, McNicoll's successor as Chief of Naval Staff. He believed that the inquiry was the best thing that had happened to the Navy for many years.

Whitlam had dissected the report with a lawyer's incisive mind. He proceeded to expose its weaknesses and to identify the failures of the government, the Navy and of the individual ministers who had misled parliament and the people of Australia during earlier debates. He named the Attorney-General, Nigel Bowen, and the Minister for the Navy, Don Chipp, as having deliberately stated that there was no corroboration for my statement in the full knowledge that there was. He also found it difficult to understand why Burbury and Asprey should have taken such great pains to denigrate me. He contrasted their description of me as 'an unreliable witness' with his own view that 'in many instances he emerged as an entirely reliable witness on detailed objective facts. Actually, the overwhelming majority of statements of fact contained in the Cabban statement were proved correct. Nobody who gave evidence before this commission required corroboration less.' When the Opposition leader declared that a great deal of corroboration existed at the time of the May 1967 debate, the Treasurer, William McMahon, made himself look even sillier than usual by interjecting, 'None!'

Whitlam described as 'distasteful' the fact that the commissioners devoted three pages of their report to 'what it describes as a histrionic metaphor about Cabban's vision of himself' (referring to the *Caine Mutiny* scenario). The Opposition leader went so far as to say that if I had indeed seen myself as the instrument for achieving justice for Captain Robertson, then I was right, 'because that is precisely the role he filled'. Later in his speech Whitlam said, 'The Parliament and this nation is deeply in Cabban's debt.' That was an extremely kind sentiment to express, but I did not see it that way. I was just grateful to have survived. I was indebted to my wife for her vital support as well as to my legal advisers, particularly Ted St John, Jack Hiatt and Chester Porter in the front line, and Gordon Beard and Tony McDonald facilitating our efforts. Nobody owed me anything. Then, in full rhetorical flight, Whitlam indulged himself in a flourish that allowed the government an opening. He described the most blatant of all of the purveyors of false information, Samuel Landau, as 'this creature'. They were accurate and reasonable words, but they were also unparliamentary.

The new Prime Minister, John Gorton, seized on Whitlam's sarcastic description of one of the nation's most senior civil servants in an obvious endeavour to divert the debate away from the embarrassing substance of Burbury's report. But Gorton was never a terribly convincing debater. As a previous Navy Minister, he also carried the baggage of old loyalties that were no longer sensible. The Prime Minister inadvertently proved Whitlam right by attempting to deny evidence that had already been accepted as sound. He claimed that the allegations in the Cabban Statement were 'misleading', conveniently forgetting that the royal commission had been sufficiently convinced by the substance of my assertions to find Stevens unfit to command and to overthrow the Spicer conclusions. In his book *A Time to Speak*, Edward St John condemned this shameless action by Gorton.

Lance Barnard, deputy Leader of the Opposition, spoke brilliantly, I thought. He went straight to the heart of the matter by declaring, '. . . the dominant emphasis of this report is that the *Voyager* was captained by a very ill man who never should have been in tactical command of a naval vessel at sea.' I was touched when he said, 'It should never be forgotten that the new findings . . . which will bring us as close to the truth of the *Voyager* as we will ever get, derive solely from the courage and persistence of Lieutenant Commander Cabban.' But my actions were not prompted by courage. I had certainly received ample advice from those whose counsel I trusted most to 'leave it alone'. Yet although I appreciated the probable consequences of my persistence, I could not stop. I was driven from within by an irresistible compulsion to assuage my consuming guilt and to ensure, as far as it was within my power, that such a tragedy could not recur through similar circumstances. 'Conscience' is perhaps too bald and melodramatic a word to describe my feelings, but the impulse to see the matter out was overwhelming.

When McMahon rose to speak, he, too, latched on to the unfortunate word 'creature' and prolonged the tirade. But hypocrisy has a way of asserting itself. After his snide attack on me during the original debate, McMahon had the hide to claim, 'I feel that it is wrong to attack anyone who cannot come into this House and defend himself.' Always quick to defend the Canberra mandarins who actually did the work of running the country, the Treasurer was pleased to quote the commissioners' unctuous absolution of Landau. ('We think it proper to add that no sinister motive can possibly be attributed to Mr Landau in destroying Dr Tiller's original sketchy comments.') Nevertheless, it fell to McMahon to announce the one cabinet decision that the press and public had been waiting for. As an inevitable response to the overthrow of Spicer's findings in relation to *Melbourne*, the government had now decided to pay Captain Robertson $60,000, free of tax, as an 'act of grace' in recognition of his forgone pension. McMahon read out Robertson's letter of thanks to the Prime Minister and cabinet, which the former captain had punctiliously addressed to Landau.

Kelly and Bate had already been promoted, said the Treasurer, and would not be impeded. Lieutenant Bate's promotion was in fact automatic, yet McMahon implied that it was on a higher plane than that (presumably quoting from a Naval Board memorandum). The remainder of his speech was a fawning reiteration of the Gorton line and added nothing to the image of a government desperate to continue denying that it had been caught out in its attempts to hide the truth from parliament and the nation. Why could they not see that the game was up? Forty years later we know that this vain perversity on the part of the government and the Naval Board would have massively negative consequences. Had they been gracious and positive, there is no doubt the healing process could have been accelerated and the nation might have avoided the sickening and expensive spectacle of decades of litigation from many of the unfortunate survivors.

While McMahon's performance might have been the epitome of slimy politics, Don Chipp, now no longer Navy Minister and recently demoted to the backbench, defended his former departmental secretary with almost pathetic fulsomeness. He deplored the abuse being heaped on Landau during the debate, claiming, 'In all my human experience – I say this with deep sincerity – I have never met a man of more integrity or more honesty than Mr Landau.' To me, this defined the former minister more completely than anything he ever said or wrote. Quoting extensively from the commissioners' report, Chipp continued the government's attack on me. These were slings and arrows to which I had almost become accustomed, but Chipp then wildly overplayed his hand at the conclusion of his speech when he insisted on paying tribute to Duncan Stevens. Wiser political heads in his own party had resisted such dangerous grandstanding, but Chipp ploughed ahead. He quoted from the commission report:

> . . . the evidence enables us to make a clear affirmative finding that at all times other than the few occasions to which we have referred, Captain Stevens conducted himself with complete propriety and sobriety and carried out his manifold duties (both at sea and in harbour) with considerable credit to himself and to the entire satisfaction of those having administrative and operational command over him. He showed high qualities of leadership and the morale of the ship was good.

Blind to the tacit warning behind the judges' careful qualification 'other than the few occasions to which we have referred', Chipp blundered on to favour the parliament with his own interpretation of those incidents. 'On only three occasions in the whole of his service which has been under microscopic examination was he found to be moderately affected by alcohol. On the first occasion, illness was a substantially contributing factor; on the second, he was mildly intoxicated, and on the third was slightly intoxicated.' Joining the dots, it could only be presumed that Chipp was referring, in order, to the birthday dinner (where Duncan was drunk to the point of collapsing), the 'Lost in *Yarra*' fiasco (when the captain did not know where he was and shouted 'You're not going to get me!'), and the Army party in Hong Kong (when Stevens whistled drunkenly at stewards and was improperly dressed in front of civilian and military guests). If that is 'moderate', 'mild' and 'slight', we should all be grateful that Chipp chose politics as a career and not the police force. Not many drunk drivers would have been charged while Constable Chipp was on duty!

Bill O'Connor, the Labor Member for Dalley, focused on the failure of Smyth QC to call me, and then on the damning affidavit of Judge Hicks and its rebuttal by Justice Street. (This did not, however, prevent him from taking time to rebuke government speakers who had self-righteously condemned attacks on those who could not protect themselves. He pointedly cited Chipp's own propensity to do just that.) Coming to the reliance placed on the evidence of Sir William Morrow, O'Connor considered that faith to be far too generous. He referred to Dr Birrell's disagreement with certain conclusions by Morrow, and said that he had spoken to other doctors who had laughed at Morrow's evidence. O'Connor was also scathing of the commissioners' going to extreme lengths to throw doubt on Hyland's evidence, three years after he had first given it with the benefit of a fresh memory. Making a commentary on the implications of the report for the Navy, O'Connor addressed the key question that I believed had been overlooked by the commissioners: how is a junior officer to deal with a senior officer? He concluded, 'I am certain that the type of situation that prevailed in Stevens' case will continue.'

Finally, reading from page 143 of the report, he said, 'Stevens was the bluff outgoing naval captain, impatient of formality and unwilling to stand on ceremony. Cabban was almost his complete opposite, quietly efficient but reserved and inclined to be self-centred and uncompromising, a near perfectionist to whom any departure by his captain or fellow naval officer from rigid standards of propriety he set for himself were abhorrent and inexcusable.' He finished on that note, saying,

> If that was the approach of Cabban and the House accepts it as such, is that to the detriment of Cabban? Have we reached the stage in society or in life where people who hold such ideals – ideals which may be a nuisance to some people – are to be castigated and thrown out because of their attitude? Quite frankly I say that it would be far better for all if there were more Cabbans around than there are at present.

John Jess entered the debate to support Robertson and me, as well as to castigate Admiral McNicoll and the commissioners. (It was typical of

Jess's character that he would now be dissatisfied with the findings of the same inquiry he had so strenuously fought to establish.) He was, to my mind, on firmer ground when he attacked McNicoll's failure to call me and his pompous dismissal of the suggestion when replying to Jack Hiatt. Jess made the rather tart observation that the admiral might change his views in the light of the report. He highlighted the telling evidence concerning the request by Osborne (solicitor for the Stevens family in the initial inquiry) for a character reference for Stevens. McNicoll had replied, 'I asked not to be pressed, as I could not describe him as in any way outstanding.' But then, in the second commission, McNicoll said, 'A perusal of his "flimsies" indicates a long, satisfactory and indeed distinguished service in the various capacities in which he served from time to time.' This, said Jess, was a fair indication of the kinds of flimsies that are written: 'the last of which was from Admiral McNicoll re service in *Voyager* from January 1963 to January 1964; "has conducted himself to my entire satisfaction. A keen and enthusiastic captain of HMAS *Voyager*".'

Jess found Smyth QC's lack of action in raising matters of alcohol on the night of the collision to be astounding. Now warming to his task of exposing weaknesses in the inquiry process, Jess reminded parliament of the paragraph in Landau's letter written to Commodore Dacre Smyth, in London, asking him to destroy both the letter (which alerted the commodore to Jess's impending visit) and the Cabban Statement. Jess asked the obvious question: how many other documents were destroyed? Concerning me, he asserted that the inquiry was 'the trial of Cabban more than anybody else'. I could only agree. Debate was adjourned following the Jess speech and resumed the following afternoon.

Harry Turner, one of the 'dissident' Liberals who had helped force the government towards a second inquiry, made a carefully considered and balanced speech. Turner gave credit for what he saw as findings that vindicated his stand alongside Ted St John against the prevailing party view. I was proud to have had his courageous support. The Liberal Member for Swan, Richard Cleaver, made a useful contribution to the debate when he briefly listed the positives to emerge from the commission. As he saw them, they were: an injustice to Robertson and others had been corrected; the medical reporting actions of two naval doctors as well as review procedures had been exposed as deficient; and social pressures on captains on operational cruises might be modified. Although I differed on the last, I appreciated his intentions. He could not have known that it was only Stevens who found these social pressures so debilitating.

The entry into the debate of Edward St John was anticipated keenly, both inside and outside parliament. First praising the speech of John Jess, Ted attributed to him a wider and nobler cause – that of truth and justice – rather than the more personal motive of assisting his cousin, John Robertson. With a barrister's instinct for persuasive analogy, St John suggested that if either of the commissioners were in an aircraft flown by a pilot with Captain Stevens' history for the previous year, they could not land fast enough to complain to the airline that employed him. Coming to the criticisms levelled at me, he rejected entirely the judges' statement that casting myself in a dramatic role was 'a complete flight from reality'. Ted said:

> The telling of the truth often requires great moral courage. If it hurts, as it often does, it will frequently trigger off what learned counsel assisting the commission described as a defence mecha- nism. The man who tries to tell the truth will find himself denigrated in every possible way, subjected to personal attacks, accused of malicious motives, mental instability, self-righteous egomania, deliberate lying and fabrication or whatever else appears to present itself as a weapon against him. All these things have happened to Cabban, and perhaps the hardest to take is the lack of real appreciation even from those who should be most grateful. Throughout all this Peter Cabban, with support of his loyal wife, has conducted himself with dignity and courage . . . Without his evidence none of this would have been achieved.

Ted drew attention to the unexplained preference for the evidence of Sir William Morrow and lack of comment on the contrary evidence of Dr Birrell. As he said, the interpretation that I placed on my observa- tions of Stevens was that which any layman, unaware of his medical condition, would have attributed to them. Most importantly, St John stated that the two inquiries would have been in vain if all officers and men of the armed services did not learn the lesson of loyalty. This was that loyalty to their service, and to the nation, must take precedence over loyalty to their comrades or fellow officers, or the desire to advance their careers. 'Particularly when lives may be imperilled by the failure to perform their duty, let *Voyager* remind them to perform it. When public interest requires them to tell the truth, even if it may reflect adversely on others either dead or alive, let *Voyager* remind them to tell it. Lest we forget.' I could not have better summarised my own convictions.

The Queensland Liberal, Jim Killen, gave a speech that mixed occasional touches of humour with elegantly veiled attacks on a number of targets. Himself soon to be given the Navy portfolio, Killen followed the party line of supporting the Burbury Report and denouncing all who criticised it. He was particularly unimpressed by Jess, saying, 'I doubt very much indeed whether there would have been the anxiety to have this second royal commission if Captain Robertson had received some form of superannuation.' This attempt to sweep away the importance of Stevens' unfitness to command rang an alarm bell in my mind. It also led Killen into a ludicrous exaggeration when he claimed that 'it has been by sheer chance – not through Lieutenant Commander Cabban – that any injustice has been corrected'. Parading his legal knowledge, Killen questioned the procedures of the second royal commission operating as a *de facto* appellate court, especially in relation to their revisiting of the navigational evidence. To most observers, it seemed as if the Member for Moreton regretted that *Melbourne*'s captain and bridge officers were no longer the convenient scapegoats for the disaster.

Listening to this long debate became something of an ordeal for Sue and me, but we enjoyed the acerbic wit of Clyde Cameron. He agreed with his 'Presbyterian friend, the Honourable Member for Evans' (the Reverend Dr Malcolm Mackay), that they should drop the legal talk. Referring to our meetings of twelve months earlier, Cameron said that I was not 'some simpleton who entered into and embarked upon this exercise not knowing the consequences'. He was generous in his expressed opinion of me and my attitude. But the central thrust of his speech was a powerful critique of the commission's generous findings in relation to Duncan Stevens and alcohol. Clyde was determined to cut through all the humbug and remind the nation that *Voyager*'s captain had been a drunkard.

Turning to the curious evidence of Sir William Morrow, Cameron speculated on the reason for him referring Stevens for a liver function test. If not to check for alcohol-related liver damage, what else would it be? He told parliament, 'But the remarkable thing about all this is that the two most sensitive alcohol tests that should be taken in conjunction with a liver function test were either not taken, or the results were suppressed.' Sir William might have considered himself lucky that Clyde Cameron MHR had not been counsel assisting the commission.

The Opposition front-bencher had some more sharp questions for the knighted physician. Cameron raised the birthday dinner incident of which Morrow had said that, apart from some horseplay, on hands and knees, Stevens had been able to walk across the wardroom. But Morrow had said, 'I am convinced that this condition was mainly due to his ulcer.' Cameron asked, 'What is this condition? He could not stand up and was able only to mumble a reply.' Then he suggested that members look at Birrell's statement, exhibit No. 183, where the doctor stated, 'I consider this man to be suffering from alcoholism, there being no reasonable alternative.' (Dr Birrell based this on the accepted clinical definition of alcoholism: 'Drinking in amounts sufficient to interfere with the drinker's health or social functioning.') 'Dr Birrell,' said Cameron, 'referred to the great discovery by Dr Morrow that he [Stevens] had not been drinking to the extent that there had been cerebral damage.' What a relief! The captain had apparently not become mentally defective through drinking. Birrell described the crawling incident as acting like a sixteen-year-old schoolboy being drunk and not like an adult non-alcoholic. Yet, as Cameron now noted, the commission cast all of this aside rather than acknowledge that it supported my evidence. Clyde raised another relevant remark of Birrell's concerning brandy in Stevens' coffee in the mornings, a habit he believed was brought on primarily by alcohol misuse. Cameron suggested, 'Even the worst of us here has not reached the point of wanting brandy in our coffee in the morning.'

The recently appointed Minister for the Navy, Bert Kelly (later replaced by Killen), was left until last and proceeded to mop up as best he could after the mess the debate had become for the government. He attempted to put a gloss on the actions the Navy had taken in light of the findings and recommendations of the commissioners, but without great success. I was intrigued by his announcement that there was now an amendment to instructions, issued to facilitate procedures under which naval personnel may by-pass their immediate superiors to make complaints and representations. I have since heard, first hand, of one such successful action in a shore establishment. But it would still be very difficult at sea.

The debate on the Burbury Report concluded at 11.00 p.m. What had all these words achieved? The management of speeches by the Opposition had the semblance of an extremely disciplined and efficient allocation of responsibilities. Each speaker appeared to have researched the transcript of evidence relating to his specific aspects of the report so that he could speak with authority and effect. They landed telling blows on the government, drawing extravagant personal attacks and repeated references to the many insupportable conclusions in the report. Their targeting of the commissioners' reliance on Sir William Morrow was well directed and obviously informed. The Stevens family had attended parliament during the debate, but their presence did not subdue members, as I am sure the government hoped it would. At least in my view, the late Duncan Stevens received far more respect than was accorded me by the government in both debates, and his memory was also respected by the majority of the other side. But eighty-one other men died through the actions of Captain Stevens on the night of 10 February 1964, and their memory also deserves respect.

44
Aftermath

And that was that. Four years of anguish, doubt, self-recrimination and relentless public scrutiny were brought to an abrupt full stop. The *Voyager* disaster swiftly disappeared from the headlines, and I could return to the welcome anonymity of private life. Copies of the inquiry report were filed away and forgotten in the nation's libraries. I was the survivor of a royal commission that bore my name, but if there were any victors in this saga they certainly did not include me. I had been complimented, by each QC, as 'the best witness' they had ever seen (with the typically irreverent exception of Burt, who said that he had known one witness, a murderer, with a better recall). Yet the two commissioners, Burbury and Asprey, remained unconvinced of my reliability. In the public mind, there was little doubt that the inquiry had established that Stevens' excessive drinking contributed to the collision. There was a similar recognition – especially in press commentary – that both the Navy and the government had conspired to cover up the truth behind the disaster. But that still was not full vindication, and it did little to lift my persisting sense of guilt. Meanwhile, I received no thanks or any acknowledgement from John Robertson. (He obtained substantial compensation, and he was now indifferent to my fate.)

My family and I began picking up the pieces of our lives, and I was aware that Sue had protected me from the realities of the pressures they had endured throughout the commission. We received some wonderful support from a few stalwart friends, a great deal of supporting mail from strangers, and some anonymous criticism to ensure that we were never in doubt that not everyone appreciated our situation. My clients seemed pleased to see me back at work, and I was immediately immersed consulting to hospitals, principally in New South Wales, and for the New South Wales Department of Public Works.

I can confess now that while overseas during seven months of study of hospital staffing and design in 1969, I often hoped that I might be killed in an accident. I had lost my own purpose in living. Family and a few friends were the sole reason for continuing. I kept going through the motions, but was far more fragile than they could possibly know. The suppressed guilt continued to haunt me. When *Melbourne* sliced through a second destroyer, USS *Frank E. Evans*, while I was in the USA, Sue was frightened of the effect the tragedy might have on me. But I knew that it was almost impossible in a 'dry' US warship (where no alcohol is permitted) for the cause to be identical. The only similarity in the collision was the lack of attention from the captain, who had turned in, and the ineptitude of his inexperienced watch-keepers. Remarkably, the behaviour of our Naval Board was no more commendable in the treatment of the new captain of *Melbourne* than it had been for Robertson in 1964. Despite being cleared by court martial, his career was also blighted.

As the years passed I found myself able to slowly push the pain of *Voyager* into the middle distance. The traumas never left me entirely, but they were manageable, and I had the welcome distraction of a challenging professional career. Admiral McNicoll, who had retired at the end of the second commission, was not having such an enjoyable time. His reward from a grateful government was the diplomatic posting as our ambassador to Turkey. He filled that decidedly uncoveted position from 1968 to 1973, but the *Voyager* scandal clearly continued to rankle. A year after his return to Australia the former Naval Board member who had most probably done more than anyone to cover up Stevens' deficiencies burst into print. He wrote a long and bitter article, published prominently in both the *Age* and *Sydney Morning Herald*. In it he abused the commissioners, the Robertson finding in great detail and me in particular. McNicoll's diatribe could not be allowed to stand, and Ted St John responded in typically erudite manner, pointing out the ridiculous, erroneous and abusive nature of the article. To me, this unseemly episode revealed two things: first, the lingering depth of the 'traditional' Navy's resentment of any external inquiry into its conduct and second, McNicoll's need to publicly avenge himself on those he clearly thought had put a permanent stain on his career. It did the man little credit.

It took many more years before fragmentary new evidence began to emerge confirming the depth of the cover-up. On ABC Radio on 12 February 1992, in the wake of a *Four Corners* report on the aftermath of the *Voyager* disaster, Andrew Olle interviewed Dr Malcolm Mackay, who'd been Minister for the Navy in 1970–71. Mackay made some startling revelations, supporting the claim that justice had not been done to the survivors and many others who'd suffered as a result of government and Naval Board actions. He said that conflicting loyalties had come into play, producing 'something less than justice for a number of people. Not just the survivors of the *Voyager*, but also Captain Roberson of the *Melbourne*.'

Mackay attributed the apparent cover-up 'to the appointment of the captain of the *Voyager*', saying that it was 'fairly well known throughout the Navy that he had, shall we say, a tendency to drink unwisely, if not a drinking problem'. He went on to say, 'Other things came together at that time to mean that all the rules were broken.' Then, 'at the crucial moment the con was taken over by the captain of the ship, and in an irrational way, he gave an order which brought her right under the bows of *Melbourne*'. Asked what caused this behaviour, Mackay said that it was known by some that Stevens was prone to seasickness and was medicated for this with a barbiturate or Pethidine, 'which destroys judgement, anyway'.

Dr Mackay cited quite sensational corroboration for his assertions. He confirmed that while he was Minister, his 'great friend', the Secretary to the Naval Board, Samuel Landau (now deceased), had unburdened himself to Mackay. Landau told him that before the second royal commission he was aware that on the night of the collision, Captain Stevens was taking medication, 'Pethidine, or it's equivalent'. Mixed with the triple brandy this was 'an explosive combination' that would have rendered him unfit to be anywhere near the bridge. The drug was supposedly for seasickness, although it was known that Duncan had been regularly at sea for the past thirteen months and had suffered no seasickness – but had been drinking the previous day.

It can reasonably be assumed that the drug to which Landau referred was amphetamine, as disclosed by Don Chipp in his book and confirmed in an interview with John Penlington on *This Day Tonight* on 24 May 1978. Chipp said, 'On the amphetamine thing, there was not a shred of evidence that had anything to do with the Commission and the

Commissioners said so. There is not a shred of evidence that it had any effect on his behaviour at sea. It did have an affect on his behaviour on shore when mixed with a minute quantity of alcohol.' But when asked, 'Are you sure, though, that he didn't take amphetamines when he was at sea?' Chipp replied, 'I am not sure, no I'm sure he did not take alcohol at sea and it is the mixture of the two that can be quite dangerous and cause erratic behaviour.'

Around this time, the producer of the *Four Corners* report, Harvey Broadbent, received a brief telephone call from a women who identifed herself as a former medical records librarian at Concord Repatriation General Hospital. She claimed to have been conscience-stricken since 1967 when two officers from the Naval Board visited the hospital and removed the medical records of Duncan Herbert Stevens. These, she assured Broadbent, had detailed his psychiatric treatment for alcoholism. What telling exhibits they would have been at the second royal commission!

Obviously, I found a great sense of fulfilment in my profession, and enjoyed sharing this with the special people with whom I worked – both my colleagues and the staff members of our clients at every level. Yet none of this, nor a rich and happy home life, could fully lift my feelings of in-adequacy deeply rooted in the guilt of Subic Bay. I was forever haunted by the spectre of the collision. All my instincts were to push it away as a dark memory, not to be revisited. When, in 2003, preparation began on a new documentary for the ABC on the tragedy, a researcher asked if I would participate in the program. I gave a categorical refusal, but agreed later to meet the producer, David Salter, and was persuaded that I would be in safe hands. We recorded a long interview that centred on my memories from 1963 to 1968. The finished documentary – titled *Unfit to Command* – was broadcast in late 2003 and has acted like a circuit-breaker for me. I am so relieved and grateful to have at last stopped dreaming every night, as I did for forty years, that I was still in the Navy and could not leave. I am equally relieved and grateful that I do not feel guilty any more.

Many individuals whom fate casts in the role of 'whistleblower' grow to regret their period of public prominence, and even question their original decision to break ranks and expose the truth. I do not regret that the royal commission was held, but my reasons are highly personal. Had it not been, I would probably have never recovered from the hysterical amnesia that overtook my mind on the night that I first became aware of the collision. It was only the stark shock of seeing the punishment returns, handed to me in the witness box, that unlocked the vault in which my memories were buried. Those falsified returns were the very basis of my guilt. I had signed them because, at the time, I believed Duncan Stevens had the power to have me rendered unconscious and transported to an institution where my mind might be destroyed by shock treatment. It might seem far-fetched today, but in the isolation of an RAN destroyer anchored off a jungle in the North Pacific, that threat was all too real. My knowledge of regulations told me that making just one move to seek help would give the paranoid Stevens the trigger he needed to set that horrific plan in motion. It was too hideous to ignore, and I had succumbed. A few months later, on first hearing of the collision, I believed that my action in signing those false returns had condemned eighty-two men to death. Some might still think I did. Until a year ago I was myself uncertain, but I do not believe that any more.

If Captain Willis had reported Captain Stevens' ill health (let alone his alcoholism) in Tokyo, Duncan would have been removed from the ship and the tragedy almost certainly could not have occurred. As the naval historian Tom Frame has written, Willis, for that failure to report, was liable to severe disciplinary action. Pondering the sequence of events in retrospect, I cannot help wondering whether Willis and Dollard did in fact report and that their reports were destroyed after the collision. Plenty of other vital documents relating to the circumstances surrounding the collision have disappeared or were destroyed. We'll never know, but Willis certainly enjoyed subsequent success in his naval career.

There is another evocative memory I retain from the conclusion of the commission hearings. As we were saying our temporary farewells in Hiatt's chambers, Jack turned and asked me what he described as a stupid question, but one that he had to ask anyway. 'If you had known at the beginning what this would entail, would you have gone ahead?'

'A stupid question deserves a stupid answer, Jack,' I responded, after only a moment's hesitation. 'Yes! Someone had to do it, and I could not have subjected another living soul to what I have endured. But I survived.'

The RAN also survived, but still appears to have learned little about loyalty and the absolute obligation of officers to their men over the forty ensuing years of periodic calamities. Two sailors were lost through neglect from *Oxley*; four young people perished through negligence in *Westralia*. More recently a sailor was inexplicably lost overboard, with not even a hint of suspicion that it might have been murder. The whole system of order within the service depends on the notion of unquestioning obedience, inculcated from the moment of enlistment and fostered by idealism to manifest itself in loyalty right up the chain of command. But there it stops. This duty of care and respect is purportedly even stronger towards the lower echelons, for those seamen and women do not enjoy the briefings, the specialised knowledge and experience, the education or the privileges of their senior officers. It is unquestionably right that the junior officers and the sailors look to their seniors for support and guidance, in the confident expectation that if they are in peril then they will find protection and comfort from those who command them. But to my mind there is no evidence, except evidence just as poor as the evidence that I witnessed from the majority of serving personnel in the royal commission, that the men and women of our Navy can expect any better.

Acknowledgements

It is important that acknowledgement be given to those friends whose support and encouragement motivated me in unburdening myself publicly in writing the material in this book.

David Salter, in persuading me to participate in the comprehensive documentary, *Unfit to Command*, provided the initial catharsis that released me from much of the depression that resided in me for forty years. His initial editing of my freewheeling manuscript, both ruthless and incisive, prevented me from wallowing in detail and losing reader interest. It is a privilege to have worked with him as co-writer.

Chester Porter, who introduced me to Random House, provided unswerving criticism to prevent me from legal blunders as well as counselling compassion and understanding when I may have been unforgiving. Jack Hiatt encouraged me to be forthright in identification of corrupt conduct where it was clearly displayed. To both of these eminent counsel who represented me at considerable personal risk and cost to their careers, I owe an immense debt.

Jeanne Ryckmans, publisher at Random House, showed faith in this book and encouraged me from the outset, and with project editor Lydia Papandrea became a dear friend and gentle mentor.

Nothing of this story as it is told here would have been possible without the love, trust and support of my family, but particularly Sue, who read, criticised and challenged me as it developed. She expressed her embarrassment at her intimate inclusion, saying, 'It's a love story', and insisted that I delete many details of her pain. Tragically, Sue died before publication, but she was grateful to have lived to see its completion.

Index

A Time to Speak (St John) 354
ABC *Four Corners* 314, 365, 366
ABC radio 207, 353, 365
ABC *Unfit to Command* 339, 366
ACNB (Australian Commonwealth
  Naval Board) *see* Naval Board
Age 364
AIF (Australian Imperial Force) 6, 8
Amos, Dr Bernie 224
AMP Building (Circular Quay) 102
Anstruther, Mrs 197
Armstrong, J. M. 56
Ash, W. P., QC
  Landau 283–84
  Liebenschutz 321
  McNicoll 297
  medical evidence 278, 279
  PC 244, 246–49, 254, 257, 327, 349
  Peek 292, 293
  for Stevens family 221
Asprey, Justice Kenneth William 220–21,
  255, 277–78, 286, 308, 327, 330, 331,
  335, 363
Atomic, Biological and Chemical Warfare
  and Damage Control (ABCD) 136,
  165–66, 252–53
Australia House (London) 281
The Australian 195, 196

Australian Air League 5
Australian Commonwealth Naval Board
  (ACNB) *see* Naval Board
Australian Hospitals Association 224

Baird, Lieutenant 135
Balmoral Naval Hospital 185, 188, 276
barber's pole souvenirs 27
Barker, Chief Petty Officer 318
Barnard, Lance 354–55
Bate, Sub-Lieutenant 190, 203, 204, 349,
  355
Beange, Commander Guy. A. 74, 98–99
Beard, Gordon 219, 354
Beaufort Scale 76
Becher, Rear Admiral Otto H.
  background 46–47
  HMAS *Vengeance* 76–77, 338
  Royal Commission 1964 186, 190, 192,
    203, 204, 211
Benevolent Society of New South Wales
  200, 245
Benson, Sam 211–12, 215, 275
Birrell, Dr John 285–86, 357, 359, 361
Blackburn, Professor
  blood alcohol levels 211, 266, 269, 278,
    286–87

blood analysis and validity of material 286–87
nominated by Stevens family 269, 272
recommended by Osborne 278
Royal Commission 1964 263, 264, 266, 269
Stevens drinking habits 208–9
untested evidence 271
Blaikie, Lieutenant Commander Ian 126, 132–33, 143, 164, 303, 318, 319, 326, 349
Blair, George 4–5
Bowen, Nigel 202–3, 353
Bowles, Lieutenant Commander Jimmy 83
Bradman, Don 45
Braund, J. C. 262–63, 268, 270, 271, 329
bridge watch-keeping
    bridge layout 261, 338
    Cabban Statement 242
    command conditions 260, 291, 365
    effect of reduction in numbers 53–54
    'Hands to collision stations' 260–61, 338
    HMAS *Sydney* 66
    'Mark 1 eyeball' 77, 338
    PC 255, 260
    plane guard station 139, 186
    Spicer Report inconsistency 335
British Commonwealth Occupation Force 50
Britten, Captain Jeff 244, 256, 320–21, 350–51
Broadbent, Harvey 366
Bromwich, John 39
Brooks, Lieutenant E. A. 185, 241, 338
Brown, Geoff 39
Buchanan, Captain H. J. 65–67, 69–70, 73, 83, 98, 192
Burbury, Sir Stanley Charles
    'adversary' (use of the word) 273
    Britten 320
    Burbury Report 282, 345–51
    Cabban Statement 220–21

fitness to command 297
Governor of Tasmania 351
Jamieson 309
McIntyre 309
medical evidence 279
PC 249, 254, 255, 259–61, 325–26, 327, 329, 331, 363
Peek 292, 295
Spicer Report 336
Burke, Cyril 38
Burleigh, Lord 46
Burnett, Midshipman Pat 30, 32, 33, 39
Burnett, Rory 47
Burns, Ron 92
Burrows, Sir Robert and Lady 22, 46, 59, 60–61, 67–68, 78, 92–94
Burt, Francis T. P. ('Red'), QC
    appointed counsel assisting the commission 220
    background 221–22
    Cabban Statement 229–31
    Carpendale 321–22
    claim of attempt to corrupt commission 223
    Dollard 304
    final address 339–42
    Griffith 317–18
    Jamieson 309
    McNicoll 295–97
    Martin 313
    Mead 318–19
    medical evidence 275–79, 281, 282, 286
    Menkins 319
    PC 244–46, 248, 249, 254, 256–57, 260, 261, 326–28, 330, 363
    Peek 291
    Royal Commission 1964 263–69, 271
    summary 310–11
    terms of reference 337

Cabban, Christopher John 79, 106, 223
Cabban, David 72, 78–79, 85, 106, 223

Cabban, Laurie 3, 8
Cabban, Peter (*see also* subheadings PC)
  appointments, positions and ranks 5,
    22–23, 75, 80, 86, 87, 91, 102, 103,
    106–7, 108, 110, 244
  AS206 confidential reports on officers
    300
  attends parliamentary debate 202, 210,
    214–16
  Aviation course 43–45
  birth, childhood and education 3–6
  Central Air Medical Board 69–70
  defends able seaman HMAS *Vendetta*
    88–90
  executive officer HMAS *Voyager* 106–7,
    108–13
  feelings about RAN 87, 99, 172, 198,
    237
  feelings of guilt 328, 364, 366–67
  final sea command 174–80
  financial plight 266–67
  freedom of information inquiry 309
  grounding 83–84, 245
  hysterical amnesia 179, 185, 188, 261,
    348, 366–67
  letter to Jess 198, 258–59
  management consultant 253–54
  memory recall mechanism 225–26
  Perini Australia Ltd 172, 176–77, 183,
    190
  resigns 172, 180, 237, 246, 326, 348
  work study consultancy 200
  see also Cabban Statement
Cabban, Sally Jane 103, 106, 223
Cabban, Suzanne ('Sue', née Hill)
  attends parliamentary debate 202
  Bill Dunlop 80
  children 68, 71–72, 76, 78–79, 85, 97,
    106
  debt to 354, 363
  marriage to PC 60–61, 170, 179, 327,
    364
  PC's courtship of 15–17, 19–20, 48,
    58–59
  royal commission 245–46, 249–50, 267
  tape recordings 162, 199, 218, 246, 326
  Tuke 319
Cabban Statement
  conflicts of evidence 311
  Department of the Navy 281, 283
  McNicoll 300–301
  Naval Board 297–98
  order prohibiting publication 231
  PC as witness 246, 324–32
  Robertson 334
  Royal Commission 1964 196–97
  Royal Commission 1967–68 229–43
  Statement Number 78 263
  Voyager debate 206–7, 216
  wardroom mess 235
The Caine Mutiny (book and film) 128,
    249
Cameron, Clyde 207, 212–14, 360
Campbell, Lieutenant Commander Gill
    73, 82–84
Carpendale, Jenny 321
Carpendale, Lieutenant Richard 144, 145,
    147, 150, 321–22, 326–27
Carrington, Lieutenant Commander
    Bruce 179
Caws, Lieutenant Bill 83
Ceylon 123, 346
Chaney, Fred 194, 197, 211
Channel Seven 202
Cheadle, Petty Officer Gunner's Mate
    George 18
China 51
Chipp, Don
  autobiography 285, 365
  Landau 283, 356–57
  misleads parliament 284, 353
  Royal Commission 1964 312
  Stevens abuse of amphetamines 337,
    365–66
  Voyager debate 205–6, 209–12, 299
Clarke, 'Nobby' 18
Cleaver, Richard 358–59
Cleland, Lieutenant Keith 319–20

Collins, Vice Admiral Sir John 55, 323
Collins, Peter 314
collisions in navy (frequest near) 241
'colours', ceremony of 109
Commonwealth Industrial Court 189
Commonwealth Police 186–87, 190, 205,
  230, 238, 260–61, 264
  Document Examination Bureau 257
compensation 64
Concord Repatriation Hospital (Sydney)
  101, 161, 167, 366
Cook, Lieutenant Harry
  HMAS *Voyager* 136, 179, 193, 338
  HMS *Caesar* 136
Cooper, Lieutenant Peter ('Bras') 73–74,
  98
Coplans, Surgeon Rear Admiral Robert
  47, 94, 279–80
Cordell, Alan 57–58, 60, 100–101
corporal punishment 10–11
courts martial (conditions for) 89,
  164–65, 177–78, 292, 294, 297, 315,
  318
Crabb, Rear Admiral 353
Crosbie, Gordon 25
Crown Street Women's Hospital 200, 202
customs officers 120–21, 143, 169–70,
  318

Daily Telegraph 213, 252
Darwin episode 325, 346
Davidson, Commander John 186
de Lange, Adrian and Robin 99, 137
Dean, Group Captain 'Dixie' 41
Dollard, Captain A. N.
  admiral's hypotheticals 295
  Burbury Report 350
  Cabban Statement 235
  crisis in Tokyo 150, 151, 155, 307, 323,
    347
  evidence 287, 303–5, 309–10, 318, 326
  failure to report 367
  Karatsu 141, 143

Korean War 350
Donnelly, Petty Officer 110
Dovers, Captain Bill 86–87, 172, 177–78,
  347
  court martial 178, 237, 319, 348
Dowling, Lieutenant Jim 127, 239
Drax, Midshipman 'Plunkett' 30, 32–33
Dreyer, Admiral 150, 168
drinking on duty at sea
  Bowen 203
  Cabban Statement 231, 232, 239,
    240
  HMAS *Voyager* 164–65
  meaning of terms 330
  PC 253, 256, 259, 330–31
  proposed abolition of 328–29
  survivors claims 185–88
  triple brandy 191, 205–6, 264–65,
    268–69, 287, 299, 338, 365
  Voyager collision explained 338
Dunlop, Bill 74, 80
Dunlop, Dorothy 80
Duntroon Royal Military College 8
duodenal ulcer (Stevens medical
  condition)
  consequences of 280
  diagnosis 278
  evidence 304, 305, 308
  fitness to command 279, 345
  liver function test 360–61
  naval medical records 279–80
  perforation 236, 276, 279
  reporting of 275–77
  Royal Commission 1964 269
  Royal Commission 1967–68 286
  symptoms 275

Eddy, Steward 319, 326
Edward, Prince of Wales 21
electroconvulsive shock treatment
  Cordell 101
  PC threatened with 161, 179, 255, 260,
    367

Elizabeth II, Queen 70
Ennor, Able Seaman 257, 322
Evans, Signalman 272

Fairhall, Alan 328
Fairhall, David 198
Farmers and Graziers Company 195
Farrelly, Squadron Leader Maurice
   141–43, 151, 305–7, 309–11, 318, 326,
   350
Ferrier, Lieutenant 171, 251, 348
Fisher, Commander 24, 28, 37
fitness to command
   ABC *Unfit to Command* 339
   Burbury Report 345
   Cabban Statement 291–92
   duodenal ulcer (Stevens medical
      condition) 279, 345
   evidence 230–31, 265, 293–94, 297
   illness argument 230–31
   Spicer Report inconsistency 335
   Stevens 147–48, 179, 208
   Stevens diagnosed as fit 275
   'unfit' (meaning of) 274
Fitzgerald, Sergeant B. J. 257
Fleet Air Arm *see under* RAN
Flinders Naval Depot (Westernport, Vic)
   9, 87–88, 94, 96–97
Flinders Naval Hospital 94–95, 276
   Stevens 178, 252
Foreign Affairs, Department of 295, 309,
   315
Forrest, Sub-Lieutenant 322
Fowler, Lieutenant Murray 48–50, 52–55
Frame, Lieutenant Tom 285, 314, 367
Fraser of North Cape, Lord Bruce,
   Admiral of the Fleet 32–33, 45–46, 60
Freeman, Leading Steward 124, 150, 152,
   237, 238, 330, 346
French Foreign Legion 33–35
Frost, Tommy 78

Gafford, 'Snow' 100
Gale, Keith and Jenny 149, 151, 155, 307,
   330
Gannet Trainer tests 81–84
Garden Island Dockyard (Sydney) 104–6,
   118, 170, 171, 326
Gatacre, Rear Admiral 84, 120, 209
George, Captain F. Leveson 96–97, 105,
   106
George, Tony 10
George VI, King 22
Gilbreth, Frank 93–94
Gloucester Cup 53
Goble, Captain John 214
Goldrick, Lieutenant Commander Peter
   74, 83
Golsby, Ron and Barney 202
Gooch, Flight Lieutenant Jim 57
Gordon L. Beard & McDonald 219
Gordon, 'Speed' 52–53
Gorton, John 354
Goulston, Dr Kerry 276
Grant, Captain Duncan W. 21
Gregory, W. H. 221
Grey, Ernest ('Gus') 21
Griffith, Lieutenant Commander Scott
   Cabban Statement 233, 243
   crisis in Tokyo 150
   evidence 316–18, 321
   HMAS *Voyager* 112, 147, 323
   Hong Kong 130, 137–38
   medical evidence 283, 284
   PC 252–55, 327
   Royal Commission 1964 263, 268, 270,
      272
   Singapore 167, 179, 187–88
   Stevens 118, 120
   Voyager debate 207, 213
Griffith, Rear Admiral Guy 100

Hain, Commander 'Butch' 81
Hansman, Dr F. S. 286–89
Hardy's wines 112, 143, 318

Harries, Rear Admiral D. H. ('Darbo') 47, 84, 86

Harrington, Vice Admiral Sir Hastings 86–87, 91–92, 94, 97–98, 100, 119, 193–94, 295

Haughton, Surgeon Commander Tim 276–77, 349

Henchman, Humphrey 221, 244

Hiatt, J.T., QC
  Asprey 318
  Birrell 286
  Britten 320–21
  Burt 221, 313
  Cleland and Tuke 319–20
  Dollard 304
  Jamieson 308
  Landau 283–84
  Liebenschutz 321
  McIntyre 309
  McNicoll 296, 297–301, 358
  medical evidence 275–79, 282
  PC 219, 244–46, 248–52, 254, 261, 326, 327, 354, 367
  Peek 294–95
  preparation 223–25
  Royal Commission 1964 263, 265–66, 268, 269
  terms of reference 337
  Willis 316
  Wineberg 285

Hickling, Vice Admiral Harold
  Cabban Statement 195–97, 217, 222, 231, 245, 246, 329
  goldfish bowl 247
  One Minute of Time 195, 197
  PC 29, 221, 337–38
  Voyager debate 206, 210

Hicks, David, QC 191, 327, 333, 357

Hill, Suzanne see Cabban, Suzanne

HMAS Albatross 56, 64, 65, 84, 263

HMAS Anzac 170

HMAS Creswell 86, 312

HMAS Culgoa 53

HMAS Kuttabul 104

HMAS Lonsdale 175–76

HMAS Melbourne
  Beange 75
  Burbury Report 349
  commissioned 75
  evidence 259
  Hong Kong 132
  McNeill 130–31, 274–77
  mentioned 135
  Pakistan Shield 172
  PC on 79–80, 97–98
  Peek commands 106, 128
  Royal Commission 1964 190, 192, 193, 265, 270–71
  Royal Commission 1967–68 333–38
  Sea Venoms fatalities 80–81
  Stevens as executive officer 215
  USS Frank E. Evans 364
  Voyager collision 184–86, 190, 288, 337–38
  witnesses 263

HMAS Oxley 368

HMAS Parramatta 100, 316

HMAS Penguin 101, 102

HMAS Perth 122

HMAS Quickmatch 89, 175, 179

HMAS Rushcutter 7

HMAS Shoalhaven 48, 50, 51, 53, 55, 206, 295, 296

HMAS Stuart 8

HMAS Sydney
  817 Squadron 73
  Cleland and Tuke 319–20
  commissioned 46
  coronation cruise 66, 70
  customs 169
  Dovers 177–78, 237
  McMahon 212
  mentioned 75, 170
  PC appointed to 55–56, 113, 232, 235, 254
  recommissioning 103, 104–7, 120
  Robertson 192, 237
  Stevens 56

HMAS *Tobruk* 85, 102–3
HMAS *Vampire*
  Cabban Statement 234
  Commander Errol Stevens 322–23
  crisis in Tokyo 153–54, 156, 159, 304,
    308
  deck log 256, 317–18
  HMAS *Voyager* collides with 118,
    233
  mentioned 138
  report of proceedings for March 1963
    325, 346
  Singapore 166–67
  Sydney 170, 172
  Willis 236, 280, 282
HMAS *Vendetta* 88–90, 192, 209
HMAS *Vengeance* 75–77
HMAS *Voyager*
  Cabban Statement 233, 234, 236–37,
    260
  collision in Hong Kong 132
  collision with *Melbourne* 184–86, 190,
    288, 337–38
  crew 110, 133, 135, 140–42, 147, 167
  damage control teams 148
  deck log 230, 256, 257
  discipline 118
  HMS *Hermes* 145–47
  HMS *Rothesay* 147
  inquiry *see* Royal Commission of
    Inquiry into the Loss of HMAS
    Voyager
  Mad Chemist of Wanchai 138–39
  mentioned 96
  near collisions 241
  Operation Sea Serpent 134–36
  painted 168–69
  parliamentary debate 199–216
  parliamentary post-mortem 352–62
  PC appointed to 106–7, 231
  PC commands 121, 154, 156–59,
    165–66, 174–80, 266, 326
  PC leaves 179–80
  refit returns 251–52

  report of proceedings for March 1963
    230, 283, 295–96, 325
  reports of proceedings for June 1963
    256, 318
  side parties 119–20, 129, 137
  stand-in commander 315
  survivors 185–87, 223, 234, 259, 271,
    355, 365
  Sydney 236–37, 251
  victims 231, 239, 241, 292, 362, 367
  wardroom mess 110–11, 117, 125–27,
    143, 179–80
  welfare fund dinner dance 175–76
  witnesses 263
  work-up 111, 170–75, 184, 239
HMAS *Warramunga* 84, 85, 244, 254
HMAS *Watson* 193–94, 206, 242
HMAS *Westralia* 48–50, 368
HMAS *Yarra* 128, 178, 237–38
  'lost in *Yarra*' incident 133, 285, 294,
    319, 320, 346
HMS *Alert* 149, 150
HMS *Ark Royal* 68, 233
HMS *Barossa* 322
HMS *Battleaxe* 185, 241, 338
HMS *Birmingham* 77
HMS *Cadiz* 33
HMS *Caesar* 124, 136, 138, 241, 268–69,
    346
HMS *Colossus* 27
HMS *Dolphin* 92–93
HMS *Duke of York* 32, 33
HMS *Excellent* 42
HMS *Gabbard* 33
HMS *Gamecock* 78
HMS *Glasgow* 27
HMS *Glory* 46
HMS *Hermes* 135, 138–39, 145–47, 158
HMS *Howe* 27–28
HMS *King George V* 19, 22–24, 26–29,
    37, 146
HMS *Lincoln* 325
HMS *Lion* 124, 157–58, 237, 316, 325,
    346

HMS *Mull of Kintyre* 133
HMS *Nelson* 25, 36–37
HMS *Penelope* 22
HMS *Rothesay* 138, 147, 233, 236, 285, 287, 304, 326, 346
HMS *Siskin* 43, 68
HMS *Sluys* 30, 33, 37
HMS *Triumph* 62–63
HMS *Vanguard* 31
HMS *Vengeance* 27, 338
HMS *Vernon* 45
Hogg, Commander Ian 22
Holmes, Lieutenant 171, 251, 347
Holt, Harold 195–98, 200–201, 213–16
Hong Kong 119–20, 129, 137–39, 235, 236, 255
Hong Kong Naval Hospital 278
Hospitals and Charities Commissioners, Victorian 95
Hospitals Commission 200
Howland, Sub-Lieutenant 167, 179, 255, 322
Hyland, Officer's Steward Barry 185, 187, 191, 193, 254, 264, 266, 268, 272, 287, 357

initiation ceremonies 11–12
introversion/extroversion 253–54, 348–49
Irwin, Commander T. P. ('Peter') 138, 236, 326, 347

Jamieson, A. B. ('Jim') 150, 304, 305, 307–9, 310–11
    Burbury Report 350
Japan
    British Commonwealth Occupation Force 50
    conflicting evidence 302–11
    Karatsu 141–44, 318, 347
    Maritime Self-Defence Force 304, 307
    Nagasaki 51
    Nagoya 139, 141
    Okinawa 322
    submarines in Australian waters 13
    Tokyo 149–55, 184, 235, 270, 347
    Zero fighter propeller trophy 29
Jeffrey, Philip 220–21, 231, 307–9, 319, 333–34
Jenkyn, Norman, QC 187, 189, 191, 192, 240
Jervis Bay (NSW) 71–72
Jess, John, MHR 194–206, 211, 213, 216, 257–59, 328, 357–58, 360
Jude, George 81

Kelly, Bert (Minister for the Navy) 361
Kelly, Commander 203, 204, 349, 355
Kemp, Suzanne 221
Killen, James 210–11, 360
Kingsford Smith, Sir Charles 6
Kyd, Surgeon Lieutenant Allan 121, 281, 284–85, 288

Lake, Father Grantly 101
Lamb, Charles 59–61
Landau, Samuel 271, 272, 281, 283–84, 295, 298, 317, 326, 354–58, 365
Larkin, Commander Tom 30, 31, 33, 36, 37
Leach, David 39–40, 45, 100
Leung, Sophia 200, 218, 267
Liebenschutz, Piet 99, 130, 137, 221, 321
Loxton, Commander B. H. 178, 214, 237–38, 299, 326
Lucas, Justice Geoffrey George 220–21, 261, 292, 297, 298, 331
Lunberg, Lieutenant Commander 43, 45, 65

McCaffrey, Dr Chris. J. 95–96, 102, 112, 172, 183, 200
McDermott royal commission 219

McDonald, Tony 219, 223, 250, 354

McEwen, Lieutenant 'Soapy' 100

Macgregor, Lieutenant Commander 179,
239, 338

McIntyre, Sir Laurence 155, 295, 304, 309

Mackay, Reverend Dr Malcolm, MHR
201, 299–300, 360, 365

McMahon, William 212–13, 353, 355

McNeill, Surgeon Commander J. R.
130–31, 256–57, 274–79, 288, 346
  Burbury Report 350

McNicoll, Vice Admiral Sir Alan W. R.
  background 53–55
  evidence 295–301
  FOCAF 128
  Hong Kong 132, 135
  parliamentary post-mortem 357–58
  PC 96, 170
  Robertson 194
  Royal Commission 1964 223, 265
  Voyager debate 205–7, 212–14
  writes article for the press 364

Mad Chemist of Wanchai 138–39

Manual of Court Martial Proceedings 89

Manus Island 275–77

Martin, Lieutenant Commander David
  Dovers 347
  evidence 246, 312–14, 321, 346, 348
  Governor of New South Wales 314,
  351
  Hong Kong 130, 133, 137–38
  leaves HMAS *Voyager* 175
  medical evidence 281
  Pakistan Shield 251
  PC 76–77, 247
  promotions 351
  punishment returns 158, 160–62
  reports on seaman officers 173
  Singapore 166
  Stevens 147, 174
  Sydney 171, 172
  Voyager debate 207
  Voyager wardroom mess 127

Martin, Susie 133, 170, 246

Matthew, Commander John 10, 57,
60–61, 187, 316

Matthews, Leading Seaman A. B. 320–21

Mead, Able Seaman Peter A. 318–19, 320,
346

Melbourne Cricket Ground 178

Melbourne *Truth* 199–200, 346

Menkins, Desmond 319

Menzies, Sir Robert, and government
189, 192, 195–97, 203–4, 214

Mikado (theatre restaurant, Tokyo)
151–52, 155, 305

Money, Commander Bill 126, 132–33,
143, 151, 303, 306, 310, 318, 319, 326,
349

Morrell, Frank 45

Morris, William (Lord Nuffield) 64

Morrow, Sir William 171, 264, 266,
277–79, 285–87, 348, 357, 359–62

Murphy, Peter, QC
  Britten 320–21
  claim of attempt to corrupt
  commission 223
  Griffith 317
  Landau 283–84
  Liebenschutz 321
  McNicoll 297, 298
  Osborne 265
  PC 244, 248, 253–56, 328, 329, 349
  for RAN 221, 225
  Spicer Report 336–37

mutiny charges 129, 154, 161, 167, 207,
212

Nakayama, Admiral 151, 235, 304

Naval Board (Australian Commonwealth
  Naval Board, ACNB)
  Burbury Report 350
  Cabban Statement 297–98, 299–301
  cover up *see under* RAN
  HMAS *Melbourne* 364
  Landau (secretary to) 283
  Murphy (counsel for the Navy) 297

PC 60, 63, 87–88, 175, 245
record-keeping 256, 295–96
removes medical records 366
reporting systems 279–80, 328–29, 350
reports of proceedings 230
reports to 315
Royal Commission 1964 189, 191, 192,
    194, 195, 203, 204, 212, 265
Spicer Report 258–59
Stevens 158, 204, 209, 365
see also RAN (Royal Australian Navy)
Naval College *see* RANC
Naval Discipline Act 295
Navy, Department of 271, 281, 283,
    320–21
Navy News 257, 298
near collisions in navy (frequent) 241
night orders 159
nuclear attack exercises 136, 165–66,
    252–53
Nuffield, Lord (William Morris) 64

Oakley, Les 70
O'Connor, Bill 357
Oldham, Rear Admiral G. C. 75, 107, 120
Olle, Andrew 365
One Minute of Time (Hickling) 195, 197
Orontes (ship) 64
Orr, Professor 221
Osborne, Frederick Meares 187, 240, 253,
    264–66, 278, 358

Packer, Sir Frank 213
Pakistan Shield 172, 251, 348
Parker, Able Seaman 213
Parker, Commander Vernon 102
Pathfinder Club (London) 41, 61
Peek, Rear Admiral R. I.
    background 55–56
    becomes Second Naval Member 353
    Cabban Statement 234–35
    commands HMAS *Melbourne* 106–7

fitness to command 290–95, 297
    medical evidence 275
    mentioned 85
    PC 120, 128, 130–31, 346
    Royal Commission 1964 190, 192, 269,
        290–91
    Voyager debate 212
Penlington, John 365
pension eligibility 276
Perini Australia Ltd 172, 176–77, 183, 225
Perini, Louis 190
Pfafflin, Gus 112
Pinklao (Thai Navy frigate) 134–35
Place, Captain 347
Plunkett-Cole, Commodore J. 87, 94–95
Plunkett-Ernle-Erle-Drax, Admiral Sir
    Reginald Aylmer Ranfurly 33
Pope, Lieutenant Johnny 62
Porter, Chester, QC
    background 202
    Burt 221
    Kyd 284–85
    Martin 313
    medical evidence 288
    PC 219, 222, 245, 246, 249–51, 339,
        354
    preparation 223–25
    Royal Commission 1964 271–72
Power, Acting Commander R. T.
    ('Potter') 83
press 249, 260, 270–71
Price, Lieutenant 179, 189, 192, 193, 221,
    338
Public Works (NSW), Department of 364
Pulau Tioman island 135
punishment returns
    confrontation with Tapp, Griffith and
        Howland 167, 179, 188
    falsified 162, 185, 295–97, 367
    'For Captain (Sick)' notation 158, 160
    Martin 158, 160–62
    Naval Board instruction to Stevens 158
    out of serial number sequence and date
        order 257

PC 248–52, 322
    retyped 322

RAAF (Royal Australian Air Force) 38
RAF airfield (Weston-Super-Mare) 69
Raine, E. P. T. 221
RAN (Royal Australian Navy)
    admiral's hypotheticals 290–301
    alcohol consumption aboard ships 211,
        215, 269
    AS206 confidential reports on officers
        296
    becoming a midshipman 8–9
    cover up 262, 267, 269, 283, 337, 351,
        365, 367
    Far East General Orders 141
    Far East Strategic Reserve 118–19, 128
    Fleet Air Arm 43, 56, 63–66, 68, 84,
        214, 263
    Flinders Naval Depot see Flinders Naval
        Depot (Westernport, Vic)
    machinery of rank 290, 302–3
    Navy Office 105–6
    obligation of officers to their men 167,
        367–68
    'Pompey' (Portsmouth) courses 42
    promotions 221
    record-keeping 256, 295–96
    reporting systems 279–80, 328–29, 350
    Royal Commission 1964 see under
        Naval Board
    Royal Navy 19, 65
    Voyager debate 208, 216
    see also Naval Board (ACNB)
RANC (Royal Australian Naval College)
    7–18, 21, 38, 265
Redfern Mail Exchange 176–77
Redman, Terry 164–65, 318
Reed, John 197
Rees, Peter 50, 52–53
Reid, Alan 213
Reynolds, R. G., QC 221, 263, 266, 270,
    272–73, 292–93, 335–36

Richelieu (French battleship) 27
RMS Arcadia 80
RMS Himalaya 79, 80
RMS Orcades 47, 58
RMS Strathaird 47
RNAS Culdrose 60
RNAS Eglinton 60, 63
RNAS Lossiemouth 59–60
Robertson, Commander Andrew 67, 89
Robertson, Bettine 66, 194, 310
Robertson, David 68
Robertson, Captain Ronald John
    Dollard 235
    Hickling 195
    HMAS Vendetta 88–90, 209
    HMAS Watson 193–94, 206
    Jess 357–59
    Mackay 365
    mystique of high rank 333
    parliamentary debate 204, 208, 211
    PC 66, 71, 178, 220, 253, 259–60, 354,
        363
    PC offers to give evidence 195–96,
        240–41, 349
    pension 194–95, 355, 360
    resigns 194
    Royal Commission 1964 189–98, 202,
        220, 267, 270–73
    Royal Commission 1967–68 309–10,
        333–38
    Samuels 332
    Stevens 327
Rogers, Chief Petty Officer Jonathan
    162, 257
Royal Australian Navy see RAN
Royal Ceylon Navy 123
Royal Commission of Inquiry into the
    Allegations of Lieutenant Commander
    Cabban and Matters Incidental Thereto
    'adversary' (use of the word) 273
    advice on answering questions
        224–25
    announced 258
    breaking point 303, 311

Chairman *see* Burbury, Sir Stanley
Charles
commissioners 220, 263, 272, 283–84,
286, 288–89, 297, 313–14, 321, 327,
357–58, 364
conflicts of evidence 310–11, 339–42,
365
hearsay evidence, trial-law test of
231
medical evidence 274–89
operation of royal commissions 217–18
PC as witness 244–61, 308, 324–32
proceedings 229
terms of reference 220, 262, 291–92,
302, 327, 332, 333, 337, 349
witnesses (general references to) 222,
320–21, 323, 350–51
Royal Commission of Inquiry into the
Loss of HMAS *Voyager*
announced 186
Chairman *see* Spicer, Honourable Sir
John Armstrong
commissioners 285
interviewing process 263, 270, 271
PC not called 262–63, 265–66, 270,
271
proceedings 186, 189–98
Royal Commission 1967 229
secret session 285, 288–89
Spicer Report *see* Spicer Report
Royal Dutch Inter-ocean Line 130
Royal Marine Barracks (Eastney) 45
Royal Navy
attitude to crew 62–63
Central Air Medical Board 69–70
Naval Base Portsmouth 42, 97
Naval College Dartmouth 21
Naval College Greenwich 38, 54–55
provisioning of aircraft carriers 100
RAN 19, 65
restructuring 97
Royal Newcastle Hospital 95–96,
102
Royal North Shore Hospital 224

Russell, Lieutenant Des 43–44
Ryder, Lady Francis 20–21, 38

St John, Edward, QC
medical evidence 285–86
parliamentary post-mortem 354,
358–60
PC 218–19, 223, 332, 364
A Time to Speak 354
Voyager debate 201–2, 207–10, 212–16
Sallmann, Tony 54–55
Salter, David 366
Samuels, Gordon, QC 286, 331–32,
336–37
Sangster, Lieutenant 53, 54
Scatchard, Rear Admiral Jack 145, 147
Schmitzer, Clem 50
seasickness 13
SEATO (South East Asia Treaty
Organisation) 98, 118, 134
service attire 129
Shand, Jack, KC 219
Shands, Commander Ken 106–7
Sheppard, Ian Fitzharding 271–73, 329
ship handling 233, 242, 296
shock therapy *see* electroconvulsive shock
treatment
signal communications 97–98
Sinatra, Frank 16
Sinclair, Ian 10
Sinclair, John Bowditch 187–88, 221,
264–65, 266
Singapore 166–67, 179, 255
Skinner, Lieutenant Bernard 19
Smith, Commander V. A. T. 75, 84, 99,
194, 353
Smyth, Commodore Dacre 265, 281, 358
Smyth, John William, QC
Burbury Report 349, 358
Cabban Statement 230
Griffith 316
medical evidence 287
PC 236, 238, 240, 253, 260, 329, 357

Robertson 334
Royal Commission 1964 187–88, 190, 193, 195, 262, 265, 267, 272–73
Voyager debate 204–5, 208–9, 212, 214
Snedden, Billy 192
Snowy Mountains Scheme 183–84, 190
Spicer, Honourable Sir John Armstrong 189–90, 192–93, 214, 253, 259, 265, 349
  assistants 262–73
  cover up 351
Spicer Report 193–95, 208–9, 211, 332
  navigational aspects 310, 334–42, 349
  RAN and Crown support for 336–37
Spurgeon, Commander S. H. K. 7–8
Sri Lanka 123, 346
station-keeping 31–32, 233, 259
Stevens, Beatrice
  alcoholism 201–2
  destroys Duncan's letters 252
  Manus Island 277
  marriage to Duncan Stevens 120, 170, 173, 185, 234
  PC and 247, 252, 326
  Royal Commission 1967–68 244
  see also Stevens family
Stevens, Captain Duncan Herbert
  alcoholism 201–2, 285–86, 287, 345, 365, 366
  ambition for promotion 277, 280
  amphetamine abuse 172, 178, 251, 284–85, 287–89, 337–38, 348, 365–66
  Amphogel 278, 285
  Ceylon 124
  China Fleet Club 131–32, 346
  Chipp pays tribute to 356–57
  commands HMAS *Sydney* 56
  commands HMAS *Voyager* 109, 117, 156, 176, 206, 338
  cricketer 122, 234
  Dovers court martial 178
  executive officer HMAS *Melbourne* 215
  HMAS *Vampire* 118

HMAS *Yarra* 133
HMS *Hermes* 146–47
HMS *Rothesay* 138
Hong Kong 120–21, 130, 137–38, 199
illness 121, 152–53, 167, 174
Karatsu 142
Martin 314
medical examinations 130, 152–53, 171, 235–36
medical records 366
Mikado (theatre restaurant) 155
nicknames 109
nuclear attack exercises 165–66
Pinklao incident 134–35
report summaries on 215, 269–70
reports on seaman officers 173
ship handling 118, 147, 157, 233
stood down from command 153–59, 256, 266, 269, 326
Sydney 170, 171
temperament 146–47, 233, 242, 280–81, 338
Tokyo 150–55
wardroom mess 125–27, 280, 293, 322
work-up 173
Stevens, Commander Errol 322–23
Stevens, Sir Jack and Lady 207, 244
Stevens family
  legal expenses 190
  parliamentary post-mortem 362
  Royal Commission 1964 187–90, 192, 205
Strachan, Petty Officer W. S. 320–21
Street, Laurence, QC 187, 190, 264–66, 327, 334, 357
Subic Bay 160–63, 167, 179, 184, 218, 246, 250–51, 255, 260, 261, 366
Sunda Strait 122
Sydney Morning Herald 249, 364
Syfrett, Admiral Sir Neville 22

Synnot, Commander A. M. 84, 85, 118, 132

Tapp, Lieutenant Commander Keith 50–51, 86, 167, 179, 239, 255, 282–83
Taylor, Joe and Betty 38
Templeton, Lord 46
This Day Tonight 365
Thomas Hardy & Sons 112
Thomas, Robert ('Bob') 102, 172, 176, 183, 185, 190
Thompson, Commander Ron. H. 91
Thorne, Squadron Leader Alex 41
Tiller, Surgeon Lieutenant Michael ('Mick')
  admiral's hypotheticals 298, 299
  Burbury Report 350
  Cabban Statement 236–37
  career 280
  crisis in Tokyo 152–54
  diagnosis 278
  Dollard 304
  evidence 280–84, 305, 308
  HMAS *Voyager* 121, 164
  Hong Kong 130
  Landau 355
  leaves HMAS *Voyager* 174–75
  McNeill 274–75
  medical evidence 288
  Stevens stood down 157
  Stevens wardroom party 127
Trafalgar, Battle of 79
Truth 199–200, 346
Tuke, Lieutenant Commander Barry 272, 319–20
Turner, Harry 201, 210, 216, 358
Turner, Sergeant 205, 260–61, 263, 264
Typhoon Polly 149
Typhoon Rose 157–59, 256, 317, 322

Unfit to Command 339, 366
US Navy 52, 71, 100, 162

US Navy's Guam weather station 256
USS *Frank E. Evans* 364

Vasey, Lieutenant Commander Russell 126, 129–30
venturi effect 157
Veterans' Affairs, Department of 276
Victoria and Albert (royal yacht) 42
Victoria Police 286

Wallabies 38
watch-keeping *see* bridge watch-keeping
Watson, Mrs Darsie 21
Watson, Elizabeth 35
Webster, Able Seaman 261
Wells, Commander David 87–88, 108
Whitlam, E. G. 216, 284, 353–54
Williams, Esther 52
Williamstown dockyard 174, 237, 251, 317, 319, 322, 325–26, 348
Willis, Captain G. J.
  actions analysed 315
  admiral's hypotheticals 295, 299
  Burbury Report 350
  Cabban Statement 236
  crisis in Tokyo 150, 151
  Dollard's evidence 303–4
  evidence 305, 308, 310–11, 314–16
  failure to report 367
  HMAS *Vampire* 118, 323
  medical evidence 282
  mentioned 122
  PC 153–59, 179, 247, 255, 260
  promotions 350
  Singapore 166
  Stevens 179, 349
  Subic Bay 161
  Sydney 172
  Tiller 280
  Voyager debate 207, 212, 213
Willis, Commander Alan A. 109, 111–12, 117, 152, 206, 213, 231–32, 255, 283

Wilson, Lieutenant John 19, 68
Wilson, Petty Officer Sick Berth
   Attendant 175, 178, 238
Wineberg, R. H. 221, 285
Winter, John 46
Wolcott, Surgeon Commander 46–47
Women's Hospital Crown Street 200, 202

Wren, P. C. 34
Wright, Lieutenant 122, 346
Wright, Senior Constable G. E. 264

Yates, Captain G. D. 22
Young, Nancy and Evelyn 221